Test Bank

for

Berk

Infants, Children, and Adolescents

Seventh Edition

prepared by

Kimberly Michaud

Sara Harris
Illinois State University

Allyn & Bacon

Boston   Columbus   Indianapolis   New York   San Francisco   Upper Saddle River
Amsterdam   Cape Town   Dubai   London   Madrid   Milan   Munich   Paris   Montreal   Toronto
Delhi   Mexico City   Sao Paulo   Sydney   Hong Kong   Seoul   Singapore   Taipei   Tokyo

10 9 8 7 6 5 4 3 2 1   14 13 12 11 10

Allyn & Bacon
is an imprint of

www.pearsonhighered.com

ISBN-10: 0-205-01052-0
ISBN-13: 978-0-205-01052-3

CONTENTS

CHAPTER 1
HISTORY, THEORY, AND RESEARCH STRATEGIES

MULTIPLE CHOICE

1) The central questions addressed by the field of child development
    A) are primarily of scientific interest.
    B) have applied, or practical, importance.
    C) are based exclusively on research conducted by psychologists.
    D) involve all changes a person experiences throughout the lifespan.
Answer: B
Page Ref: 4
Skill: Factual
Objective: 1.1

2) Our large storehouse of information about child development
    A) is scientifically important, but has only limited practical value.
    B) has grown solely through the contributions of child development investigators.
    C) has grown through the combined efforts of people from many fields.
    D) is relevant and practical, but has limited scientific value.
Answer: C
Page Ref: 4
Skill: Factual
Objective: 1.1

3) Which of the following is true regarding the major domains of development?
    A) The domains of development are separate and distinct.
    B) Each period of development is made up of a new set of domains.
    C) The physical domain has little influence on the other domains.
    D) Development is divided into three broad domains: physical, cognitive, and emotional and social.
Answer: D
Page Ref: 5
Skill: Conceptual
Objective: 1.2

4) During which period of development does a sense of morality become evident?
    A) infancy and toddlerhood
    B) early childhood
    C) middle childhood
    D) adolescence
Answer: B
Page Ref: 6
Skill: Conceptual
Objective: 1.2

5) Which of the following is true about emerging adulthood?
    A) It is a period of development that spans ages 16 to 22 years.
    B) It is a period of development unique to underdeveloped nations.
    C) Although emerging adults have moved beyond adolescence, they have not yet fully assumed adult roles.
    D) It is mostly limited to young people in developing nations.
Answer: C
Page Ref: 6
Skill: Conceptual
Objective: 1.2

6) Theories are vital tools because they
    A) provide organizing frameworks for our observations of children.
    B) provide the ultimate truth about child development.
    C) do not require scientific verification.
    D) are resistant to the influence of cultural values and belief systems.
Answer: A
Page Ref: 7
Skill: Conceptual
Objective: 1.3

7) In what important way do theories differ from mere opinion or belief?
    A) They are influenced by cultural values.
    B) They depend on scientific verification.
    C) Singular theories can explain all aspects of development.
    D) They cannot be tested using a fair set of research procedures.
Answer: B
Page Ref: 7
Skill: Conceptual
Objective: 1.3

8) Reid believes that the difference between the immature and the mature being is simply one of amount or complexity. Reid views development as
    A) discontinuous.
    B) determined by nature.
    C) continuous.
    D) determined by nurture.
Answer: C
Page Ref: 7
Skill: Applied
Objective: 1.3

9) Jessica believes that development takes place in stages where children change rapidly as they step up to a new level and then change very little for a while. Jessica views development as
    A) discontinuous.
    B) determined by nature.
    C) continuous.
    D) determined by nurture.
Answer: A
Page Ref: 8
Skill: Applied
Objective: 1.3

10) The stage concept assumes that
    A) development is a smooth, continuous process.
    B) change is fairly sudden rather than gradual and ongoing.
    C) infants and preschoolers respond to the world in much the same way as adults do.
    D) development is a process of gradually adding more of the same types of skills that were there to begin with.
    Answer: B
    Page Ref: 8
    Skill: Conceptual
    Objective: 1.3

11) The stage concept assumes that change is
    A) gradual.
    B) ongoing.
    C) fairly sudden.
    D) unique for each child.
    Answer: C
    Page Ref: 8
    Skill: Factual
    Objective: 1.3

12) In her research, Dr. Rosenblum explores why shy children develop differently from their outgoing agemates. Dr. Rosenblum most likely emphasizes _____ in her research.
    A) the role of distinct contexts
    B) the nature–nurture controversy
    C) the concept of stage
    D) continuous development
    Answer: A
    Page Ref: 8
    Skill: Applied
    Objective: 1.3

13) Charlene believes that her daughter's ability to think in complex ways is largely the result of an inborn timetable of growth. Charlene's view emphasizes
    A) nurture.
    B) nature.
    C) plasticity.
    D) early experiences.
    Answer: B
    Page Ref: 9
    Skill: Applied
    Objective: 1.3

14) Theorists who believe that children who are high or low in a characteristic will remain so at later ages typically stress the importance of
    A) heredity.
    B) stages.
    C) nurture.
    D) plasticity.
    Answer: A
    Page Ref: 9
    Skill: Factual
    Objective: 1.3

15) Dr. Kudrow views development as open to change in response to influential experiences. Dr. Kudrow probably emphasizes
    A) stability.
    B) heredity.
    C) stages.
    D) plasticity.
Answer: D
Page Ref: 9
Skill: Applied
Objective: 1.3

16) According to research on resilience, which of the following children has an increased chance of offsetting the impact of a stressful home life?
    A) John, who is a talented musician
    B) Mary, who is an only child
    C) Luke, who is shy
    D) Jane, who comes from a blended family
Answer: A
Page Ref: 10–11 Box: B&E: Resilient Children
Skill: Applied
Objective: 1.3

17) The most consistent asset of resilient children is
    A) high self-esteem.
    B) access to high-quality child care.
    C) a strong bond to a competent, caring adult.
    D) being identified as gifted.
Answer: C
Page Ref: 11 Box: B&E:Resilient Children
Skill: Factual
Objective: 1.3

18) During medieval times,
    A) children dressed and acted like adults.
    B) childhood was regarded as a separate period of life.
    C) a child was viewed as a tabula rasa.
    D) childhood was not regarded as a distinct developmental period.
Answer: B
Page Ref: 11
Skill: Factual
Objective: 1.4

19) During the Reformation, the Puritans
    A) characterized children as innocent and close to angels.
    B) regarded children as fully mature by the time they were 7 or 8 years old.
    C) recommended permissive child-rearing practices.
    D) believed that children were born evil and had to be civilized.
Answer: D
Page Ref: 12
Skill: Factual
Objective: 1.4

20) As the Puritans emigrated from England to America, they brought the belief that
   A) children were born innocent and self-reliant.
   B) child rearing was one of adults' most important obligations.
   C) children were naturally endowed with a sense of right and wrong.
   D) children's characters were shaped entirely by experience.
   Answer: B
   Page Ref: 12
   Skill: Factual
   Objective: 1.4

21) According to John Locke's view, children begin
   A) with a soul tainted by original sin.
   B) as nothing at all.
   C) as noble savages.
   D) as evil and stubborn.
   Answer: B
   Page Ref: 12
   Skill: Factual
   Objective: 1.4

22) John Locke opposed the use of
   A) praise as a reward.
   B) negative reinforcement.
   C) physical punishment.
   D) any form of discipline.
   Answer: C
   Page Ref: 12
   Skill: Factual
   Objective: 1.4

23) John Locke regarded development as
   A) continuous.
   B) mostly influenced by nature.
   C) discontinuous.
   D) highly stable.
   Answer: A
   Page Ref: 12
   Skill: Factual
   Objective: 1.4

24) All contemporary child development theories view children as
   A) naturally endowed with a sense of right and wrong.
   B) passive and emotionally fragile.
   C) adults in training.
   D) active, purposeful beings.
   Answer: D
   Page Ref: 12
   Skill: Factual
   Objective: 1.4

25) According to Jean-Jacques Rousseau, children are
   A) born evil and stubborn and have to be civilized.
   B) born as blank slates to be filled by adult instruction.
   C) naturally endowed with a sense of right and wrong.
   D) passive and do little to influence their own destinies.
   Answer: C
   Page Ref: 13
   Skill: Conceptual
   Objective: 1.4

26) Dr. Thigpen views development as a discontinuous, stagewise process that follows a single, unified course mapped out by nature. Dr. Thigpen's views are most aligned with which perspective?
   A) Jean-Jacques Rousseau's view of the child as a noble savage
   B) John Locke's view of the child as a tabula rasa
   C) The Puritans' view of the child as evil and stubborn
   D) Charles Darwin's view of survival of the fittest
   Answer: A
   Page Ref: 13
   Skill: Applied
   Objective: 1.4

27) Which of the following is true about Charles Darwin's contribution to developmental theories?
   A) He proved that the development of the human child followed the same general plan as the evolution of the human species.
   B) Scientific child study was born out of his first attempts to document an idea about development.
   C) He launched the normative approach, in which measures of behavior are taken on large numbers of individuals and age-related averages are computed to represent typical development.
   D) He proved that human development is a genetically determined process that unfolds automatically, much like a flower.
   Answer: B
   Page Ref: 13
   Skill: Conceptual
   Objective: 1.4

28) _____ is generally regarded as the founder of the child-study movement.
   A) John Locke
   B) Jean-Jacques Rousseau
   C) Charles Darwin
   D) G. Stanley Hall
   Answer: D
   Page Ref: 13
   Skill: Factual
   Objective: 1.4

29) Inspired by Charles Darwin's work, G. Stanley Hall and his student, Arnold Gesell,
   A) were the first theorists to focus on the role of nurture in human development.
   B) collected detailed normative information on children's behavior and characteristics.
   C) developed the concept of a sensitive period in human development.
   D) constructed the first intelligence test.
   Answer: B
   Page Ref: 13
   Skill: Factual
   Objective: 1.4

30) Along with Benjamin Spock's Baby and Child Care, _____'s books became a central part of a rapidly expanding popular literature for parents.
   A) G. Stanley Hall
   B) Alfred Binet
   C) Theodore Simon
   D) Arnold Gesell
Answer: D
Page Ref: 14
Skill: Factual
Objective: 1.4

31) Alfred Binet and Theodore Simon's intelligence test was developed as a way to
   A) identify children with learning problems who needed to be placed in special classes.
   B) accurately predict school achievement and vocational success.
   C) document developmental improvements in children's intellectual functioning.
   D) measure individual differences in development as a function of race, gender, and birth order.
Answer: A
Page Ref: 14
Skill: Factual
Objective: 1.4

32) The psychoanalytic perspective emphasizes
   A) normative information that represents typical development.
   B) the unique history of each child.
   C) stimuli and responses.
   D) modeling or imitation.
Answer: B
Page Ref: 15
Skill: Conceptual
Objective: 1.5

33) Sigmund Freud's psychosexual theory
   A) was developed through careful observations of his own children.
   B) emphasizes that how parents manage their child's fears is crucial for healthy sexual development.
   C) emphasizes five parts of the personality that become integrated during a sequence of three stages.
   D) was developed through having emotionally troubled adults talk freely about painful events of their childhoods.
Answer: D
Page Ref: 15
Skill: Factual
Objective: 1.5

34) According to Freud, the _____ is the conscious, rational part of personality.
   A) id
   B) ego
   C) superego
   D) superid
Answer: B
Page Ref: 15
Skill: Factual
Objective: 1.5

35) Freud's theory was the first to stress the influence of _____ on development.
   A) observational learning
   B) rewards and punishment
   C) cultural norms
   D) the early parent–child relationship
Answer: D
Page Ref: 15
Skill: Factual
Objective: 1.5

36) Erik Erikson was one of the first theorists to
   A) study the nature–nurture controversy.
   B) focus on the impact of early experiences on later behavior.
   C) recognize the lifespan nature of development.
   D) view children as passive beings.
Answer: C
Page Ref: 15
Skill: Factual
Objective: 1.5

37) Which of the following is a reason the psychoanalytic perspective is no longer in the mainstream of child development research?
   A) Many psychoanalytic ideas, such as ego functioning, are too vague to be tested empirically.
   B) Psychoanalytic theorists accept the clinical method in which age-related averages are computed to represent typical development.
   C) Modern researchers have demonstrated that personality development does not take place in stages.
   D) Psychoanalytic theorists became isolated from the rest of the field because they failed to consider the early parent–child relationship.
Answer: A
Page Ref: 17
Skill: Conceptual
Objective: 1.5

38) According to behaviorism, _____ are the appropriate focus of psychological research.
   A) stimuli and responses
   B) unconscious impulses and drives
   C) adaptive evolutionary behavior patterns
   D) nonobservable events
Answer: A
Page Ref: 17
Skill: Factual
Objective: 1.5

39) Ivan Pavlov taught dogs to salivate at the sound of a bell by using
   A) operant conditioning.
   B) classical conditioning.
   C) innate reflexes.
   D) modeling.
Answer: B
Page Ref: 17
Skill: Factual
Objective: 1.5

40) When John Watson taught Albert, an 11-month-old infant, to fear a neutral stimulus by presenting it several times with a sharp, loud sound, Watson applied _____ to children's behavior.
    A) innate reflexes
    B) observational learning
    C) classical conditioning
    D) operant conditioning
Answer: C
Page Ref: 17
Skill: Factual
Objective: 1.5

41) Consistent with Locke's tabula rasa, John Watson concluded that _____ is the supreme force in development.
    A) nature
    B) early experience
    C) environment
    D) cognition
Answer: C
Page Ref: 17
Skill: Conceptual
Objective: 1.5

42) On a few occasions, Jack's mother gave him candy to keep him quiet when she took him to the doctor's office. Now every time Jack goes to the doctor's office, he asks his mother for candy. This is an example of
    A) classical conditioning.
    B) operant conditioning.
    C) observational learning.
    D) modeling.
Answer: B
Page Ref: 17
Skill: Applied
Objective: 1.5

43) According to B. F. Skinner, the frequency of a behavior can be increased by following it with a wide variety of
    A) punishments.
    B) negative stimuli.
    C) stimulus–response associations.
    D) reinforcers.
Answer: D
Page Ref: 17
Skill: Conceptual
Objective: 1.5

44) Every time 10-month-old Rita eats a pea, her father claps and says, "Good girl!" In response to her father's praise, Rita excitedly eats the remaining peas. Rita's behavior is an example of
    A) classical conditioning.
    B) modeling.
    C) behavior modification.
    D) operant conditioning.
Answer: D
Page Ref: 17
Skill: Applied
Objective: 1.5

45) Which of the following is true about social learning theory?
  A) It emphasizes modeling, also known as imitation or observational learning, as a powerful source of development.
  B) It maintains that behaviorism offers little or no effective explanation of the development of children's social behavior.
  C) It is criticized because it places little emphasis on how children are influenced by the behavior of their parents and peers.
  D) It emphasizes classical over operant conditioning and relies heavily on the precise concepts of psychoanalytic theory.
Answer: A
Page Ref: 18
Skill: Factual
Objective: 1.5

46) At home, Paul's parents hit him as punishment for misbehavior. At preschool, Paul angrily hits a playmate who takes his toy. According to social learning theory, Paul is displaying
  A) classical conditioning.
  B) operant conditioning.
  C) behavior modification.
  D) observational learning.
Answer: D
Page Ref: 18
Skill: Applied
Objective: 1.5

47) The most recent revision of Albert Bandura's theory places such a strong emphasis on how children think about themselves and other people that he calls it a(n) _____ rather than a(n) _____ approach.
  A) observational learning; social-cognitive
  B) social-cognitive; social learning
  C) social learning; cognitive
  D) social learning; observational learning
Answer: B
Page Ref: 18
Skill: Factual
Objective: 1.5

48) Which of the following is an example of behavior modification?
  A) letting children with acute burn injuries play a virtual reality game while nurses engage in the painful process of changing their bandages
  B) modeling quiet reading for children to teach them to sit quietly while they read
  C) talking with children about fears in an attempt to uncover the underlying cause of thumb sucking
  D) taking away a treasured toy for an increased amount of time each time a child bites his or her nails
Answer: A
Page Ref: 18
Skill: Applied
Objective: 1.5

49) Both behaviorism and social learning theory have been criticized for
  A) overestimating children's contributions to their own development.
  B) presenting ideas that are too vague to test empirically.
  C) emphasizing nature over nurture.
  D) underestimating children's contributions to their own development.
Answer: D
Page Ref: 18–19
Skill: Conceptual
Objective: 1.5

50) According to Jean Piaget's cognitive-developmental theory,
 A) development must be understood in relation to each child's culture.
 B) children's sense of self-efficacy guides their responses in particular situations.
 C) children actively construct knowledge as they interact with their world.
 D) children's learning depends on reinforcers, such as rewards from adults.
 Answer: C
 Page Ref: 19
 Skill: Conceptual
 Objective: 1.5

51) The biological concept of _____ is central to Piaget's theory.
 A) reinforcement
 B) adaptation
 C) imitation
 D) physical growth
 Answer: B
 Page Ref: 19
 Skill: Factual
 Objective: 1.5

52) According to Piaget, _____ lead(s) to more advanced ways of thinking.
 A) children's observation of adults
 B) brain growth
 C) punishment and reinforcement
 D) children's efforts to achieve equilibrium
 Answer: D
 Page Ref: 19
 Skill: Conceptual
 Objective: 1.5

53) Development of language and make-believe play take place in Piaget's _____ stage.
 A) sensorimotor
 B) preoperational
 C) concrete operational
 D) formal operational
 Answer: B
 Page Ref: 19
 Skill: Factual
 Objective: 1.5

54) According to Piaget's theory, in the sensorimotor stage, children
 A) can think of all possible outcomes in a scientific problem.
 B) organize objects into hierarchies of classes and subclasses.
 C) think by acting on the world with their eyes, ears, hands, and mouth.
 D) can evaluate the logic of verbal statements without referring to real-world circumstances.
 Answer: C
 Page Ref: 19
 Skill: Conceptual
 Objective: 1.5

55) Children can evaluate the logic of verbal statements without referring to real-world circumstances in Piaget's
_____ stage.
   A) sensorimotor
   B) preoperational
   C) concrete operational
   D) formal operational
Answer: D
Page Ref: 19
Skill: Factual
Objective: 1.5

56) A classroom environment based on Piaget's theory of cognitive development would likely emphasize
   A) joint problem solving with older children or adults.
   B) reinforcing children with tokens they could exchange for treats.
   C) formal mathematics and language drills.
   D) discovery learning and direct contact with the environment.
Answer: D
Page Ref: 20
Skill: Applied
Objective: 1.5

57) Which of the following is a limitation of Piaget's theory?
   A) He overestimated the competencies of infants and young children.
   B) Adolescents generally reach their full intellectual potential in all areas, regardless of education and experience.
   C) Children's performance on Piagetian problems can be improved with training.
   D) Piaget's stagewise account overemphasizes social and cultural influences on development.
Answer: C
Page Ref: 21
Skill: Conceptual
Objective: 1.5

58) Dr. Brewer views the human mind as a symbol-manipulating system through which information flows. Dr. Brewer's view is consistent with
   A) information processing.
   B) ethology.
   C) behaviorism.
   D) sociocultural theory.
Answer: A
Page Ref: 21
Skill: Applied
Objective: 1.6

59) Information-processing researchers often use _____ to map the precise steps individuals use to solve problems and complete tasks.
   A) clinical interviews
   B) flowcharts
   C) imprinting
   D) social mediation
Answer: B
Page Ref: 21
Skill: Factual
Objective: 1.6

60) In a research study, 10-year-old Joe was given a pile of blocks varying in size, shape, and weight and was asked to build a bridge over a "river" (painted on a floor map) that was too wide for any single block to span. The researcher carefully tracked Joe's efforts using a flowchart. The researcher was probably applying which recent theoretical perspective?
  A) ecological systems theory
  B) evolutionary developmental psychology
  C) information processing
  D) sociocultural theory
Answer: C
Page Ref: 22
Skill: Applied
Objective: 1.6

61) Both Piaget's theory and the information-processing perspective
  A) regard children as active beings who modify their own thinking in response to environmental demands.
  B) focus on the development of imagination and creativity.
  C) regard perception, memory, and problem solving as similar at all ages.
  D) emphasize the importance of equilibration in producing higher levels of thinking.
Answer: A
Page Ref: 22
Skill: Conceptual
Objective: 1.6

62) A great strength of the information-processing approach is its commitment to
  A) field work.
  B) clinical interviews.
  C) rigorous research methods.
  D) structured observations.
Answer: C
Page Ref: 22
Skill: Conceptual
Objective: 1.6

63) The information-processing perspective has little to say about
  A) linear cognition.
  B) how children think at different ages.
  C) logical cognition.
  D) imagination and creativity.
Answer: D
Page Ref: 23
Skill: Conceptual
Objective: 1.6

64) Dr. Grief studies the relationship between changes in the brain and the developing child's cognitive processing and behavior patterns. Dr. Grief would most likely consider herself to be a(n)
  A) behaviorist.
  B) developmental cognitive neuroscientist.
  C) evolutionary developmental psychologist.
  D) information-processing researcher.
Answer: B
Page Ref: 23
Skill: Applied
Objective: 1.6

65) Sociocultural theory, ethology, ecological systems theory, and dynamic system theory all focus on
    A) contexts for development.
    B) the adaptive value of behavior.
    C) children's biological makeup.
    D) how culture is transmitted to the next generation.
Answer: A
Page Ref: 23–29
Skill: Conceptual
Objective: 1.6

66) Which recent theoretical perspective is concerned with the adaptive, or survival, value of behavior and its evolutionary history?
    A) information processing
    B) ethology
    C) sociocultural theory
    D) ecological systems theory
Answer: B
Page Ref: 23
Skill: Conceptual
Objective: 1.6

67) Observations of imprinting led to which of the following major concepts in child development?
    A) behavior modification
    B) observational learning
    C) the critical period
    D) the chronosystem
Answer: C
Page Ref: 23
Skill: Conceptual
Objective: 1.6

68) Why does the term sensitive period apply better to human development than does the notion of a critical period?
    A) Its boundaries are less well-defined than are those of a critical period.
    B) Its boundaries are more well-defined than are those of a critical period.
    C) There are more sensitive periods than critical periods in human development.
    D) Sensitive periods, but not critical periods, have been empirically tested.
Answer: A
Page Ref: 23–24
Skill: Conceptual
Objective: 1.6

69) Dr. McMath is an evolutionary developmental psychologist. Which of the following is probably true about Dr. McMath?
    A) He is primarily concerned with the genetic and biological basis of development.
    B) He wants to understand the entire organism–environment system.
    C) He is primarily concerned with environmental influences on development.
    D) He focuses on how culture is transmitted to the next generation.
Answer: B
Page Ref: 24
Skill: Applied
Objective: 1.6

70) According to Vygotsky's theory,
    A) today's lifestyles differ so radically from those of our evolutionary ancestors that certain evolved behaviors are no longer adaptive.
    B) children shape their own development during both sensitive and critical developmental periods.
    C) children revise incorrect ideas in their ongoing efforts to achieve equilibrium between internal structures and everyday information.
    D) social interaction is necessary for children to acquire the ways of thinking and behaving that make up a community's culture.
Answer: D
Page Ref: 25
Skill: Conceptual
Objective: 1.6

71) Vygotsky's theory has been especially influential in the study of children's
    A) physical growth.
    B) cognition.
    C) emotional development.
    D) gender identity.
Answer: B
Page Ref: 25
Skill: Conceptual
Objective: 1.6

72) Unlike Piaget, Vygotsky
    A) emphasized children's capacity to shape their own development.
    B) viewed cognitive development as a socially mediated process.
    C) believed that children undergo certain stagewise changes.
    D) focused on discontinuous change.
Answer: B
Page Ref: 25
Skill: Conceptual
Objective: 1.6

73) Which of the following behaviors is consistent with Vygotsky's theory?
    A) When his mother takes him to the grocery store, Tom is well-behaved because he knows that his mother will reward him with candy.
    B) When playing in her sandbox, Amy builds the same sort of castle that she observed her best friend building yesterday.
    C) Yesica, a child candy seller with no schooling, develops sophisticated mathematical abilities as a result of her work.
    D) When working on her math homework, Michelle tries several solutions before she arrives at the correct answer.
Answer: C
Page Ref: 25
Skill: Applied
Objective: 1.6

74) Which of the following is a limitation of Vygotsky's sociocultural theory?
    A) It neglects the biological side of development.
    B) It overemphasizes the biological side of development.
    C) It overemphasizes children's capacity to shape their own development.
    D) It places little emphasis on joint experiences.
Answer: A
Page Ref: 25
Skill: Conceptual
Objective: 1.6

75) Which recent theoretical perspective views children as developing within a complex system of relationships affected by multiple levels of the surrounding environment?
   A) information processing
   B) ethology
   C) sociocultural theory
   D) ecological systems theory
   Answer: D
   Page Ref: 25–26
   Skill: Conceptual
   Objective: 1.6

76) In Bronfenbrenner's ecological systems theory, the _____ includes interactions between the child and the immediate environment.
   A) microsystem
   B) mesosystem
   C) exosystem
   D) macrosystem
   Answer: A
   Page Ref: 26
   Skill: Conceptual
   Objective: 1.6

77) In Bronfenbrenner's ecological systems theory, the _____ encompasses connections between microsystems, such as home, school, and neighborhood.
   A) mesosystem
   B) exosystem
   C) macrosystem
   D) chronosystem
   Answer: A
   Page Ref: 26
   Skill: Conceptual
   Objective: 1.6

78) According to ecological systems theory, a parent's workplace is in the
   A) microsystem.
   B) mesosystem.
   C) exosystem.
   D) macrosystem.
   Answer: C
   Page Ref: 27
   Skill: Conceptual
   Objective: 1.6

79) According to Urie Bronfenbrenner, the environment
   A) is a static force.
   B) is ever-changing.
   C) affects children in a uniform way.
   D) is less important to development than heredity.
   Answer: B
   Page Ref: 27
   Skill: Conceptual
   Objective: 1.6

80) Dr. Jones believes that a child's mind, body, and physical and social worlds form an integrated system that guides mastery of new skills. The system is constantly in motion. His view is consistent with which recent theoretical perspective?
   A) evolutionary developmental psychology
   B) sociocultural theory
   C) ecological systems theory
   D) dynamic systems perspective
Answer: D
Page Ref: 28
Skill: Applied
Objective: 1.6

81) Dynamic systems theorists emphasize that
   A) children are driven mainly by instincts and unconscious motives.
   B) different skills vary in maturity within the same child.
   C) sensitive periods are key to understanding development.
   D) development can be best understood in terms of its adaptive value.
Answer: B
Page Ref: 28
Skill: Conceptual
Objective: 1.6

82) Which of the following recent theoretical perspectives can best explain why Easton never crawled on his hands and knees before he learned how to walk?
   A) ecological systems theory
   B) sociocultural theory
   C) evolutionary developmental psychology
   D) dynamic systems perspective
Answer: D
Page Ref: 28
Skill: Applied
Objective: 1.6

83) Which major theory focuses on emotional development?
   A) psychoanalytic theory
   B) ethology
   C) behaviorism
   D) ecological systems theory
Answer: A
Page Ref: 29
Skill: Conceptual
Objective: 1.7

84) Both _____ and _____ stress changes in thinking.
   A) behaviorism; social learning theory
   B) cognitive-developmental theory; information-processing theory
   C) ethology; psychoanalytic theory
   D) dynamic systems theory; ecological systems theory
Answer: B
Page Ref: 29
Skill: Conceptual
Objective: 1.7

85) Both _____ and _____ emphasize many possible courses of development.
   A) the psychoanalytic perspective; ethology
   B) ethology; evolutionary developmental psychology
   C) Piaget's cognitive-developmental theory; behaviorism
   D) behaviorism; social learning theory
Answer: D
Page Ref: 29
Skill: Conceptual
Objective: 1.7

86) A major limitation of naturalistic observation is that
   A) the findings cannot be generalized beyond the participants and settings in which the research was originally conducted.
   B) researchers cannot control the conditions under which participants are observed.
   C) the research may not yield observations typical of participants' behavior in everyday life.
   D) participants may not accurately report their thoughts, feelings, and experiences.
Answer: B
Page Ref: 31, 32
Skill: Conceptual
Objective: 1.8

87) Dr. Brown observes behavior in a laboratory, where conditions are the same for all participants. This is an example of
   A) the clinical method.
   B) a structured observation.
   C) a naturalistic observation.
   D) an ethnography.
Answer: B
Page Ref: 31–32
Skill: Applied
Objective: 1.8

88) A major advantage of structured observation is that it
   A) is useful for studying behaviors that investigators rarely have an opportunity to see in everyday life.
   B) permits participants to display their thoughts in terms that are as close as possible to the way they think in everyday life.
   C) yields richly detailed narratives that offer valuable insight into the many factors that affect development.
   D) allows researchers to see the behavior of interest as it occurs in natural settings.
Answer: A
Page Ref: 32
Skill: Conceptual
Objective: 1.8

89) Dr. Kempsell combines interviews, observations, and test scores to obtain a full picture of one individual's psychological functioning. This is an example of
   A) naturalistic observation.
   B) structured observation.
   C) a structured interview.
   D) the clinical method.
Answer: D
Page Ref: 32
Skill: Applied
Objective: 1.8

90) Dr. Stephens would like to obtain rich, descriptive insights into processes of development of one individual. Which of the following methods is best suited to meet Dr. Stephens' needs?
    A) naturalistic observation
    B) a case study
    C) structured observation
    D) a clinical interview
Answer: B
Page Ref: 32
Skill: Applied
Objective: 1.8

91) Which of the following is true about structured observation?
    A) It permits greater control over the research situation than does naturalistic observation.
    B) It is especially useful for studying behaviors commonly seen in everyday life.
    C) It usually takes place in the field, or natural environment, rather than in the laboratory.
    D) It provides rich, descriptive insights into processes of development of one individual.
Answer: A
Page Ref: 32
Skill: Conceptual
Objective: 1.8

92) Self-reports
    A) are usually very accurate.
    B) ask research participants to provide information on their thoughts, beliefs, and experiences.
    C) tell researchers little about the reasoning behind how participants behave.
    D) are always highly structured.
Answer: B
Page Ref: 32, 33
Skill: Conceptual
Objective: 1.8

93) A strength of the clinical interview is that
    A) it can provide a large amount of information in a fairly brief period.
    B) it provides highly objective and generalizable data.
    C) it accurately assesses even those participants who have low verbal ability and expressiveness.
    D) each participant is asked the same questions in the same way.
Answer: A
Page Ref: 33
Skill: Factual
Objective: 1.8

94) One major limitation of the clinical interview is
    A) it does not provide much insight into participants' reasoning or ideas.
    B) it requires extensive training to interpret.
    C) the questions are phrased the same for each participant, regardless of verbal ability.
    D) participants are not always accurate when they report their thoughts, feelings, and experiences.
Answer: D
Page Ref: 33
Skill: Factual
Objective: 1.8

95) Structured interviews are limited because they
   A) are less efficient than clinical interviews.
   B) do not yield the same depth of information as clinical interviews.
   C) are more time consuming to carry out compared to clinical interviews.
   D) are overly flexible and sometimes confusing.
Answer: B
Page Ref: 33
Skill: Factual
Objective: 1.8

96) Dr. Jaster is interested in children's dreams. He recruits students from two public schools in his community and administers the same questionnaire to several large groups. Dr. Jaster is using a(n)
   A) biased interviewing technique.
   B) case study method.
   C) structured interview.
   D) ethnographic approach.
Answer: C
Page Ref: 33
Skill: Applied
Objective: 1.8

97) The clinical method is well-suited to
   A) studying a culture or a distinct social group through participant observation.
   B) providing a large amount of information in a relatively brief period.
   C) studying the development of certain types of individuals who are few in number but vary widely in characteristics.
   D) asking multiple participants the same questions in the same way.
Answer: C
Page Ref: 34
Skill: Factual
Objective: 1.8

98) Dr. Snyder used the clinical method to obtain a richly detailed case narrative about Charlie, a 10-year-old college student. Dr. Snyder should be aware that
   A) information collected using the clinical method cannot offer insight into factors affecting development.
   B) he cannot assume that his conclusions apply, or generalize, to anyone other than Charlie.
   C) the information will help him understand the cultural group to which Charlie belongs.
   D) ethical guidelines will limit their contact to one or two sessions.
Answer: B
Page Ref: 34
Skill: Applied
Objective: 1.8

99) Dr. Newman spent three years in Botswana, participating in the daily life of a community there. She gathered extensive field notes, consisting of a mix of self-reports from members of the community and her own observations. Which research method did Dr. Newman most likely use in her research?
   A) ethnography
   B) structured observation
   C) the microgenetic design
   D) the case study method
Answer: A
Page Ref: 34–35
Skill: Applied
Objective: 1.8

100) Which of the following research methods utilizes participant observation?
   A) the clinical method
   B) naturalistic observation
   C) ethnography
   D) structured observation
   Answer: C
   Page Ref: 34–35
   Skill: Conceptual
   Objective: 1.8

101) Which of the following is a limitation of the ethnographic method?
   A) Research may not yield observations typical of participants' behavior in everyday life.
   B) Research does not yield as much information as naturalistic observations or structured interviews.
   C) Commonly used research techniques tend to ignore cultural and social influences that affect development.
   D) Investigators' cultural values and theoretical commitments sometimes lead them to observe selectively or misinterpret what they see.
   Answer: D
   Page Ref: 35
   Skill: Conceptual
   Objective: 1.8

102) In the United States, children who are first-generation and second-generation immigrants
   A) are more likely than children of native-born parents to use drugs and alcohol.
   B) report lower self-esteem as compared to children of native-born parents.
   C) graduate from high school at similar or greater overall rates than students of native-born parents.
   D) are more likely than children of native-born parents to commit delinquent acts.
   Answer: C
   Page Ref: 36 Box: CI: Immigrant Youths: Adapting to a New Land
   Skill: Conceptual
   Objective: 1.8

103) Immigrant parents of successful youths typically
   A) view school successes as less important than native-born parents.
   B) develop close ties to an ethnic community.
   C) encourage full assimilation into the majority culture.
   D) stress individualistic values over collectivist values.
   Answer: B
   Page Ref: 36 Box: CI: Immigrant Youths: Adapting to a New Land
   Skill: Conceptual
   Objective: 1.8

104) Which of the following is true about the correlational design?
   A) Researchers gather information on individuals, generally in natural life circumstances, and make no effort to alter their experiences.
   B) Unlike the experimental design, it permits inferences of cause and effect.
   C) Researchers use an evenhanded procedure to assign people to two or more treatment conditions.
   D) In an experiment, the events and behaviors of interest are divided into independent and dependent variables.
   Answer: A
   Page Ref: 37
   Skill: Conceptual
   Objective: 1.9

105) The major limitation of correlational studies is that
    A) the findings do not provide information about how people behave outside the laboratory.
    B) the findings do not reveal relationships between participants' characteristics and their behavior.
    C) researchers cannot make inferences about cause and effect.
    D) the results cannot be generalized to other people and settings.
Answer: C
Page Ref: 37
Skill: Conceptual
Objective: 1.9

106) In interpreting a correlation coefficient,
    A) the magnitude of the number shows the direction of the relationship.
    B) the sign of the number shows the strength of the relationship.
    C) a positive sign means that as one variable increases, the other decreases.
    D) a zero correlation indicates no relationship.
Answer: D
Page Ref: 37
Skill: Factual
Objective: 1.9

107) Dr. Brenneman's research shows that participation in music programs is positively related to grades in school. Based on the findings from this one study, what can Dr. Brenneman conclude?
    A) Participating in music programs causes grades to decrease.
    B) Participating in music programs causes grades to increase.
    C) Children who participate in music programs have higher grades.
    D) Children who participate in music programs have lower grades.
Answer: C
Page Ref: 37
Skill: Applied
Objective: 1.9

108) A correlation of +.55 between preschool attendance and self-esteem indicates that children who attend preschool have
    A) moderately higher self-esteem scores than children who do not attend preschool.
    B) significantly higher self-esteem scores than children who do not attend preschool.
    C) have significantly lower self-esteem scores than children who do not attend preschool.
    D) have moderately lower self-esteem scores than children who do not attend preschool.
Answer: A
Page Ref: 37
Skill: Applied
Objective: 1.9

109) A(n) _____ permits inferences about cause and effect.
    A) correlation coefficient
    B) experimental design
    C) correlational design
    D) case study
Answer: B
Page Ref: 37
Skill: Factual
Objective: 1.9

110) The independent variable is the one that
    A) the investigator expects to be influenced by another variable.
    B) is randomly assigned.
    C) shows the strength of the correlational relationship.
    D) the investigator expects to cause changes in another variable.
Answer: D
Page Ref: 37
Skill: Factual
Objective: 1.9

111) In an experiment examining whether a specific type of intervention improves the psychological adjustment of shy children, the independent variable would be the
    A) type of intervention.
    B) number of children in the subject pool who are shy.
    C) number of shy children who benefit from the intervention.
    D) measure of psychological adjustment.
Answer: A
Page Ref: 37
Skill: Applied
Objective: 1.9

112) In the same experiment examining whether a specific type of intervention improves the psychological adjustment of shy children, the dependent variable would be the
    A) type of intervention.
    B) number of children in the subject pool who are shy.
    C) number of shy children who benefit from the intervention.
    D) measure of psychological adjustment.
Answer: D
Page Ref: 37
Skill: Applied
Objective: 1.9

113) When a researcher directly controls or manipulates changes in an independent variable by exposing participants to the treatment conditions,
    A) she is conducting a correlational study.
    B) cause-and-effect relationships can be detected.
    C) the correlational coefficient should be zero.
    D) she is using a technique called matching.
Answer: B
Page Ref: 37–38
Skill: Conceptual
Objective: 1.9

114) Professor Hudgens is studying the impact of adults' angry interactions on children's adjustment. To determine which participants are exposed to each treatment condition, Professor Hudgens draws the participants' names out of a hat. Professor Hudgens is using
    A) matching.
    B) random assignment.
    C) experimental assignment.
    D) cross-sectioning.
Answer: B
Page Ref: 38
Skill: Applied
Objective: 1.9

115) Dr. Riley wanted to know if adolescent computer use has an immediate effect on their sustained attention. Dr. Riley assigned participants into one of two groups (computer use vs. no computer use) by flipping a coin. Dr. Riley used
   A) matching.
   B) random assignment.
   C) a correlational design.
   D) a field experiment.
   Answer: B
   Page Ref: 38
   Skill: Applied
   Objective: 1.9

116) One way Professor Hudgens could use the matching technique to assign the participants to the experimental conditions would be to
   A) flip a coin or draw names out of a hat.
   B) let the parents choose in which experimental group they would like their children to participate.
   C) assign equal numbers of children with high and low parental conflict to each treatment condition.
   D) let the children choose in which experimental group they would like to participate.
   Answer: C
   Page Ref: 38
   Skill: Applied
   Objective: 1.9

117) Professor Spinner wanted to compare how children from different family environments made friends at school. He carefully chose participants to ensure that their characteristics were as much alike as possible. Professor Spinner observed the participants in the school setting. Professor Spinner used
   A) a laboratory experiment.
   B) random assignment.
   C) a field experiment.
   D) a correlational design.
   Answer: C
   Page Ref: 38
   Skill: Applied
   Objective: 1.9

118) In _____ experiments, control over the treatment is usually weaker than in _____ experiments.
   A) laboratory; natural
   B) laboratory; field
   C) field; laboratory
   D) correlational; field
   Answer: C
   Page Ref: 39
   Skill: Factual
   Objective: 1.9

119) In quasi-experiments,
   A) random assignment helps protect against reduction in the accuracy of the findings.
   B) researchers combine random assignment with the matching technique.
   C) cause-and-effect inferences cannot be made.
   D) lack of random assignment substantially reduces the precision of the research.
   Answer: D
   Page Ref: 39
   Skill: Conceptual
   Objective: 1.9

120) Professor Yang wondered if parenting style is related children's achievement test scores. Professor Yang gathered information on the participants, but made no effort to alter their experiences. Professor Yang used
    A) a correlational design.
    B) random assignment.
    C) experimental design.
    D) a natural experiment.
Answer: A
Page Ref: 39
Skill: Applied
Objective: 1.9

121) In a _____, participants are studied repeatedly, and changes are noted as they get older.
    A) correlational design
    B) longitudinal design
    C) cross-sectional study
    D) sequential design
Answer: B
Page Ref: 39
Skill: Factual
Objective: 1.10

122) One limitation of the longitudinal design is it
    A) does not permit the study of individual development.
    B) requires intensive study of participants' moment-by-moment behaviors.
    C) may distort age-related changes because of biased sampling or cohort effects.
    D) is more efficient than cross-sectional design, but less efficient than microgenetic design.
Answer: C
Page Ref: 39
Skill: Conceptual
Objective: 1.10

123) Two strengths of longitudinal design are that researchers can _____ and _____.
    A) collect a large amount of data in a short time span; identify both common patterns and individual differences
    B) explore similarities among children of different ages at the same time; examine relationships between early and later behaviors
    C) collect a large amount of data in a short time span; explore similarities among children of different ages at the same time
    D) identify both common patterns and individual differences; examine relationships between early and later behaviors
Answer: D
Page Ref: 39
Skill: Conceptual
Objective: 1.10

124) To examine whether children's popularity was stable or changed across the years, Dr. Clique followed a group of children from ages 5 to 18 years. This is an example of a _____ design.
    A) sequential
    B) microgenetic
    C) cross-sectional
    D) longitudinal
Answer: D
Page Ref: 39, 40
Skill: Applied
Objective: 1.10

125) Dr. Stamina's longitudinal study on Native American personality styles was criticized because he failed to enlist participants who adequately represented the Native American population. This limitation is known as
    A) cohort effects.
    B) selective attrition.
    C) practice effects.
    D) biased sampling.
Answer: D
Page Ref: 39, 40
Skill: Applied
Objective: 1.10

126) The most widely discussed threat to the accuracy of longitudinal findings is
    A) practice effects.
    B) cohort effects.
    C) selective attrition.
    D) biased sampling.
Answer: B
Page Ref: 41
Skill: Factual
Objective: 1.10

127) Cohort effects occur when
    A) participants in longitudinal studies become "test-wise."
    B) specific experiences influence some children but not others in the same generation.
    C) participants move away or drop out of a longitudinal study.
    D) participants in a research study have a special appreciation for the scientific value of research.
Answer: B
Page Ref: 41
Skill: Conceptual
Objective: 1.10

128) Dr. Kirk wants to study sibling relationships at differing ages. Dr. Kirk has children with one or more siblings in grades 3, 6, 9, and 12 complete his questionnaire. This is an example of a _____ study.
    A) cross-sectional
    B) longitudinal
    C) microgenetic
    D) sequential
Answer: A
Page Ref: 41
Skill: Applied
Objective: 1.10

129) Because participants are measured only once in the cross-sectional design, researchers need not be concerned about difficulties like _____ and _____.
    A) cohort effects; practice effects
    B) selective attrition; cohort effects
    C) cohort effects; biased sampling
    D) participant dropout; practice effects
Answer: D
Page Ref: 41
Skill: Factual
Objective: 1.10

130) A disadvantage of cross-sectional research is that
    A) it is more inefficient and inconvenient than longitudinal research.
    B) it does not provide evidence about change at the individual level.
    C) it can be threatened by practice effects and participant dropout.
    D) age-related changes cannot be examined.
Answer: B
Page Ref: 41
Skill: Conceptual
Objective: 1.10

131) In an effort to overcome some of the limitations of traditional developmental designs, Dr. Francisco conducted several similar cross-sectional studies at varying times. Dr. Francisco used the _____ design.
    A) longitudinal
    B) experimental
    C) sequential
    D) correlational
Answer: C
Page Ref: 42
Skill: Applied
Objective: 1.10

132) One advantage of the sequential design is that
    A) researchers can find out whether cohort effects are operating by comparing participants of the same age who were born in different years.
    B) it permits cause-and-effect inferences by studying groups of people differing in age at the same point in time.
    C) it presents participants with a novel task and follows their mastery over a series of closely spaced sessions.
    D) it is especially useful for studying the strategies children use to acquire new knowledge in reading and science.
Answer: A
Page Ref: 42
Skill: Conceptual
Objective: 1.10

133) Using the _____ design, researchers observe how developmental change occurs.
    A) longitudinal
    B) cross-sectional
    C) sequential
    D) microgenetic
Answer: D
Page Ref: 43
Skill: Factual
Objective: 1.10

134) Professor Story is interested in studying how children acquire new reading strategies. The best design for Professor Story to use would be the _____ design.
    A) longitudinal
    B) microgenetic
    C) cross-sectional
    D) sequential
Answer: B
Page Ref: 43
Skill: Applied
Objective: 1.10

135) One limitation of microgenetic studies is that
    A) participant dropout often distorts developmental trends.
    B) they are difficult to carry out.
    C) they often create ethical issues.
    D) cohort effects often limit the generalizability of the findings.
Answer: B
Page Ref: 43
Skill: Conceptual
Objective: 1.10

136) When children take part in research, the ethical concerns are especially complex because
    A) children are less vulnerable than adults to physical harm.
    B) immaturity makes it difficult for children to evaluate for themselves what participation in research will mean.
    C) while adults are more vulnerable to psychological harm, children are sometimes exploited.
    D) children do not have the same privacy rights as adults.
Answer: B
Page Ref: 43
Skill: Factual
Objective: 1.11

137) The "Mozart effect"
    A) only applies to infants and young toddlers.
    B) lasts only about 15 minutes.
    C) is easily replicated in participants of all ages.
    D) results in IQ gains of 10 to 15 points.
Answer: B
Page Ref: 44 Box: SI: Education: Can Musical Experiences Enhance Intelligence?
Skill: Conceptual
Objective: 1.10

138) Sustained musical experiences, such as music lessons, can lead to
    A) substantial increases in intelligence that do not arise from comparable drama lessons.
    B) substantial decreases in social maturity that do not arise from comparable drama lessons.
    C) small increases in intelligence that do not arise from comparable drama lessons.
    D) small increases in social maturity that do not arise from comparable drama lessons.
Answer: C
Page Ref: 44 Box: SI: Education: Can Musical Experiences Enhance Intelligence?
Skill: Conceptual
Objective: 1.10

139) An investigator wanted to speak candidly with high school students about their drug use. He felt that the students would be more honest if their parents were unaware that they were participating in the study. If the investigator chooses to interview the students without their parents' knowledge, he will violate which of the following children's research rights?
    A) privacy
    B) protection from harm
    C) informed consent
    D) beneficial treatments
Answer: C
Page Ref: 45
Skill: Applied
Objective: 1.11

140) A researcher studying the effects of a certain pain reliever on children with chronic pain gave one group of children the pain medication and gave a placebo (or sugar pill) to another group of children. This violates which of the following children's research rights?
   A) privacy
   B) beneficial treatments
   C) informed consent
   D) knowledge of results
   Answer: B
   Page Ref: 45
   Skill: Applied
   Objective: 1.11

141) The ultimate responsibility for the ethical integrity of research with children lies with the
   A) investigator.
   B) institutional review board.
   C) child.
   D) child's parents.
   Answer: A
   Page Ref: 45
   Skill: Factual
   Objective: 1.11

142) After Dr. Busch completes his research interviews, he provides each participant with a full account and justification of the activities. Dr. Busch is engaging in
   A) debriefing.
   B) informed consent.
   C) presenting research results.
   D) unethical research methods.
   Answer: A
   Page Ref: 46
   Skill: Applied
   Objective: 1.11

ESSAY

143) Describe the five periods of development, and identify the new capacities and social expectations that serve as important transitions during each period.

Answer:

- *The prenatal period: from conception to birth.* In this nine-month period, the most rapid time of change, a one-celled organism is transformed into a human baby with remarkable capacities for adjusting to life in the surrounding world.
- *Infancy and toddlerhood: from birth to 2 years.* This period brings dramatic changes in the body and brain that support the emergence of a wide array of motor, perceptual, and intellectual capacities; the beginnings of language; and first intimate ties to others. Infancy spans the first year; toddlerhood spans the second, during which children take their first independent steps, marking a shift to greater autonomy.
- *Early childhood: from 2 to 6 years.* The body becomes longer and leaner, motor skills are refined, and children become more self-controlled and self-sufficient. Make-believe play blossoms, supporting every aspect of psychological development. Thought and language expand at an astounding pace, a sense of morality becomes evident, and children establish ties with peers.
- *Middle childhood: from 6 to 11 years.* Children learn about the wider world and master new responsibilities that increasingly resemble those they will perform as adults. Hallmarks of this period are improved athletic abilities; participation in organized games with rules; more logical thought processes; mastery of reading, writing, math, and other academic knowledge and skills; and advances in understanding the self, morality, and friendship.
- *Adolescence: from 11 to 18 years.* This period initiates the transition to adulthood. Puberty leads to an adult-sized body and sexual maturity. Thought becomes abstract and idealistic, and schooling is increasingly directed toward preparation for higher education and the world of work. Young people begin to establish autonomy from the family and to define personal values and goals.

Page Ref: 6

144) What is resilience? What are the four broad factors that seem to offer protection from the damaging effects of stressful life events? What is the most consistent asset of resilient children?

Answer: Resilience is the ability to adapt effectively in the face of threats to development. Four broad factors seem to offer protection from the damaging effects of stressful life events:

1. *Personal characteristics:* A child's biologically endowed characteristics can reduce exposure to risk or lead to experiences that compensate for early stressful events.
2. *A warm parental relationship:* A close relationship with at least one parent who provides warmth, appropriately high expectations, monitoring of the child's activities, and an organized home environment fosters resilience.
3. *Social support outside the immediate family:* For children who do not have a close bond with either parent, a grandparent, aunt, uncle, or teacher who forms a special relationship with the child can promote resilience.
4. *Community resources and opportunities:* Good schools, convenient and affordable healthcare and social services, libraries, and recreation centers foster both parents' and children's well-being.

The most consistent asset of resilient children is a strong bond to a competent, caring adult.

Page Ref: 10–11

145) Compare and contrast the terms critical period and sensitive period, and discuss how observations of imprinting led to the development of these concepts.
Answer: Watching diverse animal species in their natural habitats, European zoologists Konrad Lorenz and Niko Tinbergen developed the concept of imprinting to describe the early following behavior of certain baby birds, which ensures that the young will stay close to the mother and be fed and protected from danger. Imprinting takes place during an early, restricted time period of development. If the mother is absent during this time but an object resembling her in important features is present, young birds may imprint on it instead.

The term *critical period* refers to a limited time span during which the child is biologically prepared to acquire certain adaptive behaviors but needs the support of an appropriately stimulating environment. A *sensitive period* refers to a time that is biologically optimal for certain capacities to emerge because the individual is especially responsive to environmental influences. The idea of a sensitive period offers a better account of human development than does the strict notion of a critical period. However, its boundaries are less well-defined than are those of a critical period. Development may occur later, but it is harder to induce.
Page Ref: 23–24

146) Describe the similarities and differences between Jean Piaget's cognitive-developmental theory and Lev Vygotsky's sociocultural theory.
Answer: Piaget did not regard direct teaching by adults as important for cognitive development. Instead, he emphasized children's active, independent efforts to make sense of their world. Vygotsky agreed with Piaget that children are active, constructive beings. But whereas Piaget emphasized children's independent efforts to make sense of their world, Vygotsky viewed cognitive development as a socially mediated process, in which children depend on assistance from adults and more expert peers as they tackle new challenges. Both Vygotsky and Piaget believed that children undergo certain stagewise changes. But Vygotsky did not regard all children as moving through a universal sequence of stages of cognitive development as Piaget did. Vygotsky believed that as soon as children acquire language, their enhanced ability to communicate with others leads to continuous changes in thought and behavior that can vary greatly from culture to culture. Unlike Piaget, Vygotsky also emphasized that children in every culture develop unique strengths that are not present in other cultures because different cultures select and value different tasks for children's learning.
Page Ref: 19–21, 24–25

147) Discuss ecological systems theory, and describe each level of the environment.
Answer: Ecological systems theory views the child as developing within a complex system of relationships affected by multiple levels of the surrounding environment. Since the child's biologically influenced dispositions join with environmental forces to mold development, Urie Bronfenbrenner characterized his perspective as a bioecological model. He envisioned the environment as a series of interrelated, nested structures that form a complex functioning whole, or system. The microsystem concerns relations between the child and the immediate environment; the mesosytem includes connections among immediate settings; the exosystem includes social settings that affect but do not contain the child; and the macrosystem consists of the values, laws, customs, and resources of the culture that affect activities and interactions at all inner layers. The chronosystem is not a specific context. Instead, it refers to the dynamic, ever-changing nature of child development.
Page Ref: 25–27

148) Two types of systematic observation used in child development research are naturalistic and structured observation. Explain the benefits and limitations of each.
Answer: Naturalistic observation involves viewing behavior in natural contexts. The great strength of naturalistic observation is that investigators can see directly the everyday behaviors they hope to explain. One limitation of this research method is that not all children have the same opportunity to display a particular behavior in everyday life. Researchers commonly deal with this difficulty by making structured observations in a laboratory, where conditions are the same for all participants. In this approach, the investigator sets up a situation that evokes the behavior of interest so that every participant has equal opportunity to display the behavior of interest. The major benefit of this method is that it permits greater control over the research situation than does naturalistic observation. In addition, structured observation is especially useful for studying behaviors that investigators rarely have an opportunity to see in everyday life. A limitation of structured observation is that participants may not behave in the laboratory as they typically behave in their natural environment.
Page Ref: 31–33

149) Summarize research on the academic achievement and adjustment of immigrant youths in the United States.

Answer: Research reveals that many children of immigrant parents from diverse countries adapt amazingly well. Students who are first generation or second generation often achieve in school as well as or better than students of native-born parents, graduating from high school at similar or greater overall rates. Findings on psychological adjustment are similar. Compared with their agemates, adolescents from immigrant families are less likely to commit delinquent and violent acts, to use drugs and alcohol, or to have early sex. They are also less likely to be obese or to have missed school because of illness. They also tend to report just as favorable, and at times higher, self-esteem as do young people with native-born parents.

Page Ref: 36

150) Explain why inferences about cause and effect can be made in experiments but not in correlational studies.

Answer: Correlational studies do not permit inferences about cause-and-effect relationships; they simply permit study of the strength and direction of an association between variables. For example, a positive correlation indicates that as one variable increases, the other also increases. A negative correlation indicates that as one variable increases, the other decreases. In experimental design, inferences about cause-and-effect relationships are possible because the researcher uses an evenhanded procedure to assign people to two or more treatment conditions. Cause-and-effect relationships can be detected because the researcher directly controls or manipulates changes in the independent variable by exposing participants to treatment conditions. Random assignment of participants to treatment conditions increases the chances that the characteristics of participants will be equally distributed across treatment groups. Random assignment also increases the likelihood that any differences in the dependent variable will be due to the manipulation of the independent variable rather than systematic differences in composition of the treatment groups.

Page Ref: 37–39

151) Describe some problems investigators face in conducting longitudinal research.

Answer: Despite its strengths, longitudinal research poses a number of problems. First, investigators sometimes fail to enlist participants who adequately represent the population of interest, making a biased sample. People who willingly participate in long-term research are likely to have distinctive characteristics, such as a special appreciation for the scientific value of research. Furthermore, longitudinal samples generally become more biased with time because of selective attrition. Participants may move away or drop out of the study, and the ones who remain are likely to differ in important ways from the ones who leave. Also, from repeated study, participants may become "test-wise." Their performance may improve as a result of practice effects—better test-taking skills and increased familiarity with the test—not because of factors commonly associated with development. Finally, the most widely discussed threat to the accuracy of longitudinal findings is cultural–historical change, commonly called cohort effects. Longitudinal studies examine the development of cohorts—children born at the same time, who are influenced by particular cultural and historical conditions. Results based on one cohort may not apply to children developing at other times.

Page Ref: 40–41

152) Why are ethical concerns heightened when children take part in research? How is informed consent used with children?

Answer: Sometimes the quest for scientific knowledge can exploit people. When children take part in research, the ethical concerns are especially complex. Children are more vulnerable than adults to physical and psychological harm. Additionally, immaturity makes it hard or even impossible for children to evaluate for themselves what participation in research will mean. Thus, special ethical guidelines for research on children have been developed.

All research participants have the right to have all aspects of the research explained to them in language appropriate to their level of understanding. When children are participants, informed consent of parents as well as other adults (such as school officials) should be obtained, preferably in writing. As soon as children are old enough to do so, their own informed consent should be obtained in addition to parental consent. Extra care should be taken to ensure that children understand that they have the right to discontinue participation in the research at any time.

Page Ref: 43, 45–46

CHAPTER 2
GENETIC AND ENVIRONMENTAL FOUNDATIONS

MULTIPLE CHOICE

1) Hair color is an example of a
   A) karotype.
   B) phenotype.
   C) gamete.
   D) genotype.
   Answer: B
   Page Ref: 51
   Skill: Applied
   Objective: 2.1

2) Directly observable characteristics are affected by an individual's lifelong history of experiences and also by the individual's
   A) karotype.
   B) phenotype.
   C) gamete.
   D) genotype.
   Answer: D
   Page Ref: 51
   Skill: Conceptual
   Objective: 2.1

3) The nucleus of a cell contains
   A) karotypes.
   B) chromosomes.
   C) genotypes.
   D) phenotypes.
   Answer: B
   Page Ref: 52
   Skill: Factual
   Objective: 2.2

4) Chromosomes
   A) store and transmit genetic information.
   B) come in 46 matching pairs.
   C) are inherited from the mother only.
   D) are inherited from the father only.
   Answer: A
   Page Ref: 52
   Skill: Factual
   Objective: 2.2

5) Each rung of the DNA ladder
   A) is made up of thousands of chromosomes.
   B) contains 20,000 genes.
   C) consists of a pair of chemical substances called bases.
   D) contains 23 matching pairs.
   Answer: C
   Page Ref: 52
   Skill: Factual
   Objective: 2.2

6) Individuals around the world are about _____ percent genetically identical.
   A) 39.1
   B) 59.1
   C) 79.1
   D) 99.1
   Answer: D
   Page Ref: 52–53
   Skill: Factual
   Objective: 2.2

7) On the DNA ladder, adenine always appears
   A) alone.
   B) with thymine.
   C) with cytosine.
   D) with guanine.
   Answer: B
   Page Ref: 53
   Skill: Factual
   Objective: 2.2

8) DNA duplicates itself during
   A) mitosis.
   B) osmosis.
   C) meiosis.
   D) gamete formation.
   Answer: A
   Page Ref: 53
   Skill: Factual
   Objective: 2.3

9) Research demonstrates that
   A) it takes a change in several base pairs to influence human traits.
   B) approximately 75 percent of chimpanzee and human DNA is identical.
   C) even at the microscopic level, biological events are the result of both genetic and nongenetic forces.
   D) simpler species have far more proteins than humans or primates.
   Answer: C
   Page Ref: 53
   Skill: Conceptual
   Objective: 2.3

10) Gametes
    A) are formed during mitosis.
    B) contain only 23 chromosomes.
    C) contain 46 chromosomes.
    D) determine directly observable characteristics, like eye color.
Answer: B
Page Ref: 53
Skill: Factual
Objective: 2.4

11) _____ halves the number of chromosomes normally present in body cells.
    A) Mitosis
    B) Osmosis
    C) Meiosis
    D) Autosome formation
Answer: C
Page Ref: 53
Skill: Factual
Objective: 2.4

12) Which of the following is true about crossing over?
    A) It results in a new cell called a zygote.
    B) It creates new hereditary combinations.
    C) It increases the probability that nontwin siblings will be genetically identical.
    D) It decreases the chances that some members of a species will survive ever-changing environments.
Answer: B
Page Ref: 53
Skill: Conceptual
Objective: 2.4

13) Meiosis results in _____ in the male and _____ in the female.
    A) four sperm; one ovum
    B) one sperm; four ova
    C) millions of sperm; about 40,000 ova
    D) four sperm; millions of ova
Answer: A
Page Ref: 54
Skill: Factual
Objective: 2.4

14) Twenty-two matching pairs of chromosomes are
    A) sex chromosomes.
    B) XX.
    C) autosomes.
    D) XY.
Answer: C
Page Ref: 54
Skill: Factual
Objective: 2.5

15) Taylor's twenty-third pair of chromosome is XY. Taylor
    A) has PKU.
    B) has Down syndrome.
    C) is male.
    D) is female.
Answer: C
Page Ref: 54
Skill: Applied
Objective: 2.5

16) Which of the following is true about sex chromosomes?
    A) The Y chromosome is large and long, and the X chromosome carries most of the genetic material.
    B) Both boys and girls are born with several pairs of X and Y chromosomes.
    C) When gametes form in females, the X and Y chromosomes separate into different cells.
    D) The sex of a baby is determined by whether an X-bearing or a Y-bearing sperm fertilizes the ovum.
Answer: D
Page Ref: 55
Skill: Conceptual
Objective: 2.5

17) Dizygotic twins
    A) have the same genetic makeup.
    B) result from a zygote that separates into two clusters.
    C) are the most common type of multiple birth.
    D) are more alike than ordinary siblings.
Answer: C
Page Ref: 55
Skill: Factual
Objective: 2.6

18) The release and fertilization of two ova results in
    A) identical twins.
    B) fraternal twins.
    C) PKU.
    D) miscarriage.
Answer: B
Page Ref: 55
Skill: Factual
Objective: 2.6

19) Which of the following is a major cause of the dramatic rise in fraternal twinning in industrialized nations?
    A) temperature changes
    B) older maternal age
    C) late fertilization of the ovum
    D) variation in oxygen levels
Answer: B
Page Ref: 55
Skill: Conceptual
Objective: 2.6

20) Which of the following individuals is most likely to have fraternal twins?
    A) Marlie, a 25-year-old Caucasian American
    B) Janie, a 30-year-old Caucasian American
    C) Jessi, a 30-year-old Asian American
    D) Rhoda, a 30-year-old African American
Answer: D
Page Ref: 55
Skill: Applied
Objective: 2.6

21) Which of the following environmental influences contributes to monozygotic twinning?
    A) early fertilization of the ovum
    B) poor maternal nutrition
    C) temperature change
    D) high-fructose diet
Answer: C
Page Ref: 55
Skill: Conceptual
Objective: 2.6

22) If the alleles from both parents are alike, the child is
    A) homozygous.
    B) female.
    C) heterozygous.
    D) a monozygotic twin.
Answer: A
Page Ref: 56
Skill: Conceptual
Objective: 2.7

23) Heterozygous individuals with just one recessive allele
    A) cannot pass that trait to their children.
    B) may be carriers of the trait.
    C) will pass the dominant trait to their children.
    D) will pass the recessive trait to their children.
Answer: B
Page Ref: 56
Skill: Conceptual
Objective: 2.7

24) Which of the following is a recessive trait?
    A) curly hair
    B) facial dimples
    C) double-jointedness
    D) red hair
Answer: D
Page Ref: 56
Skill: Applied
Objective: 2.7

25) One of the most frequently occurring recessive disorders is
   A) phenylketonuria.
   B) Huntington disease.
   C) Marfan syndrome.
   D) Down syndrome.
Answer: A
Page Ref: 56
Skill: Factual
Objective: 2.7

26) All U.S. states require that each newborn be given a blood test for
   A) cystic fibrosis.
   B) PKU.
   C) sickle cell anemia.
   D) Tay-Sachs disease.
Answer: B
Page Ref: 56
Skill: Factual
Objective: 2.7

27) _____ enhance or dilute the effects of other genes.
   A) Alleles
   B) Trait genes
   C) Sickle cells
   D) Modifier genes
Answer: D
Page Ref: 57
Skill: Factual
Objective: 2.7

28) Which of the following serious diseases is due to dominant alleles?
   A) Cooley's anemia
   B) sickle cell anemia
   C) Huntington disease
   D) hemophilia
Answer: C
Page Ref: 57
Skill: Conceptual
Objective: 2.7

29) In incomplete dominance,
   A) both alleles are expressed in the phenotype.
   B) children have a 25 percent chance of being carriers.
   C) children have a 50 percent chance of inheriting the disorder.
   D) one allele is expressed in the phenotype.
Answer: A
Page Ref: 57
Skill: Conceptual
Objective: 2.7

30) Sickle cell anemia
  A) is common among Jews of European descent.
  B) is common in children whose parents are of Mediterranean descent.
  C) occurs in full form when a child inherits two recessive alleles.
  D) is a homogeneous condition.
Answer: C
Page Ref: 57
Skill: Conceptual
Objective: 2.7

31) The average life expectancy of a North American with sickle cell anemia is
  A) 18.
  B) 35.
  C) 55.
  D) 62.
Answer: C
Page Ref: 57
Skill: Factual
Objective: 2.7

32) When a harmful allele is carried on the X chromosome,
  A) females are more likely to be affected.
  B) males are more likely to be affected.
  C) 50 percent of the female children are likely to have the disorder.
  D) 50 percent of the male children are likely to be carriers of the disorder.
Answer: B
Page Ref: 57
Skill: Factual
Objective: 2.7

33) Which of the following statements is true about sex differences?
  A) Rates of miscarriage are higher for girls, while rates of birth defects are higher for boys.
  B) Rates of miscarriage, mental retardation, and birth defects are all higher for girls.
  C) Worldwide, about 106 girls are born for every 100 boys.
  D) Rates of miscarriage, mental retardation, and birth defects are all higher for boys.
Answer: D
Page Ref: 59
Skill: Conceptual
Objective: 2.7

34) Genomic imprinting
  A) can be triggered by smoking or exposure to environmental pollutants, such as mercury or lead.
  B) occurs when alleles are chemically marked in such a way that one pair member is activated, regardless of its makeup.
  C) is more likely to affect males because their sex chromosomes do not match.
  D) is always permanent, cannot be erased in the next generation, and occurs in all offspring if it occurs in one.
Answer: B
Page Ref: 59
Skill: Conceptual
Objective: 2.7

35) Fragile X syndrome
    A) is an example of polygenic inheritance.
    B) occurs when there is a sudden but permanent change in a segment of DNA.
    C) is the most common inherited cause of mental retardation.
    D) occurs more often in females than males because the disorder is X-linked.
    Answer: C
    Page Ref: 59
    Skill: Factual
    Objective: 2.7

36) Mutations
    A) rarely occur spontaneously.
    B) can be caused by hazardous environmental agents.
    C) affect only one gene.
    D) cannot occur after birth.
    Answer: B
    Page Ref: 60
    Skill: Factual
    Objective: 2.7

37) In somatic mutations,
    A) the defective DNA is passed on to the next generation.
    B) cells that give rise to gametes mutate.
    C) the event giving rise to the mutation occurs at conception.
    D) the DNA defect appears in every cell derived from the affected body cell.
    Answer: D
    Page Ref: 60
    Skill: Factual
    Objective: 2.7

38) Personality variations among siblings is due to
    A) germline mutation.
    B) dominant–recessive inheritance.
    C) polygenic inheritance.
    D) homozygotic inheritance.
    Answer: C
    Page Ref: 60
    Skill: Factual
    Objective: 2.7

39) Most chromosomal defects result from
    A) mistakes during meiosis.
    B) germline mutations.
    C) mistakes during mitosis.
    D) somatic mutations.
    Answer: A
    Page Ref: 60
    Skill: Factual
    Objective: 2.8

40) Mr. and Mrs. White are told that their son has the most common chromosomal disorder. The Whites' son has _____ syndrome.
    A) Klinefelter
    B) Down
    C) Triple X
    D) Turner
    Answer: B
    Page Ref: 60
    Skill: Applied
    Objective: 2.8

41) The most frequently occurring form of Down syndrome results from
    A) an extra broken piece of a twenty-first chromosome attaching to another chromosome.
    B) an error during the early stages of mitosis.
    C) a failure of the twenty-first pair of chromosomes to separate during meiosis.
    D) the inheritance of an extra X chromosome.
    Answer: C
    Page Ref: 60–61
    Skill: Conceptual
    Objective: 2.8

42) Which of the following individuals has the highest probability of having a child with Down syndrome?
    A) Isabella, who is 15 years old
    B) Bonny, who is 24 years old
    C) Raelyn, who is 33 years old
    D) Katrina, who is 42 years old
    Answer: D
    Page Ref: 61
    Skill: Applied
    Objective: 2.8

43) Most children with sex chromosome disorders
    A) suffer from mental retardation.
    B) have verbal difficulties.
    C) have trouble with spatial relations.
    D) have very specific intellectual problems.
    Answer: D
    Page Ref: 62
    Skill: Conceptual
    Objective: 2.8

44) Mr. and Mrs. Sedgwick's child was diagnosed with Turner syndrome. Their child has a(n) _____ chromosome.
    A) extra X
    B) missing X
    C) missing Y
    D) extra Y
    Answer: B
    Page Ref: 62
    Skill: Applied
    Objective: 2.8

45) Angela and Tony's first child died in infancy. They badly want to have another child, but are worried about Angela's family history of genetic disorders. They want to find out if Angela is a carrier. Angela and Tony are candidates for
   A) in vitro fertilization.
   B) genetic counseling.
   C) donor insemination.
   D) amniocentesis.
Answer: B
Page Ref: 63
Skill: Applied
Objective: 2.9

46) Except for _____, prenatal diagnosis should not be used routinely, since other methods have some chance of injuring the developing organism.
   A) maternal blood analysis
   B) amniocentesis
   C) chorionic villus sampling
   D) ultrasound
Answer: A
Page Ref: 63
Skill: Factual
Objective: 2.9

47) Which of the following is a risk associated with frequent ultrasound use?
   A) premature labor
   B) miscarriage
   C) low birth weight
   D) limb deformities
Answer: C
Page Ref: 64
Skill: Conceptual
Objective: 2.9

48) In proteomics,
   A) researchers map the sequence of all human DNA base pairs.
   B) scientists modify gene-specified proteins involved in disease.
   C) doctors correct genetic abnormalities by delivering DNA carrying a functional gene to the cells.
   D) the fetus is inspected for defects of the limbs and face using a small tube with a light source.
Answer: B
Page Ref: 65
Skill: Conceptual
Objective: 2.9

49) Which of the following is true about adoption?
   A) In North America, more unwed mothers give up their babies than in the past.
   B) Children adopted after infancy fare as well or better than those adopted as infants.
   C) In North America, the availability of healthy babies has declined.
   D) Fewer adoptive parents are accepting children who have known developmental problems.
Answer: C
Page Ref: 65
Skill: Conceptual
Objective: 2.9

50) Most adopted children
   A) fare well and make rapid progress.
   B) have persistent cognitive delays.
   C) suffer from severe emotional problems.
   D) have persistent social problems.
   Answer: A
   Page Ref: 66
   Skill: Conceptual
   Objective: 2.9

51) _____ of all couples who try to conceive discover that they are infertile.
   A) One-third
   B) One-fourth
   C) One-sixth
   D) One-eighth
   Answer: C
   Page Ref: 66 Box: SI: Health: The Pros and Cons of Reproductive Technologies
   Skill: Factual
   Objective: 2.9

52) Children conceived through assisted reproductive techniques
   A) may receive caregiving that is somewhat warmer than children who are conceived naturally.
   B) are at greater risk for genetic disorders than their naturally conceived counterparts.
   C) tend to experience severe adjustment problems throughout childhood, including insecure attachment to caregivers.
   D) are usually well-adjusted until adolescence when they experience a significant rise in psychological problems.
   Answer: A
   Page Ref: 66 Box: SI: Health: The Pros and Cons of Reproductive Technologies
   Skill: Conceptual
   Objective: 2.9

53) Which of the following is true about surrogate motherhood?
   A) Most surrogates have no children of their own.
   B) Surrogates cannot be paid for their childbearing services.
   C) It usually involves the wealthy as contractors for infants and the less economically advantaged as surrogates.
   D) It usually involves younger couples as contractors and older women as surrogates.
   Answer: C
   Page Ref: 67 Box: SI: Health: The Pros and Cons of Reproductive Technologies
   Skill: Conceptual
   Objective: 2.9

54) In power and breadth of influence, no other microsystem context equals the
   A) school.
   B) church.
   C) family.
   D) peer group.
   Answer: C
   Page Ref: 69
   Skill: Factual
   Objective: 2.10

55) Contemporary researchers view the family as
   A) a network of interdependent relationships.
   B) primarily influenced by third parties.
   C) a macrosystem.
   D) a chronosystem.
   Answer: A
   Page Ref: 70
   Skill: Conceptual
   Objective: 2.10

56) Jonelle can promote her grandchildren's development indirectly by
   A) responding warmly to the children.
   B) gently reprimanding the children when they misbehave.
   C) providing financial assistance to their parents.
   D) implementing a reward system for the children's good behavior.
   Answer: C
   Page Ref: 71
   Skill: Applied
   Objective: 2.10

57) People who work in skilled and semiskilled manual occupations tend to _____ than people in professional and technical occupations.
   A) marry later
   B) have more children
   C) have fewer children
   D) have children later
   Answer: B
   Page Ref: 71
   Skill: Factual
   Objective: 2.11

58) In diverse cultures around the world, _____ in particular fosters patterns of thinking and behaving that greatly improve quality of life, for both parents and children.
   A) education of women
   B) collectivism
   C) living near extended family
   D) having one stay-at-home parent
   Answer: A
   Page Ref: 72
   Skill: Conceptual
   Objective: 2.11

59) Affluent parents
   A) too often fail to engage in family interaction and parenting that promote favorable development.
   B) are less likely than low-SES parents to have children who use alcohol and drugs.
   C) are less likely than low-SES parents to have children who report high levels of depression.
   D) are more likely than low-SES parents to engage in family interaction and parenting that promote favorable development.
   Answer: A
   Page Ref: 72
   Skill: Conceptual
   Objective: 2.11

60) _____ strongly predicts women's preventive health behavior.
   A) Age
   B) Marital status
   C) IQ
   D) Years of schooling
Answer: D
Page Ref: 73 Box: SI: Education: Worldwide Education of Girls: Transforming Current and Future Generations
Skill: Conceptual
Objective: 2.11

61) The largest barrier to the education of girls worldwide is/are
   A) cultural beliefs about gender roles.
   B) a reluctance to give up a daughter's work at home.
   C) that many schools charge parents a fee for each child enrolled.
   D) a limited number of schools in developing areas.
Answer: C
Page Ref: 73 Box: SI: Education: Worldwide Education of Girls: Transforming Current and Future Generations
Skill: Factual
Objective: 2.11

62) In the United States, poverty rates
   A) have declined in recent years.
   B) are lower among children than any other age group.
   C) are lower for African Americans than for Caucasian Americans.
   D) have risen in recent years.
Answer: D
Page Ref: 74
Skill: Factual
Objective: 2.11

63) Neighborhood resources
   A) have a greater impact on economically disadvantaged than on well-to-do young people.
   B) contribute to favorable development in preschoolers, but not in adolescents.
   C) are rarely needed in middle-income areas.
   D) have a greater impact on affluent than on low-SES young people.
Answer: A
Page Ref: 76
Skill: Factual
Objective: 2.12

64) Which of the following children is least likely to participate in an available neighborhood organization?
   A) Meagan, who lives in a lower-middle class area
   B) Francois, who lives in a low-income area
   C) Chantel, who lives in an upper-middle class area
   D) Lucius, who lives in an affluent area
Answer: B
Page Ref: 76
Skill: Applied
Objective: 2.12

65) Nate, whose parents are involved in his school activities, probably
    A) resents his parents' involvement in his education.
    B) shows better academic achievement than his agemates whose parents are uninvolved.
    C) lives in a low-SES household with many siblings.
    D) attends a private school in a large city.
Answer: B
Page Ref: 77
Skill: Applied
Objective: 2.12

66) Parent–teacher contact is more frequent in
    A) small towns.
    B) large cities.
    C) low-SES schools.
    D) small schools.
Answer: A
Page Ref: 77
Skill: Factual
Objective: 2.12

67) Which of the following statements reflects a widely held opinion in the United States?
    A) "The government should help poor parents raise their children."
    B) "Most people are content with others intruding into family life as long as help is needed."
    C) "If you decide to have a baby, you should be ready to care for it."
    D) "People should try to define themselves as part of a group."
Answer: C
Page Ref: 78
Skill: Applied
Objective: 2.13

68) In _____ societies, people stress group over individual goals.
    A) individualistic
    B) independent
    C) collectivist
    D) industrialized
Answer: C
Page Ref: 78
Skill: Factual
Objective: 2.13

69) In individualistic societies, people
    A) define themselves as part of a group.
    B) are largely concerned with their own personal needs.
    C) value an interdependent self.
    D) readily endorse public policies for low-SES families.
Answer: B
Page Ref: 78
Skill: Conceptual
Objective: 2.13

70) _____ tends to increase as cultures become more complex.
    A) Collectivism
    B) Interdependence
    C) Individualism
    D) Social harmony
Answer: C
Page Ref: 78
Skill: Factual
Objective: 2.13

71) In the United States today, African-American parents _____ than Caucasian-American parents.
    A) live farther away from extended-family members
    B) see fewer relatives during the week
    C) perceive their relatives as less important in their lives
    D) more often live in extended-family households
Answer: D
Page Ref: 79 Box: CI: The African-American Extended Family
Skill: Factual
Objective: 2.13

72) Extended-family living is associated with
    A) more positive mother–child interaction during the preschool years.
    B) increased antisocial behavior in adolescents.
    C) decreased self-reliance in adolescents.
    D) lower rates of adolescent pregnancy and parenthood.
Answer: A
Page Ref: 79 Box: CI: The African-American Extended Family
Skill: Conceptual
Objective: 2.13

73) Which of the following is true about how the United States ranks on key measures of children's health and well-being?
    A) The United States ranks in the top 10 on most key measures of children's health.
    B) The United States ranks higher than Poland and Germany on the childhood poverty indicator.
    C) The United States ranks higher than Canada in public expenditure on children's healthcare.
    D) The United States does not rank well on any key measure of children's health and well-being.
Answer: D
Page Ref: 79
Skill: Conceptual
Objective: 2.13

74) In the United States, affordable child care is
    A) usually high in quality.
    B) fairly easy to find.
    C) in short supply.
    D) the norm.
Answer: C
Page Ref: 79
Skill: Factual
Objective: 2.13

75) Which of the following is a reason why attempts to help children and youths have been difficult to realize in the United States?
   A) While good social programs are inexpensive, they must compete for a share of the country's economic resources.
   B) Cultural values of interdependence and responsibility to others have made federal programs unnecessary.
   C) Children cannot vote or lobby to protect their own interests.
   D) Public policies aimed at fostering children's development do not yield valuable returns.
   Answer: C
   Page Ref: 80
   Skill: Conceptual
   Objective: 2.13

76) Which of the following is an accurate statement about the Convention on the Rights of the Child?
   A) The United States was one of the first countries in the world whose legislature ratified it.
   B) Opponents maintain that the Convention's provisions would shift the burden of child rearing from the state to the family.
   C) Although it includes the rights to freedom of thought and freedom of religion, it does not include the right to a free compulsory education.
   D) The United States is one of only two countries in the world whose legislature has not yet ratified it.
   Answer: D
   Page Ref: 81
   Skill: Conceptual
   Objective: 2.13

77) In the United States,
   A) a significant portion of government spending is devoted to improving quality of child care.
   B) the Children's Defense Fund is the most vigorous special interest group devoted to the well-being of children.
   C) the Convention on the Rights of the Child engages in research, public education, and legal action on behalf of children.
   D) UNICEF is the most vigorous special interest group devoted to the well-being of American children.
   Answer: B
   Page Ref: 81
   Skill: Conceptual
   Objective: 2.13

78) Behavioral geneticists
   A) have identified the variations in DNA sequences associated with most psychological disorders.
   B) argue that the effects of the environment account for only a small amount of variation in behavior.
   C) are still limited to investigating the impact of genes on complex characteristics indirectly.
   D) have identified the genes that underlie most polygenic traits, such as intelligence and personality.
   Answer: C
   Page Ref: 82
   Skill: Factual
   Objective: 2.14

79) Dr. Dimera is interested in measuring the extent to which individual differences in complex traits in a specific population are due to genetic factors. When conducting research, Dr. Dimera will most likely rely on
   A) heritability estimates.
   B) epigenesis.
   C) canalization.
   D) genetic–environmental correlation.
   Answer: A
   Page Ref: 82
   Skill: Applied
   Objective: 2.14

80) In a kinship study of intelligence, which of the following sibling pairs will likely share a high correlation?
    A) Max and Martin, nontwin brothers
    B) Jabar and Tobias, identical twins
    C) Marci and Sonia, fraternal twins
    D) Mary Jane and Susan, nontwin sisters
Answer: B
Page Ref: 82–83
Skill: Applied
Objective: 2.14

81) A heritability estimate of .3 for activity level would indicate that differences in _____ could explain ____ percent of the variation in activity level.
    A) the environment; 30
    B) heredity; 70
    C) heredity; 30
    D) the environment; 3
Answer: C
Page Ref: 83
Skill: Applied
Objective: 2.14

82) Heritability estimates
    A) give precise information on how personality traits develop.
    B) are likely to diminish the role of heredity because the environments of twin pairs are less diverse.
    C) tell researchers how environment can modify genetic influences.
    D) are controversial measures because they can easily be misapplied.
Answer: D
Page Ref: 83
Skill: Factual
Objective: 2.14

83) In an extremely understimulating environment, both Bella and Alice would have low intelligence. However, in a highly stimulating environment, Alice's performance would greatly exceed Bella's performance. This is an example of
    A) canalization.
    B) niche-picking.
    C) reaction range.
    D) genetic–environmental correlation.
Answer: C
Page Ref: 84
Skill: Applied
Objective: 2.14

84) Range of reaction reveals that
    A) individuals usually respond similarly to the same environment.
    B) unique blends of heredity and environment lead to both similarities and differences in behavior.
    C) twins are more alike than other siblings because they are raised in the same environment.
    D) our genes influence the environments to which we are exposed.
Answer: B
Page Ref: 84
Skill: Conceptual
Objective: 2.14

85) A behavior that is strongly canalized
    A) is easily modified by environmental conditions.
    B) varies greatly with changes in the environment.
    C) develops similarly in a wide range of environments.
    D) influences the environment to which the individual is exposed.
Answer: C
Page Ref: 84
Skill: Factual
Objective: 2.14

86) Which of the following seems to be strongly canalized?
    A) intelligence
    B) motor development
    C) personality
    D) emotional development
Answer: B
Page Ref: 84
Skill: Conceptual
Objective: 2.14

87) According to the concept of genetic–environmental correlation,
    A) the environments to which we are exposed determine which genes are expressed in our phenotypes.
    B) our genes influence the environments to which we are exposed.
    C) heredity restricts the development of some behaviors to just one or a few outcomes.
    D) our genes influence how we respond to the environment.
Answer: B
Page Ref: 85
Skill: Conceptual
Objective: 2.14

88) Denyse and David are both actors and have enrolled their children in acting classes. This is an example of a(n) _____ genetic–environmental correlation.
    A) passive
    B) evocative
    C) active
    D) dynamic
Answer: A
Page Ref: 85
Skill: Applied
Objective: 2.14

89) Marcus, a cooperative, attentive child, receives more patient and sensitive interactions from his parents than they give to Erica, his distractible, inattentive sister. This is an example of a(n) _____ genetic–environmental correlation.
    A) passive
    B) evocative
    C) active
    D) dynamic
Answer: B
Page Ref: 85
Skill: Applied
Objective:2.14

90) Grace, a musically talented youngster, joins the school orchestra and practices her violin. This is an example of a(n) _____ genetic–environmental correlation.
   A) passive
   B) evocative
   C) active
   D) dynamic
   Answer: C
   Page Ref: 85
   Skill: Applied
   Objective: 2.14

91) Niche-picking is an example of a(n) _____ genetic–environmental correlation.
   A) passive
   B) evocative
   C) active
   D) dynamic
   Answer: C
   Page Ref: 85
   Skill: Conceptual
   Objective: 2.14

92) Which of the following age groups does the most niche-picking?
   A) infants
   B) toddlers
   C) preschoolers
   D) adolescents
   Answer: D
   Page Ref: 85
   Skill: Conceptual
   Objective: 2.14

93) Niche-picking helps us understand why _____ pairs report similar stressful life events influenced by personal decisions and actions more often than other pairs.
   A) same-sex fraternal twin
   B) other-sex fraternal twin
   C) identical twin
   D) adopted sibling
   Answer: C
   Page Ref: 85
   Skill: Conceptual
   Objective: 2.14

94) The relationship between heredity and the environment is
   A) a one-way street.
   B) strongest for intelligence.
   C) best measured using heritability estimates.
   D) bidirectional.
   Answer: D
   Page Ref: 86
   Skill: Conceptual
   Objective: 2.14

95) According to the concept of epigenesis,
A) development results from ongoing bidirectional interactions between heredity and all levels of the environment.
B) children's genetic makeup causes them to receive, evoke, and seek experiences that actualize their inborn tendencies.
C) heredity restricts the development of some behaviors to just one or a few outcomes.
D) children's genetic inheritance constrains their responsiveness to varying environments.
Answer: A
Page Ref: 86
Skill: Factual
Objective: 2.14

96) Jada provides her baby with a healthy diet, which promotes brain growth, leading to new connections among nerve cells, which transform gene expression. This sequence opens the door to new gene–environment exchanges, such as advanced exploration of objects and interaction with caregivers. This is an example of
A) niche-picking.
B) canalization.
C) epigenesis.
D) range of reaction.
Answer: C
Page Ref: 86
Skill: Applied
Objective: 2.14

97) Research suggests that by itself, the DD genotype is
A) related to impulsivity.
B) unrelated to impulsivity, overactivity, or oppositional behavior.
C) related to overactivity.
D) related to oppositional behavior.
Answer: B
Page Ref: 87 Box: B&E: A Case of Epigenesis: Smoking During Pregnancy Alters Gene Expression
Skill: Factual
Objective: 2.14

98) Which of the following individuals is the most likely to score high in impulsivity, according to research on smoking?
A) Daniel, who has a DD genetic makeup and a mother who smoked during pregnancy
B) Reba, who has a DD genetic makeup and a nonsmoking mother
C) John, who has a DD genetic makeup and a mother who smoked prior to becoming pregnant
D) Samantha, who has a DB genetic makeup and a mother who smoked during pregnancy
Answer: C
Page Ref: 87 Box: B&E: A Case of Epigenesis: Smoking During Pregnancy Alters Gene Expression
Skill: Applied
Objective: 2.14

ESSAY

99) Summarize factors that account for the dramatic rise in fraternal twinning and other multiple births in industrialized nations over the past several decades.
Answer: Currently, fraternal twins account for 1 in about every 60 births in the United States. Older maternal age, fertility drugs, and in vitro fertilization are major causes of the dramatic rise in fraternal twinning and other multiple births in the past several decades. The rate of fraternal twinning rises with maternal age, peaking between 35 and 39 years, and then rapidly falls. Multiple births occur less often among women with poor diets, and occur more often among women who are tall and overweight or of normal weight. Multiple births are more likely with fertility hormones and in vitro fertilization. A variety of environmental influences prompt identical twinning, including temperature changes, variation in oxygen levels, and late fertilization of the ovum.
Page Ref: 55

100) List and describe the steps that prospective parents can take before conception to increase their chances of having a healthy baby.

Answer: *Arrange for a physical exam.* A physical exam permits detection of diseases and other medical problems that might reduce fertility, be difficult to treat during pregnancy, or affect the developing organism.

Consider their genetic makeup. Find out if anyone in their families has had a child with a genetic disease or disability. If so, seek genetic counseling before conception.

Reduce or eliminate toxins. The developing organism is highly sensitive to damaging environmental agents during the early weeks of pregnancy. Couples trying to conceive should avoid drugs, alcohol, cigarette smoke, radiation, pollution, chemical substances in the home and workplace, and infectious diseases. Furthermore, stay away from ionizing radiation and some industrial chemicals that are known to cause mutations.

Ensure proper nutrition. Taking a vitamin–mineral supplement containing folic acid before conception helps prevent many prenatal problems. Folic acid reduces the chances of neural tube defects, prematurity, and low birth weight.

Consult a doctor after 12 months of unsuccessful efforts at conception. Long periods of infertility may be due to undiagnosed spontaneous abortions, which can be caused by genetic defects in either partner. If a physical exam reveals a healthy reproductive system, seek genetic counseling.

Page Ref: 68

101) Discuss direct and indirect influences on family functioning, and provide an example of each.

Answer: Contemporary researchers view the family as a network of interdependent relationships. Bidirectional influences exist in which the behaviors of each family member affect those of others. Direct influences occur when the behavior of one family member helps sustain a form of interaction in the other that either promotes or undermines psychological well-being. For example, when warmth and affection accompany parents' requests, children tend to cooperate. When children willingly comply, their parents are likely to be warm and gentle in the future. In contrast, parents who discipline with hostility usually have children who refuse and rebel. Because children's misbehavior is stressful for parents, they may increase their use of punishment, leading to more unruliness by the children. In these examples, each of the children's reactions, in turn, prompts a new link in the interactive chain. Indirect influences occur when interactions between any two family members are affected by others, known as third parties, who are present in the setting. For example, when the parents' marital relationship is warm and considerate, mothers and fathers praise and stimulate their children more, and nag and scold them less. In contrast, when a marriage is tense and hostile, parents are likely to express anger, criticize, and punish.

Page Ref: 69–71

102) How does educating girls impact the welfare of families, societies, and future generations? What impact does it have on family health?

Answer: Although schooling is vital for all children, educating girls has an especially powerful impact on the welfare of families, societies, and future generations. The diverse benefits of girls' schooling largely accrue in two ways: (1) through enhanced verbal skills—reading writing, and oral communication; and (2) through empowerment—a growing desire to improve their life conditions.

Education gives girls the communicative skills and confidence to seek health services and to benefit from public health information. Years of schooling strongly predicts women's preventive health behavior. Because educated women have more life opportunities, they are more likely to take advantage of family planning services, delay marriage and childbearing, and have more widely spaced and fewer children. All these practices are linked to increased maternal and child survival and family health.

Page Ref: 73

103) Summarize the benefits of establishing family–neighborhood ties.

Answer: Family–neighborhood ties reduce parental stress and promote child development. They provide social support, which leads to the following benefits:

- *Parental self-worth.* A neighbor or relative who listens and tries to relieve a parent's concern enhances her self-esteem. The parent, in turn, is likely to interact in a more sensitive and involved manner with her children.
- *Parental access to valuable information and services.* A friend who suggests where a parent might find a job, housing, and affordable child care and youth activities helps make the multiple roles of spouse, parent, and provider easier to fulfill.
- *Child-rearing controls and role models.* Friends, relatives, and other community members may encourage and demonstrate effective parenting practices and discourage ineffective practices.
- *Direct assistance with child rearing.* As children and adolescents participate in their parents' social networks and in neighborhood settings, other adults can influence children through warmth, stimulation, and exposure to a wider array of competent models. In this way, family–neighborhood ties can reduce the impact of ineffective parenting. Nearby adults can also intervene when they see young people skipping school or behaving antisocially.

Page Ref: 76

104) Describe range of reaction and canalization, including how each of these concepts helps us to understand how heredity and the environment interact.

Answer: Range of reaction refers to each person's unique, genetically determined response to a range of environmental conditions. Reaction range can apply to any characteristic. Reaction range highlights two important points about the relationship between heredity and the environment. First, it shows that because each of us has a unique genetic makeup, we respond differently to the same environment. Second, sometimes different genetic–environmental combinations can make two people look the same.

Canalization refers to the tendency of heredity to restrict the development of some characteristics to just one or, at most, a few outcomes. A behavior that is strongly canalized develops similarly in a wide range of environments; only strong environmental forces can change it. Canalization is highly adaptive. Through it, nature ensures that children will develop certain species-typical skills under a wide range of rearing conditions, thereby promoting survival.

Page Ref: 84

105) Define and provide an example of niche-picking.

Answer: Niche-picking is the tendency to actively choose environments that complement our heredity. It is an example of active genetic–environmental correlation. As children extend their experiences beyond the immediate family and are given the freedom to make more choices, they actively seek environments that fit with their genetic tendencies. For example, a well-coordinated, muscular child joins an after-school sports team. Infants and young children cannot do much niche-picking because adults select environments for them. In contrast, older children and adolescents are much more in charge of their environments.

Page Ref: 85

CHAPTER 3
PRENATAL DEVELOPMENT

MULTIPLE CHOICE

1) Today, the issue of whether to have children is a
   A) biological given.
   B) compelling social expectation.
   C) matter of true individual choice.
   D) matter of legacy.
   Answer: C
   Page Ref: 92
   Skill: Conceptual
   Objective: 3.1

2) In the United States today, _____ percent of married couples bear children.
   A) 50
   B) 60
   C) 70
   D) 80
   Answer: C
   Page Ref: 92
   Skill: Factual
   Objective: 3.1

3) When asked about the disadvantages of parenthood, Americans cite _____ most often.
   A) loss of freedom
   B) financial strain
   C) loss of privacy
   D) work conflicts
   Answer: A
   Page Ref: 92
   Skill: Conceptual
   Objective: 3.1

4) The average number of children per couple in North America today is
   A) 3.1.
   B) 2.7.
   C) 2.2.
   D) 1.8.
   Answer: D
   Page Ref: 93
   Skill: Factual
   Objective: 3.2

5) Which of the following was a finding by the U.S. National Longitudinal Survey of Youth?
   A) Mothers with lower intelligence test scores tend to have larger families than mothers with higher scores.
   B) Mothers with small families are usually less well-off economically than mothers with larger families.
   C) First-born children in large families are more intelligent than their younger siblings.
   D) Only children have lower intelligence test scores than children with siblings.
   Answer: A
   Page Ref: 94
   Skill: Conceptual
   Objective: 3.2

6) Which of the following statements is supported by research on family size?
   A) Parental quality declines as new children are born.
   B) New births lead to an increase in maternal affection toward older siblings.
   C) Limiting family size increases the chances of having children with high intelligence scores.
   D) Parents who have many children tend to reallocate their energies.
   Answer: D
   Page Ref: 94
   Skill: Conceptual
   Objective: 3.2

7) Which of the following statements is true about only children?
   A) They are more intelligent than children with siblings.
   B) They are as well-adjusted as children with siblings.
   C) They have more emotional problems than children with siblings.
   D) They are less intelligent than children with siblings.
   Answer: B
   Page Ref: 94
   Skill: Conceptual
   Objective: 3.2

8) Which of the following statements is true about birthrate trends between 1970 and 2008?
   A) The birthrate increased during this period for women 20 to 24 years of age.
   B) The birthrate decreased during this period for women 25 years of age and older.
   C) For women in their thirties, the birthrate more than doubled during this period.
   D) The greatest decline in the birthrate during this period was for women in their thirties.
   Answer: C
   Page Ref: 95
   Skill: Conceptual
   Objective: 3.2

9) Research on childbearing reveals that
   A) fertility problems do not increase for men between ages 25 and 45.
   B) fertility problems among women do not show any increase until age 40.
   C) reproductive technologies are equally successful among younger and older parents.
   D) a 45-year-old man is less fertile than a 25-year-old man.
   Answer: D
   Page Ref: 95
   Skill: Conceptual
   Objective: 3.2

10) The _____ secretes hormones that prepare the lining of the uterus to receive a fertilized ovum.
   A) ovaries
   B) corpus luteum
   C) fallopian tubes
   D) cervix
Answer: B
Page Ref: 96
Skill: Factual
Objective: 3.3

11) Sperm can survive for up to
   A) twelve hours.
   B) two days.
   C) four days.
   D) six days.
Answer: D
Page Ref: 96
Skill: Factual
Objective: 3.3

12) The ovum can survive for _____ after it is released into the fallopian tube.
   A) a couple of hours
   B) one day
   C) four days
   D) six days
Answer: B
Page Ref: 96
Skill: Factual
Objective: 3.3

13) Most conceptions result from intercourse during the
   A) first week of the menstrual cycle.
   B) last week of the menstrual cycle.
   C) day of ovulation and the two days following it.
   D) two days preceding ovulation and the day of ovulation.
Answer: D
Page Ref: 96
Skill: Factual
Objective: 3.3

14) Following conception, the one-celled _____ multiplies and forms a(n) _____.
   A) blastocyst; zygote
   B) blastocyst; embryo
   C) zygote; blastocyst
   D) embryo; fetus
Answer: C
Page Ref: 97
Skill: Factual
Objective: 3.3

15) The period of the zygote lasts
    A) for about 13 weeks, or a trimester.
    B) from fertilization to implantation.
    C) for about 6 weeks.
    D) from conception to fertilization.
Answer: B
Page Ref: 97
Skill: Factual
Objective: 3.3

16) The _____ becomes the new organism.
    A) embryonic disk
    B) trophoblast
    C) amnion
    D) chorion
Answer: A
Page Ref: 98
Skill: Factual
Objective: 3.3

17) Between the seventh and the ninth days after fertilization, _____ occurs.
    A) the period of the embryo
    B) the period of the fetus
    C) implantation
    D) cell duplication
Answer: C
Page Ref: 98
Skill: Factual
Objective: 3.3

18) The _____ produces blood cells until the developing liver, spleen, and bone marrow are mature enough to take over this function.
    A) amnion
    B) chorion
    C) placenta
    D) yolk sac
Answer: D
Page Ref: 98
Skill: Factual
Objective: 3.3

19) As many as _____ percent of zygotes do not survive the first two weeks.
    A) 20
    B) 30
    C) 40
    D) 50
Answer: B
Page Ref: 98
Skill: Factual
Objective: 3.3

20) Valerie, 2-months pregnant, wonders how food and oxygen are delivered to the developing organism. You should tell Valerie that the _____ performs this function.
   A) chorion
   B) amnion
   C) placenta
   D) neural tube
   Answer: C
   Page Ref: 98
   Skill: Applied
   Objective: 3.3

21) The placenta is connected to the developing organism by the
   A) uterine wall.
   B) amnion.
   C) chorion.
   D) umbilical cord.
   Answer: D
   Page Ref: 98
   Skill: Factual
   Objective: 3.3

22) The most rapid prenatal changes take place during the
   A) period of the zygote.
   B) period of the fetus.
   C) period of the embryo.
   D) final trimester.
   Answer: C
   Page Ref: 99
   Skill: Conceptual
   Objective: 3.3

23) The _____ becomes the nervous system.
   A) ectoderm
   B) mesoderm
   C) endoderm
   D) trophoblast
   Answer: A
   Page Ref: 99
   Skill: Factual
   Objective: 3.3

24) At the beginning of the embryonic period, the _____ system develops fastest.
   A) nervous
   B) circulatory
   C) digestive
   D) skeletal
   Answer: A
   Page Ref: 99
   Skill: Factual
   Objective: 3.3

25) During the second month of pregnancy, the
 A) embryo reacts to light.
 B) embryo kicks and bends its arms.
 C) heart begins to pump blood.
 D) heart develops separate chambers.
Answer: D
Page Ref: 99
Skill: Conceptual
Objective: 3.3

26) The developing organism responds to touch during the _____ month of pregnancy.
 A) first
 B) second
 C) third
 D) fourth
Answer: B
Page Ref: 99
Skill: Factual
Objective: 3.3

27) During the period of the fetus, the
 A) developing organism increases rapidly in size.
 B) most rapid prenatal changes take place.
 C) heart begins to pump blood.
 D) brain is formed.
Answer: A
Page Ref: 100
Skill: Conceptual
Objective: 3.3

28) During the third month of pregnancy,
 A) the fetus can suck its thumb.
 B) tiny buds become arms, legs, fingers, and toes.
 C) neuron production begins.
 D) the eyes, ears, and nose form.
Answer: A
Page Ref: 100
Skill: Conceptual
Objective: 3.3

29) Mel wonders when he will be able to find out the sex of his baby. You tell him that he should be able to detect the sex with ultrasound as early as the _____ week of pregnancy.
 A) ninth
 B) twelfth
 C) fifteenth
 D) eighteenth
Answer: B
Page Ref: 100
Skill: Applied
Objective: 3.3

30) Which of the following statements is true about Zola's third month of pregnancy?
    A) She should be able to feel the baby move.
    B) She should avoid regular exercise.
    C) She should be able to hear the heartbeat through a stethoscope.
    D) She should have gained at least 10 pounds since becoming pregnant.
    Answer: C
    Page Ref: 100
    Skill: Applied
    Objective: 3.3

31) During her first prenatal visit, LaToya's doctor explains that the _____ prevent(s) the skin from chapping during the long months spent bathing in the amniotic fluid.
    A) villi
    B) vernix
    C) glial cells
    D) chorion
    Answer: B
    Page Ref: 100
    Skill: Applied
    Objective: 3.3

32) During the second trimester,
    A) convolutions appear on the surface of the brain.
    B) the fetus takes on the beginnings of a personality.
    C) lanugo appears over the entire body.
    D) the fetus can distinguish the tone and rhythm of different voices.
    Answer: C
    Page Ref: 100
    Skill: Conceptual
    Objective: 3.3

33) From the twentieth week until birth,
    A) brain weight increases tenfold.
    B) glial cells decrease at a rapid rate.
    C) the fetus is viable.
    D) brain growth slows.
    Answer: A
    Page Ref: 100
    Skill: Conceptual
    Objective: 3.3

34) Sara's doctor is looking inside her uterus using fetoscopy. Her 22-week-old fetus may react by
    A) grabbing at the light.
    B) holding its toes.
    C) shielding its eyes.
    D) kicking its legs.
    Answer: C
    Page Ref: 100
    Skill: Applied
    Objective: 3.3

35) The age of viability occurs sometime between _____ and _____ weeks.
    A) 18; 22
    B) 20; 24
    C) 22; 26
    D) 26; 30
Answer: C
Page Ref: 100
Skill: Factual
Objective: 3.3

36) Carmen is prematurely delivering her baby at 28 weeks. The baby will probably
    A) not survive.
    B) need oxygen assistance to breathe.
    C) experience intense pain.
    D) spend the next few weeks with no periods of alertness.
Answer: B
Page Ref: 100
Skill: Applied
Objective: 3.3

37) Synchrony between fetal heart rate and motor activity peaks between _____ and _____ weeks.
    A) 20; 22
    B) 24; 26
    C) 27; 29
    D) 30; 34
Answer: D
Page Ref: 101
Skill: Factual
Objective: 3.3

38) In one study, more active fetuses during the third trimester became 1-year-olds who _____ than those who were less active prenatally.
    A) could better handle frustration
    B) less readily interacted with unfamiliar adults
    C) were more fearful
    D) less readily interacted with toys
Answer: A
Page Ref: 101
Skill: Conceptual
Objective: 3.3

39) During the third trimester,
    A) the fetus spends the majority of the day awake.
    B) painkillers should be used during any surgical procedures performed on a fetus.
    C) fetuses can hear bodily noises but not noises that occur outside of the womb.
    D) higher fetal activity is linked with abnormal neurological development.
Answer: B
Page Ref: 101
Skill: Conceptual
Objective: 3.3

40) A study involving the fetal heart rate's response to auditory stimuli during the third trimester suggests that fetuses
   A) cannot hear sounds from the outside world.
   B) can remember for at least a brief period.
   C) cannot distinguish between their mother's voice and a stranger's voice.
   D) cannot distinguish between familiar and unfamiliar melodies.
   Answer: B
   Page Ref: 101
   Skill: Conceptual
   Objective: 3.3

41) Monica provides her fetus with stimulation specially designed to enhance later mental development. Monica should know that
   A) playing classical music is likely to have a long-lasting impact on cognitive development.
   B) reading aloud is likely to have a long-lasting impact on cognitive development.
   C) later experiences can override the impact of fetal stimulation.
   D) prolonged exposure to sounds is just as harmless to fetal inner-ear structure as they are to the mature ear.
   Answer: C
   Page Ref: 102
   Skill: Applied
   Objective: 3.3

42) During the final months of pregnancy, the fetus
   A) gains more than 5 pounds and grows 7 inches.
   B) spends the majority of the day awake.
   C) assumes a right-side-up position.
   D) gains less than 2 pounds and grows less than 3 inches.
   Answer: A
   Page Ref: 102
   Skill: Conceptual
   Objective: 3.3

43) The harm done by teratogens
   A) is simple and straightforward.
   B) always creates a "monstrosity" or malformation.
   C) depends on dose, heredity, age, and other negative influences.
   D) can rarely be prevented.
   Answer: C
   Page Ref: 102–103
   Skill: Conceptual
   Objective: 3.4

44) The _____ have a long period of sensitivity to teratogens.
   A) hands and feet
   B) palate and mouth
   C) arms and legs
   D) brain and eyes
   Answer: D
   Page Ref: 103
   Skill: Factual
   Objective: 3.4

45) The _____ is the time when serious defects from teratogens are most likely to occur.
    A) period of the zygote
    B) period of the embryo
    C) second trimester
    D) third trimester
Answer: B
Page Ref: 104
Skill: Conceptual
Objective: 3.4

46) During the fetal period,
    A) teratogens rarely have any impact.
    B) teratogens are most likely to cause serious defects.
    C) the ears can be strongly affected by teratogens.
    D) teratogenic damage usually causes miscarriage.
Answer: C
Page Ref: 104
Skill: Conceptual
Objective: 3.4

47) The effects of teratogens
    A) may not show up for decades.
    B) rarely go beyond physical damage.
    C) are always immediate.
    D) are always obvious.
Answer: A
Page Ref: 104
Skill: Conceptual
Objective: 3.4

48) _____ is associated with _____ in adulthood.
    A) Low birth weight; breast cancer
    B) High birth weight; diabetes
    C) High birth weight; Alzheimer's disease
    D) Low birth weight; cardiovascular disease
Answer: D
Page Ref: 104 Box: B&E: The Prenatal Environment and Health in Later Life
Skill: Conceptual
Objective: 3.4

49) Jesse weighed 3.3 pounds when he was born. Research shows that he is at an increased risk of _____ in adulthood.
    A) prostate cancer
    B) diabetes
    C) lymphatic cancer
    D) Alzheimer's disease
Answer: B
Page Ref: 104 Box: B&E: The Prenatal Environment and Health in Later Life
Skill: Applied
Objective: 3.4

50) Sophie weighed 8.9 pounds when she was born. Research shows that she is at an increased risk of _____ in adulthood.
    A) breast cancer
    B) lung cancer
    C) heart disease
    D) stroke
Answer: A
Page Ref: 105 Box: B&E: The Prenatal Environment and Health in Later Life
Skill: Applied
Objective: 3.4

51) Children exposed to thalidomide were often born
    A) with noncancerous tumors.
    B) six to eight weeks premature.
    C) with gross deformities of the arms and legs.
    D) with severe cognitive delays.
Answer: C
Page Ref: 105
Skill: Conceptual
Objective: 3.5

52) Daughters of mothers who took diethylstilbestrol to prevent miscarriages
    A) were born with gross deformities of the arms and legs.
    B) showed unusually high rates of vaginal cancer.
    C) had abnormally high-pitched and shrill cries.
    D) often developed diabetes in adulthood.
Answer: B
Page Ref: 105–106
Skill: Conceptual
Objective: 3.5

53) The most widely used potent teratogen is prescribed
    A) as a sedative.
    B) to treat severe acne.
    C) to prevent miscarriages.
    D) to treat depression.
Answer: B
Page Ref: 106
Skill: Conceptual
Objective: 3.5

54) Although it has been linked to low birth weight, infant death, and lower intelligence test scores in early childhood, _____ is/are one of the most common over-the-counter medications taken by pregnant women.
    A) cough syrup
    B) antacids
    C) aspirin
    D) antihistamines
Answer: C
Page Ref: 106
Skill: Conceptual
Objective: 3.5

55) Caffeine use during pregnancy
    A) can result in low birth weight.
    B) is only safe during the first trimester.
    C) can result in gross fetal abnormalities.
    D) is linked to respiratory distress in childbirth.
Answer: A
Page Ref: 106
Skill: Conceptual
Objective: 3.5

56) Which of the following statements is true about illegal drug use during pregnancy?
    A) Motor development is rapid in children who are prenatally exposed to illegal drugs.
    B) Children who are prenatally exposed to illegal drugs can have long-term difficulties.
    C) The difficulties of prenatally exposed children disappear once the drugs are out of their systems.
    D) The effects of illegal drugs on the developing organism are consistent.
Answer: B
Page Ref: 106–107
Skill: Conceptual
Objective: 3.5

57) Today, an estimated _____ percent of U.S. women smoke during pregnancies.
    A) 4
    B) 10
    C) 14
    D) 20
Answer: C
Page Ref: 107
Skill: Factual
Objective: 3.5

58) Beatrice has smoked throughout her pregnancy. Now in her seventh month, Beatrice is considering quitting. You can tell her that
    A) the damage was already done during the zygotic period.
    B) if she quits now, she reduces the likelihood that her baby will be born underweight.
    C) the damage was already done during the embryonic period.
    D) quitting now will not reduce the likelihood that her baby will have colic.
Answer: B
Page Ref: 107
Skill: Applied
Objective: 3.5

59) From one-third to one-half of nonsmoking pregnant women
    A) use alcohol regularly.
    B) smoked prior to finding out they were pregnant.
    C) take antidepressants.
    D) are "passive smokers."
Answer: D
Page Ref: 108
Skill: Conceptual
Objective: 3.5

60) Jenna's physical growth is slow. She has short eyelid openings, a thin upper lip, a flattened philtrum, and brain injury. Jenna's mother probably _____ during pregnancy.
   A) drank heavily
   B) smoked cigarettes
   C) used cocaine
   D) used methadone
Answer: A
Page Ref: 108
Skill: Applied
Objective: 3.5

61) Matthew was prenatally exposed to alcohol. His physical growth is typical and he has no facial abnormalities. However, he has impaired motor coordination, attention span, and memory. Matthew was probably born with
   A) fetal alcohol syndrome.
   B) alcohol-related neurodevelopmental disorder.
   C) partial fetal alcohol syndrome.
   D) a genetic disorder.
Answer: B
Page Ref: 109
Skill: Applied
Objective: 3.5

62) It is safe to drink _____ during pregnancy.
   A) no amount of alcohol
   B) one alcoholic beverage per day
   C) 3 to 5 alcoholic beverages per week
   D) a few alcoholic beverages per month
Answer: A
Page Ref: 109
Skill: Factual
Objective: 3.5

63) Which of the following statements is true about radiation exposure during pregnancy?
   A) Low-level radiation from medical X-rays is safe.
   B) When mothers are exposed to radiation during pregnancy, the risk of miscarriage increases.
   C) The effects of radiation exposure are immediate and apparent.
   D) Radiation exposure affects physical development, but not cognitive or emotional development.
Answer: B
Page Ref: 110
Skill: Conceptual
Objective: 3.5

64) Pregnant women are wise to avoid _____ to reduce the likelihood of mercury exposure.
   A) getting X-rays
   B) changing cat litter boxes
   C) painting
   D) eating long-lived predatory fish
Answer: D
Page Ref: 110
Skill: Conceptual
Objective: 3.5

65) In Taiwan, prenatal exposure to very high levels of _____ in rice oil resulted in low birth weight, discolored skin, and delayed cognitive development.
    A) dioxins
    B) mercury
    C) PCBs
    D) lead
Answer: C
Page Ref: 110
Skill: Factual
Objective: 3.5

66) Joslyn, a school custodian, is pregnant and works in an old school building where multiple layers of paint are flaking off the walls. To be safe, Joslyn should have the paint tested for
    A) polychlorinated biphenyls (PCBs).
    B) mercury.
    C) dioxins.
    D) lead.
Answer: D
Page Ref: 111
Skill: Applied
Objective: 3.5

67) Dioxin seems to impair the fertility of _____ prior to conception.
    A) X-bearing ova
    B) Y-bearing sperm
    C) X-bearing sperm
    D) Y-bearing ova
Answer: B
Page Ref: 111
Skill: Factual
Objective: 3.5

68) The greatest damage from rubella occurs when it strikes pregnant mothers during the
    A) zygotic period.
    B) embryonic period.
    C) second trimester.
    D) third trimester.
Answer: B
Page Ref: 111
Skill: Conceptual
Objective: 3.5

69) Which of the following statements is true about HIV and AIDS?
    A) HIV-positive pregnant women pass the virus to their fetus 20 to 30 percent of the time.
    B) About 25 to 35 percent of prenatal AIDS babies die by 1 year of age.
    C) There are no antiviral drugs that reduce prenatal AIDS transmission without harmful consequences.
    D) Most infant HIV cases are curable if caught and treated early.
Answer: A
Page Ref: 112
Skill: Conceptual
Objective: 3.5

70) Kelly, a pregnant 30-year-old, has contracted the most common parasitic infection. Kelly has
   A) rubella.
   B) toxoplasmosis.
   C) cytomegalovirus.
   D) herpes simplex 2.
   Answer: B
   Page Ref: 112
   Skill: Applied
   Objective: 3.5

71) Expectant mothers can prevent toxoplasmosis by
   A) making sure the vegetables they eat are clean.
   B) avoiding exposure to X-rays.
   C) avoiding eating swordfish.
   D) making sure that the meat they eat is well-cooked.
   Answer: D
   Page Ref: 112
   Skill: Conceptual
   Objective: 3.5

72) In healthy, physically fit women, _____ exercise is related to _____.
   A) aerobic; low birth weight
   B) vigorous; a reduction in the risk of high blood pressure
   C) moderate; a reduction in the risk of maternal diabetes
   D) frequent; high birth weight
   Answer: C
   Page Ref: 113
   Skill: Conceptual
   Objective: 3.6

73) Marzanne is pregnant and wonders how much weight she should gain. Her doctor will probably recommend that she gain _____ to _____ pounds.
   A) 10; 15
   B) 20; 25
   C) 25; 30
   D) 30; 35
   Answer: C
   Page Ref: 113
   Skill: Applied
   Objective: 3.6

74) A severe famine in the Netherlands during World War II revealed that
   A) the sensitive-period concept operates with nutrition.
   B) malnutrition during the first trimester is not associated with miscarriage.
   C) malnutrition in the second trimester is associated with large head size.
   D) malnutrition during the third trimester is associated with physical defects.
   Answer: A
   Page Ref: 113
   Skill: Conceptual
   Objective: 3.6

75) Taking a folic acid supplement around the time of conception reduces the risk of
   A) miscarriage.
   B) spina bifida.
   C) Down syndrome.
   D) cytomegalovirus.
Answer: B
Page Ref: 114
Skill: Factual
Objective: 3.6

76) Enriching women's diets with calcium
   A) can cause miscarriages in the zygotic period.
   B) helps prevent neural tube defects.
   C) eliminates the risk of osteoporosis in offspring.
   D) helps prevent maternal high blood pressure.
Answer: D
Page Ref: 114
Skill: Factual
Objective: 3.6

77) Prenatal maternal stress is
   A) especially damaging during the first trimester.
   B) related to pyloric stenosis.
   C) associated with emotional, but not physical, difficulties.
   D) related to neural tube defects.
Answer: B
Page Ref: 114
Skill: Conceptual
Objective: 3.6

78) The relationship between social support, positive pregnancy outcomes, and subsequent child development is
   A) strongest for affluent women.
   B) moderate for minority women.
   C) particularly strong for low-income women.
   D) strongest for middle-income women.
Answer: C
Page Ref: 115
Skill: Conceptual
Objective: 3.6

79) Which of the following statements is true about Rh factor incompatibility?
   A) The damage caused by Rh incompatibility can be avoided if the mother receives a blood transfusion during delivery.
   B) Rh-positive blood is dominant and Rh-negative blood is recessive, so the chances are good that a baby will be Rh-positive.
   C) Rh-positive babies are routinely given a vaccine at birth to prevent the buildup of harmful Rh antibodies.
   D) The harmful effects of Rh incompatibility can be prevented if the newborn is immediately placed on a diet low in phenylalanine.
Answer: B
Page Ref: 115
Skill: Conceptual
Objective: 3.6

80) Rh factor incompatibility
   A) affects Rh positive mothers.
   B) can result in infant death.
   C) cannot be prevented in most cases.
   D) usually affects firstborn children.
Answer: B
Page Ref: 115
Skill: Conceptual
Objective: 3.6

81) Danica is a healthy 35-year-old woman who is pregnant with her first child. Danica is
   A) more likely than a younger woman to have a low birth-weight baby.
   B) likely to have a longer and more difficult labor than a younger woman.
   C) more likely to have prenatal complications than a woman in her twenties.
   D) as likely as a younger women to have no prenatal or birth complications.
Answer: D
Page Ref: 115
Skill: Applied
Objective: 3.6

82) The Nurse–Family Partnership is a
   A) health-care program currently implemented in developing countries.
   B) voluntary home visiting program for first-time, low-income expectant mothers.
   C) mandatory home visiting program for new mothers with special needs infants.
   D) community service program available for pregnant teens in urban areas.
Answer: B
Page Ref: 116 Box: SI: Health: The Nurse–Family Partnership: Reducing Maternal Stress and Enhancing Child Development Through Social Support
Skill: Factual
Objective: 3.6

83) Which of the following statements is true about the effectiveness of the Nurse–Family Partnership?
   A) The benefits of the intervention were greater for children from high-SES families than for children from low-SES families.
   B) Trained paraprofessionals were more effective than professional nurses in preventing delayed mental development.
   C) As kindergartners, children in the program scored higher in language, but lower in intelligence than comparison children.
   D) At both ages 6 and 9, children of home-visited mothers in the poorest mental health during pregnancy exceeded comparison children in academic achievement.
Answer: D
Page Ref: 116 Box: SI: Health: The Nurse–Family Partnership: Reducing Maternal Stress and Enhancing Child Development Through Social Support
Skill: Conceptual
Objective: 3.6

84) Infants born to teenagers have a higher rate of problems because
   A) teenagers' reproductive organs are not yet mature enough to support a pregnancy.
   B) teenagers are not yet physically ready to give birth.
   C) many pregnant teenagers do not receive adequate prenatal care.
   D) teenagers are exposed to more teratogens than other pregnant mothers.
Answer: C
Page Ref: 116
Skill: Conceptual
Objective: 3.6

85) Kali's face, hands, and feet began to swell in the second half of her pregnancy. Kali's doctor began to monitor her blood pressure. The doctor was probably concerned about
   A) toxoplasmosis.
   B) maternal diabetes.
   C) Rh incompatibility.
   D) preeclampsia.
   Answer: D
   Page Ref: 117
   Skill: Applied
   Objective: 3.7

86) Nearly 30 percent of adolescent mothers
   A) receive inadequate prenatal care.
   B) give birth at home.
   C) give up their babies for adoption.
   D) develop preeclampsia in the third trimester.
   Answer: A
   Page Ref: 117
   Skill: Factual
   Objective: 3.7

87) In the early weeks of pregnancy, a diabetic mother's out-of-control blood glucose _____ the risk of _____.
   A) increases; birth defects
   B) decreases; birth defects
   C) increases; low birth weight
   D) increases; chromosomal abnormalities
   Answer: A
   Page Ref: 118 Box B&E: Prenatal Iron Deficiency and Memory Impairments in Infants of Diabetic Mothers
   Skill: Conceptual
   Objective: 3.7

88) Which of the following statements is true about research on memory impairments in infants of diabetic mothers?
   A) Prenatal iron depletion interferes with the cerebral cortex, causing long-term learning and academic problems in children of diabetic mothers.
   B) Damage to the hippocampus is not linked to long-term learning and academic problems in children of diabetic mothers.
   C) Diabetes-linked prenatal brain damage is linked to short-term memory impairments that can often be reversed with medication.
   D) As a result of iron depletion in critical brain areas, a diabetic pregnancy places the fetus at risk for lasting memory deficits.
   Answer: D
   Page Ref: 118 Box B&E: Prenatal Iron Deficiency and Memory Impairments in Infants of Diabetic Mothers
   Skill: Conceptual
   Objective: 3.7

89) In group prenatal care,
   A) expectant mothers are grouped by age, and each group is seen by an assigned health-care provider.
   B) trained leaders provide minority expectant mothers with a group discussion session after each medical checkup.
   C) expectant mothers and fathers take turns facilitating group discussions.
   D) whole families are included in prenatal visits, including mothers, fathers, and siblings.
   Answer: B
   Page Ref: 119
   Skill: Conceptual
   Objective: 3.7

90) The more a pregnant woman seeks information by reading or accessing websites, the
    A) more confident she tends to feel about parenting.
    B) less anxious she tends to feel about parenting.
    C) less likely she will ask questions to medical professionals.
    D) more likely she will be dissatisfied with her parenting experience.
    Answer: A
    Page Ref: 120
    Skill: Conceptual
    Objective: 3.8

91) Which of the following statements about models of effective parenthood is true?
    A) Overall, men are more likely than women to come to terms with negative experiences in their own childhoods and build helathier and happier relationships with their children.
    B) In most cases, people who have negative experiences in their own childhoods have conflicted relationships with their children.
    C) Many people come to terms with negative experiences in their own childhoods and build healthier and happier relationships with their children.
    D) Most people are unable to come to terms with negative experiences in their own childhoods and have conflicted relationships with their own children.
    Answer: C
    Page Ref: 121
    Skill: Conceptual
    Objective: 3.8

92) The most important preparation for parenthood
    A) takes place in the context of the parents' relationship.
    B) is having a positive relationship with one's own parents.
    C) involves attending prenatal classes.
    D) is having support from extended family.
    Answer: A
    Page Ref: 121
    Skill: Conceptual
    Objective: 3.8

ESSAY

93) When Americans are asked about their desire to have children, what are the most frequent advantages and disadvantages they list?
    Answer: Although some ethnic and regional differences exist, reasons for having children that are most important to all groups include the warm, affectionate relationship and the stimulation and fun that children provide. Also frequently mentioned are growth and learning experiences that children bring into the lives of adults, the desire to have someone carry on after one's own death, and feelings of accomplishment and creativity that come from helping children grow. Among the disadvantages of parenthood, they cite loss of freedom most often, followed by financial strain. Many adults also worry greatly about family–work conflict—not having enough time to meet both child-rearing and job responsibilities.
    Page Ref: 93

94) The average number of children per North American has decreased since 1960 from 3.1 to 1.8. What are some reasons for this decline?
    Answer: One of the main reasons for the decline in birth rate is the availability of more effective birth control. Another major reason for this decline is that a family size of one or two children is more compatible with a woman's decision to divide her energies between family and career. Marital instability has also contributed to smaller families: More couples today get divorced before their childbearing plans are complete.
    Page Ref: 93

95) Describe the period of the zygote, including the major developments that occur during this period.

Answer: The period of the zygote lasts about two weeks, from fertilization until implantation. The zygote's first cell duplication is long and drawn out; it is not complete until about 30 hours after conception. Gradually, new cells are added at a faster rate. By the fourth day, 60 to 70 cells exist that form a blastocyst. The cells on the inside of the blastocyst, called the embryonic disk, will become the new organism. The thin outer ring of cells, termed the trophoblast, will become the structures that provide protective covering and nourishment. Between the seventh and ninth days, implantation occurs: The blastocyst burrows into the uterine lining. Structures that feed and protect the developing organism begin to form—amnion, chorion, yolk sac, placenta, and umbilical cord.

Page Ref: 97–98

96) What are teratogens? What factors determine their impact?

Answer: The term *teratogen* refers to any environmental agent that causes damage during the prenatal period. The harm done by teratogens is not always simple and straightforward. It depends on the following factors:

- *Dose.* Larger doses over longer time periods usually have more negative effects.
- *Heredity.* The genetic makeup of the mother and the developing organism plays an important role. Some individuals are better able than others to withstand harmful environments.
- *Other negative influences.* The presence of several negative influences at once, such as additional teratogens, poor nutrition, and lack of medical care, can worsen the impact of a single harmful agent.
- *Age.* The effects of teratogens vary with the age of the organism at the time of exposure. Some parts of the body, such as the brain and eye, have long sensitive periods that extend throughout prenatal development. Others are much shorter. In the zygotic period, before implantation, teratogens rarely have any impact. If they do, the damage is usually so severe that a miscarriage occurs. The embryonic period is the time when serious defects are most likely to occur. During the fetal period, teratogenic damage is usually minor. However, organs such as the brain, ears, eyes, teeth, and genitals can still be strongly affected.

Page Ref: 102–104

97) What is Accutane? How does it affect a developing organism?

Answer: The most widely used potent teratogen is a vitamin A derivative called Accutane, known by the generic name *isotretinoin.* Accutane is prescribed to hundreds of thousands of women of childbearing age in industrialized nations to treat severe acne. Exposure during the first trimester results in eye, ear, skull, brain, heart, and immune system abnormalities. Accutane's packaging warns users to avoid pregnancy by using two methods of birth control, but many women do not heed this advice.

Page Ref: 106

98) Describe the effects of exercise during pregnancy.

Answer: An expectant mother who remains fit experiences fewer physical discomforts, such as back pain, upward pressure on the chest, or breathing difficulties. In healthy, physically fit women, regular moderate exercise, such as walking, swimming, or aerobics, is related to increased birth weight and a reduction in the risk of maternal diabetes and high blood pressure. However, frequent, vigorous, extended exercise, especially late in pregnancy, results in lower birth weight. During the last trimester, when the abdomen grows very large, mothers often must cut back on exercise because they have difficulty moving freely. Most women do not engage in sufficient moderate exercise during pregnancy. Pregnant women with circulatory difficulties, a history of miscarriages, or other health problems, should consult a doctor about a physical fitness routine. The wrong kind of exercise can endanger the pregnancy.

Page Ref: 113

99) Cite reasons that some women do not seek prenatal care.

Answer: Inadequate care is far more common among adolescent and low-income, ethnic minority mothers. One reason they delay going to the doctor is that they lack health insurance. Besides financial hardship, some mothers have situational barriers, including difficulty finding a doctor, getting an appointment, and arranging transportation, and insensitive or unsatisfying experiences with clinic staff. Other mothers have personal barriers, including psychological stress, the demands of taking care of other young children, family crises, lack of knowledge about the signs of pregnancy and benefits of prenatal care, and ambivalence about the pregnancy. Many also engage in high-risk behaviors, such as smoking and drinking, which they do not want to reveal to health professionals.

Page Ref: 117

100) Cynthia and Todd are having marital difficulties. Cynthia decides to have a baby, hoping parenthood will improve their relationship. What advice can you offer them?

Answer: Deciding to have a baby in hopes of improving a troubled relationship is a serious mistake. The most important preparation for parenthood takes place in the context of the parents' relationship. Expectant couples who are unhappy in their marriages and who have difficulty working out their differences continue to be distant, dissatisfied, and poor problem solvers after childbirth. In a distressed marriage, pregnancy adds to rather than lessens family conflict. Only when a couple's relationship is faring well and both partners want and plan for the baby, is the excitement of a first pregnancy likely to bring the husband and wife closer.

Page Ref: 121

CHAPTER 4
BIRTH AND THE NEWBORN BABY

MULTIPLE CHOICE

1) As pregnancy advances, the placenta releases increasing amounts of
   A) CRH.
   B) cortisol.
   C) insulin.
   D) thyroxine.
   Answer: A
   Page Ref: 126
   Skill: Factual
   Objective: 4.1

2) Lightening occurs when the
   A) amniotic sac is ruptured.
   B) mucus plug is released from the cervix.
   C) fetus's head drops low into the uterus.
   D) first uterine contractions take place.
   Answer: C
   Page Ref: 126
   Skill: Factual
   Objective: 4.1

3) A sure sign that labor is only hours or days away is
   A) contractions in the upper part of the uterus.
   B) the bloody show.
   C) lightening.
   D) frequent urination.
   Answer: B
   Page Ref: 126
   Skill: Factual
   Objective: 4.1

4) The first stage of labor
   A) is the shortest.
   B) involves delivery of the baby.
   C) climaxes with a brief phase called transition.
   D) involves birth of the placenta.
   Answer: C
   Page Ref: 126
   Skill: Conceptual
   Objective: 4.1

5) During transition, the
   A) baby is forced down and out of the birth canal.
   B) placenta is delivered.
   C) cervix opens completely.
   D) cervix begins to dilate and efface.
   Answer: C
   Page Ref: 126
   Skill: Conceptual
   Objective: 4.1

6) The infant is born during
   A) the first stage of labor.
   B) the second stage of labor.
   C) transition.
   D) the third stage of labor.
   Answer: B
   Page Ref: 127
   Skill: Factual
   Objective: 4.1

7) _____ occurs when the vaginal opening is stretched around the baby's entire head.
   A) Lightening
   B) Bloody show
   C) Crowning
   D) Transition
   Answer: C
   Page Ref: 127
   Skill: Factual
   Objective: 4.1

8) The placenta is delivered during
   A) the first stage of labor.
   B) the second stage of labor.
   C) crowning.
   D) the third stage of labor.
   Answer: D
   Page Ref: 128
   Skill: Factual
   Objective: 4.1

9) The third stage of labor typically lasts
   A) 5 to 10 minutes.
   B) 15 to 30 minutes.
   C) 45 minutes to one hour.
   D) one to two hours.
   Answer: A
   Page Ref: 128
   Skill: Factual
   Objective: 4.1

10) Which of the following statements is true about the average newborn infant?
    A) Girls are slightly heavier than boys.
    B) The average newborn is 23 inches long.
    C) Boys are slightly longer than girls.
    D) The average newborn weighs 6½ pounds.
Answer: C
Page Ref: 128
Skill: Conceptual
Objective: 4.2

11) Which of the following statements is true about the newborn baby's appearance?
    A) Proportionally, if an adult head were as large as that of a newborn infant, it would be the size of an orange.
    B) Their round faces, chubby cheeks, large foreheads, and big eyes make adults feel like picking them up and cuddling them.
    C) They may not match their parents' idealized image because they have a combination of a small head and a long torso.
    D) Their legs are long and bowed, and their heads are small compared to the rest of the body.
Answer: B
Page Ref: 128
Skill: Conceptual
Objective: 4.2

12) A combined Apgar score of ____ or better indicates that an infant is in good physical condition.
    A) 4
    B) 5
    C) 6
    D) 7
Answer: D
Page Ref: 128
Skill: Factual
Objective: 4.3

13) Two Apgar ratings are given because
    A) one is given by the pediatrician, and one is given by the labor and delivery nurse.
    B) one score is for appearance, pulse, and grimace, and the other score is for activity and respiration.
    C) some babies have trouble adjusting at first but do quite well after a few minutes.
    D) one is taken immediately after birth, and the other is taken just before the newborn is released from the hospital.
Answer: C
Page Ref: 128
Skill: Conceptual
Objective: 4.3

14) Devin is given a combined Apgar score of 7. The medical professionals should
    A) immediately provide medical attention because he is in serious danger.
    B) tell Devin's parents that he is in good physical condition.
    C) provide assistance in establishing breathing and other vital signs.
    D) immediately put him on a ventilator and monitor his situation closely.
Answer: B
Page Ref: 128
Skill: Applied
Objective: 4.3

15) Dorita is given an Apgar appearance rating of 1. This means her
    A) body is pink with blue arms and legs.
    B) body, arms, and legs are all blue.
    C) body, arms, and legs are all pink.
    D) body is blue with pink arms and legs.
Answer: A
Page Ref: 129
Skill: Applied
Objective: 4.3

16) In South America, the Jarara mother
    A) leans against the body of the "head helper" to give birth.
    B) gives birth in full view of the entire community.
    C) gives birth in a hammock with a crowd of women close by.
    D) gives birth in a freestanding birth center.
Answer: B
Page Ref: 129
Skill: Conceptual
Objective: 4.4

17) Prepared childbirth
    A) includes routine use of strong pain-relieving drugs.
    B) does not allow family members and friends to participate in the birth.
    C) always takes place outside of a hospital setting.
    D) involves techniques aimed at reducing pain and medical intervention.
Answer: D
Page Ref: 130
Skill: Conceptual
Objective: 4.4

18) Most natural childbirth programs draw on methods developed by Grantly Dick-Read and Fernand Lamaze, who recognized that
    A) new labor medications could be used to reduce the pain of childbirth.
    B) hospital costs could be saved if women used prepared childbirth methods.
    C) cultural attitudes had taught women to fear the birth experience.
    D) the mother's home was the safest and least painful place to give birth.
Answer: C
Page Ref: 130
Skill: Conceptual
Objective: 4.4

19) Mothers who are supported during labor by a doula
    A) often do not have access to other forms of support.
    B) usually give birth at home or at the home of the doula.
    C) have fewer birth complications than women who do not have supportive companionship.
    D) give birth lying flat on their backs with their feet in stirrups.
Answer: C
Page Ref: 130
Skill: Conceptual
Objective: 4.4

20) When mothers are upright during labor, they are
    A) more likely to have a longer labor.
    B) likely to need an episiotomy.
    C) less likely to use pain-relieving medication.
    D) more likely to deliver a breech baby.
Answer: C
Page Ref: 131
Skill: Conceptual
Objective: 4.4

21) Which of the following statements is true regarding home delivery?
    A) It is often attended by a certified nurse-midwife.
    B) It is more popular in the United States than in England and Sweden.
    C) It poses no additional risks to the mother and the baby.
    D) It is almost always dangerous for mothers and babies.
Answer: A
Page Ref: 131–132
Skill: Conceptual
Objective: 4.5

22) Which mother is a good candidate for a home delivery?
    A) Heather, a healthy 43-year-old who previously had a cesarean delivery
    B) Helena, a first-time mom who wants to deliver her own baby unassisted
    C) Prudence, a 30-year-old second-time mom, assisted by a certified nurse-midwife
    D) Donna, a fifth-time mom whose baby is in a breech position
Answer: C
Page Ref: 132
Skill: Applied
Objective: 4.5

23) Continuous fetal monitoring
    A) measures the baby's blood oxygen levels during labor.
    B) is required in most U.S. hospitals and used in over 80 percent of U.S. births.
    C) is linked to a decreased rate of cesarean deliveries.
    D) reduces the rate of infant brain damage and death in all pregnancies.
Answer: B
Page Ref: 132
Skill: Conceptual
Objective: 4.6

24) Fetal monitoring is linked to a(n)
    A) reduction in the rates of infant brain damage.
    B) reduction in the rates of infant death.
    C) reduction in the use of instrumental deliveries.
    D) increase in the number of cesarean deliveries.
Answer: D
Page Ref: 132–133
Skill: Conceptual
Objective: 4.6

25) The most common approach to controlling pain during labor is
    A) epidural analgesia.
    B) pitocin.
    C) a spinal block.
    D) meditation.
Answer: A
Page Ref: 133
Skill: Factual
Objective: 4.6

26) Epidural analgesia
    A) numbs the entire lower half of the body.
    B) limits pain reduction to the pelvic region.
    C) strengthens uterine contractions.
    D) reduces the chances of cesarean delivery.
Answer: B
Page Ref: 133
Skill: Factual
Objective: 4.6

27) Henrietta is concerned about using epidural analgesia during labor. You can tell her that newborns exposed to epidural analgesia tend to
    A) have trouble falling asleep.
    B) be hyperactive and animated.
    C) have lower Apgar scores.
    D) suck more aggressively when feeding.
Answer: C
Page Ref: 133
Skill: Applied
Objective: 4.6

28) _____ is appropriate if the mother's pushing during the second stage of labor does not move the baby through the birth canal in a reasonable period of time.
    A) Instrument delivery
    B) Epidural analgesia
    C) Use of an anesthetic
    D) Induced labor
Answer: A
Page Ref: 133
Skill: Conceptual
Objective: 4.6

29) Vacuum extractors
    A) are not as safe as forceps.
    B) are more likely than forceps to tear the mother's tissues.
    C) have been used since the sixteenth century to speed up delivery.
    D) can cause bleeding beneath the baby's skin and on the outside of the skull.
Answer: D
Page Ref: 133
Skill: Conceptual
Objective: 4.6

30) About ___ percent of American labors are induced.
    A) 8
    B) 14
    C) 22
    D) 28
Answer: C
Page Ref: 134
Skill: Factual
Objective: 4.6

31) Induced labors are justified when
    A) continuing the pregnancy threatens the well-being of the mother or baby.
    B) the baby has not arrived by its due date.
    C) the doctor determines that it is a convenient time to deliver the baby.
    D) the mother and father want the baby to arrive on a particular date.
Answer: A
Page Ref: 134
Skill: Conceptual
Objective: 4.6

32) In induced labors,
    A) contractions are shorter and more widely spaced apart than in spontaneous labors.
    B) the rate of cesarean delivery is less than in spontaneous labors.
    C) the mother is given a synthetic hormone that simulates contractions.
    D) the chances of an instrument delivery are less than in spontaneous labors.
Answer: C
Page Ref: 134
Skill: Conceptual
Objective: 4.6

33) The rate of cesarean delivery is
    A) substantially higher in induced than spontaneous labors.
    B) lower today than it was forty years ago.
    C) currently about 10 percent in the United States.
    D) lower in the United States than in other industrialized countries.
Answer: A
Page Ref: 134
Skill: Conceptual
Objective: 4.6

34) Which of the following statements is true about the breech position?
    A) Cesarean delivery is never justified when the baby is in the breech position.
    B) The breech position decreases the chance of oxygen deprivation.
    C) Certain breech babies fare just as well with vaginal delivery as with a cesarean.
    D) Babies in the breech position are turned facing toward the mother's back rather than facing outward.
Answer: C
Page Ref: 134
Skill: Conceptual
Objective: 4.6

35) Tonya is pregnant for a second time. She hopes to have a vaginal delivery, although her first delivery was cesarean. You should advise Tonya that
    A) she will be required to have a second cesarean delivery.
    B) a natural labor after a cesarean is associated with slightly increased rates of maternal death.
    C) a natural labor after a cesarean is just as safe as a repeated cesarean delivery.
    D) a natural labor after a cesarean is associated with slightly increased rates of rupture of the uterus.
Answer: D
Page Ref: 134
Skill: Applied
Objective: 4.6

36) Cerebral palsy
    A) affects one out of every 300 American children.
    B) can range from very mild tremors to mental retardation.
    C) is especially common in water births.
    D) is caused by either placenta abruptio or placenta previa.
Answer: B
Page Ref: 135
Skill: Factual
Objective: 4.7

37) _____ during pregnancy is associated with premature separation of the placenta.
    A) Tobacco and cocaine use
    B) Exposure to PCBs
    C) High maternal stress
    D) HIV infection
Answer: A
Page Ref: 135
Skill: Conceptual
Objective: 4.7

38) _____ results when the blastocyst implants so low in the uterus that the placenta covers the cervical opening.
    A) Toxemia
    B) Placenta previa
    C) Placenta abruptio
    D) Toxoplasmosis
Answer: B
Page Ref: 135
Skill: Factual
Objective: 4.7

39) Which of the following statements is true about anoxia?
    A) After initial brain injury from anoxia, another phase of cell death can occur several weeks later.
    B) Whole-body cooling involves immersing a newborn with an initial brain injury in freezing water from the neck down.
    C) The effects of mild or even moderate anoxia rarely persist beyond infancy.
    D) Healthy newborns can survive periods of little or no oxygen longer than adults can.
Answer: D
Page Ref: 135
Skill: Conceptual
Objective: 4.7

40) Abbie was born seven weeks premature. Her tiny lungs were so poorly developed that the air sacs collapse. A mechanical respirator is being used to keep Abbie breathing. Abbie suffers from
    A) cerebral palsy.
    B) toxemia.
    C) hyaline membrane disease.
    D) acidosis.
Answer: C
Page Ref: 136
Skill: Applied
Objective: 4.7

41) Birth weight is the best available predictor of
    A) childhood obesity.
    B) adolescent anorexia.
    C) myopia.
    D) infant survival.
Answer: D
Page Ref: 136
Skill: Factual
Objective: 4.7

42) Travis is born three days after his due date and weighs five pounds. Travis is a(n) _____ infant.
    A) preterm
    B) small-for-date
    C) average-weight
    D) anoxic
Answer: B
Page Ref: 137
Skill: Applied
Objective: 4.7

43) Which of the following statements is true about preterm infants?
    A) They are born below their expected weight considering the length of the pregnancy.
    B) They usually have more serious problems than small-for-date infants.
    C) Although they are small, their weight may still be appropriate, based on time spent in the uterus.
    D) They are more likely than small-for-date infants to show evidence of brain damage.
Answer: C
Page Ref: 137
Skill: Conceptual
Objective: 4.7

44) Compared to full-term infants, preterm babies are
    A) at a greater risk for child abuse.
    B) more often held close.
    C) talked to more gently.
    D) more often touched.
Answer: A
Page Ref: 138
Skill: Conceptual
Objective: 4.7

45) Which of the following statements is true about interventions for preterm infants?
    A) Air is filtered before it enters an isolette, but temperature cannot be controlled.
    B) Simulating preterm infants is harmful because the tiny babies are fragile.
    C) Touch is the least important form of infant stimulation.
    D) When preterm infants are gently massaged several times each day, they gain weight faster.
Answer: D
Page Ref: 138
Skill: Conceptual
Objective: 4.8

46) Kangaroo skin-to-skin contact
    A) is not commonly used in developing nations where hospitalization is not always possible.
    B) fosters improved oxygenation of the baby's body, temperature regulation, and infant survival.
    C) is rarely used in Western nations where preterm infants are placed in hospital intensive care units.
    D) provides babies with touch stimulation but neglects the other sensory modalities.
Answer: B
Page Ref: 138–139
Skill: Conceptual
Objective: 4.8

47) Dawn and Richard have the economic and personal resources to care for Amelia, their preterm infant. Research shows that
    A) interventions are not usually needed for economically advantaged parents like Dawn and Richard to promote healthy development.
    B) Dawn and Richard will need extensive coaching in recognizing and responding to Amelia's needs.
    C) just a few sessions of coaching in recognizing and responding to Amelia's needs could reduce Amelia's crying and improve her sleep.
    D) Dawn and Richard will need comprehensive long-term, intensive intervention to meet Amelia's needs.
Answer: C
Page Ref: 139
Skill: Applied
Objective: 4.8

48) _____ has the most up-to-date health-care technology in the world.
    A) The United States
    B) China
    C) Sweden
    D) Canada
Answer: A
Page Ref: 140 Box: SI: Health: A Cross-National Perspective on Health Care and Other Policies for Parents and Newborn Babies
Skill: Factual
Objective: 4.8

49) In international rankings, the infant death rate in the United States has slipped from seventh in the 1950s to _____ in 2009.
    A) tenth
    B) fourteenth
    C) twentieth
    D) twenty-eighth
Answer: D
Page Ref: 140 Box: SI: Health: A Cross-National Perspective on Health Care and Other Policies for Parents and Newborn Babies
Skill: Factual
Objective: 4.8

50) African-American and Native-American babies are more than ____ as likely as white infants to be born early and underweight and are _____ as likely as white infants to die in the first year.
A) twice; half
B) twice; twice
C) three times; twice
D) three times; half

Answer: B

Page Ref: 140 Box: SI: Health: A Cross-National Perspective on Health Care and Other Policies for Parents and Newborn Babies
Skill: Factual
Objective: 4.8

51) The two factors that are largely responsible for neonatal mortality are
A) birth defects and sudden infant death syndrome.
B) child abuse and sudden infant death syndrome.
C) serious physical defects and low birth weight.
D) unintentional injuries and low birth weight.

Answer: C

Page Ref: 140 Box: SI: Health: A Cross-National Perspective on Health Care and Other Policies for Parents and Newborn Babies
Skill: Conceptual
Objective: 4.8

52) Each country that outranks the United States in infant survival provides its citizens with
A) government-sponsored health-care benefits.
B) stronger crime prevention and family planning programs.
C) more up-to-date health-care technology.
D) higher numbers of well-trained medical professionals.

Answer: A

Page Ref: 140 Box: SI: Health: A Cross-National Perspective on Health Care and Other Policies for Parents and Newborn Babies
Skill: Conceptual
Objective: 4.8

53) Carol lives in Wyoming and works for a small company with 12 employees. Carol hopes to take 12 weeks of maternity leave. What advice can you give Carol?
A) The United States mandates 12 weeks of paid maternity leave for all new mothers.
B) Federal law mandating unpaid maternity leave does not apply to her employer.
C) The United States mandates six weeks of paid maternity leave for all new mothers.
D) The United States mandates 12 weeks of unpaid maternity leave for all new mothers.

Answer: B

Page Ref: 141 Box: SI: Health: A Cross-National Perspective on Health Care and Other Policies for Parents and Newborn Babies
Skill: Applied
Objective: 4.8

54) The Kauai study tells us that
    A) even children who experience mild birth trauma and grow up in stable families do not do as well on measures of intelligence as children with no birth problems.
    B) as long as birth injuries are not overwhelming, a supportive home can restore children's growth.
    C) a supportive home environment does little to alleviate the effects of birth trauma, as brain injuries are often permanent.
    D) children who experience moderate birth trauma and are exposed to poverty will have serious learning difficulties even if they are otherwise resilient.
    Answer: B
    Page Ref: 142
    Skill: Conceptual
    Objective: 4.9

55) In several studies, fathers showed slight increases in _____ and _____ when holding their newborn babies that were comparable with those of mothers.
    A) oxytocin; prolactin
    B) prolactin; estrogens
    C) androgens; oxytocin
    D) estrogens; androgens
    Answer: B
    Page Ref: 143
    Skill: Conceptual
    Objective: 4.10

56) Current evidence on bonding shows that
    A) the human mother–infant relationship depends largely on what happens during a sensitive period immediately after birth.
    B) the human parent–infant relationship does not depend on a precise, early period of togetherness.
    C) skin-to-skin contact between parent and baby is vital for the parent to feel affection and concern for the infant.
    D) adoptive parents have difficulty developing warm, affective relationships when the infant enters the family months after birth.
    Answer: B
    Page Ref: 143
    Skill: Conceptual
    Objective: 4.10

57) Contact with the baby after birth
    A) guarantees immediate emotional closeness between the new mother and the newborn.
    B) is vital for fathers so they can bond with the baby.
    C) may be one of several factors that help build a good parent–infant relationship.
    D) is essential for maternal bonding because birth-related hormones facilitate responsiveness to the infant.
    Answer: C
    Page Ref: 143
    Skill: Conceptual
    Objective: 4.10

58) Research shows that mothers learn to discriminate their newborn baby from other infants on the basis of touch, smell, and sight after as little as _____ of contact.
   A) 15 minutes
   B) 30 minutes
   C) one hour
   D) two hours
Answer: C
Page Ref: 143
Skill: Factual
Objective: 4.10

59) Unlike her two sisters, when Teresa gives birth, she does not choose rooming in. Teresa should know that
   A) her ability to bond with the baby will be compromised as a result of this decision.
   B) her baby will suffer emotionally as a result of this decision.
   C) her competence as a caregiver will be compromised as a result of this decision.
   D) there is no evidence that her parenting ability or her baby's emotional well-being will be affected.
Answer: D
Page Ref: 143
Skill: Applied
Objective: 4.10

60) Baby Sunni quickly closes her eyelids when her father claps his hands near her head. The function of this reflex is to
   A) stimulate the eye muscle.
   B) protect the infant from a blow to the head.
   C) protect the infant from strong stimulation.
   D) communicate irritation toward a caregiver.
Answer: C
Page Ref: 144
Skill: Applied
Objective: 4.11

61) A baby will display the Moro reflex when his caregiver
   A) shines a bright light at his eyes.
   B) produces a sudden loud sound against the surface supporting him.
   C) places him face down in a pool of water.
   D) strokes his cheek near the corner of his mouth.
Answer: B
Page Ref: 144
Skill: Conceptual
Objective: 4.11

62) The stepping reflex
   A) is permanent.
   B) appears at around 3 months.
   C) reveals the health of the leg muscles.
   D) disappears at around 2 months.
Answer: D
Page Ref: 144
Skill: Factual
Objective: 4.11

63) The function of the Babinski reflex is
   A) unknown.
   B) to prepare the infant for voluntary walking.
   C) to prepare the infant for voluntary reaching.
   D) to help the infant cling to its mother.
   Answer: A
   Page Ref: 144
   Skill: Factual
   Objective: 4.11

64) Which of the following statements is true about reflexes and the development of motor skills?
   A) The stepping reflex appears only when the newborn's body is in upright position.
   B) Certain reflexes drop out early, but the motor functions involved are renewed later.
   C) Parents should deliberately exercise newborn stepping reflexes to encourage early walking.
   D) The tonic neck reflex may prepare the baby for voluntary walking.
   Answer: B
   Page Ref: 144
   Skill: Conceptual
   Objective: 4.11

65) Pediatricians usually test newborn reflexes carefully because reflexes can reveal
   A) ineffective parenting.
   B) the baby's temperament.
   C) a compromised circulatory system.
   D) the health of the baby's nervous system.
   Answer: D
   Page Ref: 145
   Skill: Conceptual
   Objective: 4.11

66) The most fleeting state of arousal is
   A) NREM sleep.
   B) REM sleep.
   C) drowsiness.
   D) quiet alertness.
   Answer: D
   Page Ref: 146
   Skill: Factual
   Objective: 4.12

67) Although Baby Irina's eyelids are closed, occasional rapid eye movements can been seen beneath them. Her breathing is irregular. She stirs occasionally and grimaces while she sleeps. Irina is MOST likely in which of the following states of arousal?
   A) regular sleep
   B) drowsiness
   C) quiet alertness
   D) REM sleep
   Answer: D
   Page Ref: 146
   Skill: Applied
   Objective: 4.12

68) REM sleep accounts for ____ percent of a newborn baby's sleep time.
   A) 20
   B) 30
   C) 50
   D) 70
Answer: C
Page Ref: 146
Skill: Factual
Objective: 4.12

69) Researchers believe that the stimulation of REM sleep is
   A) necessary to refine fine muscle development of the eye.
   B) more important in adolescence than in infancy.
   C) more important for adults than for babies.
   D) vital for growth of the central nervous system.
Answer: D
Page Ref: 146
Skill: Conceptual
Objective: 4.12

70) Which of the following individuals is the most likely to spend the greatest amount of time in REM sleep?
   A) Trevor, a preterm baby
   B) Alice, a five-year-old
   C) Henry, a full-term infant
   D) Erica, a 13-year-old
Answer: A
Page Ref: 146
Skill: Applied
Objective: 4.12

71) In infants who have experienced serious birth trauma,
   A) sleep behavior is organized and patterned.
   B) disturbed REM–NREM sleep cycles are often present.
   C) NREM sleep occurs, but REM sleep does not.
   D) sleep–wake cycles are affected more by darkness–light than by fullness–hunger.
Answer: B
Page Ref: 146
Skill: Conceptual
Objective: 4.12

72) The leading cause of infant mortality between 1 week and 12 months in industrialized nations is
   A) birth trauma.
   B) congenital defects.
   C) child abuse.
   D) sudden infant death syndrome.
Answer: D
Page Ref: 147 Box: SI: Health: The Mysterious Tragedy of Sudden Infant Death Syndrome
Skill: Factual
Objective: 4.12

73) SIDS victims usually
   A) have normal sleep–wake patterns.
   B) have normal Apgar scores.
   C) show physical problems from the beginning.
   D) were full-term, normal-weight newborns.
   Answer: C
   Page Ref: 147 Box: SI: Health: The Mysterious Tragedy of Sudden Infant Death Syndrome
   Skill: Conceptual
   Objective: 4.12

74) _____ doubles the risk of SIDS.
   A) Placing a sleeping baby on her back
   B) Prenatal abuse of drugs
   C) Placing a sleeping infant on his side
   D) Maternal cigarette smoking
   Answer: D
   Page Ref: 147 Box: SI: Health: The Mysterious Tragedy of Sudden Infant Death Syndrome
   Skill: Factual
   Objective: 4.12

75) Arthur wakes frequently to check to see if his sleeping infant, Sam, is breathing. Arthur can reduce the risk of SIDS by
   A) wrapping Sam in very warm clothing and blankets.
   B) placing Sam to sleep on his stomach.
   C) placing Sam to sleep on his back.
   D) providing Sam with soft bedding and taking away his pacifier.
   Answer: C
   Page Ref: 147 Box: SI Health: The Mysterious Tragedy of Sudden Infant Death Syndrome
   Skill: Applied
   Objective: 4.12

76) Young infants most often cry because they are
   A) cold.
   B) scared.
   C) in pain.
   D) hungry.
   Answer: D
   Page Ref: 148
   Skill: Factual
   Objective: 4.12

77) Crying usually peaks at about
   A) 6 weeks.
   B) 12 weeks.
   C) 6 months.
   D) 18 months.
   Answer: A
   Page Ref: 148
   Skill: Factual
   Objective: 4.12

78) Maddy is babysitting an infant for the first time. What can you tell her is the most effective way to soothe the baby if she cries?
   A) Sing to her softly.
   B) Lift her to the shoulder and rock or walk with her.
   C) Swaddle her.
   D) Take her for a ride in her stroller.
   Answer: B
   Page Ref: 148
   Skill: Applied
   Objective: 4.12

79) When parents hold their babies extensively, the amount of crying in the early months is reduced by about
   A) one-fourth.
   B) one-third.
   C) one-half.
   D) two-thirds.
   Answer: B
   Page Ref: 149
   Skill: Factual
   Objective: 4.12

80) The cause of colic is
   A) central nervous system damage.
   B) unknown.
   C) unpleasant stimuli.
   D) gas.
   Answer: B
   Page Ref: 149
   Skill: Conceptual
   Objective: 4.12

81) Newborn babies
   A) are not particularly sensitive to touch.
   B) are not particularly sensitive to pain.
   C) can distinguish the shapes and textures of small objects.
   D) are especially sensitive to touch around the torso.
   Answer: C
   Page Ref: 149
   Skill: Conceptual
   Objective: 4.13

82) Wanda is concerned that her son, Max, will be in pain during his circumcision. You can tell Wanda that
   A) newborn males do not experience much pain during circumcision.
   B) offering a nipple that delivers a sugar solution reduces discomfort during circumcision.
   C) local anesthetics cannot be used during newborn circumcisions because they elevate the heart rate.
   D) local anesthetics can actually cause increased pain during minor procedures like circumcision.
   Answer: B
   Page Ref: 150
   Skill: Applied
   Objective: 4.13

83) Newborns relax their facial muscles in response to a _____ taste.
A) salty
B) sour
C) bitter
D) sweet
Answer: D
Page Ref: 150
Skill: Factual
Objective: 4.13

84) Which of the following statements is true regarding taste in newborns?
A) Newborns can readily learn to like a taste that first evoked either a neutral or a negative response.
B) Newborns do not exhibit taste preferences until a few weeks after birth.
C) Not until 6 months do babies prefer a salty taste to plain water.
D) Newborns respond to sour tastes by showing a distinct archlike mouth opening.
Answer: A
Page Ref: 150
Skill: Conceptual
Objective: 4.13

85) Which of the following statements is supported by research on newborn odor preferences?
A) Most newborns cannot distinguish between the smell of their mother's breast and that of an unfamiliar lactating woman.
B) Bottle-fed newborns orient more to the smell of formula milk than to unfamiliar human milk.
C) Even without postnatal exposure, the odor of human milk is attractive to newborns.
D) Only breastfed babies prefer the smell of a lactating mother's breast to formula.
Answer: C
Page Ref: 151
Skill: Conceptual
Objective: 4.13

86) At birth, infants prefer
A) pure tones.
B) nonspeech sounds.
C) simple sounds.
D) voices.
Answer: D
Page Ref: 151
Skill: Factual
Objective: 4.13

87) Research on hearing shows that newborns
A) can perceive only those sounds that are found in their own native language.
B) prefer pure tones to complex sounds, such as human language.
C) can tell the difference between a series of tones arranged in ascending versus descending order.
D) cannot distinguish happy-sounding speech from speech with negative emotional qualities.
Answer: C
Page Ref: 151
Skill: Conceptual
Objective: 4.13

88) _____ is the least developed of the newborn baby's senses.
   A) Hearing
   B) Taste
   C) Vision
   D) Touch
   Answer: C
   Page Ref: 151
   Skill: Factual
   Objective: 4.13

89) At birth, visual structures in
   A) the eyes are fully formed, but those in the brain are not yet fully formed.
   B) both the eyes and the brain are fully formed.
   C) the brain are fully formed, but those in the eyes are not yet fully formed.
   D) both the eyes and the brain are not yet fully formed.
   Answer: D
   Page Ref: 151
   Skill: Conceptual
   Objective: 4.13

90) Newborn babies
   A) see nearby objects most clearly.
   B) see unclearly across a wide range of distances.
   C) cannot detect human faces.
   D) have finely attuned visual acuity.
   Answer: B
   Page Ref: 152
   Skill: Conceptual
   Objective: 4.13

91) Which of the following statements is true about vision in newborn babies?
   A) Newborns are attracted to muted colors, such as gray, rather than colored stimuli.
   B) Newborns' eye movements are slow and inaccurate.
   C) Newborns tend to look at entire shapes rather than a single feature of an object.
   D) Newborns see more clearly at far distances than up close.
   Answer: B
   Page Ref: 152
   Skill: Conceptual
   Objective: 4.13

92) The Neonatal Behavioral Assessment Scale (NBAS)
   A) evaluates reflexes, muscle tone, state changes, and responsiveness to stimuli.
   B) is specially designed for use with newborns at risk for developmental problems.
   C) evaluates appearance, pulse, grimace, activity, and respiration.
   D) evaluates vision, touch sensitivity, hearing, and odor sensitivity.
   Answer: A
   Page Ref: 152
   Skill: Factual
   Objective: 4.14

93) In some hospitals, health professionals use the NBAS to
    A) offer parents an early intelligence test score for their newborn.
    B) measure the newborn's physical condition at 1 and 5 minutes after birth.
    C) demonstrate to parents the capacities of their newborn infant.
    D) teach new mothers how to bond with their babies.
    Answer: C
    Page Ref: 153
    Skill: Conceptual
    Objective: 4.14

94) Dagwood and Marcia postponed parenthood until Dagwood was 32 and Marcia was 31. They have a happy marriage and both have fulfilling careers. Compared to younger parents, which of the following statements is most likely to be true?
    A) Dagwood will be less enthusiastic about being a father.
    B) Marcia is less likely to encourage Dagwood to share in child care.
    C) Dagwood will be more willing to participate in parenting.
    D) Marcia will be less likely to encourage Dagwood to share housework.
    Answer: C
    Page Ref: 154
    Skill: Applied
    Objective: 4.15

95) Couples can ease the transition to parenthood by
    A) being more willing to take on traditional gender roles.
    B) sharing child care right after the baby arrives.
    C) returning to work shortly after the baby is born.
    D) imposing their parenting standards on each other.
    Answer: B
    Page Ref: 154
    Skill: Conceptual
    Objective: 4.15

96) Postpartum depression
    A) occurs only in first-time mothers.
    B) fails to subside as a new mother adjusts to hormonal changes in her body.
    C) affects 15 to 20 percent of women.
    D) usually subsides after a week or two.
    Answer: B
    Page Ref: 155 Box: Biology and Environment: Parental Depression and Child Development
    Skill: Conceptual
    Objective: 4.15

97) Compared to infants of mothers who are not depressed, infants of depressed mothers
    A) have patterned sleep–wake cycles.
    B) are less attentive to their surroundings.
    C) have depleted cortisol levels.
    D) cry less often.
    Answer: B
    Page Ref: 155 Box: Biology and Environment: Parental Depression and Child Development
    Skill: Conceptual
    Objective: 4.15

98) Persistent paternal depression is linked to
    A) aggression in boys.
    B) colic in infants.
    C) anorexia in girls.
    D) childhood autism.
    Answer: A
    Page Ref: 155 Box: Biology and Environment: Parental Depression and Child Development
    Skill: Conceptual
    Objective: 4.15

99) Laura is the nanny of Jackson, a six-month-old infant, whose single mother is depressed. You can tell Laura that
    A) therapy is unlikely to alleviate parental depression.
    B) antidepressant medication is unlikely to help Jackson's mother.
    C) Jackson's mother will probably need long-term treatment.
    D) a warm relationship with her can safeguard Jackson's development.
    Answer: D
    Page Ref: 155 Box: Biology and Environment: Parental Depression and Child Development
    Skill: Applied
    Objective: 4.15

100) Which of the following statements is supported by research on new parenthood?
    A) After the birth of a baby, the gender roles of husband and wife generally become less traditional.
    B) For most new parents, the arrival of a baby causes significant marital strain.
    C) Sharing caregiving predicts greater parental happiness and sensitivity to the baby.
    D) New parents in troubled marriages usually show an increase in marital satisfaction after a baby is born.
    Answer: C
    Page Ref: 156
    Skill: Conceptual
    Objective: 4.15

101) Nearly 39 percent of babies in the United States are born to single mothers, one-third of whom are
    A) teenagers.
    B) ethnic minorities.
    C) low-income Caucasians.
    D) 30- to 45-year-olds.
    Answer: A
    Page Ref: 156
    Skill: Factual
    Objective: 4.15

102) Older single women in well-paid occupations who choose parenthood
    A) often lack emotional and parenting support.
    B) experience a stressful transition to parenthood.
    C) have a hard time coping effectively with parenting challenges.
    D) may encounter fewer parenting difficulties than married couples.
    Answer: D
    Page Ref: 156
    Skill: Conceptual
    Objective: 4.15

103) Studies on new parent intervention programs demonstrate that
    A) many low-income parents require tangible support to ease stress and allow them to engage in effective caregiving.
    B) counselor-led parent groups are not effective for parents who are at low risk for problems.
    C) home visits do little to boost the effectiveness of programs for high-risk parents struggling with a child with disabilities.
    D) counselor-led parent groups can ease the stress of parenting among fathers but usually not among mothers.
    Answer: A
    Page Ref: 157
    Skill: Conceptual
    Objective: 4.15

ESSAY

104) What is CRH? Describe its role in initiating labor.
    Answer: CRH, corticotrophin-releasing hormone, is a hormone involved in the stress response. As pregnancy advances, the placenta releases increasing amounts of CRH. High levels of CRH trigger additional placental hormone adjustments that induce uterine contractions. As CRH rises in the fetal bloodstream in the final prenatal weeks, it stimulates fetal production of the stress hormone cortisol, which promotes development of the lungs in preparation for breathing. An abnormal increase in maternal CRH in the third trimester is currently being evaluated as an early predictor of premature birth.
    Page Ref: 126

105) Describe the signs that indicate that labor is near.
    Answer:
    - *Prelabor contractions.* These are felt in the upper part of the uterus and are often called false labor because they remain brief and unpredictable for several weeks.
    - *Lightening.* About two weeks before birth, lightening occurs—the baby's head drops low into the uterus. Placental hormone changes cause the cervix to soften, and it no longer supports the baby's weight so easily.
    - *Bloody show.* A sure sign that labor is only hours or days away is the bloody show. As the cervix begins to open, the plug of mucus that sealed it during pregnancy is released, producing a reddish discharge. Soon after, uterine contractions become more frequent, and mother and baby enter the first stage of labor—dilation and effacement of the cervix.
    Page Ref: 126

106) Discuss the use of epidural analgesia to control pain during labor, noting the pros and cons of its use.
    Answer: The most common approach to controlling pain during labor is epidural analgesia, a pain-relieving drug that may be given in mild doses during labor to help a mother relax. The regional pain-relieving drug is delivered continuously through a catheter into a small space in the lower spine. Unlike older spinal block procedures, which numb the entire lower half of the body, epidural analgesia limits pain reduction to the pelvic region. Because the mother retains the capacity to feel the pressure of the contractions and to move her trunk and legs, she is able to push during the second stage of labor.
    Epidural analgesia helps women cope with childbirth and enables doctors to perform essential medical interventions. However, it also can cause problems. It weakens uterine contractions and, as a result, labor is prolonged, and the chances of cesarean delivery increase. Also, because the drug crosses the placenta, exposed newborns tend to have lower Apgar scores, to be sleepy and withdrawn, to suck poorly during feedings, and to be irritable when awake. Some researchers have claimed that heavy doses have a lasting impact on physical and mental development, but their findings have been challenged.
    Page Ref: 133

107) What is "kangaroo care"? When and how is it used? What are its benefits?

Answer: Skin-to-skin "kangaroo care" is the most readily available intervention for promoting the survival and recovery of preterm babies. It involves placing the infant in a vertical position between the mother's breasts or next to the father's chest (under the parent's clothing) so the parent's body functions as a human incubator. Kangaroo care offers fathers a unique opportunity to increase their involvement in caring for preterm infants. Because of its diverse benefits, more than 80 percent of U.S. hospitals offer it to preterm infants. It is also used often in developing countries where hospital intensive care is not readily available.

Kangaroo contact fosters improved oxygenation of the baby's body, temperature regulation, sleep, breastfeeding, alertness, and infant survival. It also provides babies with gentle stimulation of all sensory modalities. Studies show that parents practicing kangaroo care feel more confident about caring for their fragile babies, interact more sensitively and affectionately, and feel more attached to them.

Page Ref: 138–139

108) Explain the concepts of bonding and rooming in. Is immediate physical contact necessary for bonding to occur? Is there a sensitive period for bonding?

Answer: Bonding is a feeling of affection and concern for the infant. Current evidence shows that the human parent–infant relationship does not depend on a precise, early period of togetherness. Some parents report sudden, deep feelings of affection on first holding their babies. For others, these emotions emerge gradually. As successful adoption reveals, humans can parent effectively without experiencing birth-related hormonal changes. Human bonding is a complex process that depends on many factors, not just on what happens during a short sensitive period. Still, contact with the baby after birth may be one of several factors that help build a good parent–infant relationship. Early parental recognition probably facilitates responsiveness to the infant.

Early contact supports parental engagement with the newborn, although it is neither necessary nor a guarantee of it. Hospitals today offer rooming in, in which the infant stays in the mother's hospital room all or most of the time. If parents do not choose this option or cannot do so for medical reasons, there is no evidence that their competence as caregivers will be compromised or that the baby will suffer emotionally.

Page Ref: 143

109) Describe ways parents and caregivers can soothe a crying baby, and explain how or why each technique works.

Answer:

- *Lift the baby to the shoulder and rock or walk.* This is the most effective technique and the one that Western parents usually try first. The combination of physical contact, upright position, and motion causes the baby to become quietly alert.
- *Swaddle the baby.* Restricting movement and increasing warmth often soothes a young infant.
- *Offer a pacifier.* Sucking helps babies control their own level of arousal.
- *Talk softly or play rhythmic sounds.* Continuous, monotonous, rhythmic sounds are more effective than intermittent sounds.
- *Take the baby for a short car ride or a walk in a baby carriage; swing the baby in a cradle.* Gentle, rhythmic motion of any kind helps lull the baby to sleep.
- *Massage the baby's body.* Stroking the baby's torso and limbs with continuous, gentle motions relaxes the baby's muscles.
- *Combine several methods.* Stimulating several of the baby's senses at once is often more effective than stimulating only one.
- *If nothing works, let the baby cry for a short period.* Occasionally, a baby responds well to just being put down and will, after a few minutes, fall asleep.

Page Ref: 148–149

110) Describe several strategies that couples can use to ease the transition to parenthood.

Answer:

- *Devise a plan for sharing household tasks.* As soon as possible, discuss division of household responsibilities. Decide who does a particular chore based on who has the needed skill and time, not gender. Schedule regular times to reevaluate your plan to fit changing family circumstances.
- *Begin sharing child care right after the baby's arrival.* For fathers, strive to spend equal time with the baby early. For mothers, refrain from imposing your standards on your partner. Instead, share the role of "child-rearing expert" by discussing parenting values and concerns often. Attend a new-parenthood course together.
- *Talk over conflicts about decision making and responsibilities.* Face conflict through communication. Clarify your feelings and needs, and express them to your partner. Listen and try to understand your partner's point of view. Then be willing to negotiate and compromise.
- *Establish a balance between work and parenting.* Critically evaluate the time you devote to work in view of new parenthood. If it is too much, try to cut back.
- *Press for workplace and public policies that assist parents in rearing children.* Difficulties faced by new parents may be partly due to lack of workplace and societal supports. Encourage your employer to provide benefits that help combine work and family roles, such as paid employment leave, flexible work hours, and on-site high-quality, affordable child care. Communicate with lawmakers and other citizens about improving policies for children and families, including paid, job-protected leave to support the transition to parenthood.

Page Ref: 156

CHAPTER 5
PHYSICAL DEVELOPMENT
IN INFANCY AND TODDLERHOOD

MULTIPLE CHOICE

1) Which of the following statements is true about changes in body size during the first two years of life?
   A) Infants and toddlers make steady gains in growth.
   B) By the end of the second year, a typical toddler is 36 inches tall.
   C) By five months of age, birth weight typically has tripled.
   D) An average 1-year-old's height is 75 percent greater than at birth.
   Answer: B
   Page Ref: 162
   Skill: Conceptual
   Objective: 5.1

2) By the end of the first year, a typical child's weight has _____ since birth.
   A) doubled
   B) tripled
   C) quadrupled
   D) quintupled
   Answer: B
   Page Ref: 162
   Skill: Factual
   Objective: 5.1

3) "Baby fat"
   A) helps the infant maintain a constant body temperature.
   B) peaks at about 6 months.
   C) increases very slowly during infancy.
   D) helps the infant gain strength and physical coordination.
   Answer: A
   Page Ref: 162
   Skill: Conceptual
   Objective: 5.1

4) Throughout childhood, girls
   A) are slightly taller than boys.
   B) are slightly heavier than boys.
   C) have a higher ratio of fat to muscle than boys.
   D) have more "baby fat" than boys.
   Answer: C
   Page Ref: 162
   Skill: Conceptual
   Objective: 5.1

5) Considering the average growth norms, which child will probably be the smallest?
    A) Timmy, a Caucasian-American boy
    B) June, an African-American girl
    C) Freddy, an African-American boy
    D) Kim, an Asian boy
Answer: D
Page Ref: 162
Skill: Applied
Objective: 5.1

6) Which of the following statements demonstrates the cephalocaudal trend?
    A) During infancy and childhood, the legs and arms grow faster than the trunk.
    B) At birth, the head takes up one-fourth of total body length, the legs only one-third.
    C) In the prenatal period, the head, chest, and trunk grow first, then the arms and legs.
    D) During infancy and childhood, the hands and feet grow ahead of the fingers and toes.
Answer: B
Page Ref: 162
Skill: Conceptual
Objective: 5.1

7) Which of the following statements is consistent with the proximodistal trend of body growth?
    A) In the prenatal period, the head, chest, and trunk grow first, then the arms and legs.
    B) At birth, the head takes up one-fourth of total body length, the legs only one-third.
    C) In the prenatal period, the trunk grows first, followed by the chest and the head.
    D) During infancy and childhood, the hands and feet develop more rapidly than the trunk.
Answer: A
Page Ref: 162
Skill: Conceptual
Objective: 5.1

8) The best estimate of a child's physical maturity is
    A) height.
    B) weight.
    C) skeletal age.
    D) chronological age.
Answer: C
Page Ref: 163
Skill: Factual
Objective: 5.1

9) _____ can be estimated by X-raying the bones and seeing the number of epiphyses and the extent to which they are fused.
    A) Chronological age
    B) Skeletal age
    C) Adult height
    D) Bone pliability
Answer: B
Page Ref: 164
Skill: Factual
Objective: 5.1

10) Which of the following statements is true about skeletal age?
    A) Caucasian-American children tend to be slightly ahead of African-American children in skeletal age.
    B) At birth, the sexes differ by about 2 to 3 weeks in skeletal age.
    C) Girls are considerably ahead of boys in skeletal age.
    D) The gap between the sexes in skeletal age closes during toddlerhood.
Answer: C
Page Ref: 164
Skill: Conceptual
Objective: 5.1

11) Skull growth is especially rapid
    A) between birth and age 2 years.
    B) during the preschool years.
    C) between age 3 and 5 years.
    D) during adolescence.
Answer: A
Page Ref: 164
Skill: Factual
Objective: 5.1

12) The bones of the skull
    A) begin to grow around age 2.
    B) never completely grow together.
    C) are fused at birth.
    D) are separated by six fontanels at birth.
Answer: D
Page Ref: 164
Skill: Factual
Objective: 5.1

13) Fontanels
    A) cannot be felt after four or five months.
    B) prevent the brain from growing too large.
    C) permit the bones to overlap during childbirth.
    D) gradually close by adolescence.
Answer: C
Page Ref: 164
Skill: Conceptual
Objective: 5.1

14) At birth, the _____ is nearer to its adult size than any other physical structure.
    A) heart
    B) liver
    C) brain
    D) skull
Answer: C
Page Ref: 164
Skill: Factual
Objective: 5.2

15) Neurons
    A) store and transmit information.
    B) are tightly packed together.
    C) do not directly connect with each other.
    D) that are stimulated too soon lose their synapses.
Answer: A
Page Ref: 164
Skill: Factual
Objective: 5.2

16) A surprising aspect of brain growth is that
    A) the neural tube produces far less neurons than the brain will need.
    B) as synapses form, 20 to 80 percent of the surrounding neurons die.
    C) during infancy and toddlerhood, neural fibers stagnate.
    D) neurons send messages to one another through neuroimaging.
Answer: B
Page Ref: 165
Skill: Conceptual
Objective: 5.2

17) Which of the following statements is true about stimulation of neurons?
    A) Neurons that are stimulated return to an uncommitted state so they can support future development.
    B) Appropriate stimulation of the brain is vital during periods in which synaptic pruning is at its peak.
    C) An early overabundance of synapses ensures that infants will acquire motor, cognitive, and social skills.
    D) Overstimulation of synapses leads to synaptic pruning during childhood and adolescence.
Answer: C
Page Ref: 164
Skill: Conceptual
Objective: 5.2

18) In all, about _____ percent of synapses are pruned during childhood and adolescence.
    A) 20
    B) 40
    C) 60
    D) 80
Answer: B
Page Ref: 165
Skill: Factual
Objective: 5.2

19) _____ improves the efficiency of message transfer.
    A) Stimulation
    B) Synaptic pruning
    C) Tomography
    D) Myelination
Answer: D
Page Ref: 165
Skill: Factual
Objective: 5.2

20) _____ are responsible for coating neural fibers with an insulating fatty sheath.
    A) Glial cells
    B) Neurotransmitters
    C) Brain waves
    D) Synapses
Answer: A
Page Ref: 165
Skill: Factual
Objective: 5.2

21) Gains in _____ and _____ are responsible for the extraordinary gain in overall size of the brain during the first 2 years.
    A) neurons; synapses
    B) neural fibers; myelination
    C) glial cells; synapses
    D) muscle; fat
Answer: B
Page Ref: 165
Skill: Factual
Objective: 5.2

22) When measuring brain functioning with _____, researchers use a geodesic sensor net to hold interconnected electrodes in place.
    A) the EEG
    B) fMRI
    C) PET
    D) NIRS
Answer: A
Page Ref: 166
Skill: Factual
Objective: 5.3

23) Damon is injected with a radioactive substance and then lies on an apparatus with a scanner that emits fine streams of X-rays, which detect increased blood flow and oxygen metabolism in areas of the brain as Damon processes particular stimuli. Damon's brain functioning is being measured using
    A) an electroencephalogram.
    B) event-related potentials.
    C) functional magnetic resonance imaging.
    D) position emission tomography.
Answer: D
Page Ref: 166
Skill: Applied
Objective: 5.3

24) Near-infrared spectroscopy
    A) enables identification of general regions of stimulus-induced activity.
    B) detects changes in electrical brain-wave activity in the cerebral cortex.
    C) is appropriate for infants and young children, who can move within a limited range during testing.
    D) records the frequency and amplitude of brain waves in response to particular stimuli using the EEG.
Answer: C
Page Ref: 166
Skill: Factual
Objective: 5.3

25) Which of the following is a limitation of neurophysiological methods?
   A) They cannot uncover relationships between the brain and psychological development and, therefore, have limited practical value.
   B) Researchers have yet to devise a method for detecting changes in electrical brain-wave activity in the cerebral cortex.
   C) Even though a stimulus produces a consistent pattern of brain activity, investigators cannot be certain that an individual has processed it in a certain way.
   D) They are largely ineffective for studying preverbal infants' responsiveness to various stimuli.
   Answer: C
   Page Ref: 167
   Skill: Conceptual
   Objective: 5.3

26) The cerebral cortex
   A) contains the greatest number of neurons and synapses in the brain.
   B) is the first part of the brain to stop growing.
   C) is less sensitive to environmental influences than other parts of the brain.
   D) fully develops during the third trimester of pregnancy.
   Answer: A
   Page Ref: 167
   Skill: Conceptual
   Objective: 5.4

27) The cortical regions with the most extended period of development are the _____ lobes.
   A) occipital
   B) frontal
   C) temporal
   D) parietal
   Answer: B
   Page Ref: 168
   Skill: Factual
   Objective: 5.4

28) The _____ cortex is responsible for consciousness, inhibition of impulses, and use of memory.
   A) occipital
   B) temporal
   C) parietal
   D) prefrontal
   Answer: D
   Page Ref: 168
   Skill: Factual
   Objective: 5.4

29) For most people, the left hemisphere of the cerebral cortex is responsible for
   A) judging distances.
   B) negative emotion.
   C) verbal abilities.
   D) recognizing geometric shapes.
   Answer: C
   Page Ref: 168
   Skill: Conceptual
   Objective: 5.4

30) Studies using fMRI reveal that the right hemisphere is specialized for processing information in a(n) _____ manner.
   A) sequential
   B) analytical
   C) piece-by-piece
   D) integrative
   Answer: D
   Page Ref: 168
   Skill: Factual
   Objective: 5.4

31) In a highly plastic cerebral cortex,
   A) the areas of the brain are strongly committed to specific functions, and there is a high capacity for learning.
   B) if a part of the cortex is damaged, other parts can take over the tasks it would have handled.
   C) spatial skills develop more rapidly than language skills and are easier to recover after injury.
   D) the right and left hemispheres of the brain have become strongly lateralized.
   Answer: B
   Page Ref: 168
   Skill: Conceptual
   Objective: 5.4

32) Most newborns show greater activation in the left hemisphere while
   A) displaying a positive state of arousal.
   B) listening to nonspeech sounds.
   C) drinking a sour-tasting fluid.
   D) feeling distress.
   Answer: A
   Page Ref: 168
   Skill: Conceptual
   Objective: 5.4

33) When a 1-month-old kitten is put in the dark and kept there during the fourth week of life and beyond, damage to visual centers of the brain is permanent. This example provides evidence of
   A) brain plasticity.
   B) synaptic pruning.
   C) lateralization of the cerebral cortex.
   D) sensitive periods in brain development.
   Answer: D
   Page Ref: 169
   Skill: Applied
   Objective: 5.5

34) Alexia was born with cataracts in both eyes. What can you tell her parents about when she should have corrective surgery?
   A) Alexia should wait to have corrective surgery until adulthood when her eyes are fully mature.
   B) Alexia should not have corrective surgery during the first six months of life because her vision would be severely and permanently impaired.
   C) The longer cataract surgery is postponed beyond infancy, the less complete Alexia's recovery in visual skills.
   D) Alexia should wait until later in childhood to have corrective surgery because there are no sensitive periods in visual development.
   Answer: C
   Page Ref: 169
   Skill: Applied
   Objective: 5.5

35) In a large study of children with injuries to the cerebral cortex that occurred before birth or in the first six months of life,
    A) delays in language development persisted into adolescence if injury occurred in the left hemisphere.
    B) delays in language development persisted into adolescence if injury occurred in the right hemisphere.
    C) undamaged areas in either the left or the right hemisphere took over vocabulary and grammatical skills by age 5.
    D) language skills were more likely to be permanently damaged than spatial skills.
Answer: C
Page Ref: 170 Box: B&E: Brain Plasticity: Insights from Research on Brain-Damaged Children and Adults
Skill: Conceptual
Objective: 5.4

36) Research reveals that
    A) plasticity declines during synaptic pruning.
    B) plasticity is greatest while the brain is forming new neurons.
    C) brain plasticity is restricted to early childhood.
    D) the adult brain cannot produce new neurons.
Answer: A
Page Ref: 170 Box: B&E: Brain Plasticity: Insights from Research on Brain-Damaged Children and Adults
Skill: Conceptual
Objective: 5.4

37) A study of children who had spent their first eight months or more in Romanian institutions before being adopted into Canadian homes found that
    A) the longer the children spent in orphanage care, the higher their cortisol levels—even 6½ years after adoption.
    B) the children had abnormally high levels of oxytocin in their blood, regardless of when they were adopted.
    C) children who experienced adequate early nutrition were not negatively affected by early orphanage rearing.
    D) depression only appeared in those children who spent more than 2 years in an orphanage.
Answer: A
Page Ref: 171
Skill: Conceptual
Objective: 5.5

38) Sensitive adult care
    A) may overwhelm institutionalized infants beyond their capacities and interfere with the brain's potential.
    B) seems to protect the young brain from the potentially damaging effects of inadequate stress-hormone exposure.
    C) has little impact on brain development in traumatized infants and young children.
    D) may help institutionalized infants grow physically, but will not aid in cognitive development.
Answer: B
Page Ref: 171
Skill: Conceptual
Objective: 5.5

39) Nicole is considering sending her 8-month-old son Austin to a new academic learning center where infants are trained with letter and number flash cards. You can advise Nicole that
    A) Austin will likely score 10 to 15 points higher in IQ than agemates who attend traditional early child-care programs.
    B) although this program will not likely raise Austin's IQ, it will probably help him learn to read more quickly.
    C) this program is probably as effective as a traditional early childhood development program in promoting cognitive development.
    D) this program could overwhelm Austin and cause him to withdraw, thereby threatening his interest in learning.
Answer: D
Page Ref: 172
Skill: Applied
Objective: 5.5

40) Experience-expectant brain growth
    A) is a result of specific learning experiences that vary widely across cultures.
    B) usually occurs later than experience-dependent brain growth.
    C) occurs naturally as caregivers engage babies in enjoyable daily routines.
    D) provides mastery of skills that depend on extensive training.
Answer: C
Page Ref: 172
Skill: Conceptual
Objective: 5.5

41) Which of the following is an activity associated with experience-expectant brain growth?
    A) coloring a picture
    B) playing peekaboo
    C) learning to ride a bike
    D) playing the piano
Answer: B
Page Ref: 172
Skill: Applied
Objective: 5.5

42) Experience-dependent brain growth
    A) takes place through naturally occurring interactions with caregivers.
    B) provides a foundation for later-occurring, experience-expectant development.
    C) depends on ordinary experiences, such as moving about and exploring the environment.
    D) relies on specific learning experiences that differ widely across individuals.
Answer: D
Page Ref: 172
Skill: Conceptual
Objective: 5.5

43) Which of the following is an activity associated with experience-dependent brain growth?
    A) writing a poem
    B) singing a song
    C) imitating facial expressions
    D) playing peekaboo
Answer: A
Page Ref: 172
Skill: Applied
Objective: 5.5

44) The average 2-year-old needs _____ to _____ hours of sleep.
    A) 16; 18
    B) 14; 15
    C) 12; 13
    D) 10; 11
Answer: B
Page Ref: 172
Skill: Factual
Objective: 5.6

45) Between ages _____ and _____, napping subsides.
   A) 1; 3
   B) 2; 4
   C) 3; 5
   D) 4; 6
   Answer: C
   Page Ref: 172
   Skill: Factual
   Objective: 5.6

46) The American Academy of Pediatrics issued a controversial warning that parent–infant bedsharing may increase the risk of
   A) excessive dependency.
   B) SIDS.
   C) suffocation.
   D) adjustment problems.
   Answer: B
   Page Ref: 173 Box: CI: Cultural Variation in Infant Sleep Arrangements
   Skill: Factual
   Objective: 5.6

47) Cross-cultural research shows that cosleeping
   A) is the norm for approximately 90 percent of the world's population.
   B) is uncommon in U.S. ethnic minority families.
   C) babies breastfeed for shorter time periods than independent sleepers.
   D) children are at risk for later social problems, especially dependency.
   Answer: A
   Page Ref: 173 Box: CI: Cultural Variation in Infant Sleep Arrangements
   Skill: Conceptual
   Objective: 5.6

48) One possible explanation for the high frequency of bedtime struggles in American homes is that American children
   A) are much more dependent than children from other cultures.
   B) are expected to sleep for more hours than children from other cultures .
   C) often eat late in the evening, which interferes with sleep.
   D) may feel stressed when they must fall asleep without assistance.
   Answer: D
   Page Ref: 173 Box: CI: Cultural Variation in Infant Sleep Arrangements
   Skill: Conceptual
   Objective: 5.6

49) In cultures where parent–child cosleeping is widespread,
   A) the rate infant mortality from SIDS is high.
   B) parents and infants usually sleep on soft mattresses.
   C) infants often sleep in a cradle or hammock next to the parents' bed.
   D) infants tend to lie on their stomach or side facing the mother.
   Answer: C
   Page Ref: 173 Box: CI: Cultural Variation in Infant Sleep Arrangements
   Skill: Conceptual
   Objective: 5.6

50) As long as negative environmental influences such as poor nutrition or illness are not severe,
    A) children and adolescents typically show catch-up growth once conditions improve.
    B) adopted children typically reach a height closer to their adoptive than biological parents' heights.
    C) body weight is influenced by eating habits rather than heredity.
    D) height and rate of physical growth are largely determined by the environment.
Answer: A
Page Ref: 174
Skill: Conceptual
Objective: 5.7

51) Pound for pound, a young infant's energy needs are at least __ times those of an adult.
    A) 2
    B) 3
    C) 4
    D) 5
Answer: A
Page Ref: 174
Skill: Factual
Objective: 5.8

52) Which of the following statements is true about breastfeeding?
    A) Human milk is lower in fat and higher in protein than the milk of other mammals.
    B) A mother who breastfeeds needs to add solid foods to her infant's diet around 4 months.
    C) Breastfed babies suffer from more gastrointestinal problems than bottle-fed infants.
    D) Breastfed infants generally accept new solid foods more easily than bottle-fed infants.
Answer: D
Page Ref: 175
Skill: Conceptual
Objective: 5.8

53) Breastfed babies in poverty-stricken regions of the world
    A) are more likely than bottle-fed babies to be malnourished.
    B) should be given a vitamin-enriched supplement of commercial formula at least weekly.
    C) are far more likely than bottle-fed babies to survive the first year of life.
    D) should be breastfed until age 2 years, with solid food added at 3 months of age.
Answer: C
Page Ref: 175
Skill: Conceptual
Objective: 5.8

54) The World Health Organization recommends breastfeeding until age ___, with solid foods added at ____.
    A) 3 months; 4 months
    B) 6 months; 6 months
    C) 1 year; 4 months
    D) 2 years; 6 months
Answer: D
Page Ref: 175
Skill: Factual
Objective: 5.8

55) Which of the following statements is true regarding breastfeeding?
    A) Breastfeeding should be combined with formula for a balanced diet.
    B) Breastfeeding helps increase spacing among siblings.
    C) Breastfeeding has become less common in industrialized nations.
    D) Breastfeeding is a reliable method of birth control.
    Answer: B
    Page Ref: 175
    Skill: Conceptual
    Objective: 5.8

56) In the United States,
    A) nearly 75 percent of mothers breastfeed, but half of them stop after a few months.
    B) most mothers follow the advice of the World Health Organization regarding when to stop breastfeeding.
    C) breastfeeding has become more common, especially among low-income minority women.
    D) only 25 percent of preterm babies are breastfed at hospital discharge.
    Answer: A
    Page Ref: 175
    Skill: Conceptual
    Objective: 5.8

57) The U.S. Department of Health and Human Services advises
    A) exclusive breastfeeding for the first 2 years.
    B) exclusive breastfeeding for the first 12 months.
    C) inclusion of breast milk in the baby's diet until at least 1 year.
    D) weaning from breast milk by age 6 months.
    Answer: C
    Page Ref: 176
    Skill: Conceptual
    Objective: 5.8

58) Garrett, 2 months, is an enthusiastic eater who nurses vigorously and gains weight quickly. Garrett's mom, Christine, is concerned that Garrett might be at risk of being permanently overweight. You can advise Christine that
    A) most chubby babies will continue to gain weight during toddlerhood and the preschool years.
    B) there is no evidence that rapid weight gain in infancy is related to later obesity.
    C) she should start supplementing Garrett's diet with cereal.
    D) breastfeeding for the first six months is associated with a leaner body build through early childhood.
    Answer: D
    Page Ref: 176
    Skill: Applied
    Objective: 5.8

59) Zahara, age 3 months, is painfully thin. Her mother is too malnourished to produce enough breast milk and the supply of formula is inadequate for bottle-feeding. Zahara is probably in danger of dying from
    A) marasmus.
    B) growth faltering.
    C) kwashiorkor.
    D) nonorganic failure to thrive.
    Answer: A
    Page Ref: 177
    Skill: Applied
    Objective: 5.9

60) Bulous is 20 months old and was recently weaned. He has an unbalanced diet very low in protein. Bulous has an enlarged belly, swollen feet, a skin rash, and thinning hair. Bulous most likely has
    A) iron-deficiency anemia.
    B) kwashiorkor.
    C) nonorganic failure to thrive.
    D) marasmus.
Answer: B
Page Ref: 177
Skill: Applied
Objective: 5.9

61) Osita is a 4-year-old Ethiopian boy. He survived kwashiorkor and was recently adopted by a Canadian couple. Osita will probably
    A) continue to undereat even when food is plentiful.
    B) gain very little weight as his diet improves.
    C) have an average to high basal metabolism rate.
    D) suffer from lasting damage to the brain, heart, or other organs.
Answer: D
Page Ref: 177
Skill: Applied
Objective: 5.9

62) An estimated 22 percent of U.S. children suffer from
    A) marasmus.
    B) food insecurity.
    C) kwashiorkor.
    D) iron deficiency anemia.
Answer: B
Page Ref: 178
Skill: Factual
Objective: 5.9

63) Six-month-old Luka's weight, height, and head circumference are substantially below age-related growth norms. Luka is withdrawn and apathetic. A disturbed parent–infant relationship contributed to Luka's failure to grow normally. Luka most likely suffers from
    A) growth faltering.
    B) malnutrition.
    C) marasmus.
    D) food insecurity.
Answer: A
Page Ref: 178
Skill: Applied
Objective: 5.10

64) If growth faltering is corrected in infancy, most babies
    A) remain small.
    B) show lasting cognitive difficulties.
    C) show quick catch-up growth.
    D) show lasting emotional difficulties.
Answer: C
Page Ref: 178
Skill: Conceptual
Objective: 5.10

65) Classical conditioning
   A) helps infants anticipate what is about to happen next.
   B) disappears once reflexive behaviors become voluntary.
   C) plays a vital role in the formation of social relationships.
   D) emerges only after newborn reflexes have begun to wane.
   Answer: A
   Page Ref: 179
   Skill: Conceptual
   Objective: 5.11

66) Baby Paul's mother strokes his hair just before he eats. Now when Paul's mother strokes his hair, Paul begins to suck. Paul's response to the stroking illustrates
   A) habituation.
   B) recovery.
   C) operant conditioning.
   D) classical conditioning.
   Answer: D
   Page Ref: 179
   Skill: Applied
   Objective: 5.11

67) Baby Paul's mother strokes his hair just before he eats. Now when Paul's mother strokes his hair, Paul begins to suck. The stroking is the _____, and the taste of milk is the _____.
   A) conditioned stimulus; neutral stimulus
   B) unconditioned stimulus; conditioned stimulus
   C) neutral stimulus; unconditioned stimulus
   D) neutral stimulus; conditioned response
   Answer: C
   Page Ref: 179
   Skill: Applied
   Objective: 5.11

68) In classical conditioning, if learning occurs, the neutral stimulus alone produces a(n)
   A) unconditioned response.
   B) neutral response.
   C) unconditioned stimulus.
   D) conditioned response.
   Answer: D
   Page Ref: 179
   Skill: Conceptual
   Objective: 5.11

69) In classical conditioning, if a conditioned stimulus is presented alone enough times, without being paired with the unconditioned stimulus, _____ occurs.
   A) habituation
   B) extinction
   C) imitation
   D) recovery
   Answer: B
   Page Ref: 180
   Skill: Conceptual
   Objective: 5.11

70) Prim has classically conditioned young Rue to suck when Prim touches Rue's stomach during feeding. If Prim repeatedly touches Rue's stomach without feeding her, Rue will
    A) gradually stop sucking in response to having her stomach touched.
    B) learn to suck without having her stomach touched.
    C) stop eating until Prim touches her stomach and feeds her again.
    D) increase her level of sucking in response to having her stomach touched.
Answer: A
Page Ref: 180
Skill: Applied
Objective: 5.11

71) Young infants can be classically conditioned most easily when
    A) a conditioned stimulus is no longer paired with an unconditioned stimulus.
    B) the conditioned response is fear.
    C) the association between two stimuli has survival value.
    D) a neutral stimulus is paired with an unconditioned response.
Answer: C
Page Ref: 180
Skill: Conceptual
Objective: 5.11

72) _____ is a very difficult response to classically condition in young infants because they _____.
    A) Hunger; are almost always hungry
    B) Fear; do not have the motor skills to escape unpleasant events
    C) Happiness; express happiness only in familiar contexts
    D) Anger; do not yet have the capacity to express anger
Answer: B
Page Ref: 180
Skill: Conceptual
Objective: 5.11

73) In operant conditioning, a(n) _____ increases the occurrence of a response.
    A) neutral stimulus
    B) conditioned stimulus
    C) reinforcer
    D) unconditioned stimulus
Answer: C
Page Ref: 180
Skill: Factual
Objective: 5.11

74) Baby Calinda sucks on a bottle. The taste of the sweet liquid increases Calinda's sucking. This is an example of
    A) operant conditioning.
    B) habituation.
    C) classical conditioning.
    D) extinction.
Answer: A
Page Ref: 180
Skill: Applied
Objective: 5.11

75) As Baby Harriet smiles and laughs, her mother responds by smiling, laughing, and talking gently to her. This makes Harriet smile and laugh more often. The mother's behavior is an example of
   A) habituation.
   B) a reinforcer.
   C) recovery.
   D) extinction.
Answer: B
Page Ref: 180
Skill: Applied
Objective: 5.11

76) When Baby Rico whimpers and whines, his mother responds by ignoring him and refusing to pick him up. This decreases Rico's whining. The mother's behavior is an example of
   A) habituation.
   B) a reinforcer.
   C) recovery.
   D) punishment.
Answer: D
Page Ref: 180
Skill: Applied
Objective: 5.11

77) At birth, the human brain is set up to be
   A) attracted to novelty.
   B) wary of change.
   C) attracted to familiarity.
   D) bored by repetition.
Answer: A
Page Ref: 180
Skill: Factual
Objective: 5.11

78) At first, Baby Marcia wakes up from her nap when she hears the noise of the dishwasher. After several weeks, Marcia sleeps through the noise of the dishwasher. This is an example of
   A) imitation.
   B) recovery.
   C) reinforcement.
   D) habituation.
Answer: D
Page Ref: 180–181
Skill: Applied
Objective: 5.11

79) Once habituation occurs, _____ causes responsiveness to return to a high level.
   A) imitation
   B) recovery
   C) extinction
   D) punishment
Answer: B
Page Ref: 181
Skill: Factual
Objective: 5.11

80) _____ preference assesses infants' _____.
   A) Familiarity; recent memory
   B) Novelty; remote memory
   C) Novelty; recent memory
   D) Familiarity; reflexes
Answer: C
Page Ref: 181
Skill: Factual
Objective: 5.11

81) The newborn's capacity to imitate
   A) has primarily been observed in Western cultures.
   B) disappears by two weeks of age.
   C) has been demonstrated in many ethnic groups and cultures.
   D) is limited to tongue protrusions.
Answer: C
Page Ref: 181
Skill: Conceptual
Objective: 5.11

82) According to Andrew Meltzoff, newborns imitate
   A) more at 2 to 3 months old than just after birth.
   B) more often for their mothers than for their fathers.
   C) random movements and facial expressions.
   D) much as older children and adults do.
Answer: D
Page Ref: 182
Skill: Conceptual
Objective: 5.11

83) Scientists believe that _____ are the biological basis of imitation.
   A) mirror neurons
   B) motor neurons
   C) pruned synapses
   D) neurotransmitters
Answer: A
Page Ref: 182
Skill: Conceptual
Objective: 5.11

84) Which of the following is an example of a gross-motor skill?
   A) climbing
   B) pointing
   C) reaching
   D) scribbling
Answer: A
Page Ref: 183
Skill: Applied
Objective: 5.12

85) Which of the following is an example of a fine-motor skill?
    A) standing
    B) throwing
    C) sitting up
    D) grasping
Answer: D
Page Ref: 183
Skill: Applied
Objective: 5.12

86) Which of the following motor skills typically develops first?
    A) rolling from back to side
    B) building a tower of two cubes
    C) grasping a cube
    D) playing pat-a-cake
Answer: C
Page Ref: 184
Skill: Applied
Objective: 5.12

87) Which of the following motor skills typically develops the latest?
    A) building a tower of two cubes
    B) scribbling vigorously
    C) walking on tiptoe
    D) jumping in place
Answer: C
Page Ref: 184
Skill: Applied
Objective: 5.12

88) Baby Issac learned to combine control of his head and upper chest into sitting with support. This is an example of
    A) coordinated trends.
    B) fine-motor coordination.
    C) gross-motor coordination.
    D) dynamic systems of action.
Answer: D
Page Ref: 184–185
Skill: Applied
Objective: 5.13

89) Dynamic systems theory provides convincing evidence that motor development
    A) is generally slower in females than males.
    B) is hardwired into the nervous system.
    C) always follows the cephalocaudal trend.
    D) cannot be genetically determined.
Answer: D
Page Ref: 185
Skill: Conceptual
Objective: 5.13

90) In James Galloway and Esther Thelen's microgenetic study following babies from their first attempts until skill mastery, the infants
   A) scooted before crawling.
   B) first explored the toys with their feet.
   C) violated the proximodistal trend.
   D) required adult instruction to acquire motor skills.
   Answer: B
   Page Ref: 185–186
   Skill: Conceptual
   Objective: 5.13

91) In Wayne Dennis's study of infants in Iranian orphanages, only 15 percent of the orphans were walking alone by 3 to 4 years of age because
   A) they spent the first year of their lives being carried by caregivers.
   B) they were malnourished and unable to acquire the strength to walk.
   C) they spent their days lying on their backs in cribs.
   D) rapid motor progress was actively discouraged by caregivers.
   Answer: C
   Page Ref: 186
   Skill: Conceptual
   Objective: 5.13

92) Which of the following motor skills do infants usually skip in the Kenyan and Jamaican cultures as compared to Western nations?
   A) crawling
   B) rolling from side to back
   C) sitting alone
   D) pulling to a stand
   Answer: A
   Page Ref: 186
   Skill: Conceptual
   Objective: 5.13

93) Which of the following motor skills is believed to play the greatest role in infant cognitive development?
   A) crawling
   B) reaching
   C) rolling from back to side
   D) walking
   Answer: B
   Page Ref: 186
   Skill: Conceptual
   Objective: 5.14

94) In a dimly lit room, Baby Ursula actively works to bring her hands into her field of vision. She makes poorly coordinated swipes toward objects in front of her. Ursula is demonstrating
   A) the ulnar grasp.
   B) voluntary reaching.
   C) the pincer grasp.
   D) prereaching.
   Answer: D
   Page Ref: 187
   Skill: Applied
   Objective: 5.14

95) At about ____ to ____ months, reaching appears as purposeful, forward arm movements and gradually improves in accuracy.
   A) 1; 2
   B) 2; 3
   C) 3; 4
   D) 4; 6
Answer: C
Page Ref: 187
Skill: Factual
Objective: 5.14

96) Reaching is largely controlled by
   A) hand-eye coordination.
   B) gross-motor development.
   C) proprioception.
   D) vision.
Answer: C
Page Ref: 187
Skill: Factual
Objective: 5.14

97) Five-month-old Raelle can be expected to _____ when an object is moved beyond her reach.
   A) extend one arm rather than both
   B) reduce her efforts
   C) revert to prereaching
   D) increase her efforts
Answer: B
Page Ref: 187
Skill: Applied
Objective: 5.14

98) One-year-old Manny pulls up an individual blade of grass. He is probably using
   A) the pincer grasp.
   B) prereaching.
   C) gross-motor skills.
   D) the ulnar grasp.
Answer: A
Page Ref: 188
Skill: Applied
Objective: 5.14

99) In cultures where mothers carry their infants on their hips or in slings for most of the day,
   A) infants are delayed in reaching and grasping.
   B) manual skills develop later than in Western infants.
   C) infants are advanced in reaching and grasping.
   D) the overstimulation causes babies to cry a great deal.
Answer: C
Page Ref: 188
Skill: Conceptual
Objective: 5.14

100) Research suggests that the best time to begin toilet training is when infants
  A) can walk without assistance.
  B) are around 18 months of age.
  C) are around 27 months of age.
  D) have turned 3 years old.
Answer: C
Page Ref: 188
Skill: Factual
Objective: 5.15

101) Children whose parents postpone intensive toilet training until the beginning or middle of the third year are generally trained
  A) within 2 to 3 weeks.
  B) within 4 months.
  C) within 6 months.
  D) by age 4.
Answer: B
Page Ref: 188
Skill: Factual
Objective: 5.15

102) Between 6 and 8 months, babies
  A) become sensitive to syllable stress patterns in foreign languages.
  B) start to "screen out" sounds not used in their own language.
  C) do not yet recognize familiar words in spoken passages.
  D) prefer listening to a foreign language than their own language.
Answer: B
Page Ref: 189
Skill: Conceptual
Objective: 5.16

103) Research indicates that around 7 to 9 months, infants
  A) detect when words are deliberately mispronounced.
  B) begin to divide the speech stream into wordlike structures.
  C) become sensitive to syllable stress patterns in their own language.
  D) detect words that start with weak syllables.
Answer: B
Page Ref: 190
Skill: Conceptual
Objective: 5.16

104) Which of the following statements is true about how infants perceive the structure of speech?
  A) Rules that infants extract from the speech stream do not generalize to nonspeech sounds.
  B) Parents must directly teach word-order rules for infants to understand the basic grammar of their language.
  C) Infants locate words by discriminating syllables that often occur together from syllables that seldom occur together.
  D) Infants do not become sensitive to the speech structure of individual words until after their first birthday.
Answer: C
Page Ref: 190
Skill: Conceptual
Objective: 5.16

105) For exploring the environment, humans depend on _____ more than any other sense.
    A) vision
    B) touch
    C) hearing
    D) instinct
Answer: A
Page Ref: 190
Skill: Factual
Objective: 5.17

106) Color vision is adultlike by
    A) birth.
    B) 1 month.
    C) 2 months.
    D) 4 months.
Answer: D
Page Ref: 190
Skill: Factual
Objective: 5.17

107) In a study of face perception, by 9 months, infants
    A) could discriminate the individual faces of both humans and monkeys.
    B) no longer showed a novelty preference when viewing monkey pairs.
    C) showed a novelty preference only when viewing monkey pairs.
    D) could not yet discriminate the individual faces of humans or monkeys.
Answer: B
Page Ref: 191 Box: B&E: "Tuning in" to Familiar Speech, Faces, and Music: A Sensitive Period for Culture-Specific
        Learning
Skill: Conceptual
Objective: 5.16

108) Studies of perception demonstrate that
    A) Western adults, but not infants, can detect rhythmic-pattern deviations of non-Western music.
    B) Western children retain the ability to detect deviations in foreign musical rhythms throughout childhood.
    C) Western babies lose their ability to detect deviations in foreign musical rhythms by 12 months of age.
    D) several weeks of daily opportunities to listen to non-Western music restores Western adults' sensitivity to music
       rhythms.
Answer: C
Page Ref: 191 Box: B&E: "Tuning in" to Familiar Speech, Faces, and Music: A Sensitive Period for Culture-Specific
        Learning
Skill: Conceptual
Objective: 5.16

109) Researchers using Gibson and Walk's visual cliff found that
    A) depth perception first appears after babies begin to walk.
    B) most babies avoided the deep side of the cliff.
    C) most babies avoided the shallow side of the cliff.
    D) depth perception first appears after babies begin to crawl.
Answer: B
Page Ref: 192
Skill: Conceptual
Objective: 5.17

110) _____ is/are the first depth cues to which infants are sensitive.
   A) Motion
   B) Binocular depth cues
   C) Pictorial depth cues
   D) Spatial relationships
Answer: A
Page Ref: 192
Skill: Factual
Objective: 5.17

111) _____ arise because our two eyes have slightly different views of the visual field.
   A) Pictorial depth cues
   B) Dimensions
   C) Binocular depth cues
   D) Receding lines
Answer: C
Page Ref: 192
Skill: Factual
Objective: 5.17

112) Which of the following infants is most likely to refuse to cross the deep side of the visual cliff?
   A) Abbie, who has 3 days of crawling experience
   B) Bart, who has 4 weeks of crawling experience
   C) Crystal, who has 2 months of crawling experience
   D) Din, who has 4 months of crawling experience
Answer: D
Page Ref: 192
Skill: Applied
Objective: 5.17

113) Research indicates that _____ probably strengthens certain neural connections, especially those involved in vision and _____.
   A) crawling; pattern perception
   B) sitting; understanding of space
   C) sitting; pattern perception
   D) crawling; understanding of space
Answer: D
Page Ref: 193
Skill: Conceptual
Objective: 5.17

114) Baby Alfredo looks more intensely at a checkerboard with large black and white squares rather than one with smaller gray and white squares. Alfredo is demonstrating
   A) contrast sensitivity.
   B) sensitivity to pictorial depth cues.
   C) proprioception.
   D) sensitivity to the visual cliff.
Answer: A
Page Ref: 193
Skill: Applied
Objective: 5.17

115) Compared to older babies, very young babies prefer to look at large, bold checkerboards over checkerboards with many small squares. This is because very young infants
    A) are overstimulated by more complex checkerboard patterns.
    B) prefer the pattern with the least contrast.
    C) are more sensitive to the greater contrast in complex patterns.
    D) cannot resolve the small features in more complex patterns.
Answer: D
Page Ref: 193
Skill: Conceptual
Objective: 5.17

116) Infants with severe visual impairments are not motivated to move independently until
    A) "reaching on sound" is achieved.
    B) their parents push them to do so.
    C) they have received extensive mobility training.
    D) they receive vision correction through eyeglasses or surgery.
Answer: A
Page Ref: 194 Box: SI: Education: Development of Infants with Severe Visual Impairments
Skill: Conceptual
Objective: 5.17

117) Seven-month-old Tyrese was born with a severe visual impairment. Research suggests that
    A) Tyrese will use sound to establish a shared focus of attention with his caregivers.
    B) once language emerges, Tyrese is likely to make impressive developmental rebounds.
    C) Tyrese will be as effective at communicating with caregivers as sighted infants.
    D) until his vision is restored, Tyrese will not benefit from stimulating, responsive interaction.
Answer: C
Page Ref: 194 Box: SI: Education: Development of Infants with Severe Visual Impairments
Skill: Applied
Objective: 5.17

118) At 2 to 3 months of age, infants
    A) can detect objects represented by incomplete drawings.
    B) perceive subjective boundaries that really are not present.
    C) prefer the walking-human display.
    D) explore the internal features of a pattern.
Answer: D
Page Ref: 195
Skill: Conceptual
Objective: 5.17

119) Which picture is newborn Rori most likely to prefer?
    A) a facelike drawing with the features arranged naturally
    B) a facelike drawing with the features arranged upside down
    C) a facelike drawing with the features arranged sideways
    D) a complex drawing of a face
Answer: A
Page Ref: 195
Skill: Applied
Objective: 5.17

120) As early as 3 months, infants prefer and more easily discriminate among
   A) male adults than boys.
   B) female faces than male faces.
   C) members of other races than members of their own race.
   D) unfamiliar faces than familiar faces.
   Answer: B
   Page Ref: 196
   Skill: Conceptual
   Objective: 5.17

121) Habituation research reveals that size and shape constancy are present as early as
   A) the first week of life.
   B) 3 months of age.
   C) 6 months of age.
   D) 1 year of age.
   Answer: A
   Page Ref: 196
   Skill: Factual
   Objective: 5.18

122) As infants become familiar with many types of objects, they rely more on _____ and less on _____.
   A) motion; size
   B) motion; shape
   C) motion; surface pattern
   D) object features; motion
   Answer: D
   Page Ref: 197
   Skill: Conceptual
   Objective: 5.18

123) _____ enhances older infants' attention to an object's surface features.
   A) Motion
   B) Perception
   C) The environment
   D) Experience
   Answer: D
   Page Ref: 197
   Skill: Conceptual
   Objective: 5.18

124) Baby Wanda uses _____ to learn that dropping her heavy plastic dish on the hardwood flood will cause a loud, banging sound.
   A) depth perception
   B) intermodal perception
   C) differentiation theory
   D) affordances
   Answer: B
   Page Ref: 197
   Skill: Applied
   Objective: 5.19

125) Research reveals that babies perceive input from different sensory systems in a unified way by detecting
    A) amodal sensory properties.
    B) invariant features of the environment.
    C) affordances.
    D) pictorial depth cues.
Answer: A
Page Ref: 197
Skill: Factual
Objective: 5.19

126) Between 3 and 4 months, babies can
    A) discriminate positive from negative emotion in voices.
    B) match faces with voices on the basis of lip–voice synchrony.
    C) discriminate positive from negative emotion in faces.
    D) remember the unique face–voice pairings of unfamiliar adults.
Answer: B
Page Ref: 198
Skill: Conceptual
Objective: 5.19

127) According to the Gibsons' differentiation theory, infants actively search for _____ of the environment in a constantly changing perceptual world.
    A) novel features
    B) detailed associations
    C) variations in patterns
    D) invariant features
Answer: D
Page Ref: 198
Skill: Conceptual
Objective: 5.20

128) Eleanor and James Gibson describe their theory as_____ because over time a baby detects finer and finer invariant features among stimuli.
    A) differentiation
    B) discontinuous
    C) dynamic
    D) bidirectional
Answer: A
Page Ref: 198
Skill: Conceptual
Objective: 5.20

129) One way of understanding perceptual development is to think of it as a built-in tendency to seek
    A) risk.
    B) novelty.
    C) order.
    D) change.
Answer: C
Page Ref: 198–199
Skill: Conceptual
Objective: 5.20

130) According to the Gibsons, perception is guided by the discovery of
   A) failure.
   B) success.
   C) dynamic relationships.
   D) affordances.
   Answer: D
   Page Ref: 199
   Skill: Conceptual
   Objective: 5.20

ESSAY

131) Define and compare the cephalocaudal and prosimodistal trends of growth.
   Answer: The name *cephalocaudal* is Latin for "head to tail." During the prenatal period, in this growth trend, the head develops more rapidly than the lower part of the body. At birth, the head takes up one-fourth of total body length, the legs only one-third. But the lower portion of the body catches up. By age 2, the head accounts for only one-fifth and the legs for nearly one-half of total body length.
   In the second pattern, the proximodistal trend, growth proceeds, literally, from "near to far"—from the center of the body outward. In the prenatal period, the head, chest, and trunk grow first, then the arms and legs, and finally the hands and feet. During infancy and childhood, the arms and legs continue to grow somewhat ahead of the hands and feet.
   Page Ref: 162

132) What is lateralization of the brain, and why does it occur?
   Answer: The cerebral cortex has two hemispheres, or sides, that differ in their functions. The specialization of functions is called lateralization. Studies using fMRI reveal that the left hemisphere is better at processing information in a sequential, analytic way, a good approach for dealing with communicative information—both verbal and emotional. In contrast, the right hemisphere is specialized for processing information in a holistic, integrative manner, ideal for making sense of spatial information and regulating negative emotion. A lateralized brain may have evolved because it enabled humans to cope more successfully with changing environmental demands. It permits a wider array of functions to be carried out effectively than if both sides processed information in exactly the same way. However, the popular notion of a "right-brained" or "left-brained" person is an oversimplification. The two hemispheres communicate and work together, doing so more rapidly and effectively with age.
   Page Ref: 168–169

133) Describe some common forms of inadequate nutrition in the United States.
   Answer: While severe extreme forms of malnutrition, such as kwashiorkor and marasmus, are not common in the United States, *iron-deficiency anemia* is common among poverty-stricken infants and children. It is a condition that interferes with the central nervous system processes. Withdrawal and listlessness reduce the nutritionally deprived child's ability to pay attention, explore, and evoke sensitive caregiving from parents, whose lives are already disrupted by poverty and stressful living conditions.
   Because government-supported supplementary food programs do not reach all families in need, an estimated 22 percent of U.S. children suffer from *food insecurity*—uncertain access to food for a healthy, active life. Food insecurity is especially high among single-parent families and low-income ethnic minority families. Children who suffer from food insecurity are affected in their physical growth and ability to learn.
   Page Ref: 177–178

134) Describe growth faltering, including factors that contribute to it. What interventions are used to treat this disorder?

Answer: *Growth faltering* is a term applied to infants whose weight, height, and head circumference are substantially below age-related growth norms and who are withdrawn and apathetic. Affection is as vital for healthy physical growth as food. In as many as half of growth faltering cases, a disturbed parent–infant relationship contributes to a failure to grow normally. Often an unhappy marriage and parental psychological disturbance contribute. Most of the time, the baby is irritable and displays abnormal feeding behaviors, such as poor sucking or vomiting, that both disrupt growth and lead parents to feel anxious and helpless, which stress the parent–infant relationship further. When treated early, by intervening in infant feeding problems, helping parents with their own life challenges, and encouraging sensitive caregiving, babies show quick catch-up growth. But if the disorder is not corrected in infancy, most of these children remain small and show lasting cognitive and emotional difficulties.

Page Ref: 178

135) Using examples from the text, explain how cultural variations in infant-rearing practices affect motor development.

Answer: Early movement opportunities and a stimulating environment contribute to motor development. In some cultures, sitting, crawling, and walking are deliberately discouraged or encouraged. Japanese mothers, for example, believe that it is unnecessary to deliberately encourage motor skills. The Zinacanteco Indians of southern Mexico and the Gusii of Kenya actively discourage rapid motor progress because babies who walk before they know enough to keep away from cooking fires and weaving looms are viewed as dangerous to themselves and disruptive to others. In contrast, among the Kipsigis of Kenya and the West Indians of Jamaica, babies hold their heads up, sit alone, and walk considerably earlier than North American infants. Kipsigi parents deliberately teach these motor skills. In the first few months, babies are seated in holes dug in the ground, with rolled blankets to keep them upright. Walking is promoted by frequently standing babies in adults' laps and bouncing them on their feet. Infants respond with stepping movements. These infants often skip crawling because they are rarely put on the floor.

Page Ref: 186

136) Define size and shape constancy, and explain how they contribute to infants' perception of objects.

Answer: The images that objects cast on our retina constantly change in size and shape. To perceive objects as stable and unchanging, we must translate these varying retinal images into a single representation. *Size constancy*—perception of an object's size as the same, despite changes in the size of its retinal image—is evident in the first week of life. Perception of an object's shape as stable, despite changes in the shape projected on the retina is called *shape constancy*. Habituation research reveals that it, too, is present within the first week of life, long before babies can actively rotate objects with their hands and view them from different angles. Both size and shape constancy seem to be built-in capacities that assist babies in detecting a coherent world of objects. Yet they provide only a partial picture of young infants' object perception.

Page Ref: 196

CHAPTER 6
COGNITIVE DEVELOPMENT
IN INFANCY AND TODDLERHOOD

MULTIPLE CHOICE

1) In Piaget's sensorimotor stage, infants and toddlers
   A) "think" with their eyes, ears, and hands.
   B) assimilate more than they accommodate.
   C) represent their experiences in speech, gesture, and play.
   D) carry out many activities inside their heads.
   Answer: A
   Page Ref: 204
   Skill: Conceptual
   Objective: 6.1

2) According to Piaget, infants' very first schemes are
   A) disorganized bits of information.
   B) based on internal representations of experience.
   C) sensorimotor action patterns.
   D) deliberate and creative.
   Answer: C
   Page Ref: 204
   Skill: Conceptual
   Objective: 6.1

3) In Piaget's theory, _____ involves building schemes through direct interaction with the environment.
   A) disequilibrium
   B) assimilation
   C) organization
   D) adaptation
   Answer: D
   Page Ref: 204
   Skill: Factual
   Objective: 6.1

4) In Piaget's theory, during _____, toddlers use their current schemes to interpret the external world.
   A) equilibrium
   B) assimilation
   C) accommodation
   D) organization
   Answer: B
   Page Ref: 204
   Skill: Conceptual
   Objective: 6.1

5) According to Piaget, during _____, children create new schemes or adjust old ones.
   A) assimilation
   B) disequilibrium
   C) organization
   D) accommodation
   Answer: D
   Page Ref: 204
   Skill: Conceptual
   Objective: 6.1

6) At 6 months, Annabelle dropped her rattle in a fairly rigid way. By 12 months, she tossed objects down the basement stairs, bounced them off walls, and threw them in the air. Annabelle's modifications of her dropping scheme are an example of
   A) accommodation.
   B) equilibrium.
   C) organization.
   D) assimilation.
   Answer: A
   Page Ref: 204
   Skill: Applied
   Objective: 6.1

7) When children are not changing much, they
   A) are in a state of disequilibrium.
   B) assimilate more than they accommodate.
   C) experience cognitive discomfort.
   D) modify their schemes.
   Answer: B
   Page Ref: 204–205
   Skill: Conceptual
   Objective: 6.1

8) During periods of rapid cognitive change,
   A) organization predominates over adaptation.
   B) accommodation predominates over assimilation.
   C) assimilation and accommodation are balanced.
   D) adaptation and organization are balanced.
   Answer: B
   Page Ref: 205
   Skill: Conceptual
   Objective: 6.1

9) Piaget's _____ stage is the most complex period of development.
   A) sensorimotor
   B) preoperational
   C) concrete operational
   D) formal operational
   Answer: A
   Page Ref: 205
   Skill: Conceptual
   Objective: 6.1

10) According to Piaget, organization takes place
    A) apart from direct contact with the environment.
    B) only during the preoperational stage.
    C) during Substage 3 of Piaget's sensorimotor period.
    D) when new schemes are formed.
Answer: A
Page Ref: 205
Skill: Conceptual
Objective: 6.1

11) Baby Franklin practiced his dropping and throwing schemes, and eventually developed an understanding of height. This achievement is an example of
    A) organization.
    B) accommodation.
    C) equilibrium.
    D) assimilation.
Answer: A
Page Ref: 205
Skill: Applied
Objective: 6.1

12) In Piaget's sequence of sensorimotor development, newborns first develop
    A) mental representations.
    B) tertiary circular schemes.
    C) reflexive schemes.
    D) primary circular schemes.
Answer: C
Page Ref: 205
Skill: Conceptual
Objective: 6.2

13) In Piaget's theory, a circular reaction is a means of building schemes in which infants
    A) attempt to form mental symbols of the world.
    B) try to repeat chance motor activities again and again.
    C) try to imitate the behaviors of others around them.
    D) attempt to act out imaginary activities.
Answer: B
Page Ref: 205
Skill: Conceptual
Objective: 6.2

14) Baby Faith sucks, grasps, and looks in much the same way, no matter what experiences she encounters. Faith is probably in Substage _____ of Piaget's sensorimotor period.
    A) 1
    B) 2
    C) 3
    D) 4
Answer: A
Page Ref: 205
Skill: Applied
Objective: 6.2

15) During Substage ___ of the sensorimotor period, babies repeat chance behaviors largely motivated by basic needs.
    A) 1
    B) 2
    C) 3
    D) 4
    Answer: B
    Page Ref: 205
    Skill: Factual
    Objective: 6.2

16) Baby Sabrina opens her mouth differently for a nipple than for a spoon. In Piaget's theory, this is an example of a _____ circular reaction.
    A) reflexive
    B) primary
    C) secondary
    D) tertiary
    Answer: B
    Page Ref: 205
    Skill: Applied
    Objective: 6.2

17) Baby Bertha accidentally knocks a toy hung on her crib. Over the next several days, Bertha tries to repeat this effect, gradually forming a "hitting" scheme. In Piaget's theory, this is an example of a _____ circular reaction.
    A) reflexive
    B) primary
    C) secondary
    D) tertiary
    Answer: C
    Page Ref: 205
    Skill: Applied
    Objective: 6.2

18) According to Piaget, intentional, or goal-directed, behavior first occurs in Substage ____ of the sensorimotor period.
    A) 1
    B) 2
    C) 3
    D) 4
    Answer: D
    Page Ref: 205
    Skill: Conceptual
    Objective: 6.2

19) Two landmark cognitive changes that take place in Substage 4 of the sensorimotor period of Piaget's theory are _____ and _____.
    A) deferred imitation; animistic thinking
    B) intentional behavior; object permanence
    C) dual representation; intentional behavior
    D) deferred imitation; object permanence
    Answer: B
    Page Ref: 206–207
    Skill: Conceptual
    Objective: 6.2

20) Baby Jessica accidentally pushes her stuffed toy behind the couch, out of her line of vision. One possible reason Jessica begins to cry is that she has not yet developed
    A) an A-not-B search error.
    B) conservation.
    C) object permanence.
    D) animistic thinking.
Answer: C
Page Ref: 207
Skill: Applied
Objective: 6.2

21) Baby Parker's mom shows him his pacifier behind a pillow. Parker reaches for it and finds it several times. Parker's mom then shows him his pacifier hidden under a cup. Parker continues to search for it behind the pillow. This is most likely because Parker
    A) is not yet able to make an accurate A–B search.
    B) does not yet appreciate physical causality.
    C) has not yet attained even rudimentary object permanence.
    D) cannot yet engage in goal-directed behavior.
Answer: A
Page Ref: 207
Skill: Applied
Objective: 6.2

22) Piaget argued that babies make the A-not-B search error because
    A) the ability to engage in goal-directed behavior has not yet developed.
    B) they do not have a clear image of the object as persisting when hidden from view.
    C) appreciation of physical causality has not yet been attained.
    D) they cannot yet coordinate means–end action sequences.
Answer: B
Page Ref: 207
Skill: Conceptual
Objective: 6.2

23) Baby Manny discovered how to use a stick to get toys that were out of reach. According to Piaget, Manny's behavior would best be described as a _____ circular reaction.
    A) tertiary
    B) secondary
    C) primary
    D) reflexive
Answer: A
Page Ref: 207
Skill: Applied
Objective: 6.2

24) _____ enable(s) older toddlers to solve advanced object permanence problems involving invisible displacement.
    A) Imitation
    B) Reflexive schemes
    C) Mental representation
    D) Realistic props
Answer: C
Page Ref: 207
Skill: Conceptual
Objective: 6.2

25) Two-year-old Greta pretends to bake a cake. Greta is demonstrating
   A) object permanence.
   B) core knowledge.
   C) abstract thinking.
   D) mental representation.
   Answer: D
   Page Ref: 207
   Skill: Applied
   Objective: 6.2

26) In the violation-of-expectation method, researchers use _____ to familiarize babies with a situation in which their knowledge will be tested.
   A) reflexes
   B) imitation
   C) habituation
   D) experimentation
   Answer: C
   Page Ref: 208
   Skill: Conceptual
   Objective: 6.3

27) Some critics argue that the violation-of-expectation method is flawed because
   A) it is difficult for observers to discern when babies have habituated to the familiar event.
   B) this method cannot be used with young babies or toddlers, who easily become fatigued.
   C) babies make only subtle changes to their behaviors when they recover to a new stimulus.
   D) it reveals only babies' perceptual preference for novelty, not their understanding of experience.
   Answer: D
   Page Ref: 208
   Skill: Conceptual
   Objective: 6.3

28) In a series of studies using the violation-of-expectation method, Renée Baillargeon and her collaborators claimed to have found evidence for _____ in the first few months of life.
   A) assimilation
   B) mental representation
   C) object permanence
   D) equilibrium
   Answer: C
   Page Ref: 208
   Skill: Conceptual
   Objective: 6.3

29) Follow-up research suggests that once 8- to 12-month-olds search for hidden objects, they may make the A-not-B search error because they
   A) do not attend closely when the object is hidden at A.
   B) have trouble remembering an object's new location.
   C) lack the motor skills necessary for intentional reaching and grasping.
   D) have trouble inhibiting a previously rewarded motor response.
   Answer: D
   Page Ref: 209
   Skill: Conceptual
   Objective: 6.3

30) Laboratory research reveals that deferred imitation is present at _____ of age.
   A) 6 weeks
   B) 4 months
   C) 6 months
   D) 18 months
   Answer: A
   Page Ref: 210
   Skill: Factual
   Objective: 6.3

31) Follow-up research on deferred imitation demonstrates that toddlers
   A) are more likely to imitate accidental behaviors than purposeful behaviors.
   B) can imitate rationally, by inferring others' intentions.
   C) do not yet use intentional means–end action sequences.
   D) cannot yet imitate actions that an adult produces.
   Answer: B
   Page Ref: 210
   Skill: Conceptual
   Objective: 6.3

32) When 12-month-old Barrett's mom asks him, "Where is your teddy bear?" Barrett responds by pointing to the place on his bed where the teddy bear usually rests. Barrett is displaying
   A) habituation and recovery.
   B) inferred imitation.
   C) displaced reference.
   D) means-end problem solving.
   Answer: C
   Page Ref: 211
   Skill: Applied
   Objective: 6.3

33) Awareness of the symbolic function of pictures emerges
   A) at birth.
   B) between 4 and 6 months.
   C) between 8 and 12 months.
   D) in the second year.
   Answer: D
   Page Ref: 212
   Skill: Factual
   Objective: 6.3

34) Toddlers seem to discount information on video as relevant to their everyday experiences because
   A) people do not look at and converse with them directly.
   B) they have little experience with digital media.
   C) they are easily overstimulated by the fast-paced content.
   D) the characters are usually unfamiliar to them.
   Answer: A
   Page Ref: 213 Box: SI: Education: Baby Learning from TV and Video: The Video Deficit Effect
   Skill: Factual
   Objective: 6.3

35) Around age ____, the video deficit effect declines.
   A) 1½
   B) 2
   C) 2½
   D) 3
Answer: C
Page Ref: 213 Box: SI: Education: Baby Learning from TV and Video: The Video Deficit Effect
Skill: Factual
Objective: 6.3

36) According to the core knowledge perspective, babies
   A) construct knowledge through independent exploration of their world.
   B) internalize knowledge though social interaction with others.
   C) achieve new mental abilities through schedules of reinforcement and punishment.
   D) are born with at set of innate special-purpose knowledge systems.
Answer: D
Page Ref: 214
Skill: Conceptual
Objective: 6.4

37) According to core knowledge theorists,
   A) each "prewired" core domain of thought permits a ready grasp of new, related information and, therefore, supports early, rapid development.
   B) infants make sense of the complex stimulation around them by repeating chance behaviors again and again.
   C) infants are endowed with very little innate understanding and must rely on their interactions with the environment to construct knowledge.
   D) infants are not born with knowledge of concepts or reasoning because such ready-made knowledge would limit their ability to adapt to environmental changes.
Answer: A
Page Ref: 214
Skill: Conceptual
Objective: 6.4

38) Research involving infants' numerical knowledge suggests that babies
   A) can discriminate quantities up to five.
   B) can perform simple addition, but not subtraction.
   C) have the ability to distinguish among large sets of items.
   D) can add and subtract small sets correctly.
Answer: C
Page Ref: 214
Skill: Conceptual
Objective: 6.4

39) The core knowledge perspective emphasizes
   A) experimentation.
   B) native endowment.
   C) assimilation.
   D) accommodation.
Answer: B
Page Ref: 215
Skill: Factual
Objective: 6.4

40) According to the information-processing perspective, _____ increase(s) the chances that we will retain information and use it efficiently.
    A) autobiographical memory
    B) individual experiences
    C) use of mental strategies
    D) operant conditioning
Answer: C
Page Ref: 217
Skill: Conceptual
Objective: 6.5

41) In the information-processing system, information first enters
    A) working memory.
    B) the central executive.
    C) long-term memory.
    D) the sensory register.
Answer: D
Page Ref: 217
Skill: Factual
Objective: 6.5

42) In the information-processing system, the central executive
    A) is the conscious, reflective part of the mental system.
    B) collaborates with long-term memory to direct problem solving and reasoning.
    C) is where sights and sounds are represented directly and stored briefly.
    D) is a special part of the long-term memory that manages complex activities.
Answer: A
Page Ref: 218
Skill: Factual
Objective: 6.5

43) In the information-processing system, _____ is unlimited in capacity.
    A) working memory
    B) long-term memory
    C) the central executive
    D) the sensory register
Answer: B
Page Ref: 218
Skill: Factual
Objective: 6.5

44) According to the information-processing framework, _____ make(s) more complex forms of thinking possible with age.
    A) increases in the size of short-term memory
    B) changes in the structure of the mental system
    C) increases in the capacity of the mental system
    D) the emergence of goal-directed behavior
Answer: C
Page Ref: 218
Skill: Conceptual
Objective: 6.5

45) Research on infant attention demonstrates that _____ between birth and 4 to 5 months of age.
   A) attraction to novelty increases
   B) sustained attention declines
   C) habituation time decreases
   D) the ability to shift attention declines
Answer: C
Page Ref: 218
Skill: Conceptual
Objective: 6.6

46) The ability to shift attention from one stimulus to another improves by
   A) 1 to 2 months.
   B) 3 to 4 months.
   C) 1 to 2 years.
   D) 2 to 3 years.
Answer: B
Page Ref: 218
Skill: Conceptual
Objective: 6.6

47) After 2- to 6-month olds forget an operant response,
   A) it takes months for them to reinstate the memory.
   B) they need only a brief prompt to reinstate the memory.
   C) they reinstate the memory after a few days.
   D) they are unable to remember it without extensive training.
Answer: B
Page Ref: 219
Skill: Conceptual
Objective: 6.6

48) Infants learn and retain information
   A) only through physical activity.
   B) just by watching objects and events.
   C) only by manipulating objects.
   D) but they cannot engage in recall.
Answer: B
Page Ref: 219
Skill: Conceptual
Objective: 6.6

49) Recall memory
   A) is not as challenging as recognition memory.
   B) is the simplest form of memory.
   C) involves remembering a stimulus with perceptual support.
   D) improves steadily with age.
Answer: D
Page Ref: 220
Skill: Factual
Objective: 6.6

50) _____ increases sharply between ages 3 and 4—the period during which children "scramble over the amnesia barrier."
   A) Autobiographical memory
   B) Implicit memory
   C) Explicit memory
   D) Verbal recall
   Answer: D
   Page Ref: 221 Box: B&E: Infantile Amnesia
   Skill: Conceptual
   Objective: 6.6

51) Studies of infantile amnesia suggest that the advent of _____ contributes to the end of infantile amnesia.
   A) an autobiographical memory
   B) a clear self-image
   C) object permanence
   D) mnemonic strategies
   Answer: B
   Page Ref: 221 Box: B&E: Infantile Amnesia
   Skill: Conceptual
   Objective: 6.6

52) Which of the following statements is true about categorization?
   A) Even young infants can categorize on the basis of shape, size, and other physical properties.
   B) As infants approach their second birthday, more categories appear to be based on subtle sets of features.
   C) Older infants cannot make categorical distinctions when the perceptual contract between two categories is minimal.
   D) Not until the early preschool years can children sort people and their voices by gender and age.
   Answer: A
   Page Ref: 222
   Skill: Conceptual
   Objective: 6.6

53) Korean toddlers develop object-sorting skills later than their English-speaking counterparts because
   A) they are less likely to be given opportunities to physically manipulate objects.
   B) English-speaking children develop language skills sooner than Korean-speaking children.
   C) the English language is less complex than the Korean language.
   D) the Korean language often omits object names from sentences.
   Answer: D
   Page Ref: 223
   Skill: Conceptual
   Objective: 6.6

54) Compared with Piaget's theory of development, the information-processing approach has had more difficulty with
   A) breaking down children's thoughts into precise procedures.
   B) integrating information into a broad, comprehensive theory.
   C) reducing changes in thoughts into manageable proportions.
   D) identifying specific stages of cognitive development.
   Answer: B
   Page Ref: 224
   Skill: Conceptual
   Objective: 6.6

55) Vygotsky's sociocultural theory emphasizes that
    A) children are born with prewired understandings that permit a ready grasp of new information.
    B) children think with their eyes, ears, hands, and other sensorimotor equipment.
    C) complex mental activities have their origins in social interaction.
    D) children discover virtually all knowledge about the world through their own activity.
    Answer: C
    Page Ref: 224
    Skill: Conceptual
    Objective: 6.7

56) According to Vygotsky, children master activities and think in ways that have meaning in their culture through
    A) the physical world acting on the child.
    B) independent interaction with the physical environment.
    C) the biological unfolding of genetic structures.
    D) joint activities with more mature members of their society.
    Answer: D
    Page Ref: 224
    Skill: Conceptual
    Objective: 6.7

57) Which of the following tasks would be within Lucy's zone of proximal development?
    A) a task that Lucy cannot accomplish alone or with the help of an adult
    B) a task that Lucy has recently mastered independently following the assistance of an adult
    C) a task that Lucy cannot yet handle on her own but can do with the help of an adult
    D) a task that Lucy accomplishes through her independent activity
    Answer: C
    Page Ref: 224
    Skill: Applied
    Objective: 6.7

58) Eighteen-month-old Liam is putting together a puzzle. Liam's father begins by pointing to where each piece needs to go and then straightening out each piece as Liam places them on the puzzle board. As Liam's competence with the task increases, his father gradually withdraws support. This is an example of
    A) scaffolding.
    B) cooperative learning.
    C) reciprocal teaching.
    D) transitive inference.
    Answer: A
    Page Ref: 224
    Skill: Applied
    Objective: 6.7

59) Which of the following statements is true about the application of Vygotsy's ideas to infancy and toddlerhood?
    A) Vygotsky failed to recognize the significance of social experiences for children under the age of 5.
    B) Fine-tuned adult support during infancy and toddlerhood is related to advanced problem solving during the second year.
    C) Cultural variations in social experiences rarely affect mental strategies until children reach school age.
    D) While scaffolding promotes learning in the preschool years, it seems to inhibit learning in infancy and toddlerhood.
    Answer: B
    Page Ref: 225
    Skill: Conceptual
    Objective: 6.7

60) Vygotsky's theory emphasizes that _____ affect(s) mental strategies.
   A) development of cognitive schemes
   B) cultural differences in social experiences
   C) repetition and training
   D) cultural differences in formal schooling
Answer: B
Page Ref: 225
Skill: Conceptual
Objective: 6.7

61) Which of the following statements is supported by research on make-believe play?
   A) Early make-believe is the combined result of children's readiness to engage in it and social experiences that promote it.
   B) In cultures where make-believe play is more frequent with older siblings than with mothers, the pretend play of toddlers is hindered.
   C) Most episodes of make-believe play during toddlerhood occur when children are playing with same-aged children.
   D) Children are more likely to combine play schemes into complex sequences when they are playing with agemates than when playing with caregivers.
Answer: A
Page Ref: 226 Box: CI: Social Origins of Make-Believe Play
Skill: Conceptual
Objective: 6.7

62) Research demonstrates that make-believe play is
   A) less frequent and rich in collectivist cultures than in individualistic cultures.
   B) a major means through which children extend their cognitive and social skills.
   C) usually initiated by toddlers rather than their parents or older siblings.
   D) discovered by toddlers independently, once they are capable of representational schemes.
Answer: B
Page Ref: 226 Box: CI: Social Origins of Make-Believe Play
Skill: Conceptual
Objective: 6.7

63) Mental tests focus on
   A) the process of development.
   B) cognitive delays.
   C) how children's thinking changes.
   D) cognitive products.
Answer: D
Page Ref: 227
Skill: Factual
Objective: 6.8

64) The Bayley Scales of Infant Development test
   A) is suitable for preschool and school-age children.
   B) accurately predicts future school achievement.
   C) is suitable for children between one month and 3½ years.
   D) is a poor predictor of infants' mental development.
Answer: C
Page Ref: 227
Skill: Factual
Objective: 6.8

65) Kegan was given a test that indicates the extent to which his raw score deviates from the typical performance of same-age individuals. Kegan's score is known as a(n)
   A) normal distribution.
   B) intelligence quotient.
   C) screening quotient.
   D) standardization sample.
Answer: B
Page Ref: 227
Skill: Applied
Objective: 6.8

66) Within the standardization sample for an IQ test, performances at each age level
   A) are distributed equally among all scores.
   B) cluster around the extreme scores.
   C) form a normal distribution.
   D) infrequently fall around the mean.
Answer: C
Page Ref: 228
Skill: Factual
Objective: 6.8

67) A child's IQ score offers a way of finding out
   A) individual strengths and weaknesses, as well as the mental and chronological age of the child.
   B) whether the child is ahead, behind, or average in mental development compared to agemates.
   C) the percentage of younger and older children who fall above or below the child's score.
   D) how the child compares in mental development to younger and older children.
Answer: B
Page Ref: 228
Skill: Conceptual
Objective: 6.8

68) Molly has an IQ of 130. Molly performed better than _____ percent of her agemates.
   A) 16
   B) 50
   C) 85
   D) 98
Answer: D
Page Ref: 228
Skill: Applied
Objective: 6.8

69) Longitudinal research reveals that
   A) most infant tests accurately predict later intelligence and academic performance.
   B) the majority of children show substantial fluctuations in IQ between toddlerhood and adolescence.
   C) infant tests are somewhat better at making long-term predictions for moderate to high-scoring babies.
   D) the majority of children perform the same or slightly worse on IQ tests as they age.
Answer: B
Page Ref: 228
Skill: Conceptual
Objective: 6.8

70) Most infant tests
  A) are helpful in assessing the newborn's adjustment to life outside the womb.
  B) emphasize higher-order cognitive skills like memory and problem solving.
  C) do not tap the same dimensions of intelligence measured at older ages.
  D) show good long-term prediction of childhood intellectual functioning.
Answer: C
Page Ref: 228
Skill: Conceptual
Objective: 6.8

71) Today, infant tests are largely used for
  A) measuring higher-order cognitive skills.
  B) predicting future performance.
  C) predicting school placement.
  D) screening to identify babies in need of intervention.
Answer: D
Page Ref: 228
Skill: Conceptual
Objective: 6.8

72) Many infant test scores are labeled _____ quotients.
  A) intelligence
  B) developmental
  C) emotional
  D) cognitive
Answer: B
Page Ref: 228
Skill: Factual
Objective: 6.8

73) As an alternative to infant tests, some researchers have turned to _____ measures to assess early mental development.
  A) adult IQ
  B) operant learning
  C) information-processing
  D) classical conditioning
Answer: C
Page Ref: 228
Skill: Factual
Objective: 6.8

74) Habituation and recovery seem to be especially effective early indexes of intelligence because they
  A) indicate important sensorimotor milestones.
  B) measure higher-order cognitive skills.
  C) assess skills that underlie intelligent behavior at all ages.
  D) reveal infants' ability to process complex stimuli.
Answer: C
Page Ref: 228
Skill: Conceptual
Objective: 6.8

75) The designers of the Bayley-III included items that tap
   A) parental warmth toward the child.
   B) such cognitive skills as habituation and categorization.
   C) provision of appropriate play materials.
   D) opportunities for variety in daily stimulation.
   Answer: B
   Page Ref: 228
   Skill: Conceptual
   Objective: 6.8

76) The extent to which parents _____ contributes strongly to early language process, which, in turn, predicts intelligence and academic achievement in elementary school.
   A) engage their children in physical activity
   B) watch educational television with their children
   C) talk to their infants and toddlers
   D) teach their children specific literacy and math skills
   Answer: C
   Page Ref: 229
   Skill: Conceptual
   Objective: 6.9

77) _____ predict(s) children's IQ scores beyond the contribution of parental IQ and education.
   A) Maternal age
   B) Family living conditions
   C) Provision of age-appropriate play materials
   D) Quality child care
   Answer: B
   Page Ref: 229
   Skill: Conceptual
   Objective: 6.9

78) Research shows the young children exposed to long hours of mediocre to poor-quality child care
   A) score lower on cognitive measures only if they also come from low-SES homes.
   B) score lower on language measures, but high on social skills during the preschool years.
   C) still show gains in cognitive, emotional, and social competence in the elementary school years.
   D) score lower on measures of cognitive and language skills during the preschool and elementary school years.
   Answer: D
   Page Ref: 230
   Skill: Conceptual
   Objective: 6.9

79) In the United States, child-care settings providing the very worst care tend to
   A) serve middle-SES families.
   B) serve low-SES families.
   C) be publicly subsidized, nonprofit centers.
   D) be in family homes.
   Answer: A
   Page Ref: 230
   Skill: Factual
   Objective: 6.9

80) Which of the following statements is true about child care in the United States?
   A) Most child-care centers require that caregivers have special training in child development.
   B) Child-care centers are nationally regulated and funded to ensure their quality.
   C) In studies of quality, about 20 to 25 percent of child-care centers offer substandard care.
   D) Child-care standards are set by the individual states and vary widely.
Answer: D
Page Ref: 230
Skill: Conceptual
Objective: 6.9

81) Quality tends to be the lowest in
   A) nonprofit child-care centers.
   B) family child-care settings.
   C) for-profit child-care centers.
   D) single child-care settings.
Answer: C
Page Ref: 230
Skill: Factual
Objective: 6.9

82) Children living in poverty
   A) usually have access to free child care.
   B) are likely to show gradual declines in intelligence test scores.
   C) tend to show increases in IQ once they reach school age.
   D) are unlikely to benefit from early intervention programs.
Answer: B
Page Ref: 231
Skill: Conceptual
Objective: 6.9

83) The Carolina Abecedarian Project shows that _____ is an effective way to reduce the negative effects of poverty on children's mental development.
   A) furnishing free nutrition and health services for parents and children
   B) providing children a special resource teacher during the early elementary school years
   C) an early intervention approach that focuses on parental involvement
   D) enrollment in full-time, year-round child care through the preschool years
Answer: D
Page Ref: 231–232
Skill: Conceptual
Objective: 6.9

84) The strongest effects from Early Head Start occur at sites
   A) located in rural communities.
   B) located in the child's own neighborhood.
   C) offering a mix of center- and home-based services.
   D) located near the parent's workplace.
Answer: C
Page Ref: 232
Skill: Conceptual
Objective: 6.9

85) By age 6, children have a vocabulary of about _____ words.
   A) 1,000
   B) 5,000
   C) 10,000
   D) 50,000
   Answer: C
   Page Ref: 233
   Skill: Factual
   Objective: 6.10

86) Dr. Mastick believes that children are "prewired" to master the intricate rules of their language. Dr. Mastick's views are consistent with which theory of language development?
   A) behaviorism
   B) nativism
   C) interactionism
   D) psychoanalytic
   Answer: B
   Page Ref: 234
   Skill: Applied
   Objective: 6.10

87) Behaviorist Dr. Wechsler probably believes that language is acquired through
   A) a language acquisition device.
   B) social interactions.
   C) heredity.
   D) operant conditioning.
   Answer: D
   Page Ref: 233
   Skill: Applied
   Objective: 6.10

88) Linguist Noam Chomsky argued that all children
   A) have a language acquisition device that contains a universal grammar.
   B) acquire language through imitation and reinforcement.
   C) rely on imitation to rapidly acquire complex utterances.
   D) cue their caregivers to provide appropriate language experiences.
   Answer: A
   Page Ref: 233–234
   Skill: Conceptual
   Objective: 6.10

89) The idea that a grammatically complex language system seems to be unique to humans is consistent with
   A) Chomsky's account of language acquisition.
   B) the interactionist perspective.
   C) the dynamic systems perspective.
   D) Skinner's account of language acquisition.
   Answer: A
   Page Ref: 234
   Skill: Conceptual
   Objective: 6.10

90) Evidence that there is a sensitive period for language development has been interpreted as supporting
    A) Skinner's account of language acquisition.
    B) the sociocultural perspective of language acquisition.
    C) Chomsky's account of language acquisition.
    D) an interactionist's account of language acquisition.
    Answer: C
    Page Ref: 234
    Skill: Conceptual
    Objective: 6.10

91) Broca's area
    A) supports language production.
    B) supports grammatical processing.
    C) is mainly responsible for language comprehension.
    D) is located in the left temporal lobe.
    Answer: A
    Page Ref: 234
    Skill: Factual
    Objective: 6.10

92) Damage to the frontal-lobe area of the adult left hemisphere usually yields _____ problems.
    A) language comprehension
    B) language production
    C) no language
    D) short-term, mild language
    Answer: B
    Page Ref: 234
    Skill: Conceptual
    Objective: 6.10

93) Second-language competence
    A) drops sharply after age 18.
    B) increases continuously with age.
    C) drops sharply after age 10.
    D) decreases continuously with age.
    Answer: D
    Page Ref: 235
    Skill: Conceptual
    Objective: 6.10

94) Which of the following is a limitation of Chomsky's nativist perspective?
    A) Chomsky's theory is inconsistent with research on efforts to teach nonhuman primates language systems.
    B) Chomsky's theory cannot explain why children refine and generalize many grammatical forms gradually.
    C) Chomsky's theory overemphasizes the role of social experience in language development.
    D) Chomsky's theory fails to show that humans have evolved specialized regions in the brain that support language skills.
    Answer: B
    Page Ref: 235
    Skill: Conceptual
    Objective: 6.10

95) Dr. Rasmussen believes that language acquisition occurs through exchanges between inner capacities and environmental influences. Dr. Rasmussen is a(n)
   A) interactionist.
   B) behaviorist.
   C) nativist.
   D) acquisitionist.
   Answer: A
   Page Ref: 236
   Skill: Applied
   Objective: 6.10

96) Among social interactionists, disagreement continues over whether or not children
   A) have the necessary social skills to make sense of language.
   B) progress through distinct stages of language development.
   C) are equipped with specialized language structures.
   D) should acquire a second language before formal schooling begins.
   Answer: C
   Page Ref: 236
   Skill: Conceptual
   Objective: 6.10

97) Which of the following sounds is the best example of cooing?
   A) "oooo"
   B) "mae-do" (for "tomato")
   C) "rrrrrr"
   D) "dadada"
   Answer: A
   Page Ref: 236
   Skill: Applied
   Objective: 6.11

98) Which of the following sounds is the best example of babbling?
   A) "aaaaa"
   B) "ooooo"
   C) "rrrrr"
   D) "nanana"
   Answer: D
   Page Ref: 236
   Skill: Applied
   Objective: 6.11

99) Which of the following statements is supported by research on babbling and deaf infants?
   A) Deaf infants not exposed to sign language will stop babbling entirely.
   B) Deaf infants do not babble or coo unless they are exposed to sign language.
   C) Deaf infants start babbling much earlier than hearing infants.
   D) Deaf infants start babbling much later than hearing infants.
   Answer: A
   Page Ref: 237
   Skill: Conceptual
   Objective: 6.11

100) Ten-month-old Thaddeus and his 12-year-old brother watch their cat play with a ball. Thaddeus looks at the cat and then looks at his brother to ensure that he is also watching the cat. Thaddeus's brother labels the cat and the ball. Thaddeus and his brother are engaged in
    A) sustained attention.
    B) telegraphic speech.
    C) child-directed speech.
    D) joint attention.
Answer: D
Page Ref: 238
Skill: Applied
Objective: 6.11

101) Sally and her granddaughter play peekaboo regularly. At first, Sally starts the game and her granddaughter is an amused observer. By 12 months, the granddaughter actively participates, trading roles with Sally. Sally is helping her granddaughter
    A) learn how to overextend and underextend.
    B) understand the turn-taking pattern of human conversation.
    C) develop a referential style of communication.
    D) understand telegraphic speech.
Answer: B
Page Ref: 238
Skill: Applied
Objective: 6.11

102) Infant pointing predicts faster vocabulary development
    A) from 6 to 12 months.
    B) over the first year.
    C) from 12 to 18 months.
    D) over the second year.
Answer: D
Page Ref: 238
Skill: Conceptual
Objective: 6.11

103) Which of the following is most likely to be one of Baby Raj's first words?
    A) "table"
    B) "box"
    C) "red"
    D) "kitty"
Answer: D
Page Ref: 238–239
Skill: Applied
Objective: 6.12

104) Maxi used the word "doll" only to refer to the rag doll she carried every day. This is an example of
    A) underextension.
    B) overextension.
    C) telegraphic speech.
    D) referential speech.
Answer: A
Page Ref: 239
Skill: Applied
Objective: 6.12

105) Sophie used the word "open" to apply to opening a door, peeling fruit, and untying her shoelaces. This is an example of
    A) underextension.
    B) joint attention.
    C) overextension.
    D) telegraphic speech.
Answer: C
Page Ref: 239
Skill: Applied
Objective: 6.12

106) As vocabulary and pronunciation improve,
    A) underextensions increase.
    B) overextensions disappear.
    C) overextensions increase.
    D) underextensions replace overextensions.
Answer: B
Page Ref: 239
Skill: Conceptual
Objective: 6.12

107) Once toddlers produce about _____ words, they start to combine two words.
    A) 10
    B) 50
    C) 200
    D) 1,000
Answer: C
Page Ref: 239
Skill: Factual
Objective: 6.12

108) Two-year-old Zach utters the words "more cookie." This is an example of
    A) telegraphic speech.
    B) referential speech.
    C) expressive speech.
    D) an overextension.
Answer: A
Page Ref: 239
Skill: Applied
Objective: 6.12

109) Telegraphic speech
    A) usually contains significant grammatical errors.
    B) focuses on high-content words.
    C) emerges around age 3.
    D) focuses on smaller, less important words.
Answer: B
Page Ref: 239
Skill: Conceptual
Objective: 6.12

110) Children's language comprehension
    A) usually develops behind production.
    B) requires both recall and recognition.
    C) requires only recall, not recognition.
    D) develops ahead of production.
Answer: D
Page Ref: 240
Skill: Conceptual
Objective: 6.12

111) Comprehension requires that children
    A) recall the word and the concept for which it stands.
    B) merely recognize the meaning of a word.
    C) recognize the meaning of a word and actively retrieve it from their memories.
    D) actively retrieve a word from their memories and be able to pronounce it.
Answer: B
Page Ref: 240
Skill: Conceptual
Objective: 6.12

112) Research demonstrates that
    A) girls are slightly ahead of boys in early vocabulary growth.
    B) shy toddlers' vocabularies are typically larger than their agemates'.
    C) mothers tend to talk more to toddler-age boys than to girls.
    D) boys and girls develop their vocabularies at the same rate.
Answer: A
Page Ref: 240
Skill: Conceptual
Objective: 6.13

113) Arthur's vocabulary consists mainly of words that refer to objects. Like most toddlers, he uses
    A) an expressive style.
    B) child-directed speech.
    C) a referential style.
    D) an authoritative style.
Answer: C
Page Ref: 240
Skill: Applied
Objective: 6.13

114) Expressive-style children tend to
    A) eagerly imitate their parents' frequent naming of objects.
    B) think that words are for naming objects or people.
    C) have faster growing vocabularies than referential-style children.
    D) have parents who more often use verbal routines that support social relationships.
Answer: A
Page Ref: 240
Skill: Conceptual
Objective: 6.13

115) Baby Felix's parents talk to him using short sentences with high-pitched exaggerated expression, clear pronunciation, distinct pauses between speech segments, and repetition of new words in a variety of contexts. Felix's parents use
   A) telegraphic speech.
   B) a referential style.
   C) an expressive style.
   D) child-directed speech.
   Answer: D
   Page Ref: 241
   Skill: Applied
   Objective: 6.14

116) Studies show that children begin to prefer child-directed speech over other kinds of adult talk at
   A) birth.
   B) 3 months.
   C) 6 months.
   D) 12 months.
   Answer: A
   Page Ref: 241
   Skill: Factual
   Objective: 6.14

117) Which of the following statements is supported by research on child-directed speech?
   A) Deaf mothers lack a style of communication similar to child-directed speech.
   B) By as early as 5 months, infants are more emotionally receptive to child-directed speech.
   C) Infants begin to prefer child-directed speech over other kinds of adult talk by age 2.
   D) Child-directed speech becomes less information-laden and more emotion-laden over the first year of life.
   Answer: B
   Page Ref: 241
   Skill: Conceptual
   Objective: 6.14

118) Research on deaf children and parent–child interaction shows that deaf children
   A) of deaf parents show language and social skills that are on par with hearing children.
   B) typically lag behind their hearing agemates in school, regardless of whether their parents are hearing or deaf.
   C) of deaf parents have difficulty getting along well with adults and peers once they've entered school.
   D) of hearing parents are more cognitively advanced than deaf children of deaf parents.
   Answer: A
   Page Ref: 243 Box: SI: Education: Parent–Child Interaction: Impact on Language and Cognitive Development of Deaf Children
   Skill: Conceptual
   Objective: 6.14

119) Beginning in infancy, hearing parents of deaf children are _____ than are deaf parents of deaf children.
   A) more responsive to their child's efforts to communicate
   B) more effective at turn-taking
   C) less directive and intrusive
   D) less involved in play
   Answer: D
   Page Ref: 243 Box: SI: Education: Parent–Child Interaction: Impact on Language and Cognitive Development of Deaf Children
   Skill: Conceptual
   Objective: 6.14

ESSAY

120) Identify Piaget's substages of sensorimotor development, including the adaptive behaviors associated with each substage.

Answer:
- *Reflexive schemes* (birth–1 month): newborn reflexes
- *Primary circular reactions* (1–4 months): simple motor habits centered around the infant's own body; limited anticipation of events
- *Secondary circular reactions* (4–8 months): actions aimed at repeating interesting effects in the surrounding world; imitation of familiar behaviors
- *Coordination of secondary circular reactions* (8–12 months): intentional, or goal-directed, behavior; ability to find a hidden object in the first location in which it is hidden (object permanence); improved anticipation of events; imitation of behaviors slightly different from those the infant usually performs
- *Tertiary circular reactions* (12–18 months): exploration of the properties of objects by acting on them in novel ways; imitation of novel behaviors; ability to search in several locations for a hidden object (accurate A–B search)
- *Mental representation* (18 months–2 years): internal depictions of objects and events, as indicated by sudden solutions to problems; ability to find an object that has been moved while out of sight (invisible displacement); deferred imitation; and make-believe play.

Page Ref: 205–207

121) Explain the core knowledge perspective of cognitive development.

Answer: According to the core knowledge perspective, babies are born with a set of innate knowledge systems, or core domains of thought. Each of these "prewired" understandings permits a ready grasp of new, related information and, therefore, supports early, rapid development. Core knowledge theorists argue that infants could not make sense of the complex stimulation around them without having been genetically "set up" in the course of evolution to comprehend its crucial aspects. Core knowledge researchers have conducted studies of infants' physical, linguistic, psychological, and numerical knowledge.

Page Ref: 214

122) Describe the structure of the information-processing system.

Answer: Most information-processing researchers assume that we hold information in three parts of the mental system for processing: the sensory register; working, or short-term, memory; and long-term memory.

First, information enters the sensory register, where sights and sounds are represented directly and stored briefly. The sensory register, though limited, can take in a wide panorama of information.

In the second part of the mind, working, or short-term, memory, we actively apply mental strategies as we "work" on a limited amount of information. The capacity of working memory is restricted. The more thoroughly we learn information, the more automatically we use it. Automatic cognitive processing expands working memory by permitting us to focus on other information simultaneously. To manage the working memory's complex activities, the central executive directs the flow of information. It decides what to attend to, coordinates incoming information with information already in the system, and selects, applies, and monitors strategies. It is the conscious, reflective part of the mental system.

The third and largest storage area is long-term memory. As our permanent knowledge base, it is unlimited. In fact, we store so much in long-term memory that retrieval can be problematic. To aid retrieval, we apply mental strategies, just as we do in working memory. Information in long-term memory is categorized.

Page Ref: 217–218

123) Define and describe recognition and recall. Discuss the development of recall memory.
   Answer: Recognition is noticing when a stimulus is identical or similar to one previously experienced. It is the easiest
   form of memory. Recall is more challenging because it involves remembering something without perceptual
   support. To recall, you must generate a mental image of a past experience. By the middle of the first year,
   infants can recall. Recall memory improves steadily with age. The ability to recall modeled behaviors in the
   order in which the actions occurred strengthens over the second year. And when toddlers imitate in correct
   sequence, processing not just separate actions but relations between actions, they remember more.
   　　　Long-term recall depends on connections among multiple regions of the cerebral cortex, especially with the
   prefrontal cortex. During infancy and toddlerhood, these neural circuits develop rapidly. Infants' memory
   processing is remarkably similar to that of older children and adults: Babies acquire information quickly, retain
   it over time, and apply it flexibly—doing so more effectively with age.
   Page Ref: 220

124) How well do infant tests predict later intelligence? What are some alternatives to traditional infant tests?
   Answer: Most infant tests predict later intelligence poorly. Longitudinal research reveals that the majority of children
   show substantial fluctuations in IQ between toddlerhood and adolescence—typically 10 to 20 points, and
   sometimes much more. Infant tests are somewhat better at making long-term predictions for extremely low-
   scoring babies and are largely used for screening.
   　　　As an alternative to infant tests, some researchers have turned to information-processing measures, such as
   habituation and recovery. Piagetian object-permanence tasks are also relatively good predictors of later IQ.
   Page Ref: 227–228

125) Compare the three major theories of language development.
   Answer: According to the behaviorist perspective, language is learned through operant conditioning. As a baby makes
   sounds, parents reinforce those that are most like words with smiles, hugs, and speech in return. Some
   behaviorists believe that children rely on imitation to rapidly acquire complex utterances, such as whole phrases
   and sentences. Although reinforcement and imitation contribute to early language development, they are best
   viewed as supporting rather than fully explaining it.
   　　　Linguist Noam Chomsky's nativist view regards children as biologically equipped with a language
   acquisition device (LAD) that supports rapid mastery of the structure of language. Within the LAD is a
   universal grammar, which refers to a built-in storehouse of rules that apply to all human languages. Children's
   ability to invent new language systems, efforts to teach language to apes, evidence for specialized language
   areas in the brain, and the notion of a sensitive period for language development support a biological
   contribution to language development.
   　　　Interactionist theories emphasize the interactions between inner capacities and environmental influences.
   Information-processing theorists focus on biological abilities of the human brain to detect patterns in language,
   while social interactionists propose that native capacity, a strong desire to understand others and to be
   understood by them, and a rich language environment combine to help children discover the functions and
   regularities of language.
   Page Ref: 233–236

126) List several strategies for supporting early language learning, noting the consequences of each.
Answer:
- *Respond to coos and babbles with speech sounds and words:* encourages experimentation with sounds that can later be blended into first words; provides experience with the turn-taking pattern of human conversation
- *Establish joint attention and comment on what the child sees:* predicts earlier onset of language and faster vocabulary development
- *Play social games, such as pat-a-cake and peekaboo:* provides experience with the turn-taking pattern of human conversation
- *Engage toddlers in joint make-believe play:* promotes all aspects of conversational dialogue
- *Engage toddlers in frequent conversations:* predicts faster early language development and academic success during the school years
- *Read to toddlers often, engaging them in dialogues about picture books:* provides exposure to many aspects of language, including vocabulary, grammar, communication skills, and information about written symbols and story structures

Page Ref: 241

CHAPTER 7
EMOTIONAL AND SOCIAL DEVELOPMENT
IN INFANCY AND TODDLERHOOD

MULTIPLE CHOICE

1) One of the lasting contributions of psychoanalytic theory is its
   A) information regarding the channeling of biological drives.
   B) ability to capture the essence of personality development during each period of development.
   C) nearly exclusive focus on the importance of experiences in infancy and early childhood.
   D) emphasis on quantitative and experimental research.
   Answer: B
   Page Ref: 248
   Skill: Conceptual
   Objective: 7.1

2) According to Erikson's theory, a healthy outcome during infancy is dependent on the
   A) quantity of food offered.
   B) amount of oral stimulation provided.
   C) quality of caregiving.
   D) availability of self-soothing.
   Answer: C
   Page Ref: 248
   Skill: Conceptual
   Objective: 7.1

3) According to Erikson, the psychological conflict of the first year is
   A) autonomy versus shame and doubt.
   B) basic trust versus mistrust.
   C) initiative versus guilt.
   D) industry versus inferiority.
   Answer: B
   Page Ref: 248
   Skill: Factual
   Objective: 7.1

4) In Erikson's theory, the conflict of toddlerhood is resolved favorably when parents
   A) provide suitable guidance and reasonable choices.
   B) use appropriate and warm toilet-training techniques.
   C) employ an authoritarian child-rearing style.
   D) employ a permissive child-rearing style.
   Answer: A
   Page Ref: 249
   Skill: Conceptual
   Objective: 7.1

5) Which of the following statements is supported by research on emotional development?
   A) Infants, children, and adults use diverse responses to express a particular emotion.
   B) The emotional expressions of blind infants are exaggerated compared to infants with normal vision.
   C) Babies on the visual cliff generally display a fearful facial expression, but do not show other signs of fear.
   D) Wide cultural differences exist in the facial expressions that people associate with different emotions.
Answer: A
Page Ref: 249
Skill: Conceptual
Objective: 7.2

6) Basic emotions
   A) are not evident in nonhuman primates.
   B) are all present at birth.
   C) have no evolutionary history of promoting survival.
   D) are universal in humans.
Answer: D
Page Ref: 250
Skill: Conceptual
Objective: 7.2

7) Babies' earliest emotional life consists of which two global arousal states?
   A) happiness and sadness
   B) fullness and hunger
   C) attraction to pleasant stimuli and withdrawal from unpleasant stimuli
   D) happiness and fear
Answer: C
Page Ref: 250
Skill: Conceptual
Objective: 7.2

8) Emotional expressions are well-organized and specific
   A) at birth.
   B) by 3 months of age.
   C) by the middle of the first year.
   D) only after the start of the second year.
Answer: C
Page Ref: 250
Skill: Conceptual
Objective: 7.2

9) The social smile
   A) first appears during REM sleep.
   B) is evoked by parent–child interaction.
   C) emerges during the second week of life.
   D) first appears in response to dynamic, eye-catching sights.
Answer: B
Page Ref: 251
Skill: Factual
Objective: 7.2

10) The social smile first appears around _____ of age.
   A) 1 to 5 weeks
   B) 6 to 10 weeks
   C) 3 to 4 months
   D) 5 to 7 months
   Answer: B
   Page Ref: 251
   Skill: Factual
   Objective: 7.2

11) Laughter
   A) reflects faster processing of information than smiling.
   B) appears around 6 to 8 months of age.
   C) first occurs in response to very gentle stimuli.
   D) occurs more often when babies are interacting with new people.
   Answer: A
   Page Ref: 251
   Skill: Conceptual
   Objective: 7.2

12) Sheldon, age 1, will most likely display a _____ smile for a friendly stranger.
   A) brief, fleeting
   B) broad, "cheek-raised"
   C) reserved, muted
   D) "mouth-open"
   Answer: C
   Page Ref: 251
   Skill: Applied
   Objective: 7.2

13) Newborn babies respond with _____ to too much or too little stimulation.
   A) locked gazes
   B) generalized distress
   C) fear
   D) mouth-open smiles
   Answer: B
   Page Ref: 251
   Skill: Conceptual
   Objective: 7.2

14) Expressions of _____ are less common than those of _____.
   A) anger; fear
   B) anger; sadness
   C) sadness; anger
   D) happiness; sadness
   Answer: C
   Page Ref: 251
   Skill: Conceptual
   Objective: 7.2

15) When an unfamiliar adult picks up Louisa, age 9 months, the baby begins to cry and struggles to get down. Louisa is exhibiting
   A) stranger anxiety.
   B) avoidant attachment.
   C) insecure attachment.
   D) separation anxiety.
Answer: A
Page Ref: 252
Skill: Applied
Objective: 7.2

16) Infants raised in Israeli kibbutzim
   A) are discouraged from developing a strong emotional bond with their mother.
   B) display far greater stranger anxiety than their city-reared counterparts.
   C) are passed from one adult to another, which reduces their stranger anxiety.
   D) show very little stranger anxiety compared with agemates.
Answer: B
Page Ref: 252
Skill: Conceptual
Objective: 7.2

17) Sevan, age 11 months, is wary of strangers. However, when his mother sits on the floor, Sevan ventures a few feet away from her for a few minutes at a time, and then returns to her for emotional support. Sevan is
   A) engaging in effortful control.
   B) exhibiting unusual behavior for a toddler with stranger anxiety.
   C) using his mother as a secure base.
   D) displaying avoidance rather than approach.
Answer: C
Page Ref: 252
Skill: Applied
Objective: 7.2

18) The rise in _____ after 6 months of age keeps nearly mobile babies' enthusiasm for exploration in check.
   A) fear
   B) sadness
   C) anger
   D) emotional contagion
Answer: A
Page Ref: 252
Skill: Factual
Objective: 7.2

19) In the first few months, babies
   A) master emotional self-regulation.
   B) match the feeling tone of the caregiver in face-to-face communication.
   C) look longer at an appropriate face–voice pairing than at an inappropriate one.
   D) display empathy in most social situations.
Answer: B
Page Ref: 252
Skill: Conceptual
Objective: 7.3

20) Baby Emma is learning to stand. Each time she falls, she looks at her caregiver. If her caregiver looks concerned, Emma cries. If her caregiver smiles, Emma tries again. Emma is using
   A) a secure base.
   B) emotional self-regulation.
   C) social referencing.
   D) effortful control.
Answer: C
Page Ref: 253
Skill: Applied
Objective: 7.3

21) According to research on social referencing, which of the following responses from Tanner's mom is the *most* likely to encourage him to get up and try again after he falls down while learning to walk?
   A) a concerned look
   B) a cautious smile
   C) speaking the words "oh, no!"
   D) laughter combined with saying "oopsie-daisy"
Answer: D
Page Ref: 253
Skill: Applied
Objective: 7.3

22) Which of the following is true about social referencing?
   A) By the middle of the second year, it expands to include indirect emotional signals.
   B) A parent's use of a facial expression alone is a more effective social reference than the use of the voice.
   C) It does not allow young children to compare their own and others' assessments of events.
   D) In social referencing, toddlers simply react to others' emotional messages.
Answer: A
Page Ref: 253
Skill: Conceptual
Objective: 7.3

23) Self-conscious emotions
   A) are present at birth.
   B) are universal and basic.
   C) include happiness, fear, anger, and sadness.
   D) involve injury to or enhancement of our sense of self.
Answer: D
Page Ref: 253
Skill: Conceptual
Objective: 7.4

24) _____ are examples of self-conscious emotions.
   A) Anger and guilt
   B) Happiness and pride
   C) Shame and embarrassment
   D) Envy and sadness
Answer: C
Page Ref: 253
Skill: Conceptual
Objective: 7.4

25) Self-conscious emotions appear
    A) in the middle of the first year.
    B) at the end of the first year.
    C) in the middle of the second year.
    D) at the end of the second year.
Answer: C
Page Ref: 254
Skill: Factual
Objective: 7.4

26) Self-conscious emotions
    A) involve distinct facial expressions.
    B) do not require self-awareness.
    C) are universally experienced in response to the same types of situations.
    D) require adult instruction in when to feel proud, ashamed, or guilty.
Answer: D
Page Ref: 254
Skill: Conceptual
Objective: 7.4

27) Cross-cultural research indicates that
    A) the situations in which adults encourage various self-conscious emotions vary from culture to culture.
    B) in collectivist cultures, most children are taught to feel pride over personal achievement.
    C) nonverbal expressions of basic emotions differ widely from culture to culture.
    D) in Western individualistic nations, most children are taught to feel embarrassment over individual achievement.
Answer: A
Page Ref: 254
Skill: Conceptual
Objective: 7.4

28) Evan covered his eyes when the witch appeared on the screen while he was watching *The Wizard of Oz*. Evan was using
    A) a secure base.
    B) emotional self-regulation.
    C) social referencing.
    D) self-soothing.
Answer: B
Page Ref: 254
Skill: Applied
Objective: 7.5

29) Emotional self-regulation requires
    A) adult instruction on when to use it.
    B) goodness of fit.
    C) social referencing.
    D) effortful control.
Answer: D
Page Ref: 254
Skill: Conceptual
Objective: 7.5

30) In the early months, infants
    A) have only a limited capacity to regulate their emotional stress.
    B) are unable to regulate any form of emotional stress.
    C) are not very easily overwhelmed.
    D) rely primarily on self-soothing for distraction and reorientation of attention.
Answer: A
Page Ref: 254
Skill: Conceptual
Objective: 7.5

31) Effortful control
    A) requires adult instruction and modeling.
    B) is regarded as a major dimension of temperament.
    C) plays a limited role in mental and social development.
    D) is an ability that is present at birth.
Answer: B
Page Ref: 255
Skill: Conceptual
Objective: 7.5

32) Which of the following statements is supported by research on emotional self-regulation?
    A) Collectivist cultures usually discourage the expression of strong emotion in infants.
    B) Beginning in infancy, girls find it harder to regulate negative emotion than boys.
    C) By the second year, toddlers are quite skilled at using language to comfort themselves.
    D) Beginning in the first few months, mothers imitate their babies' negative feelings far more often than their positive
       ones.
Answer: A
Page Ref: 255
Skill: Conceptual
Objective: 7.5

33) Gil describes his son as calm and cautious. He describes his daughter as cheerful and energetic. Gil's descriptions refer to
    the children's
    A) ability to use effortful control.
    B) ability to use self-soothing.
    C) temperaments.
    D) level of reactivity.
Answer: C
Page Ref: 256
Skill: Applied
Objective: 7.6

34) Which of the following is true about the results of the longitudinal study on temperament conducted by Alexander
    Thomas and Stella Chess?
    A) Temperament can increase a child's chances of experiencing psychological problems.
    B) Because temperament is innate, parenting practices cannot modify children's emotional styles.
    C) Temperament cannot protect a child from the negative effects of a highly stressful home life.
    D) The psychological traits that make up temperament in childhood play a very small role in adult personality.
Answer: A
Page Ref: 256
Skill: Conceptual
Objective: 7.6

35) Baby Dak quickly establishes regular routines, is generally cheerful, and adapts easily to new experiences. Dak would be classified by Thomas and Chess as
   A) slow-to-warm-up.
   B) uninhibited.
   C) difficult.
   D) easy.
Answer: D
Page Ref: 256
Skill: Applied
Objective: 7.6

36) According to Thomas and Chess, the difficult child
   A) shows mild, low-key reactions to environmental stimuli.
   B) is irregular in daily routines.
   C) shows unique blends of temperamental characteristics.
   D) displays no identifiable temperamental traits.
Answer: B
Page Ref: 256
Skill: Conceptual
Objective: 7.6

37) Alice is inactive, shows mild, low-key reactions to environmental stimuli, and adjusts slowly to new experiences. In Thomas and Chess's research, Alice would be classified as
   A) slow-to-warm-up.
   B) uninhibited.
   C) difficult.
   D) easy.
Answer: A
Page Ref: 257
Skill: Applied
Objective: 7.6

38) In Thomas and Chess's research, _____ percent of children showed unique blends of temperamental characteristics and could not be classified as easy, difficult, or slow-to-warm-up.
   A) 10
   B) 25
   C) 35
   D) 50
Answer: C
Page Ref: 257
Skill: Factual
Objective: 7.6

39) In Mary Rothbart's model of temperament,
   A) distractibility and irritable distress are considered opposite ends of the same dimension.
   B) persistence and fearful distress are considered opposite ends of the same dimension.
   C) fearful distress and irritable distress distinguish between reactivity triggered by fear and reactivity due to frustration.
   D) the dimensions are overly broad, such as regularity of body functions.
Answer: C
Page Ref: 257
Skill: Conceptual
Objective: 7.6

40) According to Rothbart, individuals differ not just in their reactivity on each dimension but also in
    A) effortful control.
    B) self-concept.
    C) goodness of fit.
    D) interactional synchrony.
Answer: A
Page Ref: 257–258
Skill: Conceptual
Objective: 7.6

41) Which of the following is true about measuring temperament?
    A) Parental reports provide little information about the way parents view and respond to their babies.
    B) Parental reports have a low correlation to researchers' observations of children's behavior.
    C) Researchers can better control children's experiences in the home setting as opposed to the laboratory.
    D) Most neurophysiological research focuses on the positive-affect and fearful-distress dimensions of temperament.
Answer: D
Page Ref: 258
Skill: Conceptual
Objective: 7.7

42) Brendon reacts negatively to and withdraws from novel stimuli. He could be classified as a(n) _____ child.
    A) sociable
    B) shy
    C) easy
    D) uninhibited
Answer: B
Page Ref: 258
Skill: Applied
Objective: 7.7

43) Results of Jerome Kagan's longitudinal research on the development of shyness and sociability found that
    A) about 70 percent of 4-month-olds were easily upset by novelty.
    B) nearly all of the extreme groups retained their temperamental styles over time.
    C) most children's dispositions became less extreme over time.
    D) as infants, more children were shy than were highly sociable.
Answer: C
Page Ref: 259 Box: B&E: Development of Shyness and Sociability
Skill: Conceptual
Objective: 7.8

44) Which of the following is more likely to be found in shy, inhibited children than in highly sociable, uninhibited children?
    A) a higher heart rate from the first few weeks of life
    B) lower levels of amygdala activity in response to novel stimuli
    C) lower levels of saliva concentration of cortisol
    D) a drop in blood pressure in response to novelty
Answer: A
Page Ref: 259 Box: B&E: Development of Shyness and Sociability
Skill: Conceptual
Objective: 7.8

45) Compared to shy infants and preschoolers, highly sociable children show
    A) greater EEG activity in the right frontal lobe.
    B) greater generalized activation of the cerebral cortex.
    C) lower levels of fMRI activity in the amygdala.
    D) higher saliva concentrations of the stress hormone cortisol.
Answer: C
Page Ref: 259 Box: B&E: Development of Shyness and Sociability
Skill: Conceptual
Objective: 7.8

46) The overall stability of temperament is
    A) high in infancy.
    B) low from the preschool years on.
    C) low in infancy and toddlerhood.
    D) high from the preschool years on.
Answer: C
Page Ref: 260
Skill: Factual
Objective: 7.8

47) Which of the following statements is supported by research on the stability of temperament?
    A) Long-term prediction from early temperament is best achieved after age three.
    B) Temperament does not develop as the child ages.
    C) Most irritable infants become difficult children as they age.
    D) Childhood temperament is a fairly good predictor of personality in adulthood.
Answer: A
Page Ref: 260
Skill: Conceptual
Objective: 7.8

48) Research on the role of heredity in temperament indicates that
    A) heritability estimates derived from twin studies suggest a major role for genetic factors in temperament and personality.
    B) identical twins are more similar than fraternal twins across a wide range of temperamental traits and personality measures.
    C) only 5 to 10 percent of individual differences in temperament have been attributed to differences in genetic makeup.
    D) heritability estimates are much higher for expressions of positive emotion than for negative emotion.
Answer: B
Page Ref: 260
Skill: Conceptual
Objective: 7.8

49) Research on sex differences in temperament shows that
    A) girls are more daring than boys, and they have a large advantage in effortful control.
    B) boys are more anxious and timid than girls, and they are slightly more impulsive.
    C) girls' advantage in effortful control contributes to better school performance.
    D) boys are more active than girls, but they also tend to be more anxious and timid.
Answer: C
Page Ref: 261
Skill: Conceptual
Objective: 7.8

50) Studies on the cultural differences in temperament demonstrate that
    A) Japanese mothers usually say that babies come into the world as independent beings who must learn to rely on their parents through close physical contract.
    B) American mothers tend to interact gently, soothingly, and gesturally with their babies.
    C) Japanese mothers typically believe that they must wean babies away from dependency toward autonomy.
    D) American mothers tend to discourage babies from expressing strong emotion, which contributes to their infants' tranquility.
Answer: A
Page Ref: 261
Skill: Conceptual
Objective: 7.8

51) In families with several children,
    A) parents tend to look for similarities between siblings.
    B) parents often regard siblings as less distinct than other observers do.
    C) both identical and fraternal twins tend to become increasingly similar in personality with age.
    D) parents' tendency to emphasize each child's unique qualities affects their child-rearing practices.
Answer: D
Page Ref: 262
Skill: Conceptual
Objective: 7.8

52) Goodness of fit is
    A) only effective with sociable, securely attached children.
    B) rarely successful with difficult children.
    C) only effective with infants and toddlers.
    D) at the heart of infant–caregiver attachment.
Answer: D
Page Ref: 262
Skill: Conceptual
Objective: 7.8

53) An important criticism of the psychoanalytic theory of attachment is that it
    A) underemphasizes the importance of the mother–infant bond.
    B) overemphasizes the role of the quality of the parent–child relationship.
    C) ignores the internal representation of the attachment figure.
    D) overemphasizes the importance of feeding in attachment.
Answer: D
Page Ref: 264
Skill: Conceptual
Objective: 7.9

54) In the 1950s, a famous experiment of rhesus monkeys reared with terry-cloth and wire-mesh "surrogate mothers" provided evidence that
    A) the development of emotional ties between infant and mother does not depend on hunger satisfaction.
    B) the infant's characteristics play a larger role in the relationship than the caregiver's contributions.
    C) continuous, sensitive caregiving is key to the development of a secure attachment pattern.
    D) attachment security in infancy is highly dependent on hunger satisfaction.
Answer: A
Page Ref: 264
Skill: Conceptual
Objective: 7.9

55) The ethological theory of attachment
    A) suggests that the infant's emotional tie to the mother is the foundation of all later relationships.
    B) recognizes the infant's emotional tie to the caregiver as an evolved response that promotes survival.
    C) emphasizes the importance of feeding as the central context in which caregivers and babies build close emotional bonds.
    D) suggests that infants learn to prefer their mother because she functions as both a primary caregiver and a social partner.
Answer: B
Page Ref: 265
Skill: Conceptual
Objective: 7.9

56) Babies in John Bowlby's _____ phase display separation anxiety.
    A) preattachment
    B) "attachment in the making"
    C) "clear-cut" attachment
    D) formation of a reciprocal relationship
Answer: C
Page Ref: 265
Skill: Conceptual
Objective: 7.9

57) Baby Jane has begun to develop a sense of trust. She expects that her mother will respond when signaled. But Jane does not protest when separated from her mother. In which of Bowlby's phases does Jane best fit?
    A) preattachment
    B) "attachment in the making"
    C) "clear-cut" attachment
    D) formation of a reciprocal relationship
Answer: B
Page Ref: 265
Skill: Applied
Objective: 7.9

58) Baby Matthew recognizes his own mother's smell, voice, and face. But Matthew does not mind being left with an unfamiliar adult. In which of Bowlby's phases does Matthew best fit?
    A) preattachment
    B) "attachment in the making"
    C) "clear-cut" attachment
    D) formation of a reciprocal relationship
Answer: A
Page Ref: 265
Skill: Applied
Objective: 7.9

59) Jazmin, age 18 months, cries and climbs on her mother when she attempts to leave Jazmin with a babysitter. Jazmin is displaying
    A) an internal working model.
    B) interactional synchrony.
    C) social referencing.
    D) separation anxiety.
Answer: D
Page Ref: 265
Skill: Applied
Objective: 7.9

60) In which of Bowlby's phases do children use requests and persuasion to alter their caregiver's goals?
    A) formation of a reciprocal relationship
    B) "clear-cut" attachment
    C) "attachment in the making"
    D) preattachment
Answer: A
Page Ref: 265
Skill: Conceptual
Objective: 7.9

61) Separation protest declines during which of Bowlby's phases?
    A) preattachment
    B) "attachment in the making"
    C) "clear-cut" attachment
    D) formation of a reciprocal relationship
Answer: D
Page Ref: 265
Skill: Conceptual
Objective: 7.9

62) According to Bowlby, out of their experiences during the four attachment phases, children
    A) learn autonomy and develop self-soothing because they learn that caregivers cannot be relied upon to provide support during times of stress.
    B) move from secure attachment to insure attachment and back again.
    C) construct enduring affectionate ties to their caregivers that they can use as a secure base in the caregivers' absence.
    D) develop either avoidant or resistant attachment styles.
Answer: C
Page Ref: 266
Skill: Conceptual
Objective: 7.9

63) Troy, age 3, understands that his father goes to work in the morning and picks Troy up from his babysitter's house after naptime. Troy seeks his father's comfort during times of stress. These examples show that Troy has developed
    A) effortful control.
    B) an internal working model.
    C) interactional synchrony.
    D) a categorical self.
Answer: B
Page Ref: 266
Skill: Applied
Objective: 7.9

64) In designing the Strange Situation, Mary Ainsworth and her colleagues reasoned that securely attached infants and toddlers
    A) use the parent as a secure base from which to explore in an unfamiliar setting.
    B) are just as comforted by an unfamiliar adult as by the parent.
    C) combine anger and clinginess when reunited with a parent who has left the room for a time.
    D) do not show distress when the parent leaves the room.
Answer: A
Page Ref: 266
Skill: Conceptual
Objective: 7.10

65) During the Strange Situation, the parent leaves the room in order to assess _____, and returns again to assess the infant's _____.
   A) separation anxiety; use of a secure base
   B) use of a secure base; reaction to the reunion
   C) separation anxiety; reaction to the reunion
   D) secure base; separation anxiety
Answer: C
Page Ref: 266
Skill: Conceptual
Objective: 7.10

66) In the Strange Situation, Juan uses his mother as a secure base. When she leaves the room, Juan cries for a few minutes. When she returns, Juan seeks contact with her and then begins to explore toys once again. Juan is displaying characteristics of _____ attachment.
   A) avoidant
   B) secure
   C) disorganized/disoriented
   D) resistant
Answer: B
Page Ref: 266
Skill: Applied
Objective: 7.10

67) In the Strange Situation, Antwan ignores his mother and displays and odd, frozen posture. He does not cry when his mother leaves the room. When she returns, Antwan looks away when she is holding him. Antwan is displaying characteristics of _____ attachment.
   A) avoidant
   B) secure
   C) disorganized/disoriented
   D) resistant
Answer: C
Page Ref: 267
Skill: Applied
Objective: 7.10

68) In the Strange Situation, George clings to his mother and refuses to explore the toys. When his mother leaves, George is distressed. When his mother returns, George continues to cry, yet clings to his mother. He also struggles against her and hits her. George is demonstrating _____ attachment.
   A) secure
   B) resistant
   C) avoidant
   D) disorganized/disoriented
Answer: B
Page Ref: 267
Skill: Applied
Objective: 7.10

69) In the Strange Situation, Richard is unresponsive to his mother when she is present. When she leaves, Richard reacts to the stranger in much the same way as to his mother. When his mother returns, Richard pays no attention to her. Richard is demonstrating _____ attachment.
   A) avoidant
   B) secure
   C) disorganized/disoriented
   D) resistant
Answer: A
Page Ref: 267
Skill: Applied
Objective: 7.10

70) The Attachment Q-Sort
   A) is a quicker and more efficient method of assessing attachment than the Strange Situation.
   B) takes place in a specially designed laboratory.
   C) taps a wider array of attachment-related behaviors than the Strange Situation.
   D) differentiates between the types of insecurity.
Answer: C
Page Ref: 267
Skill: Factual
Objective: 7.10

71) Research on the stability of attachment indicates that
   A) insecurely attached babies more often maintain their attachment status than secure babies.
   B) attachment generally moves toward security in low-SES families with many daily stressors.
   C) quality of attachment is most stable for low-SES babies experiencing unfavorable family conditions.
   D) the disorganized/disoriented attachment pattern is as stable as attachment security.
Answer: D
Page Ref: 268
Skill: Conceptual
Objective: 7.11

72) Research on infant attachment of the Dogon people of Mali, Africa, revealed no _____ attachment.
   A) resistant
   B) avoidant
   C) secure
   D) disorganized/disoriented
Answer: B
Page Ref: 268
Skill: Conceptual
Objective: 7.11

73) Drawing on cross-cultural research on attachment, which of the following infants is the most likely to display an avoidant attachment?
   A) Gretel from Germany
   B) Yuri from Japan
   C) Garrett from the United States
   D) Sascha from an Israeli kibbutz
Answer: A
Page Ref: 268
Skill: Applied
Objective: 7.11

74) Japanese infants' reactions in the Strange Situation frequently show _____ attachment, but this reaction may not represent the true attachment pattern.
    A) disorganized/disoriented
    B) avoidant
    C) resistant
    D) secure

Answer: C
Page Ref: 268
Skill: Conceptual
Objective: 7.11

75) Studies of institutionalized adoptees indicate that
    A) it is imperative that the first attachment bond develop within the first year of life.
    B) late adoptees, placed in homes after age 4, do not display social or emotional problems.
    C) late adoptees are likely to shy away from adult attention once adopted.
    D) a first attachment can develop as late as 4 to 6 years of age.

Answer: D
Page Ref: 269
Skill: Conceptual
Objective: 7.11

76) Studies of adopted children who spent their first year or more in deprived Eastern European orphanages indicate that
    A) late adoptees are not able to bond with their adoptive parents.
    B) adoptees do not typically show social or emotional problems if adopted before the age of 6.
    C) fully normal emotional development depends on establishing a close tie with a caregiver early in life.
    D) adoptees' delays and impairments tend to disappear in middle childhood.

Answer: C
Page Ref: 269
Skill: Conceptual
Objective: 7.11

77) Sensitive caregiving that involves prompt, consistent, and appropriate responses to infant signals is likely to promote a(n)
    A) resistant attachment.
    B) avoidant attachment.
    C) secure attachment.
    D) difficult temperament.

Answer: C
Page Ref: 270
Skill: Conceptual
Objective: 7.11

78) Baby Ashley picks up her ball and says, "Ball!" Ashley's father responds with a big smile and an enthusiastic, "That's right! Ball!" In return, Ashley laughs. When Ashley is tired and crying, her father picks her up, rubs her back, and sings softly to her. Ashley and her father are engaged in
    A) attachment in the making.
    B) social referencing.
    C) goodness of fit.
    D) interactional synchrony.

Answer: D
Page Ref: 270
Skill: Applied
Objective: 7.11

79) _____ adult–infant coordination, in which interactional synchrony occurs, is the best predictor of attachment security.
   A) Loose
   B) Tight
   C) Moderate
   D) Variable
Answer: C
Page Ref: 270
Skill: Conceptual
Objective: 7.11

80) _____ babies tend to have mothers who overwhelm them with stimulation.
   A) Disorganized/disoriented
   B) Avoidant
   C) Resistant
   D) Secure
Answer: B
Page Ref: 270
Skill: Conceptual
Objective: 7.11

81) Which of the following children is most likely to be receiving abusive or neglectful care?
   A) Dante, whose attachment is disorganized/disoriented
   B) Sonya, whose attachment is secure
   C) Anthony, whose attachment is avoidant
   D) Riley, whose attachment is resistant
Answer: A
Page Ref: 270
Skill: Applied
Objective: 7.11

82) Which of the following statements about attachment is supported by research?
   A) Mothers of resistant infants tend to be overstimulating and intrusive.
   B) Securely attached infants often receive inconsistent care.
   C) Persistently depressed mothers tend to promote an avoidant attachment classification.
   D) Mothers of resistant infants are often unresponsive to infant signals.
Answer: D
Page Ref: 270
Skill: Conceptual
Objective: 7.11

83) Research on attachment in at-risk infants reveals that
   A) preterm birth predicts insecure attachment, regardless of maternal characteristics or other caregiving experiences.
   B) at-risk infants whose parents have adequate time and patience to care for them fare quite well in attachment security.
   C) infants with special needs rarely display secure attachment to any caregiver.
   D) mothers' experience of traumatic events is highly predictive of disorganized/disoriented attachment in preterm infants.
Answer: B
Page Ref: 271
Skill: Conceptual
Objective: 7.11

84) The heritability of attachment is
   A) virtually nil.
   B) moderately low.
   C) moderately high.
   D) very high.
   Answer: A
   Page Ref: 271
   Skill: Factual
   Objective: 7.11

85) Job loss, a failing marriage, and financial difficulties
   A) show little correlation with attachment security.
   B) are the primary causes of disoriented/disorganized attachment in infancy.
   C) can undermine attachment indirectly by interfering with parental sensitivity.
   D) tend to have indirect, but not direct, effects on attachment security.
   Answer: C
   Page Ref: 272
   Skill: Conceptual
   Objective: 7.11

86) Parents who _____ tend to have securely attached infants and to behave sensitively toward them.
   A) dismiss the importance of their early relationships
   B) discuss their childhoods with objectivity and balance
   C) report only positive childhood experiences
   D) describe their negative childhood experiences in angry, confused ways
   Answer: B
   Page Ref: 272
   Skill: Conceptual
   Objective: 7.11

87) Which of the following is true about the relationship between attachment security and infant child care?
   A) In the United States, the rate of insecurity is equal among child-care and non-child-care infants.
   B) Infants who experience daily separations from their employed parents are at risk for developmental problems.
   C) The relationship between child care and emotional well-being depends on both family and child-care experiences.
   D) All investigations report that babies in child care differ in attachment quality from those cared for solely by parents.
   Answer: C
   Page Ref: 273 Box: SI: Health: Does Child Care in Infancy Threaten Attachment Security and Later Adjustment?
   Skill: Conceptual
   Objective: 7.11

88) Research on the quality and extent of child care shows that
   A) most infants who are placed in full-time child care are insecurely attached.
   B) full-time, but not part-time, work during the first year is detrimental to attachment security.
   C) a history of higher-quality child care predicts poorer social skills.
   D) child care alone does not contribute to attachment insecurity.
   Answer: D
   Page Ref: 273 Box: SI: Health: Does Child Care in Infancy Threaten Attachment Security and Later Adjustment?
   Skill: Conceptual
   Objective: 7.11

89) Research on child care demonstrates that
   A) when caregiver–child ratios are generous and caregivers are educated about child development, children develop more favorably.
   B) the rate of insecurity is equivalent among infants in child care and those who stay at home with their mothers.
   C) mother–child interaction is not affected by the quality of child care or the time spent in child care.
   D) even children in high-quality child care have higher rates of insecurity than those who are informally cared for by friends, relatives, or babysitters.
Answer: A
Page Ref: 273 Box: SI: Health: Does Child Care in Infancy Threaten Attachment Security and Later Adjustment?
Skill: Conceptual
Objective: 7.11

90) When caring for their babies, mothers devote more time to _____ and fathers devote more time to _____.
   A) playful interactions; feeding and diaper changes
   B) feeding and diaper changes; emotional closeness
   C) playful interactions; emotional closeness
   D) physical care; playful interactions
Answer: D
Page Ref: 274
Skill: Conceptual
Objective: 7.12

91) Fathers
   A) are not as responsive as mothers to their infant's social needs.
   B) who provide sensitive caregiving and interactional synchrony with infants generally have more securely attached children.
   C) report feeling less anxiety than mothers about daily separations.
   D) more often than mothers provide toys and gently play conventional games with infants.
Answer: B
Page Ref: 274
Skill: Conceptual
Objective: 7.12

92) Of the following, which is supported by research on fathers?
   A) In the United States, Hispanic fathers spend more time engaged with their children compared to fathers in other ethnic groups.
   B) In dual-earner families, mothers and fathers devote equal time to caregiving.
   C) In the United States, high-SES fathers devote more time to their children than low-SES fathers.
   D) Fathers in Japan spend more time engaged in infant caregiving compared to fathers in the United States.
Answer: A
Page Ref: 274
Skill: Conceptual
Objective: 7.12

93) Highly involved fathers
   A) tend to lose their arousing play style as their children get older.
   B) tend to have fathers who were not involved in rearing them.
   C) are less gender-stereotyped in their beliefs than fathers who spend little time with their children.
   D) are warmer and more sensitive than working mothers.
Answer: C
Page Ref: 274
Skill: Conceptual
Objective: 7.12

94) Which of the following is a true statement about grandparents who are primary caregivers?
    A) Warm grandparent–grandchild bonds help protect children from worsening adjustment problems, even under conditions of great hardship.
    B) Less than 1 percent of the U.S. child population live apart from parents and with their grandparents.
    C) Grandparents in Caucasian families are more likely to serve as children's primary caregivers than grandparents in other ethnic groups.
    D) Grandparent caregivers rarely forge secure attachment relationships with grandchildren in their care.
Answer: A
Page Ref: 275
Skill: Conceptual
Objective: 7.12

95) Cross-cultural research demonstrates that
    A) fathers' warmth contributes greatly to children's long-term favorable development.
    B) fathers who devote little time to physical caregiving do not express parental warmth.
    C) mothers' and fathers' emotional interactions with each other and with their children are not linked.
    D) fathers' warmth cannot protect children against emotional and behavioral problems.
Answer: A
Page Ref: 276 Box: CI: The Powerful Role of Paternal Warmth in Development
Skill: Conceptual
Objective: 7.12

96) Research on the Aka of Central Africa reveals that a strong father–infant relationship is
    A) related to the strong division of male and female duties in the tribe.
    B) unrelated to the amount of time fathers spend near infants and toddlers.
    C) unrelated to the father's expressions of caring and affection.
    D) due in great part to an exceptionally cooperative and intimate marital relationship.
Answer: D
Page Ref: 276 Box: CI: The Powerful Role of Paternal Warmth in Development
Skill: Conceptual
Objective: 7.12

97) Today, about _____ percent of North American and European children grow up with at least one sibling.
    A) 85
    B) 80
    C) 75
    D) 70
Answer: B
Page Ref: 276
Skill: Conceptual
Objective: 7.12

98) Peer sociability is
    A) not present in the first two years.
    B) promoted by warm parental relationships.
    C) extremely delayed in only children.
    D) delayed in children who spend time in child care.
Answer: B
Page Ref: 278
Skill: Conceptual
Objective: 7.12

99) Mounting evidence indicates that _____ determines whether attachment security is linked to later development.
   A) child temperament
   B) heredity
   C) continuity of caregiving
   D) family size
Answer: C
Page Ref: 278
Skill: Conceptual
Objective: 7.13

100) Which of the following is true about attachment and later development?
   A) A child whose parental caregiving improves can bounce back from adversity.
   B) A child who experiences a secure attachment in infancy maintains that style, regardless of caregiving.
   C) By the end of early childhood, nearly 90 percent of U.S. children are securely attached to a caregiver.
   D) An insecure attachment in infancy almost always leads to severe behavior problems in childhood.
Answer: A
Page Ref: 278
Skill: Conceptual
Objective: 7.13

101) Newborn Uli displays a stronger rooting reflex in response to an adult's finger touching her cheek than to her own hand touching her cheek. This finding demonstrates that Uli has the beginnings of
   A) self-awareness.
   B) effortful control.
   C) an internal working model.
   D) emotional self-regulation.
Answer: A
Page Ref: 280
Skill: Applied
Objective: 7.14

102) Emmett, age 4 months, looks and smiles more at video images of others than video images of himself. This discrimination reflects an
   A) explicit sense of self–world differentiation.
   B) internal working model.
   C) implicit sense of self–world differentiation.
   D) external working model.
Answer: C
Page Ref: 280
Skill: Applied
Objective: 7.14

103) Which of the following children, when placed in front of a mirror, is the most likely to respond to the appearance of a red dot on his or her nose by touching or rubbing his or her nose?
   A) Reggie, a 10-month-old boy
   B) Benita, a 22-month-old girl
   C) Alan, a 14-month-old boy
   D) Swoosi, an 18-month-old girl
Answer: B
Page Ref: 280
Skill: Applied
Objective: 7.14

104) When asked to push a wagon while standing on a towel attached to its rear axle, 21-month-old Maximus figures out that if he removes himself from the towel, the wagon will move. Maximus is displaying
    A) effortful control.
    B) an implicit sense of self–world differentiation.
    C) a categorical self.
    D) an explicit body self-awareness.
Answer: D
Page Ref: 281
Skill: Applied
Objective: 7.14

105) Ahmed, age 2, gives his favorite stuffed toy to his little brother when his brother falls down and starts to cry. Ahmed is displaying
    A) an internal working model.
    B) empathy.
    C) a categorical self.
    D) social referencing.
Answer: B
Page Ref: 282
Skill: Applied
Objective: 7.14

106) Marnie, age 2, carries her plate to the sink and announces, "I big girl!" This statement demonstrates that Marnie is beginning to develop
    A) an internal working model.
    B) self-conscious emotions.
    C) a categorical self.
    D) empathy.
Answer: C
Page Ref: 282
Skill: Applied
Objective: 7.14

107) Dr. Kostelnik studies the early emergence of self-control by giving children a present and asking them to wait to open it until after she reads a story. Dr. Kostelnik is measuring
    A) delay of gratification.
    B) the categorical self.
    C) the internal working model.
    D) self–world differentiation.
Answer: A
Page Ref: 283
Skill: Applied
Objective: 7.14

ESSAY

108) Describe Erik Erikson's psychosocial theory as it applies to the development of infant and toddler personality.

Answer: Erikson accepted Freud's emphasis on the importance of the parent–infant relationship during feeding, but he expanded and enriched Freud's view. Erikson believed that a healthy outcome during infancy does not depend on the amount of food or oral stimulation offered but rather on the quality of caregiving. Many factors affect parental responsiveness—feelings of personal happiness, current life conditions, and culturally valued child-rearing practices. But when the balance of care is sympathetic and loving, the psychological conflict of the first year—basic trust versus mistrust—is resolved on the positive side.

The conflict of toddlerhood—autonomy versus shame and doubt—is resolved favorably when parents provide young children with suitable guidance and reasonable choices. In contrast, when parents are over- or undercontrolling, the outcome is a child who feels forced and shamed and who doubts his ability to control his impulses and act competently on his own.

In sum, basic trust and autonomy grow out of warm, sensitive parenting and reasonable expectations for impulse control starting in the second year. If children emerge from the first few years without sufficient trust in caregivers and without a healthy sense of individuality, the seeds are sown for adjustment problems.

Page Ref: 248–249

109) Describe the development of fear, noting the concepts of stranger anxiety and secure base.

Answer: Fear rises during the second half of the first year. The most frequent expression of fear is to unfamiliar adults, a response called stranger anxiety. Many infants and toddlers are quite wary of strangers, although the reaction does not always occur. It depends on several factors: temperament, past experiences with strangers, and the current situation. When an unfamiliar adult picks up the infant in a new situation, stranger anxiety is likely. But if the adult sits still while the baby moves around and a parent is nearby, infants often show positive and curious behavior. The stranger's style of interaction—expressing warmth, holding out an attractive toy, playing a familiar game, and approaching slowly rather than abruptly—reduces the baby's fear. Cross-cultural research reveals that infant-rearing practices can modify stranger anxiety.

The rise in fear after 6 months of age keeps newly mobile babies' enthusiasm for exploration in check. Once wariness develops, infants use the familiar caregiver as a secure base, or point from which to explore, venturing into the environment and then returning for emotional support. As part of this adaptive system, encounters with strangers lead to two conflicting tendencies: approach (indicated by interest and friendliness) and avoidance (indicated by fear). The infant's behavior is a balance between the two.

Page Ref: 252

110) Using Thomas and Chess's model of temperament, identify and describe the three categories of children. Do all children fit into one of these categories? Explain.

Answer: The easy child quickly establishes regular routines in infancy, is generally cheerful, and adapts easily to new experiences.

The difficult child is irregular in daily routines, is slow to accept new experiences, and tends to react negatively and intensely. The difficult child is at high risk for adjustment problems—both anxious withdrawal and aggressive behavior in early and middle childhood.

The slow-to-warm-up child is inactive, shows mild, low-key reactions to environmental stimuli, is negative in mood, and adjusts slowly to new experiences. Compared with the difficult child, the slow-to-warm-up child presents fewer problems in the early years. However, the slow-to-warm-up child tends to show excessive fearfulness and slow, constricted behavior in late preschool and school years, when they are expected to respond actively, and quickly in classrooms and peer groups.

Of the participants in Thomas and Chess's longitudinal study, 40 percent were identified as the easy child, 10 percent were identified as the difficult child, 15 percent were identified as the slow-to-warm-up child, and 35 percent did not fit any of the categories. Instead, they showed unique blends of temperamental characteristics.

Page Ref: 256–257

111) Describe how living in a family with siblings might have an influence on a child's temperament.

Answer: In families with several children, parents often look for differences between siblings. As a result, parents often regard siblings as more distinct than other observers do. In a large study of 1- to 3-year-old twin pairs, parents rated identical twins as resembling each other less in temperament than researchers' ratings indicated. And whereas researchers rated fraternal twins as moderately similar, parents viewed them as somewhat opposite in temperamental style. Parents' tendency to emphasize each child's unique qualities affects their child-rearing practices. Each child, in turn, evokes responses from caregivers that are consistent with parental beliefs and the child's developing temperament. Besides different experiences within the family, siblings have distinct experiences with teachers, peers, and others in their community that affect development. And in middle childhood and adolescence, they often seek ways to differ from one another. For all these reasons, both identical and fraternal twins tend to become increasingly dissimilar in personality with age.

Page Ref: 261–262

112) Describe the Attachment Q-Sort. Give some pros and cons of its use over the Strange Situation.

Answer: The Attachment Q-Sort measures attachment and is suitable for use with children between 1 and 4 years. The test depends on home observations. Either the parent or a highly trained observer sorts 90 behaviors—such as "Child greets mother with a big smile when she enters the room" and "Child uses mother's facial expressions as a good source of information when something looks risky or threatening"—into nine categories, ranging from "highly descriptive" to "not at all descriptive" of the child. Then a score, ranging from high to low in security, is computed. Because the Q-Sort taps a wider array of attachment-related behaviors than the Strange Situation, it may better reflect the parent–infant relationship in everyday life. However, the Q-Sort method is time-consuming, requiring a nonparent informant to spend several hours observing the child before sorting the descriptors, and it does not differentiate between types of insecurity. The Q-Sort responses of expert observers correspond well with babies' secure-base behavior in the Strange Situation, but parents' Q-Sorts do not. Parents of insecure children, especially, may have difficulty accurately reporting their child's attachment behaviors.

Page Ref: 267

113) Discuss the involvement of fathers as it relates to attachment security. How do mothers and fathers differ in their caregiving?

Answer: Fathers' sensitive caregiving and interactional synchrony with infants, like mothers', predict attachment security. When babies are not distressed, they approach, vocalize to, and smile equally often at both parents, who in turn are equally responsive to their infant's social bids. While an anxious, unhappy 1-year-old who is permitted to choose between the mother and the father as a source of comfort and security will usually choose the mother, this preference typically declines over the second year.

As infancy progresses, mothers and fathers in many cultures tend to interact differently with their babies: Mothers devote more time to physical care and expressing affection, fathers to playful interaction. Mothers and fathers also play differently. Mothers more often provide toys, talk to infants, and gently play conventional games like pat-a-cake and peekaboo. In contrast, fathers—especially with their infant sons—tend to engage in highly stimulating physical play with bursts of excitement and surprise that increase as play progresses. As long as fathers are also sensitive, this stimulating, startling play style helps babies regulate emotion in intensely arousing situations and may prepare them to venture confidently into active, unpredictable contexts, including novel physical environments and play with peers. Play is a vital context in which fathers build secure attachments.

Page Ref: 274–275, 276

114) Describe strategies that adults can use to help toddlers develop compliance and self-control.
Answer:
- *Respond to the toddler with sensitivity and encouragement.* Toddlers whose parents are sensitive and supportive at times actively resist, but they are also are more compliant and self-controlled.
- *Provide advance notice when the toddler must stop an enjoyable activity.* Toddlers find it more difficult to stop a pleasant activity that is already under way than to wait before engaging in a desired action.
- *Offer many prompts and reminders.* Toddlers' ability to remember and comply with rules is limited; they need continuous adult oversight and patient assistance.
- *Respond to self-controlled behavior with verbal and physical approval.* Praise and hugs reinforce appropriate behavior, increasing the likelihood that it will occur again.
- *Encourage selective and sustained attention.* Development of attention is related to self-control. Children who can shift attention from a captivating stimulus and focus on a less attractive alternative are better at controlling their impulses.
- *Support language development.* Early language development is related to self-control. In the second year, children begin to use language to remind themselves of adult expectations and to delay gratification.
- *Gradually increase rules in a manner consistent with the toddler's developing capacities.* As cognition and language improve, toddlers can follow more rules related to safety, respect for people and property, family routines, manners, and simple chores.

Page Ref: 283

CHAPTER 8
PHYSICAL DEVELOPMENT
IN EARLY CHILDHOOD

MULTIPLE CHOICE

1) The years from 2 to 6 are often called the _____ years.
   A) play
   B) growth
   C) beginning
   D) "me"
   Answer: A
   Page Ref: 289
   Skill: Factual
   Objective: 8.1

2) In early childhood, on average, children add _____ inches in height and about _____ pounds in weight each year.
   A) 1 to 2; 5
   B) 1 to 2; 10
   C) 2 to 3; 5
   D) 2 to 3; 10
   Answer: C
   Page Ref: 290
   Skill: Factual
   Objective: 8.1

3) During early childhood, boys _____ than girls.
   A) are less muscular
   B) are slightly larger
   C) have more body fat
   D) are much heavier
   Answer: B
   Page Ref: 290
   Skill: Factual
   Objective: 8.1

4) Growth norms
   A) for one population are not good standards for children elsewhere in the world.
   B) are very similar in every country of the world.
   C) vary from child to child in each population.
   D) are the best estimate of skeletal age.
   Answer: A
   Page Ref: 290
   Skill: Conceptual
   Objective: 8.1

5) _____ help(s) doctors measure skeletal age.
   A) Growth norms
   B) X-rays of epiphyses
   C) Height and weight
   D) Chronological age
   Answer: B
   Page Ref: 290
   Skill: Factual
   Objective: 8.1

6) _____ the appearance of permanent teeth in children.
   A) Overweight and obesity accelerate
   B) Poor dental hygiene in toddlerhood delays
   C) Prolonged malnutrition accelerates
   D) Excessive plaque on baby teeth delays
   Answer: A
   Page Ref: 290
   Skill: Factual
   Objective: 8.1

7) Between ages 2 and 6, the brain increases to _____ percent of its adult weight.
   A) 60
   B) 70
   C) 80
   D) 90
   Answer: D
   Page Ref: 291
   Skill: Factual
   Objective: 8.2

8) During early childhood,
   A) preschoolers show declines in sustained attention.
   B) the number of synapses in the prefrontal cortex is nearly double the adult value.
   C) energy metabolism in the cerebral cortex is at an all-time low.
   D) synaptic pruning decreases.
   Answer: B
   Page Ref: 292
   Skill: Factual
   Objective: 8.2

9) By age 4,
   A) many parts of the cerebral cortex have overproduced synapses.
   B) synaptic pruning is fully completed.
   C) preschoolers show declines in attention and focus.
   D) the brain is nearly half of its adult size.
   Answer: A
   Page Ref: 292
   Skill: Factual
   Objective: 8.2

10) An _____ during early childhood supports plasticity of the brain.
   A) underproduction of neurons
   B) underproduction of synapses
   C) overproduction of neurons
   D) overproduction of synapses
   Answer: D
   Page Ref: 292
   Skill: Factual
   Objective: 8.2

11) For most children,
   A) activity in the left hemisphere increases slowly throughout early and middle childhood.
   B) activity in the left hemisphere peaks between 1 and 3 years and decreases slowly.
   C) the left hemisphere shows a dramatic growth spurt between ages 3 and 6.
   D) activity in the right hemisphere increases dramatically between ages 2 and 6.
   Answer: C
   Page Ref: 293
   Skill: Conceptual
   Objective: 8.2

12) Which of the following skills develops at the fastest pace during early childhood?
   A) giving directions
   B) drawing pictures
   C) recognizing geometric shapes
   D) using language
   Answer: D
   Page Ref: 293
   Skill: Conceptual
   Objective: 8.2

13) Handedness
   A) reflects the greater capacity of one side of the brain to carry out skilled motor action.
   B) is evident in a wide range of skills from birth.
   C) is a heritable trait, especially for left-handed people.
   D) is strongest for simple, rather than complex, skills.
   Answer: A
   Page Ref: 293
   Skill: Conceptual
   Objective: 8.2

14) For the left-handed 10 percent of the population, language is
   A) always housed in the right hemisphere.
   B) always housed in the left hemisphere.
   C) most often housed in the right hemisphere.
   D) most often shared between the hemispheres.
   Answer: D
   Page Ref: 293
   Skill: Conceptual
   Objective: 8.2

15) Jim sometimes uses his right hand skillfully, but prefers his left hand. Jim
   A) is ambidextrous.
   B) has a strongly lateralized brain.
   C) is very likely to have left-handed children.
   D) probably had early damage to the left hemisphere.
Answer: A
Page Ref: 293
Skill: Applied
Objective: 8.2

16) Felicity and Samantha are identical twins. They are
   A) probably both right-handed.
   B) more likely than ordinary siblings to differ in handedness.
   C) probably both left-handed.
   D) less likely than fraternal twins to differ in handedness.
Answer: B
Page Ref: 293
Skill: Applied
Objective: 8.2

17) Growth and myelination of fibers linking the cerebellum to the cerebral cortex contributes to _____ in early childhood.
   A) a strong hand preference
   B) suppression of impulses in favor of thoughtful responses
   C) dramatic gains in motor coordination
   D) dramatic gains in spatial skills
Answer: C
Page Ref: 294
Skill: Conceptual
Objective: 8.2

18) Improvements in sustained, controlled attention are due to growth of the
   A) cerebellum.
   B) hippocampus.
   C) reticular formation.
   D) corpus callosum.
Answer: C
Page Ref: 294
Skill: Factual
Objective: 8.2

19) The _____ is sensitive to facial emotional expressions, especially fear.
   A) reticular formation
   B) amygdala
   C) hippocampus
   D) corpus callosum
Answer: B
Page Ref: 295
Skill: Factual
Objective: 8.2

20) Which of the following statements is supported by research on lead exposure during childhood?
    A) Overall, poorer mental test scores associated with lead exposure persist over time and seem permanent.
    B) Lead-exposed children given drugs to induce excretion of lead improve in long-term outcomes.
    C) Once lead-exposed children move away from contaminated areas, their mental test scores increase.
    D) Negative lead-related cognitive consequences are evident only at high levels of exposure.
    Answer: A
    Page Ref: 296 Box: B&E: Low-Level Lead Exposure and Children's Development
    Skill: Conceptual
    Objective: 8.2

21) Research on lead exposure during childhood reveals that
    A) middle-SES children are the most likely group to experience lead exposure.
    B) use of iron supplements increases lead concentration in the blood.
    C) exposed children absorb more lead when their diets contain zinc.
    D) a stressed, disorganized home life can heighten lead-induced damage.
    Answer: D
    Page Ref: 296 Box: B&E: Low-Level Lead Exposure and Children's Development
    Skill: Conceptual
    Objective: 8.2

22) The _____ plays a critical role in the rate of physical growth.
    A) pituitary gland
    B) hippocampus
    C) reticular formation
    D) corpus callosum
    Answer: A
    Page Ref: 297
    Skill: Factual
    Objective: 8.3

23) Growth hormone (GH)
    A) prompts the thyroid gland in the neck to release thyroxine, which is necessary for brain development.
    B) stimulates the liver and epiphyses of the skeleton to release insulin-like growth factor 1, which triggers cell duplication throughout the body.
    C) contributes to rapid physical growth in boys, whereas thyroid-stimulating hormone contributes to physical development in girls.
    D) is necessary during the prenatal period for development of the brain and spinal cord.
    Answer: B
    Page Ref: 297
    Skill: Factual
    Objective: 8.3

24) Thyroid-stimulating hormone (TSH) is necessary for
    A) brain development.
    B) prenatal development of the skeleton.
    C) short, normal-GH children to grow to average heights.
    D) secretion of IGF-1.
    Answer: A
    Page Ref: 297
    Skill: Factual
    Objective: 8.3

25) Dmitri, age 5, is very short in stature, shows decreased GH secretion, has an immature skeletal age, and has serious adjustment problems. Dmitri probably has
   A) a vitamin C deficiency.
   B) a thyroxine deficiency.
   C) psychosocial dwarfism.
   D) an iron deficiency.
   Answer: C
   Page Ref: 297
   Skill: Applied
   Objective: 8.4

26) When young children with psychosocial dwarfism are removed from their emotionally inadequate environments,
   A) their dwarfism is permanent, even with immediate treatment.
   B) they rarely exhibit catch-up growth.
   C) they must be given high levels of iron to prevent anemia.
   D) their GH levels quickly return to normal and they grow rapidly.
   Answer: D
   Page Ref: 297
   Skill: Conceptual
   Objective: 8.4

27) Sleep contributes to body growth because
   A) GH is released during the child's sleeping hours.
   B) rest allows the awake body to produce GH at higher levels.
   C) rest allows the awake body to produce TSH at higher levels.
   D) REM sleep heightens the impact of environmental events.
   Answer: A
   Page Ref: 298
   Skill: Conceptual
   Objective: 8.5

28) On average, 2- and 3-year-olds sleep _____ hours per day, while 4- to 6-year-olds sleep _____ hours.
   A) 10 to 11; 11 to 12
   B) 11 to 12; 10 to 11
   C) 11 to 12; 13 to 14
   D) 13 to 14; 11 to 12
   Answer: B
   Page Ref: 298
   Skill: Factual
   Objective: 8.5

29) Research on sleep demonstrates that
   A) most American parents cosleep with their children into the preschool years.
   B) sleepwalking in early childhood often signals a severe neurological problem.
   C) parent–child cosleeping is associated with sleep disorders during the preschool years.
   D) sleep terrors can be triggered by stress or extreme fatigue.
   Answer: D
   Page Ref: 299
   Skill: Conceptual
   Objective: 8.5

30) Which of the following statements is true about appetite in early childhood?
  A) Preschoolers' appetites increase because their growth is at an all-time high.
  B) Parents should be concerned if their preschooler varies the amount eaten from meal to meal.
  C) Preschoolers' wariness of new foods is normal and adaptive.
  D) Because preschoolers have smaller appetites, they need a different quality of food than adults need.
  Answer: C
  Page Ref: 299
  Skill: Conceptual
  Objective: 8.6

31) During the preschool years,
  A) children usually eat the same amount of food during each meal.
  B) the social environment powerfully influences food preferences.
  C) it is common for children's appetite to increase.
  D) children can tolerate more fats, oils, and salt.
  Answer: B
  Page Ref: 300
  Skill: Conceptual
  Objective: 8.6

32) Brianna, age 4, eats only pasta, bread, and chicken. Which of the following would you suggest to Brianna's parents to encourage their daughter to eat new foods?
  A) Serve her only new foods so that she has no other choices.
  B) Repeatedly expose her to new foods without any direct pressure to eat them.
  C) Add sugar or butter to new foods and offer dessert if she eats them.
  D) Refuse to serve pasta until she tries at least one new food.
  Answer: B
  Page Ref: 300
  Skill: Applied
  Objective: 8.6

33) Which of the following statements is supported by research on nutrition?
  A) Restricting access to tasty foods is an effective way to get young children to eat healthy foods.
  B) Adding salt or sugar is an easy way to get children to eat healthy foods.
  C) Children who are routinely offered sweet fruit or soft drinks may develop "milk avoidance."
  D) Offering bribes is an effective way to get preschoolers to eat healthy foods.
  Answer: C
  Page Ref: 300
  Skill: Conceptual
  Objective: 8.6

34) Sophia's parents will not allow her to eat any sugary foods. This practice usually
  A) prompts children to eat more healthy foods.
  B) has no effect on children's eating behavior.
  C) focuses children's attention on sugary foods.
  D) decreases children's desire to eat sugary foods.
  Answer: C
  Page Ref: 300
  Skill: Applied
  Objective: 8.6

35) By the school years, low-SES children in the United States are, on the average,
   A) no different in size than their middle-SES agemates.
   B) less likely than middle-SES children to have dietary deficiencies.
   C) much more likely to be overweight than middle-SES children.
   D) about ½ to 1 inch shorter than their economically advantaged counterparts.
Answer: D
Page Ref: 300
Skill: Factual
Objective: 8.6

36) Infectious diseases like measles
   A) do not occur until after age 3 throughout the world.
   B) occur at about the same rate in all countries.
   C) have been eradicated through mass immunization.
   D) occur much earlier in developing countries than in industrialized nations.
Answer: D
Page Ref: 301
Skill: Conceptual
Objective: 8.7

37) Poor diet
   A) is not a major contributor to susceptibility to childhood diseases.
   B) is usually unrelated to childhood disease.
   C) depresses the body's immune system, making children more susceptible to disease.
   D) can cause childhood diseases like measles and chicken pox.
Answer: C
Page Ref: 301
Skill: Conceptual
Objective: 8.7

38) Of the 10 million annual deaths of children under age 5 worldwide, ___ percent are due to infectious disease.
   A) 10
   B) 25
   C) 70
   D) 98
Answer: C
Page Ref: 301
Skill: Factual
Objective: 8.7

39) In developing countries,
   A) vaccines weaken the immune system and children's susceptibility to disease.
   B) most childhood deaths due to diarrhea can be prevented with nearly cost-free oral rehydration therapy.
   C) most children receive government-funded immunizations.
   D) widespread diarrhea leads to growth stunting but rarely to death.
Answer: B
Page Ref: 302
Skill: Conceptual
Objective: 8.7

40) Oral rehydration therapy and zinc supplements
    A) are effective for children with severe diarrhea, but they are expensive to administer.
    B) must be administered by trained medical professionals or public health workers.
    C) save the lives of millions of children each year.
    D) are less effective than immunization in preventing childhood deaths due to diarrhea.
Answer: C
Page Ref: 302
Skill: Conceptual
Objective: 8.7

41) About _____ percent of U.S. preschoolers are not fully immunized.
    A) 7
    B) 18
    C) 24
    D) 32
Answer: C
Page Ref: 302
Skill: Factual
Objective: 8.7

42) Which of the following is a true statement concerning childhood immunizations?
    A) The United States is ahead of Denmark, Norway, Great Britain, Canada, and Sweden in immunization rates.
    B) Childhood immunization rates in the United States lag behind many other industrialized nations because many U.S. children do not have access to adequate health care.
    C) Nearly 100 percent of U.S. children who receive a complete schedule of vaccinations in the first two years continue to receive the immunizations they need until school entry.
    D) Disease outbreaks of whooping cough and rubella have not occurred in the United States since the development of vaccines for these diseases.
Answer: B
Page Ref: 302
Skill: Conceptual
Objective: 8.7

43) Which of the following children is the most likely to lack immunizations?
    A) Sam from the United States
    B) Kristen from Canada
    C) Nigel from Great Britain
    D) Elsa from Sweden
Answer: A
Page Ref: 302
Skill: Applied
Objective: 8.7

44) One of the greatest immediate benefits of the U.S. Health-Care Reform Act is that
    A) all employers are required to provide affordable coverage to all workers.
    B) Medicaid will no longer be necessary for low-income families.
    C) government-sponsored health care will be provided free of charge for all families.
    D) insurance companies cannot deny coverage because of preexisting conditions.
Answer: D
Page Ref: 303 Box: CI: Child Health Care in the United States and Other Western Nations
Skill: Conceptual
Objective: 8.7

45) In the United States,
    A) the Health-Care Reform Act will ensure insurance coverage for all U.S. children.
    B) children can receive free medical examinations from birth through adolescence.
    C) about 7.3 million children do not have health insurance.
    D) businesses are required by the Health-Care Reform Act to offer health insurance to their employees.
Answer: C
Page Ref: 303 Box: CI: Child Health Care in the United States and Other Western Nations
Skill: Conceptual
Objective: 8.7

46) In the United States, under the Children's Health Insurance Program (CHIP),
    A) state control over program implementation enables each state to adapt insurance coverage to meet its unique needs.
    B) employers are required to provide paid leave for employees with a seriously ill child.
    C) the states are mandated to provide free routine medical visits for all uninsured children.
    D) well-child checkups include parental counseling in nutrition, disease prevention, and child development.
Answer: A
Page Ref: 303 Box: CI: Child Health Care in the United States and Other Western Nations
Skill: Conceptual
Objective: 8.7

47) Of the following, which is true in the United States?
    A) Under the Children's Health Insurance Program (CHIP), every uninsured child receives free medical examinations.
    B) Because of low insurance-reimbursement rates, many doctors refuse to take public-aid patients.
    C) Federal law requires that health checkups occur three times during the first year of life.
    D) Affordable health care is available to all parents of young children.
Answer: B
Page Ref: 303 Box: CI: Child Health Care in the United States and Other Western Nations
Skill: Conceptual
Objective: 8.7

48) Three-year-old Billy caught five colds during his first year in preschool. He also experiences repeated otitis media. If Billy is like other children with frequent otitis media, he may have trouble
    A) attending to others' speech.
    B) falling and staying asleep.
    C) mastering large motor skills, such as running and climbing.
    D) identifying the letters of the alphabet.
Answer: A
Page Ref: 304 Box: SI: Health: Otitis Media and Development
Skill: Applied
Objective: 8.7

49) Which of the following is true about otitis media?
    A) The insertion of plastic tubes that drain the Eustachian tubes is an ineffective treatment for otitis media.
    B) Otitis media occurs less often in children who attend child-care centers than in those who do not.
    C) Only about 20 percent of U.S. children have experienced a bout of otitis media.
    D) The incidence of otitis media is greatest between 6 months and 3 years.
Answer: D
Page Ref: 304 Box: SI: Health: Otitis Media and Development
Skill: Conceptual
Objective: 8.7

50) In the United States, nearly _____ percent of childhood deaths are due to injury.
  A) 5
  B) 10
  C) 25
  D) 35
Answer: D
Page Ref: 305
Skill: Factual
Objective: 8.8

51) In the United States, _____ are the most frequent source of injury across all ages, ranking as the leading cause of death among children more than 1 year old.
  A) birth traumas
  B) infectious diseases
  C) falls
  D) motor vehicle collisions
Answer: D
Page Ref: 305
Skill: Factual
Objective: 8.8

52) Childhood injuries
  A) are typically accidental and usually cannot be prevented.
  B) occur within a complex ecological system and can often be prevented.
  C) rank second only to cancer as a cause of childhood mortality in industrialized nations.
  D) are less common in the United States than in other industrialized nations.
Answer: B
Page Ref: 305
Skill: Conceptual
Objective: 8.8

53) _____ are at greater risk for injury than _____.
  A) Girls; boys
  B) Children with easy temperaments; irritable children
  C) Middle-SES children; low-SES children
  D) Economically advantaged U.S. children; children in Western Europe
Answer: D
Page Ref: 306
Skill: Factual
Objective: 8.8

54) Which of the following is a true statement about preventing childhood injury?
  A) During the past 30 years, parents have changed a great deal in the amount they do to protect their children from injury.
  B) In the United States, more than 80 percent of infant seats and 40 percent of child booster seats are improperly used.
  C) In the United States, about 15 percent of parents fail to place their children in car safety seats.
  D) Young children properly restrained in car safety seats have a 50 percent reduced risk of fatal injury.
Answer: B
Page Ref: 306
Skill: Conceptual
Objective: 8.8

55) Of the following, which is supported by research on injury prevention?
  A) American parents seem willing to ignore familiar safety practices, perhaps because they value individual rights and personal freedom.
  B) Parents rarely rely on children's knowledge of safety rules, rather than monitoring and controlling access to hazards.
  C) Older preschoolers spontaneously recall about 85 percent of the safety rules their parents teach them.
  D) Compared to other forms of child rearing, authoritarian parenting is linked to low overall rates of childhood injury.
Answer: A
Page Ref: 306
Skill: Conceptual
Objective: 8.8

56) Children should be in a properly installed car safety seat up to age _____ or until the child is 4 feet 9 inches tall.
  A) 4
  B) 6
  C) 8
  D) 10
Answer: C
Page Ref: 307
Skill: Factual
Objective: 8.8

57) Between the ages of 2 and 3 years, most children learn how to
  A) push a riding toy with their feet.
  B) use a knife to cut soft foods.
  C) tie their shoes.
  D) pedal and steer a tricycle.
Answer: A
Page Ref: 308
Skill: Factual
Objective: 8.9

58) Caitlyn, age 4, can probably
  A) tie her shoes.
  B) ride a bicycle with training wheels.
  C) draw a person with six parts.
  D) use scissors.
Answer: D
Page Ref: 309
Skill: Applied
Objective: 8.9

59) Harvey, age 3, can probably
  A) gallop and skip with one foot.
  B) copy some numbers and simple words.
  C) zip and unzip large zippers.
  D) ride a bicycle with training wheels.
Answer: C
Page Ref: 309
Skill: Applied
Objective: 8.9

60) Five- and 6-year-olds
   A) engage in true skipping.
   B) throw and catch with a rigid upper body.
   C) draw people using a tadpole image.
   D) catch a ball against their chest.
   Answer: A
   Page Ref: 309
   Skill: Factual
   Objective: 8.9

61) To parents, fine-motor progress in early childhood is most apparent in which two areas?
   A) reaching and grasping; independent movement
   B) self-help skills; drawing and painting
   C) writing; running
   D) intermodal perception; independent movement
   Answer: B
   Page Ref: 309
   Skill: Conceptual
   Objective: 8.9

62) Which of the following is a true statement about self-help skills?
   A) While young preschoolers can use a spoon well, they cannot serve themselves at mealtimes.
   B) The use of child-sized eating utensils is unnecessary and inhibits fine-motor progress.
   C) Between ages 4 and 5, children can dress and undress without supervision.
   D) Shoe-tying skills are typically mastered in early preschool.
   Answer: C
   Page Ref: 309
   Skill: Conceptual
   Objective: 8.9

63) Children first represent objects and events on paper by
   A) drawing only the boundaries of objects.
   B) drawing recognizable shapes.
   C) making gestures that leave marks.
   D) drawing stick figures.
   Answer: C
   Page Ref: 310
   Skill: Conceptual
   Objective: 8.9

64) When adults draw with children and point out resemblances between drawings and objects,
   A) they stifle children's self-expression.
   B) preschoolers' pictures become simpler so the adult can recognize items.
   C) preschoolers' pictures become more detailed and comprehensible.
   D) they interfere with the natural progression of childhood drawing.
   Answer: C
   Page Ref: 310
   Skill: Conceptual
   Objective: 8.9

65) Anya, age 4, is asked to draw a picture of a person. She will probably
    A) draw a body, a head, and arms and legs, and add features such as eyes and hair.
    B) make the universal tadpole-like shape or some other primitive drawing.
    C) draw a large head with facial features but no body.
    D) use depth cues, such as overlapping objects, in the background.
Answer: A
Page Ref: 310
Skill: Applied
Objective: 8.9

66) Jesi, age 3, is asked to draw a cylinder. Based on her age, she will probably draw
    A) nothing.
    B) nonrepresentational scribbles.
    C) a circle, an oval, or a rectangle.
    D) two circles and some lines.
Answer: C
Page Ref: 311
Skill: Applied
Objective: 8.9

67) In cultures with little art,
    A) children nonetheless create elaborate drawings.
    B) children still draw the universal tadpole to represent a person.
    C) the first drawings of the human figure typically emphasize the head and face over the hands and feet.
    D) even older children and adolescents produce simple forms.
Answer: D
Page Ref: 311
Skill: Conceptual
Objective: 8.9

68) Around age _____, children's writing shows some distinctive features of print, such as separate forms arranged in a line on the page.
    A) 18 months
    B) 2
    C) 3
    D) 4
Answer: D
Page Ref: 312
Skill: Factual
Objective: 8.9

69) Most 3-year-olds
    A) use an adult grip pattern to hold a pencil.
    B) vary their pencil grip, depending on the location of marks they are trying to make.
    C) use a constant pencil angle across a range of drawing and writing.
    D) grip pencils indiscriminately in either their left or right hand.
Answer: B
Page Ref: 312
Skill: Conceptual
Objective: 8.9

70) Girls
    A) run slightly faster than boys.
    B) can jump farther than boys.
    C) are ahead of boys in skills that emphasize force.
    D) are ahead of boys in drawing skills.
Answer: D
Page Ref: 313
Skill: Conceptual
Objective: 8.10

71) Which of the following statements is supported by research on sex differences in motor skills?
    A) Parents tend to foster sex-stereotypic physical activities in their children.
    B) Sex differences in motor skills are largely due to genetically based differences.
    C) Differences in physical capacity between boys and girls increase rapidly, beginning in infancy.
    D) Boys and girls are usually channeled into similar physical activities.
Answer: A
Page Ref: 313
Skill: Conceptual
Objective: 8.10

72) Direct instruction in which of the following activities is most likely to accelerate gross-motor development in early childhood?
    A) throwing
    B) running
    C) dancing
    D) tumbling
Answer: A
Page Ref: 313
Skill: Conceptual
Objective: 8.10

73) Studies of motor development in early childhood show that
    A) adult involvement in children's motor development should focus on perfecting the "correct" technique.
    B) children need direct instruction to master most gross- and fine-motor skills.
    C) playgrounds must offer a range of equipment to meet the diverse needs of individual children.
    D) daily routines, such as pouring juice and dressing, support fine- but not gross-motor skills.
Answer: C
Page Ref: 313
Skill: Conceptual
Objective: 8.10

ESSAY

74) Discuss the use of synthetic growth hormone (GH) to treat short, normal-GH children.
    Answer: The availability of synthetic GH has made it possible to treat short, normal-GH children with hormone injections, in hopes of increasing their final height. Thousand of parents, concerned with the social stigma of shortness, have sought this GH therapy. But most normal-GH children given GH treatment grow only slightly taller than their previously predicted mature height. And contrary to popular belief, normal-GH short children are not deficient in self-esteem. So, little justification exists for medically intervening in short stature that is merely the result of biologically normal human diversity.
Page Ref: 297

75) Discuss how sleep habits contribute to body growth in children, and explain how disrupted sleep affects cognitive functioning.

Answer: Sleep contributes to body growth because GH is released during the child's sleeping hours. A well-rested child is better able to play, learn, and contribute positively to family functioning. Sleep difficulties are associated with impaired cognitive performance. The impact of disrupted sleep on cognitive functioning is more pronounced for low-SES children. Perhaps insufficient sleep heightens the impact of other environmental stressors prevalent in their daily lives. Also, children who sleep poorly disturb their parents' sleep, which can generate family stress.

Page Ref: 298

76) Describe strategies for preventing early otitis media.

Answer: *Frequent screening for disease, followed by prompt medical intervention.* Plastic tubes that drain the narrow Eustachian tubes of the middle ear are often used to treat chronic otitis media in children, although their effectiveness has been disputed.

Child-care settings that control infection. Because infants and young children often put toys in their mouths, these objects should be rinsed frequently with a disinfectant. Pacifier use has also been linked to greater risk of otitis media. Spacious, well-ventilated rooms and small group sizes help limit the spread of the disease.

Verbally stimulating adult–child interaction. Developmental problems associated with otitis media are reduced or eliminated in high-quality child-care centers. When caregivers are verbally stimulating and keep noise to a minimum, children have more opportunities to hear, and benefit from, spoken language.

Vaccines. Researchers have developed several vaccines that seem to prevent otitis media. But more evidence is needed before they can be made widely available.

Page Ref: 304

77) Discuss how motor vehicle use relates to childhood injuries. What are some ways to minimize unintentional injuries during automobile travel?

Answer: Auto and traffic accidents are by far the most frequent source of injury across all ages, ranking as the leading cause of death among children more than 1 year old. Communities can help by modifying their physical environments. Providing inexpensive and widely available public transportation can reduce the amount of time that children spend in cars. Further, parents can use age-appropriate, properly installed car safety seats or booster seats up to age 8 or until the child is 4 feet 9 inches tall, and strap the child in correctly every time. Twenty-seven percent of U.S. parents fail to place their children in car safety seats, and 84 percent of infant seats and 41 percent of child booster seats are improperly used. Yet research confirms that young children properly restrained in car safety seats have an 80 percent reduced risk of fatal injury. Children should always ride in the back seat because passenger-side air bags in the front seat deploy so forcefully that they can cause injury or death of a child. Finally, children should never be left alone in a car, even on a cool sunny day. A child's core body temperature increases 3 to 5 times faster than an adult's, with the risk of permanent injury or death.

Page Ref: 305–306

78) Describe the development of drawing in children in Western nations.

Answer: Western children begin to draw during the second year. At first, children's scribbles illustrate action rather than the intended representation. For example, a series of dots may represent a rabbit's hopping. By age 3, children begin to represent objects in their drawings. Often this happens after they make a gesture with a crayon, notice that they have drawn a recognizable shape, and then decide to label it. By age 3 or 4, children reach a major milestone in drawing when they begin to use lines to represent the boundaries of objects. This permits children to draw their first image of a person, which universally resembles a tadpole image. Four-year-olds begin to add features, such as eyes, ears, hair, and fingers, to their tadpole images. Five- and 6-year olds create more complex drawings, containing more conventional human and animal figures, with the head and body differentiated. Older preschoolers' drawings still contain perceptual distortions because they have just begun to represent depth. Use of depth cues, such as overlapping objects, smaller size for distant than for near objects, diagonal placement, and converging lines, increases during middle childhood. As children's cognitive and fine-motor skills improve, they desire greater realism in their illustrations and create more complex drawings. Greater realism improves gradually. Three- to 7-year-olds draw a single unit to stand for an object. During the late preschool and school years, they represent salient object parts. Older school-age children integrate object parts into a realistic whole.

Page Ref: 309–311

CHAPTER 9
COGNITIVE DEVELOPMENT IN EARLY CHILDHOOD

MULTIPLE CHOICE

1) According to Piaget, the most obvious change during the preoperational stage is the increase in
   A) language ability.
   B) problem-solving skills.
   C) logical thought.
   D) representational activity.
   Answer: D
   Page Ref: 318
   Skill: Conceptual
   Objective: 9.1

2) Piaget acknowledged that _____ is our most flexible means of mental representation.
   A) imagery
   B) language
   C) intentional behavior
   D) deferred imitation
   Answer: B
   Page Ref: 318
   Skill: Conceptual
   Objective: 9.1

3) Piaget believed that through _____, young children practice and strengthen newly acquired representational schemes.
   A) logical reasoning
   B) language acquisition
   C) pretending
   D) physical activity
   Answer: C
   Page Ref: 318
   Skill: Conceptual
   Objective: 9.1

4) Tripp pretends to drink from a toy cup. Tripp's sister, Anna, takes the same cup and tells Tripp, "This is a hat." Tripp refuses to place the cup on his head to pretend that it is a hat. Tripp is probably
   A) younger than 2 years of age.
   B) at least 4 years old.
   C) less than 1 year of age.
   D) at least 6 years old.
   Answer: A
   Page Ref: 319
   Skill: Applied
   Objective: 9.1

5) In early pretending, toddlers
   A) direct pretend objects toward others.
   B) are detached participants.
   C) combine schemes without those of their peers.
   D) use only realistic objects.
   Answer: D
   Page Ref: 319
   Skill: Conceptual
   Objective: 9.1

6) Make-believe _____ as children realize that agents and recipients of pretend actions can be independent of themselves.
   A) attaches to the real-life conditions associated with it
   B) becomes less self-centered
   C) includes less complex combinations of schemes
   D) becomes more self-directed
   Answer: B
   Page Ref: 319
   Skill: Conceptual
   Objective: 9.1

7) Five-year-old Matthew and 6-year-old Jessica like to pretend that they live or work in a zoo. Often, Matthew will pretend to be an animal, such as an elephant and Jessica will pretend to be the zookeeper. This is an example of _____ play.
   A) parallel
   B) associative
   C) sociodramatic
   D) functional
   Answer: C
   Page Ref: 319
   Skill: Applied
   Objective: 9.1

8) Preschoolers who spend more time in sociodramatic play are seen as _____ by their teachers.
   A) more cognitively competent
   B) more socially competent
   C) less creative
   D) less verbal
   Answer: B
   Page Ref: 319
   Skill: Conceptual
   Objective: 9.1

9) Children's creation of _____ was once viewed as a sign of maladjustment, but current research challenges this assumption.
   A) imaginary companions
   B) dual representations
   C) animalistic symbols
   D) pretend themes
   Answer: A
   Page Ref: 319
   Skill: Factual
   Objective: 9.1

10) Twenty-month-old Hyrum attempts to sit in a tiny doll chair. Difficulty with _____ may contribute to Hyrum's scale error.
   A) cardinality
   B) dual representation
   C) conservation
   D) centration
   Answer: B
   Page Ref: 320
   Skill: Applied
   Objective: 9.1

11) According to Piaget, young children's thinking often is illogical because they are not capable of
   A) magical thinking.
   B) animistic thinking.
   C) mental actions that obey logical rules.
   D) centration.
   Answer: C
   Page Ref: 321
   Skill: Factual
   Objective: 9.2

12) For Piaget, the most fundamental deficiency of preoperational thinking is
   A) dual representation.
   B) egocentrism.
   C) animistic thinking.
   D) centration.
   Answer: B
   Page Ref: 321
   Skill: Factual
   Objective: 9.2

13) Four-year-old Marly is playing with her toy cars. She favors the blue car, but plays with the green car for at least a few minutes. She says, "I don't want the green one to get lonely." This is an example of
   A) dual representation.
   B) egocentrism.
   C) animistic thinking.
   D) centration.
   Answer: C
   Page Ref: 321
   Skill: Applied
   Objective: 9.2

14) Three-year-olds Artie and Kurt had identical boxes of raisins at snack time. When Kurt poured his raisins out onto the table, Artie was sure that Kurt had more raisins. This demonstrates that Artie lacks
   A) conservation.
   B) animistic thinking.
   C) hierarchical classification.
   D) dual representation.
   Answer: A
   Page Ref: 321
   Skill: Applied
   Objective: 9.2

15) Three-year-old Rachael could not solve a conservation-of-liquid task because she focused on the height of the water. Rachael's thinking is characterized by
    A) dynamic transformation.
    B) irreversibility.
    C) hierarchical classification.
    D) centration.
Answer: D
Page Ref: 322
Skill: Applied
Objective: 9.2

16) The most important illogical feature of preoperational thought is its
    A) dynamic transformation.
    B) irreversibility.
    C) class inclusion.
    D) reversibility.
Answer: B
Page Ref: 322
Skill: Conceptual
Objective: 9.2

17) During a conservation-of-liquid task, when asked why he thinks there is more water in the taller glass, 5-year-old Gus points out that the water level is higher in the taller glass than in the shorter glass but neglects to mention that this change in height is compensated by changes in width. This example demonstrates a limitation of preoperational thought known as
    A) centration.
    B) seriation.
    C) transductive reasoning.
    D) irreversibility.
Answer: A
Page Ref: 322
Skill: Applied
Objective: 9.2

18) In a conservation-of-liquid problem, young children ignore the dynamic transformation of the liquid when they
    A) center on the height of the liquid and ignore the width.
    B) treat the initial and final stages of the water as unrelated events.
    C) become distracted by the perceptual appearance of objects.
    D) mentally reverse direction, returning to the starting point.
Answer: B
Page Ref: 322
Skill: Conceptual
Objective: 9.2

19) During a _____ task, 4-year-old Marissa is asked whether there are more oranges or fruits in a group of two apples, one banana, and three oranges. She will most likely say _____.
    A) class inclusion; there are more fruits
    B) class inclusion; there are more oranges
    C) conservation-of-number; there are more fruits
    D) conservation-of-number; there are more oranges
Answer: B
Page Ref: 322
Skill: Applied
Objective: 9.2

20) Four-year-old Martha uses shorter, simpler expressions when interacting with her 2-year-old brother. This example suggests that Piaget may have
    A) overestimated preschoolers' animistic thinking.
    B) overestimated preschoolers' egocentrism.
    C) underestimated preschoolers' animistic thinking.
    D) underestimated preschoolers' egocentrism.
Answer: B
Page Ref: 323
Skill: Applied
Objective: 9.3

21) Four-year-old Matthew is shown a robot. Matthew is most likely to say that the robot cannot
    A) see.
    B) think.
    C) grow.
    D) remember.
Answer: C
Page Ref: 323
Skill: Applied
Objective: 9.3

22) Most 3- and 4-year-olds
    A) think that violations of social conventions require magic.
    B) understand that television characters are not real.
    C) believe in the supernatural powers of enchanted creatures.
    D) know that imagination cannot create reality.
Answer: C
Page Ref: 323
Skill: Conceptual
Objective: 9.3

23) Which of the following children is the most likely to express disbelief in the Tooth Fairy?
    A) Jacob, a 6-year-old Jewish boy
    B) Frank, a 6-year-old Catholic boy
    C) Luke, a 6-year-old Methodist boy
    D) Glenn, a 6-year-old Baptist boy
Answer: A
Page Ref: 324
Skill: Applied
Objective: 9.3

24) Follow-up research on preoperational thought indicates that preschoolers can successfully solve a conservation-of-number task when the task
    A) includes only three items rather than six or seven.
    B) deals with everyday objects, such as balls or dolls, rather than abstract concepts.
    C) is performed by their parents rather than unfamiliar experimenters.
    D) is performed with their own toys rather than unfamiliar objects.
Answer: A
Page Ref: 324
Skill: Conceptual
Objective: 9.3

25) Preschoolers' ability to reason about transformations is evident on
    A) conservation tasks.
    B) tasks that require reasoning by analogy.
    C) class inclusion problems.
    D) hierarchical classification tasks.
Answer: B
Page Ref: 324
Skill: Conceptual
Objective: 9.3

26) Three-year-old Audrey is presented with a picture-matching problem, "Play dough is to cut-up play dough as a loaf of bread is to . . . ?" Which answer is Audrey is most likely to select?
    A) a cut-up apple
    B) a biscuit
    C) bread crumbs
    D) a cut-up loaf of bread
Answer: D
Page Ref: 324
Skill: Applied
Objective: 9.3

27) Follow-up research indicates that by the second half of the first year, children have formed a variety of global categories, such as animals and vehicles. These findings challenge Piaget's assumption that
    A) preschoolers' thinking is wholly governed by appearances.
    B) the emergence of language brings about representational ability.
    C) preschoolers have difficulty distinguishing fantasy from reality.
    D) transitive inference emerges during the concrete operational stage.
Answer: A
Page Ref: 325
Skill: Conceptual
Objective: 9.3

28) Which of the following is most likely to be among a child's first categories?
    A) waterbirds
    B) landbirds
    C) flying creatures
    D) birds
Answer: D
Page Ref: 325
Skill: Conceptual
Objective: 9.3

29) When young children converse with adults, they ask
    A) mostly non-information-seeking questions.
    B) more than one question per minute, on average.
    C) comparatively few information-seeking questions.
    D) relatively few purposeful questions.
Answer: B
Page Ref: 326 Box: SI: Children's Questions: Catalyst for Cognitive Development
Skill: Factual
Objective: 9.3

30) By age 3½, _____ questions make up about half of children's questions.
   A) object-naming
   B) non-information-seeking
   C) building
   D) rhetorical
   Answer: C
   Page Ref: 326 Box: SI: Children's Questions: Catalyst for Cognitive Development
   Skill: Conceptual
   Objective: 9.3

31) Which of the following is true about children's questions?
   A) With age, preschoolers increasingly ask about function, activity, state, and theory of mind.
   B) At every age between 1 and 5 years, non-information-seeking questions are more often used than information-seeking questions.
   C) Children do not begin asking questions until they have the vocabulary to formulate sentences.
   D) Inquisitive children are more often merely clamoring for attention than seeking real answers to their questions.
   Answer: A
   Page Ref: 326 Box: SI: Children's Questions: Catalyst for Cognitive Development
   Skill: Conceptual
   Objective: 9.3

32) Which of the following is true about parents' answers to their children's questions?
   A) When parents do not respond informatively, most preschoolers abandon their questions.
   B) Parents adjust the complexity of their answers to fit their children's maturity.
   C) Parents rarely include additional relevant knowledge when answering their children's questions.
   D) Older children frequently get "prior cause" explanations, while younger children typically get "mechanism" explanations.
   Answer: B
   Page Ref: 326 Box: SI: Children's Questions: Catalyst for Cognitive Development
   Skill: Applied
   Objective: 9.3

33) When shown a LEGO structure made to look like a crayon, 3-year-old Astrid said that the object "really and truly" was a crayon. Astrid is having trouble with
   A) class inclusion.
   B) hierarchical classification.
   C) the appearance–reality distinction.
   D) conservation.
   Answer: C
   Page Ref: 327
   Skill: Applied
   Objective: 9.3

34) According to research, preschoolers' poor performance on appearance versus reality tasks occurs because they
   A) have an immature cerebral cortex.
   B) have trouble with the language of these tasks.
   C) are involved frequently in fantasy and pretend play.
   D) have a general difficulty in distinguishing appearance from reality.
   Answer: B
   Page Ref: 327
   Skill: Conceptual
   Objective: 9.3

35) After putting on a Halloween mask and looking at their reflection in a mirror, young preschoolers often are wary. This is because they have a fragile understanding of
   A) the appearance–reality distinction.
   B) centration.
   C) hierarchical categorization.
   D) class inclusion.
   Answer: A
   Page Ref: 327
   Skill: Conceptual
   Objective: 9.3

36) A wealth of recent research suggests that Piaget _____ preschoolers' cognitive capabilities.
   A) was completely wrong about
   B) vastly overestimated
   C) accurately estimated
   D) was partly wrong and partly right about
   Answer: D
   Page Ref: 327
   Skill: Conceptual
   Objective: 9.3

37) Evidence that logical operations develop gradually and that preschoolers can be trained to perform well on Piagetian tasks pose a serious challenge to Piaget's
   A) stage concept.
   B) notion about the constructive nature of knowledge.
   C) ideas about individual differences in cognitive development.
   D) concept of egocentrism.
   Answer: A
   Page Ref: 328
   Skill: Conceptual
   Objective: 9.3

38) Some neo-Piagetian theorists combine Piaget's stage approach with the _____ emphasis on task-specific changes.
   A) ecological systems
   B) information-processing
   C) dynamic systems
   D) Vygotskian
   Answer: B
   Page Ref: 328
   Skill: Factual
   Objective: 9.3

39) In Dino's preschool classroom, teachers evaluate each child's educational progress in relation to his or her previous development, rather than on the basis of normative standards, or average performance of same-age peers. This preschool emphasizes the Piagetian principle of
   A) sensitivity to children's readiness to learn.
   B) assisted discovery.
   C) discovery learning.
   D) acceptance of individual differences.
   Answer: D
   Page Ref: 329
   Skill: Applied
   Objective: 9.4

40) In Ms. Allison's Piagetian kindergarten classroom, teachers introduce activities that build on children's current thinking, challenging their incorrect ways of viewing the work. But they do not try to speed up development by imposing new skills before children indicate that they are interested and ready. This kindergarten emphasizes the Piagetian principle of
   A) sensitivity to children's readiness to learn.
   B) scaffolding.
   C) discovery learning.
   D) acceptance of individual differences.
Answer: A
Page Ref: 329
Skill: Applied
Objective: 9.4

41) A Piagetian classroom that emphasizes discovery learning would probably include
   A) explicit verbal teaching of ready-made information.
   B) a rich variety of activities designed to promote exploration.
   C) introduction of new skills according to normative standards of readiness.
   D) progress evaluation on the basis of average performance of same-age peers.
Answer: B
Page Ref: 329
Skill: Applied
Objective: 9.4

42) Vygotsky's theory stresses the _____ of cognitive development.
   A) physiology
   B) neuroplasticity
   C) social context
   D) egocentricity
Answer: C
Page Ref: 329
Skill: Conceptual
Objective: 9.5

43) As Sunni plays, she says: "Where's the cup? I want the cup. Oh, there it is. Now, I need the spoon." Sunni is engaging in what researchers now call _____ speech.
   A) egocentric
   B) private
   C) inner
   D) social
Answer: B
Page Ref: 330
Skill: Applied
Objective: 9.5

44) Most research indicates that young children use private speech
   A) because they have difficulty with perspective taking.
   B) when they are engaged in cooperative dialogues.
   C) when tasks are appropriately challenging.
   D) when they cannot find a conversational partner.
Answer: C
Page Ref: 330
Skill: Conceptual
Objective: 9.5

45) Children who freely use private speech during a challenging activity are _____ than their less talkative agemates.
    A) more attentive
    B) less involved
    C) less likely to perform the task well
    D) less attentive
Answer: A
Page Ref: 330
Skill: Conceptual
Objective: 9.5

46) According to Vygotsky, which of the following is within a child's zone of proximal development?
    A) a task that a child cannot accomplish alone or with the help of an adult.
    B) a task that a child has recently mastered independently following the assistance of an adult
    C) a task that a child cannot yet handle on her own, but can do with the help of an adult
    D) a task that a child figures out how to accomplish through her own independent activity
Answer: C
Page Ref: 330
Skill: Conceptual
Objective: 9.5

47) Adults try to promote _____ when they translate their own insights in ways that are within a child's grasp.
    A) transitive inference
    B) intersubjectivity
    C) guided participation
    D) scaffolding
Answer: B
Page Ref: 331
Skill: Conceptual
Objective: 9.5

48) Becca is making cookies all by herself after making them with the help of her mother many times in the past. Becca has learned this new skill through
    A) cooperative learning.
    B) intersubjectivity.
    C) guided participation.
    D) transitive inference.
Answer: C
Page Ref: 331
Skill: Applied
Objective: 9.5

49) In Mr. Naffie's Vygotskian classroom, he guides children's learning with explanations, demonstrations, and verbal prompts, tailoring his interventions to each child's zone of proximal development. This is an example of the Vygotskian principle of
    A) peer collaboration.
    B) discovery learning.
    C) independent exploration.
    D) assisted discovery.
Answer: D
Page Ref: 332
Skill: Applied
Objective: 9.6

50) Which of the following is more likely to be seen in a Vygotskian, than a Piagetian, classroom?
  A) activities to foster peer collaboration
  B) acceptance of individual differences
  C) opportunities for active participation
  D) experiences to promote independent exploration
Answer: A
Page Ref: 332
Skill: Applied
Objective: 9.6

51) Vygotsky regarded make-believe play as an important source of cognitive development because it
  A) enhances animistic thinking.
  B) is rich in private speech.
  C) fosters independent discovery learning.
  D) provides opportunities to practice representational schemes.
Answer: B
Page Ref: 332
Skill: Conceptual
Objective: 9.6

52) Critics argue that Vygotsky's theory
  A) underemphasizes the importance of pretend play.
  B) overemphasizes the role of verbal communication.
  C) emphasizes a set of experiences common to all cultures.
  D) overemphasizes the importance of independent discovery.
Answer: B
Page Ref: 332
Skill: Conceptual
Objective: 9.7

53) Compared to Yucatec Mayan preschoolers, Western preschoolers are
  A) less sophisticated with make-believe play.
  B) more able to sit quietly for long periods.
  C) more autonomous.
  D) less competent at self-care.
Answer: D
Page Ref: 333 Box: CI: Children in Village and Tribal Cultures Observe and Participate in Adult Work
Skill: Conceptual
Objective: 9.7

54) Ethnographic research has revealed that young Yucatec Mayan children
  A) rarely imitate adult work in their make-believe play.
  B) and Western children display impressive similarities in their make-believe play.
  C) decide for themselves how much to sleep and eat.
  D) tend to frequently display attention-getting behaviors.
Answer: C
Page Ref: 333 Box: CI: Children in Village and Tribal Cultures Observe and Participate in Adult Work
Skill: Conceptual
Objective: 9.7

55) Which of the following is a common criticism of Vygotsky's theory?
    A) It underemphasizes the role of verbal communication.
    B) It overemphasizes the development of basic cognitive processes.
    C) It places too much emphasis on how elementary capacities spark changes in children's social experiences.
    D) It says too little about how basic cognitive skills contribute to socially transmitted higher cognitive processes.
Answer: D
Page Ref: 333–334
Skill: Conceptual
Objective: 9.7

56) Sustained attention typically begins to improve in toddlerhood because children's ability to _____ improves.
    A) inhibit impulses
    B) plan out a sequence of acts
    C) use memory strategies
    D) think about thought
Answer: A
Page Ref: 334
Skill: Conceptual
Objective: 9.8

57) In *Tools of the Mind*—a preschool curriculum inspired by Vygotsky's theory—_____ is woven into virtually all classroom activities.
    A) discovery learning
    B) independent exploration
    C) scaffolding of attention skills
    D) overlapping-waves theory
Answer: C
Page Ref: 335
Skill: Conceptual
Objective: 9.8

58) Preschoolers become better at _____ by following directions for playing games and cooking from recipes.
    A) scaffolding
    B) planning
    C) metacognition
    D) recognition
Answer: B
Page Ref: 335
Skill: Conceptual
Objective: 9.8

59) Even preschoolers with good language skills recall poorly because they are not skilled at using
    A) memory strategies.
    B) episodic memory.
    C) autobiographical memory.
    D) scripts.
Answer: A
Page Ref: 336
Skill: Conceptual
Objective: 9.8

60) Scripts
    A) clutter long-term memory with irrelevant information.
    B) help children organize, interpret, and predict everyday experiences.
    C) hinder memory for events that are highly distinctive.
    D) facilitate recall of specific instances of repeated experiences.
Answer: B
Page Ref: 336
Skill: Conceptual
Objective: 9.8

61) Hallie acts out her _____ of putting her baby brother to bed when she plays with her doll.
    A) theory of mind
    B) autobiographical memory
    C) script
    D) recognition memory
Answer: C
Page Ref: 336
Skill: Applied
Objective: 9.8

62) After a trip to the zoo, 4-year-old Jaden is able to remember the animals he saw and the context in which he saw them. This is an example of
    A) scripts.
    B) recognition without recall.
    C) autobiographical memory.
    D) overlapping-waves.
Answer: C
Page Ref: 337
Skill: Applied
Objective: 9.8

63) After a family camping trip, Rollie's mother asks him to tell his grandmother about the trip. Rollie's response represents
    A) metacognitive knowledge.
    B) a script.
    C) recognition memory.
    D) autobiographical memory.
Answer: D
Page Ref: 337
Skill: Applied
Objective: 9.8

64) After a field trip to the museum, Leslie asks her son, "What was the first thing we did? Why weren't the trains moving? I thought that the pink airplane was really big. What did you think?" Leslie is using a(n) _____ style to elicit her son's autobiographical memory.
    A) deliberative
    B) repetitive
    C) reconstructive
    D) elaborative
Answer: D
Page Ref: 337
Skill: Applied
Objective: 9.8

65) After a trip to the supermarket, Raj asks his daughter, "Do you remember the supermarket? What did we do at the supermarket? What food did we buy at the supermarket?" Raj is using a(n) _____ style to elicit his daughter's autobiographical memory.
  A) deliberate
  B) repetitive
  C) reconstructive
  D) elaborative
Answer: B
Page Ref: 337
Skill: Applied
Objective: 9.8

66) According to _____ theory, when given challenging problems, children try out various strategies and observe which work best, which work less well, and which are ineffective.
  A) overlapping-waves
  B) metacognitive
  C) false-belief
  D) mindblindness
Answer: A
Page Ref: 338
Skill: Factual
Objective: 9.8

67) Theory of mind research indicates that by age 2, children realize that
  A) both beliefs and desires determine behavior.
  B) thinking takes place inside their heads.
  C) people can hold false beliefs.
  D) others' desires can differ from their own.
Answer: D
Page Ref: 339
Skill: Conceptual
Objective: 9.9

68) Greta has just been shown two boxes—a plain, unmarked box full of raisins and a familiar marked raisin box that is empty. Next, Greta is asked to predict where another child will look for raisins. This task assesses Greta's understanding of
  A) class inclusion.
  B) conservation.
  C) irreversibility.
  D) false belief.
Answer: D
Page Ref: 339
Skill: Applied
Objective: 9.9

69) Understanding of false belief is associated with early _____ ability.
  A) reading
  B) mathematical
  C) writing
  D) speaking
Answer: A
Page Ref: 340
Skill: Factual
Objective: 9.9

70) Chen, a preschooler, is most likely to view the mind as a(n)
   A) active machine.
   B) constructive agent that interprets information
   C) passive container of information.
   D) constantly spinning wheel.
Answer: C
Page Ref: 341
Skill: Applied
Objective: 9.9

71) Children with autism
   A) only use words to exchange ideas.
   B) have narrow and overly intense interests.
   C) engage in more make-believe play than typically developing children.
   D) show extremely rapid synaptic pruning.
Answer: B
Page Ref: 342 Box: B&E: "Mindblindness" and Autism
Skill: Factual
Objective: 9.9

72) Compared with typically developing children, children with autism
   A) more often engage in social referencing.
   B) are better at distinguishing facial expressions.
   C) more often imitate an adult's novel behaviors.
   D) rarely use mental-state words such as think, feel, and know.
Answer: D
Page Ref: 342 Box: B&E: "Mindblindness" and Autism
Skill: Factual
Objective: 9.9

73) Some researchers have suggested that children with autism are _____ and, therefore, deficient in human sociability.
   A) mindblind
   B) animistic thinkers
   C) flexible thinkers
   D) poor problem solvers
Answer: A
Page Ref: 342 Box: B&E: "Mindblindness" and Autism
Skill: Factual
Objective: 9.9

74) Three-year-old Stacy pretends to make a grocery list while in the car on the way to the grocery store. This activity reflects Stacy's
   A) emergent literacy.
   B) animistic thinking.
   C) private speech.
   D) phonological awareness.
Answer: A
Page Ref: 343
Skill: Applied
Objective: 9.10

75) Three-year-old Evan recognizes and "reads" the word "PIZZA" on a familiar sign, but thinks that his name is spelled "E." This demonstrates Evan's
    A) theory of mind.
    B) metacognition.
    C) emergent literacy.
    D) phonological awareness.
    Answer: C
    Page Ref: 343
    Skill: Applied
    Objective: 9.10

76) Anneli's 4-year-old daughter manipulates sounds within words and enjoys rhyming games. Anneli's daughter is demonstrating
    A) phonological awareness.
    B) metacognition.
    C) private speech.
    D) knowledge of cardinality.
    Answer: A
    Page Ref: 343
    Skill: Applied
    Objective: 9.10

77) Studies of literacy development show that
    A) the more informal literacy experiences young children have, the better their later reading skills.
    B) even young preschoolers are able to distinguish drawing from writing.
    C) the best method to teach children to read is the phonics approach.
    D) interactive reading hinders preschoolers' developing understanding of sound-word correspondences.
    Answer: A
    Page Ref: 343
    Skill: Conceptual
    Objective: 9.10

78) On average, a low-SES child is read to for a total of _____ hours during the preschool years, a higher-SES child for _____ hours.
    A) 25; 100
    B) 25; 1,000
    C) 250; 500
    D) 250; 1,000
    Answer: B
    Page Ref: 344
    Skill: Factual
    Objective: 9.10

79) Eighteen-month-old Jazmin is offered sets of animal crackers. Each set contains 1, 2, or 4 crackers. Jazmin consistently picks the set with the most pieces, displaying a beginning grasp of
    A) cardinality.
    B) estimation.
    C) ordinality.
    D) functionality.
    Answer: C
    Page Ref: 344
    Skill: Applied
    Objective: 9.10

80) Four-year-old Jack is a snack helper. He counts five children at his table and then retrieves five milk cartons. Jack is displaying an understanding of
   A) ordinality.
   B) functionality.
   C) estimation.
   D) cardinality.
   Answer: D
   Page Ref: 344
   Skill: Applied
   Objective: 9.10

81) Four-year-old Paytin is shown a plate of cookies. She is told that there are 10 cookies on the plate. She watches as several cookies are added to or removed from the plate. Paytin's sensible prediction as to how many cookies are left on the plate displays her understanding of
   A) ordinality.
   B) estimation.
   C) cardinality.
   D) functionality.
   Answer: B
   Page Ref: 345
   Skill: Applied
   Objective: 9.10

82) Research using the Home Observation for Measurement of the Environment (HOME) indicates that
   A) preschoolers who develop well intellectually have homes rich in educational toys and books.
   B) preschoolers who develop well intellectually have parents who resolve conflicts with punishment.
   C) HOME scores predict academic achievement better than IQ scores.
   D) the organization of the physical environment predicts IQ gains only among high-SES children.
   Answer: A
   Page Ref: 347
   Skill: Conceptual
   Objective: 9.11

83) In Haylee's preschool classroom, teachers provide activities in learning centers from which children select, and much learning takes place through play. Haylee's preschool is
   A) actually a child-care center.
   B) an academic program.
   C) a child-centered program.
   D) unlikely to foster school readiness.
   Answer: C
   Page Ref: 348
   Skill: Applied
   Objective: 9.11

84) Formal academic training during early childhood
   A) produces children who have more confidence in their academic abilities.
   B) produces children who display fewer stress behaviors, such as wiggling and rocking.
   C) enhances children's study habits throughout the school years.
   D) undermines young children's motivation and emotional well-being.
   Answer: D
   Page Ref: 348
   Skill: Conceptual
   Objective: 9.11

85) Montessori schools
    A) include multiage classrooms and specially designed teaching materials to promote exploration and discovery.
    B) undermine young children's motivation and emotional well-being.
    C) emphasize formal academic training and deemphasize social development.
    D) include repetition and drill by teachers who structure children's learning.
Answer: A
Page Ref: 348
Skill: Conceptual
Objective: 9.11

86) Of the following statements, which is supported by research on Head Start?
    A) Gains for Head Start participants are similar, though not as strong as for participants of university-based programs.
    B) All eligible preschool-age children in the United States and Canada receive Head Start services.
    C) Head Start and other similar interventions are not very cost effective.
    D) Parental involvement in Head Start has minimal impact on children's development.
Answer: A
Page Ref: 349
Skill: Conceptual
Objective: 9.11

87) Evaluations of children who experience Jumpstart show
    A) IQ gains of 10 to 15 points over a single academic year.
    B) gains in language, literacy, task persistence, and social skills.
    C) greater gains in social skills than academic skills.
    D) that children from middle-SES homes show the greatest long-term gains.
Answer: B
Page Ref: 350
Skill: Conceptual
Objective: 9.11

88) Which of the following statements is supported by research on child care?
    A) Even high-quality early intervention does not enhance the development of economically disadvantaged children.
    B) Preschoolers exposed to substandard child care, particularly for long hours, display more behavior problems.
    C) Psychological well-being improves when children experience several child-care settings.
    D) The emotional problems of temperamentally difficult preschoolers improve dramatically in child care.
Answer: B
Page Ref: 351
Skill: Conceptual
Objective: 9.11

89) About _____ percent of U.S. three-month-olds regularly watch either TV or videos.
    A) 20
    B) 30
    C) 40
    D) 50
Answer: C
Page Ref: 352
Skill: Factual
Objective: 9.11

90) Studies on computer use in early childhood demonstrate that
    A) computer storybooks and other literacy programs interfere with emergent literacy skills.
    B) children spend most of their time using computers for learning language and math skills.
    C) combining everyday and computer experiences with math manipulatives is especially effective in promoting math concepts and skills.
    D) video gaming consoles are among the bedroom furnishings of 30 percent of children age 5 and younger.
Answer: C
Page Ref: 353
Skill: Conceptual
Objective: 9.11

91) Between the ages of 2 and 6, a child's spoken vocabulary increases from an average of _____ words to an average of _____ words.
    A) 100; 1,000
    B) 100; 5,000
    C) 200; 5,000
    D) 200; 10,000
Answer: D
Page Ref: 354
Skill: Factual
Objective: 9.12

92) Jay introduced a new ball to his 2-year-old daughter, Kandi. He said, "I'm throwing the wiffle ball to you!" He then threw the new ball to Kandi. Kandi said, "Catch, wiffle, catch!" Kandi's connection of the term "wiffle" to the ball is an example of
    A) overregularization.
    B) syntactic bootstrapping.
    C) fast mapping.
    D) semantic bootstrapping.
Answer: C
Page Ref: 354
Skill: Applied
Objective: 9.12

93) Young children learning Chinese, Japanese, and Korean acquire _____ more readily than their English-speaking agemates.
    A) proper nouns
    B) verbs
    C) object nouns
    D) modifiers
Answer: B
Page Ref: 354
Skill: Factual
Objective: 9.12

94) Jade's mom told her they were going outside in the rain and needed a *bumbershoot*. Jade had never heard the word *bumbershoot* before, but she knew the word *umbrella*. Jade tries to figure out what the new word means, and eventually she decides that a *bumbershoot* must be an *umbrella*. Jade must abandon her _____ to reach this conclusion.
    A) cardinality principle
    B) shape bias
    C) overregularization principle
    D) mutual exclusivity bias
Answer: D
Page Ref: 355
Skill: Applied
Objective: 9.12

95) According to the principle of mutual exclusivity bias, toddlers
   A) assume that objects have multiple labels.
   B) connect new words with their underlying concepts after only a brief encounter.
   C) assume that words refer to nonoverlapping categories.
   D) discover the structure of sentences by relying on the meanings of words.
   Answer: C
   Page Ref: 355
   Skill: Conceptual
   Objective: 9.12

96) According to _____, preschoolers discover many word meanings by observing how words are used in the structure of sentences.
   A) fast mapping
   B) semantic bootstrapping
   C) mutual exclusivity
   D) syntactic bootstrapping
   Answer: D
   Page Ref: 355
   Skill: Conceptual
   Objective: 9.12

97) In acquiring new vocabulary, infants rely solely on
   A) perceptual features.
   B) social cues.
   C) sentence structure.
   D) intonation.
   Answer: A
   Page Ref: 356
   Skill: Conceptual
   Objective: 9.12

98) Between ages 2 and 3, English-speaking children use simple sentences that follow a(n) _____ word order.
   A) verb–subject–object
   B) subject–verb–object
   C) object–verb–subject
   D) verb–object–subject
   Answer: B
   Page Ref: 356
   Skill: Factual
   Objective: 9.12

99) Two-year-old Camden finds only one of her shoes. She says, "I need two shoes. I have two foots!" Camden's error is an example of
   A) semantic bootstrapping.
   B) underextension.
   C) overregularization.
   D) underregularization.
   Answer: C
   Page Ref: 357
   Skill: Applied
   Objective: 9.12

100) According to the _____ approach, young children rely on word meanings to figure out grammatical rules.
A) fast mapping
B) semantic bootstrapping
C) mutual exclusivity
D) syntactic bootstrapping
Answer: B
Page Ref: 357
Skill: Factual
Objective: 9.12

101) Research on pragmatics shows that by age 2, most children
A) adjust their speech to fit the age, sex, and social status of their listeners.
B) take turns in face-to-face interactions.
C) are able to maintain a topic over long periods of time.
D) adapt their language to social expectations.
Answer: B
Page Ref: 358
Skill: Conceptual
Objective: 9.12

102) When Sadie says, "I goed to the store," her mother replies, "Yes, you went to the store." Sadie's mother's response is an example of
A) fast mapping.
B) a recast.
C) an overregularization.
D) an expansion.
Answer: B
Page Ref: 359
Skill: Applied
Objective: 9.13

103) When Moses says, "My ball is a circle," his father relies, "Yes, your basketball is round, just like a circle." Moses's father's response is an example of
A) fast mapping.
B) a recast.
C) an overregularization.
D) an expansion.
Answer: D
Page Ref: 359
Skill: Applied
Objective: 9.13

ESSAY

104) Bethany, age 3, spends, a large amount of time engaged in make-believe play. Her parents are especially concerned because Bethany has a pair of imaginary mice that she talks to and talks about. Bethany's grandmother believes that this is a sign of maladjustment. What can you tell Bethany's parents and grandmother that might ease their minds?
Answer: Imaginary companions were once viewed as a sign of maladjustment, but research challenges that assumption. Between 25 and 45 percent of preschoolers and young school-age children spend much time in solitary make-believe, creating imaginary companions. Children with imaginary companions typically treat them with care and affection and say the companions offer caring, comfort, and good company, just as their real friendships do. Such children also display more complex and imaginative pretend play, are advanced in understanding others' viewpoints and emotions, and are more sociable with peers.
Page Ref: 319–320

105) Explain what Piaget's famous conservation tasks reveal about preoperational children's thinking.

Answer: Conservation refers to the idea that certain physical characteristics of objects remain the same, even when their outward appearance changes. Piaget's famous conservation tasks reveal several deficiencies of preoperational thought. First, preoperational children's understanding is centered, or characterized by centration. They focus on one aspect of a situation, neglecting other important features. In the conservation of liquid task, the child centers on the height of the water, failing to realize that changes in width compensate for the changes in height. Second, children are easily distracted by the perceptual appearance of objects. Third, they treat the initial and final states of the water as unrelated events, ignoring the dynamic transformation (pouring of water) between them. The most important illogical feature of preoperational though is its irreversibility—an inability to mentally go through a series of steps in a problem and then reverse direction, returning to the starting point. Reversibility is part of every logical operation.

Page Ref: 321–322

106) Describe a Piagetian classroom. What educational principles derived from Piaget's theory continue to influence teacher training and classroom practices?

Answer: In a Piagetian classroom, children are encouraged to discover for themselves through spontaneous interaction with the environment. Instead of presenting ready-made knowledge verbally, teachers promote *discovery learning* by providing a rich variety of activities designed to promote exploration, including art, puzzles, table games, dress-up clothing, building blocks, books, measuring tools, and musical instruments. Teachers show *sensitivity to children's readiness to learn* by introducing activities that build on children's current thinking, challenging their incorrect ways of viewing the world. But they do not try to speed up development by imposing new skills before children indicate they are interested and ready. Piaget's theory focuses on *acceptance of individual differences.* It assumes that all children go through the same sequence of development, but at different rates. Therefore, teachers must plan activities for individual children and small groups, not just for the whole class. In addition, teachers evaluate each child's educational progress in relation to the child's previous development, rather than on the basis of normative standards, or average performance of same-age peers.

Page Ref: 328–329

107) How are a Piagetian and Vygotskian classroom similar? How do they differ?

Answer: Both Piagetian and Vygotskian classrooms emphasize active participation and acceptance of individual differences. But a Vygotskian classroom goes beyond independent discovery to promote *assisted discovery.* Teachers guide children's learning with explanations, demonstrations, and verbal prompts, tailoring their interventions to each child's zone of proximal development. Assisted discovery is aided by *peer collaboration,* as children with varying abilities work in groups, teaching and helping one another.

Page Ref: 332

108) What are scripts? How do they contribute to young children's memory development?

Answer: Like adults, young children remember familiar, repeated events in terms of scripts—general descriptions of what occurs and when it occurs in a particular situation. Young children's scripts begin as a structure of main acts. Although first scripts contain only a few acts, as long as events in a situation take place in logical order, they are almost always recalled in correct sequence. With age, scripts become more spontaneous and elaborate. Scripts help children organize, interpret, and predict everyday experiences. Once formed, they can be used to predict what will happen on similar occasions in the future. Children rely on scripts to assist recall when listening to and telling stories. They also act out scripts in make-believe play as they pretend to put the baby to bed, go on a trip, or play school. And scripts support children's earliest efforts at planning by helping them represent sequences of actions that lead to desired goals.

Page Ref: 336–337

109) List strategies for supporting emergent literacy in early childhood, and explain why each strategy is useful.

Answer:
- *Provide literacy-rich home and preschool environments.* Homes and preschools with abundant reading and writing materials—including a wide variety of children's storybooks, some relevant to children's ethnic backgrounds—open the door to a wealth of language and literacy experiences. Make-believe play, in which children have many opportunities to use newly acquired literacy skills in meaningful ways, spurs literacy development.

- *Engage in interactive book reading.* When adults discuss story content, ask open-ended questions about story events, explain the meaning of words, and point out features of print, they promote language development, comprehension of story content, knowledge of story structure, and awareness of units of written language.
- *Provide outings to libraries, museums, parks, zoos, and other community settings.* Visits to child-oriented community settings enhance children's general knowledge and offer many opportunities to see how written language is used in everyday life. They also provide personally meaningful topics for narrative conversation, which promote many language skills essential for literacy development.
- *Point out letter–sound correspondences, play rhyming and other language-sound games, and read rhyming poems and stories.* Experiences that help children isolate the sounds in words foster phonological awareness— a powerful predictor of early childhood literacy knowledge and later reading and spelling achievement.
- *Support children's efforts at writing, especially narrative products.* Assisting children in their efforts to write— especially letters, stories, and other narratives—fosters many language and literacy skills.
- *Model literacy activities.* When children see adults engaged in reading and writing activities, they better understand the diverse everyday functions of literacy skills and the knowledge and pleasure that literacy brings. As a result, children's motivation to become literate is strengthened.

Page Ref: 345

110) Mr. and Mrs. Harken are looking for a developmentally appropriate early childhood program for their son Max. Describe for the Harkens what they should look for in terms of physical setting, caregiver–child ratio, teacher qualifications, and daily activities.

Answer:
- *Physical setting:* Indoor environment is clean, in good repair, and well-ventilated. Classroom space is divided into richly equipped activity areas, including make-believe play, blocks, science, math, games and puzzles, books, art, and music. Fenced outdoor play space is equipped with swings, climbing equipment, tricycles, and sandbox.
- *Caregiver–child ratio:* In preschools and child-care centers, teacher is responsible for no more than 8 to 10 children. In family child-care homes, caregiver is responsible for no more than 6 children.
- *Teacher qualifications:* Teachers have college-level specialized preparation in early childhood development, early childhood education, or a related field.
- *Daily activities:* Children mainly work individually or in small groups, selecting many of their own activities and learning through experiences relevant to their own lives. Teachers facilitate children's involvement, accept individual differences, and adjust expectations to children's developing capacities.

Page Ref: 352

111) Explain how adults can foster preschoolers' language development.

Answer: Interaction with more skilled speakers is vital in early childhood. Conversational give-and-take with adults is consistently related to language progress. Sensitive, caring adults use techniques that promote language skills. When children use words incorrectly or communicate unclearly, they give helpful, explicit feedback. But they do not overcorrect, especially when children make grammatical mistakes. Criticism discourages children from freely using language in ways that lead to new skills. Instead, adults often provide indirect feedback about grammar by using two strategies, often in combination: recasts—restructuring inaccurate speech into correct form, and expansions—elaborating on children's speech, increasing its complexity. For example, if a child says, "I gotted new red shoes," the parent might respond, "Yes, you got a pair of new red shoes." However, the impact of such feedback has been challenged. The techniques are not used in all cultures and, in a few investigations, had no impact on children's grammar. Rather than eliminating errors, perhaps expansions and recasts model grammatical alternatives and encourage children to experiment with them. Adults respond to children's desire to become competent speakers by listening attentively, elaborating on what children say, modeling correct usage, and stimulating children to talk further.

Page Ref: 359

MULTIPLE CHOICE

1) Erikson described early childhood as a period of
   A) doubt-filled industry.
   B) vigorous unfolding.
   C) trusting simplicity.
   D) autonomous initiative.
   Answer: B
   Page Ref: 364
   Skill: Factual
   Objective: 10.1

2) According to Erikson, the psychological conflict of the preschool years is
   A) trust versus mistrust.
   B) industry versus inferiority.
   C) initiative versus guilt.
   D) autonomy versus shame.
   Answer: C
   Page Ref: 364
   Skill: Factual
   Objective: 10.1

3) According to Erikson, play
   A) allows young children to escape from the demands of their lives into a fantasy world.
   B) symbolically represents preschoolers' unconscious wishes and desires.
   C) is secondary to academic learning for preschoolers.
   D) permits preschoolers to try out new skills with little risk of criticism or failure.
   Answer: D
   Page Ref: 364
   Skill: Conceptual
   Objective: 10.1

4) For Erikson, the negative outcome of early childhood is an overly
   A) strict superego.
   B) lenient id.
   C) strict ego.
   D) lenient ego.
   Answer: A
   Page Ref: 364
   Skill: Conceptual
   Objective: 10.1

5) Three-year-old Sara says, "I have three dolls. I have brown hair. I made a tall tower." This demonstrates that Sara is beginning to develop
  A) self-esteem.
  B) a self-concept.
  C) a gender identity.
  D) gender typing.
Answer: B
Page Ref: 365
Skill: Applied
Objective: 10.2

6) Preschoolers' self-concepts largely consist of
  A) talents.
  B) personality traits.
  C) observable characteristics.
  D) temperamental qualities.
Answer: C
Page Ref: 365
Skill: Factual
Objective: 10.2

7) If you asked 3-year-old Aidan to tell you about himself, which of the following is he most likely to say?
  A) "I have a new cat."
  B) "I am funny."
  C) "I am a good boy."
  D) "I am shy."
Answer: A
Page Ref: 365
Skill: Applied
Objective: 10.2

8) If you asked 4-year-old Hannah to describe herself, which of the following is she most likely to say?
  A) "I am friendly."
  B) "I am smart."
  C) "I am helpful."
  D) "I do not like bugs."
Answer: D
Page Ref: 365
Skill: Applied
Objective: 10.2

9) Reylynne describes herself by saying, "I'm helpful, but I'm shy." Reylynne is probably
  A) under 3 years old.
  B) 3 to 5 years old.
  C) 4 to 5 years old.
  D) not a preschooler.
Answer: C
Page Ref: 365
Skill: Applied
Objective: 10.2

10) _____ seems to foster a more positive, coherent early self-concept.
    A) Early birth order
    B) A warm, sensitive parent–child relationship
    C) Permissive parenting
    D) Authoritarian parenting
Answer: B
Page Ref: 365
Skill: Conceptual
Objective: 10.2

11) Research examining cultural variations in personal storytelling revealed that
    A) Irish-American parents often told stories about the child's misdeeds.
    B) Chinese parents downplayed the child's misdeeds, attributing them to assertiveness.
    C) Chinese parents did little to cultivate their child's individuality.
    D) Irish-American parents generally saw self-esteem as unimportant or even negative.
Answer: C
Page Ref: 366 Box CI: Cultural Variations in Personal Storytelling: Implications for Early Self-Concept
Skill: Conceptual
Objective: 10.2

12) According to research on cultural variations in personal storytelling, which of the following self-descriptions is most likely to come from a Chinese child?
    A) "I do lots of puzzles."
    B) "I like pigs."
    C) "I am really smart."
    D) "I help my sister wash dishes."
Answer: D
Page Ref: 366 Box CI: Cultural Variations in Personal Storytelling: Implications for Early Self-Concept
Skill: Applied
Objective: 10.2

13) Studies of self-esteem demonstrate that preschoolers
    A) tend to overestimate the difficulty of tasks.
    B) usually have an accurate understanding of their abilities.
    C) usually rate their own abilities as extremely high.
    D) give up easily when faced with a challenging task.
Answer: C
Page Ref: 366
Skill: Conceptual
Objective: 10.2

14) By age 3, children with a history of parental criticism
    A) give up easily when faced with a challenge.
    B) are usually nonemotional after failing.
    C) are nonetheless enthusiastic and highly motivated.
    D) seek approval and anticipate it.
Answer: A
Page Ref: 367
Skill: Conceptual
Objective: 10.2

15) _____ is vital for successful peer relationships and overall emotional health.
    A) Individualism
    B) Emotional competence
    C) Collectivism
    D) Mental representation
    Answer: B
    Page Ref: 367
    Skill: Conceptual
    Objective: 10.3

16) Which of the following is true about cognitive development and emotional understanding?
    A) Preschoolers cannot yet predict what a playmate expressing a certain emotion might do next.
    B) Young children focus on the most obvious aspect of a complex emotional situation to the neglect of other relevant information.
    C) Preschoolers believe that thinking and feeling are not connected.
    D) Preschoolers can usually make sense of situations with conflicting cues about how a person is feeling.
    Answer: B
    Page Ref: 368
    Skill: Conceptual
    Objective: 10.3

17) Of the following, which is supported by research on emotional understanding?
    A) Preschoolers whose mothers negotiate during conflicts with them show delayed emotional understanding.
    B) Preschoolers whose parents talk about diverse emotions are better able to judge others' emotions.
    C) With age, preschoolers engage in less emotion talk with siblings and friends.
    D) The less preschoolers refer to feelings when interacting with peers, the better they are liked by their peers.
    Answer: B
    Page Ref: 368
    Skill: Conceptual
    Objective: 10.3

18) Five-year-old Anthony and his 4-year-old sister Angela are engaged in a typical sibling dispute over a favorite chair. In order to help them gain sensitivity to their sibling's feelings, their parents should
    A) intervene with reasoning and negotiating.
    B) let them work through the dispute on their own, intervening only if there are tears involved.
    C) settle the dispute by making the children each take a turn in the chair for a set amount of time.
    D) totally ignore the dispute.
    Answer: A
    Page Ref: 369
    Skill: Applied
    Objective: 10.3

19) At a parade, 3-year-old Kyle puts his fingers in his ears when he hears the fire trucks coming down the street. Kyle is displaying
    A) scaffolding.
    B) situational empathy.
    C) social problem-solving.
    D) emotional self-regulation.
    Answer: D
    Page Ref: 369
    Skill: Applied
    Objective: 10.3

20) Four-year-old D'Andre is upset when his friends exclude him from a game. D'Andre sits in the sandbox alone and plays with the dump truck instead. D'Andre is displaying
    A) effortful control.
    B) situational empathy.
    C) scaffolding.
    D) altruistic behavior.
Answer: A
Page Ref: 369
Skill: Applied
Objective: 10.3

21) When portraying an emotion they do not feel, children of all ages find it easier to act _____ than _____.
    A) sad; pleased
    B) pleased; angry
    C) disgusted; pleased
    D) angry; pleased
Answer: B
Page Ref: 369
Skill: Conceptual
Objective: 10.3

22) By age 3,
    A) self-conscious emotions are clearly linked to self-evaluation.
    B) children no longer depend on adults to know when to feel self-conscious emotions.
    C) children are not yet sensitive to praise and blame.
    D) children have not yet developed the capacity to feel guilty or ashamed.
Answer: A
Page Ref: 370
Skill: Conceptual
Objective: 10.4

23) When 3-year-old Kaylee spills her water after filling her glass too full, her mother says, "You filled the glass very full. Next time try putting less water in the glass." Assuming that Kaylee's mother repeatedly gives this sort of feedback, which of the following is most likely to be true?
    A) Kaylee is likely to show little sympathy to others in distress.
    B) Kaylee is likely to experience self-conscious emotions intensely.
    C) Kaylee is likely to experience moderate, adaptive levels of shame and pride.
    D) Kaylee is likely to experience a low level of pride after a success.
Answer: C
Page Ref: 370
Skill: Applied
Objective: 10.4

24) When parents repeatedly comment on the worth of a child and his or her performance, that child experiences
    A) less shame after failure.
    B) less pride after success.
    C) no self-conscious emotions.
    D) self-conscious emotions intensely.
Answer: D
Page Ref: 370
Skill: Conceptual
Objective: 10.4

229

25) When guilt occurs in appropriate circumstances and is not accompanied by shame, it is related to
    A) ineffective parenting.
    B) good adjustment.
    C) poor emotional self-regulatory skills.
    D) an insecure attachment.
Answer: B
Page Ref: 370
Skill: Conceptual
Objective: 10.4

26) When her friend, Reagan, loses her favorite toy, 4-year-old Nahla puts her arm around Reagan and offers to give Reagan a cookie from her lunch. Nahla's emotional response to Reagan's loss exhibits
    A) sympathy.
    B) effortful control .
    C) emotional self-regulation.
    D) empathy.
Answer: D
Page Ref: 371
Skill: Applied
Objective: 10.4

27) _____ plays a role in whether empathy prompts sympathetic, prosocial behavior or a personally distressed, self-focused response.
    A) Effortful control
    B) Emotional masking
    C) Temperament
    D) Birth order
Answer: C
Page Ref: 371
Skill: Conceptual
Objective: 10.4

28) When parents are _____, their children are likely to react in a concerned way to the distress of others.
    A) warm and sensitive
    B) permissive
    C) authoritarian
    D) attentive, but discourage emotional expressiveness
Answer: A
Page Ref: 371
Skill: Conceptual
Objective: 10.4

29) When a peer is in distress, children who are assertive react with
    A) lip biting.
    B) a rise in heart rate.
    C) an increase in EEG brain-wave activity.
    D) sympathetic concern.
Answer: D
Page Ref: 371
Skill: Conceptual
Objective: 10.4

30) Four-year-old Rock has authoritarian parents who sometimes physically abuse him. When his friend Dax has a bad day and cries, Rock is most likely to respond with
    A) sympathetic concern.
    B) anxiety and distress.
    C) fear and anger.
    D) strong feelings of empathy.
Answer: C
Page Ref: 371
Skill: Applied
Objective: 10.4

31) Cousins Easton and Jack are both infants. Sometimes Easton watches Jack while he rolls on the floor. However, both babies engage in solitary play. This is known as
    A) parallel play.
    B) cooperative play.
    C) associative play.
    D) nonsocial activity.
Answer: D
Page Ref: 372
Skill: Applied
Objective: 10.5

32) In the sandbox, Amelia makes a pie while Franklin pours sand from one container to another. The children talk and pass tools back and forth. They are engaged in _____ play.
    A) parallel
    B) cooperative
    C) associative
    D) nonsocial
Answer: C
Page Ref: 372
Skill: Applied
Objective: 10.5

33) Twins Jillian and Wesley, 11 months old, play near each other with similar materials. However they do not try to direct each other's activities. They are engaged in _____ play.
    A) parallel
    B) cooperative
    C) associative
    D) nonsocial
Answer: A
Page Ref: 372
Skill: Applied
Objective: 10.5

34) Jade and Christiana are playing house. Jade is pretending to be the mom and Christiana is pretending to be the dad. Two dolls are used as their children. They are engaged in _____ play.
    A) parallel
    B) cooperative
    C) associative
    D) nonsocial
Answer: B
Page Ref: 372
Skill: Applied
Objective: 10.5

35) Which of the following is supported by research on peer sociability during the preschool years?
    A) All types of play coexist during early childhood.
    B) Nonsocial activity increases with age.
    C) By kindergarten age, children rarely engage in nonsocial activity.
    D) From ages 3 to 6 years, the frequency of solitary play decreases.
    Answer: A
    Page Ref: 373
    Skill: Conceptual
    Objective: 10.5

36) Two-year-old Beck runs around the room, grabs a car and rolls it on the floor, and then pokes at some play dough. Beck is engaging in _____ play.
    A) constructive
    B) functional
    C) parallel
    D) make-believe
    Answer: B
    Page Ref: 373
    Skill: Applied
    Objective: 10.5

37) Three-year-old Sasha makes a structure out of toy blocks. Sasha is engaging in _____ play.
    A) make-believe
    B) parallel
    C) constructive
    D) functional
    Answer: C
    Page Ref: 373
    Skill: Applied
    Objective: 10.5

38) With age, preschoolers' conflicts center less on _____ and more on _____.
    A) ideas; toys
    B) attitudes; resources
    C) differences of opinion; toys
    D) resources; differences of opinion
    Answer: D
    Page Ref: 373
    Skill: Conceptual
    Objective: 10.5

39) Children from 4 to 7 years old regard friendship as
    A) an understanding of thoughts and feelings.
    B) pleasurable play and sharing of toys.
    C) based on mutual trust.
    D) long-term and enduring.
    Answer: B
    Page Ref: 374
    Skill: Conceptual
    Objective: 10.6

40) Shelby and Sharon are 4 years old and are best friends. They probably
    A) count on each other's emotional support.
    B) have similar values and attitudes.
    C) feel lasting trust and caring for each other.
    D) have fun playing together.
Answer: D
Page Ref: 374
Skill: Applied
Objective: 10.6

41) Research on friendships shows that
    A) preschoolers interact in essentially the same ways with both friends and nonfriends.
    B) preschoolers give the same amount of reinforcement to nonfriends as to friends.
    C) most friendships during the preschool years are based on mutual trust.
    D) children who begin kindergarten with friends in their class adjust to school more favorably.
Answer: D
Page Ref: 375
Skill: Conceptual
Objective: 10.6

42) Which of the following children is the most likely to make gains in academic achievement during kindergarten?
    A) Allie, an impulsive girl
    B) Bert, an aggressive boy
    C) Calinda, a girl who makes friends easily
    D) Dow, a shy boy
Answer: C
Page Ref: 375
Skill: Applied
Objective: 10.6

43) Nicki Crick and Kenneth Dodge's circular model showing the steps of social problem solving takes a(n)
_____ approach to conflict resolution.
    A) Piagetian
    B) information-processing
    C) Vygotskian
    D) ethological
Answer: B
Page Ref: 376
Skill: Factual
Objective: 10.6

44) Children who get along well with agemates tend to
    A) request an explanation when they do not understand a peer's behavior.
    B) attend selectively to social cues.
    C) hover around peers' activities.
    D) barge into play groups without asking.
Answer: A
Page Ref: 376
Skill: Conceptual
Objective: 10.6

45) Silas and Jake are engaged in a conflict over a ball on the playground. Jake grabs the ball away. Silas hits Jake. Jake runs crying to the nearest adult. Silas and Jake are probably _____ years old.
   A) 4
   B) 6
   C) 8
   D) 9
Answer: A
Page Ref: 376
Skill: Applied
Objective: 10.6

46) Research shows that interventions designed to teach social problem solving
   A) do not benefit children from lower-SES homes.
   B) rarely improve peer relations.
   C) offer children a sense of mastery in the face of stressful life events.
   D) do not reduce the risk of adjustment difficulties for children from troubled families.
Answer: C
Page Ref: 376
Skill: Conceptual
Objective: 10.6

47) One of the best ways for Johann's mom to promote peer interaction skills is for her to
   A) provide opportunities for Johann to play with peers.
   B) avoid arranging frequent play dates that may overwhelm Johann.
   C) avoid providing specific suggestions to Johann on how to interact with other children.
   D) prevent Johann from interacting with children who have conflicts with Johann.
Answer: A
Page Ref: 377
Skill: Applied
Objective: 10.6

48) Which of the following types of parent–child play is most strongly linked to social competence in the child?
   A) parent-directed play
   B) mother–son play
   C) mother–daughter play
   D) father–daughter play
Answer: C
Page Ref: 377
Skill: Conceptual
Objective: 10.6

49) By age _____, children use words to evaluate their own and others' actions.
   A) 2
   B) 3
   C) 4
   D) 5
Answer: A
Page Ref: 378
Skill: Factual
Objective: 10.7

50) Most theories agree that
    A) a child's morality is regulated by inner standards from birth.
    B) truly moral individuals do the right thing to conform to others' expectations.
    C) at first, a child's morality is externally controlled by adults.
    D) conscience does not begin to take shape until age 7.
    Answer: C
    Page Ref: 378
    Skill: Conceptual
    Objective: 10.7

51) According to the psychoanalytic perspective, _____ leads to the formation of the conscience and moral behavior.
    A) the emergence of the reality principle
    B) avoidance of guilt
    C) identification with the other-sex parent
    D) repression of sexual longings for the mother or father
    Answer: B
    Page Ref: 378
    Skill: Conceptual
    Objective: 10.7

52) According to Freud, children obey the _____ to avoid guilt.
    A) id
    B) superego
    C) ego
    D) other-sex parent
    Answer: B
    Page Ref: 378
    Skill: Conceptual
    Objective: 10.7

53) Which of the following is true about the psychoanalytic perspective and the development of morality?
    A) Freud believed that young children form a superego by internalize the other-sex parent's moral standards.
    B) Most researchers today agree with Freud's view of conscience development.
    C) In Freud's theory, fear of punishment and loss of parental love motivate moral behavior.
    D) Freud believed that moral development is largely complete by 10 to 12 years of age.
    Answer: C
    Page Ref: 378–379
    Skill: Conceptual
    Objective: 10.7

54) The fact that children _____ provides evidence that Freud's account of conscience development is inaccurate.
    A) whose parents frequently use threats or physical force tend to feel little guilt following transgressions
    B) whose parents frequently use threats or physical force tend to feel overwhelming guilt when they violate standards
    C) who feel little guilt frequently have loving and nurturing parents
    D) who grow up in abusive households tend to violate standards infrequently
    Answer: A
    Page Ref: 378–379
    Skill: Conceptual
    Objective: 10.7

55) Conscience formation is promoted by _____ discipline.
   A) child-directed
   B) authoritarian
   C) permissive
   D) inductive
Answer: D
Page Ref: 379
Skill: Factual
Objective: 10.7

56) Which of the following disciplinary statements is the most likely to promote prosocial behavior?
   A) "Pushing your sister is not okay."
   B) "Your sister is crying because you pushed her and she fell down."
   C) "You should be ashamed of yourself. Good girls do not push."
   D) "Only bad girls push their sisters."
Answer: B
Page Ref: 379
Skill: Applied
Objective: 10.7

57) Inductive discipline
   A) promotes only momentary compliance, not lasting changes in behavior.
   B) teaches children to expect rewards for good behavior.
   C) helps children see how their actions affect others.
   D) often leads to high levels of self-blame among children.
Answer: C
Page Ref: 379
Skill: Conceptual
Objective: 10.7

58) Mild, patient tactics are sufficient to prompt conscience development in _____ children.
   A) all
   B) fearless
   C) impulsive
   D) anxious
Answer: D
Page Ref: 379
Skill: Conceptual
Objective: 10.7

59) Parents of impulsive children can foster conscience development by
   A) using requests, suggestions, and explanations.
   B) combining firm correction of misbehavior with induction.
   C) using gentle discipline that incorporates frequent rule reminders.
   D) asserting their power.
Answer: B
Page Ref: 380
Skill: Conceptual
Objective: 10.7

60) Malek is a fearless preschooler. What tactics would you recommend to his parents to prompt guilt reactions and conscience development?
    A) mild patient tactics such as requests, suggestions, and explanations
    B) coercive techniques that force guilt feelings onto the child
    C) discussions with Malek in which he determines the consequence for his misbehavior
    D) a combination of firm correction of misbehavior and induction
Answer: D
Page Ref: 380
Skill: Applied
Objective: 10.7

61) When Erin takes her brother's book away and makes him cry, Erin's father says, "Your brother is crying because you took his book away. Your behavior disappointed me." Erin's father is using _____ as a means of influencing Erin.
    A) coercion
    B) empathy-based guilt
    C) fear of loss of parental love
    D) shame
Answer: B
Page Ref: 380
Skill: Applied
Objective: 10.7

62) According to social learning theorists,
    A) morality has a unique course of development.
    B) reinforcement for good behavior is enough for children to acquire moral responses.
    C) moral behavior is acquired just like any other set of responses: through reinforcement and modeling.
    D) positive reinforcement for a child's character decreases a behavior's frequency.
Answer: C
Page Ref: 380
Skill: Conceptual
Objective: 10.7

63) Warmth and responsiveness, competence and power, and consistency between assertions and behavior are all
    A) characteristics of a model that increase a child's willingness to imitate the model's behavior.
    B) characteristics of emotional development that are necessary for moral behavior to occur.
    C) important characteristics of inductive discipline.
    D) characteristics of a prosocial child who has learned empathy-based guilt.
Answer: A
Page Ref: 380–381
Skill: Conceptual
Objective: 10.7

64) Models are most influential in
    A) adulthood.
    B) adolescence.
    C) middle childhood.
    D) the early years.
Answer: D
Page Ref: 381
Skill: Factual
Objective: 10.7

65) A sharp reprimand or physical force to restrain or move a child is justified only when
    A) reasoning is ineffective.
    B) the child misbehaves repeatedly.
    C) immediate obedience is necessary.
    D) the parent wishes to foster long-term goals.
Answer: C
Page Ref: 381
Skill: Conceptual
Objective: 10.7

66) Which of the following is true about harsh punishment?
    A) Although corporal punishment spans the SES spectrum, its frequency and harshness are elevated among the educated and economically advantaged parents.
    B) A punitive adult is likely to punish with greater frequency over time because harsh punishment gives adults immediate relief.
    C) Adults whose parents used corporal punishment are less accepting of such discipline because they've seen the consequences firsthand.
    D) There is no evidence that heredity contributes to the link between punitive discipline and children's adjustment difficulties.
Answer: B
Page Ref: 381
Skill: Conceptual
Objective: 10.7

67) Sending a child to her room for a few minutes
    A) is useful when a child is out of control.
    B) often generates much resentment in children.
    C) is less effective than punishment in producing the desired behavior.
    D) is the most effective form of discipline.
Answer: A
Page Ref: 382
Skill: Conceptual
Objective: 10.7

68) Which of the following uses of punishment is the most effective?
    A) Mr. Allen tells his son that he is using punishment as a last resort.
    B) Mrs. Vello allows her children to act inappropriately from time to time but scolds them at other times.
    C) Mr. Reilly uses punishment in public because his daughter is very embarrassed by being scolded around others.
    D) Mrs. Seldon, a warm parent, uses mild punishment consistently and provides reasons for the punishment.
Answer: D
Page Ref: 382
Skill: Applied
Objective: 10.7

69) Research on the consequences on punishment reveals that in African-American families,
    A) most children view spanking as a practice carried out with their best interests in mind.
    B) physical punishment is positively associated with adolescent aggression and antisocial behavior.
    C) children view spanking as an act of personal aggression.
    D) physical punishment is generally considered wrong.
Answer: A
Page Ref: 383 Box: CI: Ethnic Differences in the Consequences of Physical Punishment
Skill: Conceptual
Objective: 10.7

70) Research on punishment shows that spanking is
    A) associated with a rise in behavior problems regardless of the parents' child-rearing style.
    B) viewed by most Caucasian-American children as a practice carried out with their best interests in mind.
    C) associated with a rise in behavior problems if parents are cold and rejecting but not if they are warm and supportive.
    D) a more effective form of discipline than time out and withdrawal of privileges.
Answer: C
Page Ref: 383 Box: CI: Ethnic Differences in the Consequences of Physical Punishment
Skill: Conceptual
Objective: 10.7

71) The most effective forms of discipline encourage good conduct by
    A) only punishing children for severe misconduct.
    B) warning children that they will be punished if they act immaturely.
    C) letting children know ahead of time how to act.
    D) combining firm intervention with a temporary withdrawal of affection.
Answer: C
Page Ref: 383
Skill: Conceptual
Objective: 10.7

72) The cognitive-developmental perspective regards children as
    A) passive learners of moral standards.
    B) active thinkers about social rules.
    C) blank slates with regard to morality.
    D) prewired with moral compasses.
Answer: B
Page Ref: 384
Skill: Conceptual
Objective: 10.8

73) Three-year-old Connor is asked to choose the child who is the "most wrong." Which child is Connor the most likely to choose?
    A) a child eating ice cream with her fingers
    B) a child who does not say "please" when she asks her friend to pass the water
    C) a child who hits her sister for no reason
    D) a boy who wears his long hair in a ponytail
Answer: C
Page Ref: 384–385
Skill: Applied
Objective: 10.8

74) Three-year-old Madison is shown two pictures: one depicting a child stealing another child's toy and the other showing a child eating spaghetti with her fingers. Madison is most likely to view
    A) both actions as equally wrong.
    B) both actions as okay as long as they were not witnessed by an adult.
    C) the stealing as worse than the bad table manners.
    D) the bad table manners as worse than the stealing.
Answer: C
Page Ref: 384–385
Skill: Applied
Objective: 10.8

75) Within the moral domain, preschool and young school-age children
   A) tend to reason rigidly.
   B) rarely make judgments based on consequences.
   C) cannot distinguish social conventions from moral imperatives.
   D) tend to reason flexibly.
   Answer: A
   Page Ref: 385
   Skill: Conceptual
   Objective: 10.8

76) Which of the following is true about social experience and moral understanding?
   A) Social experiences are not vital to the development of morality.
   B) Children rarely benefit from adult-child discussions of moral issues.
   C) Children learn to care about the welfare of others from warm, sensitive parental communication.
   D) Children who verbally and physically assault others tend to have parents who tell stories with moral implications.
   Answer: C
   Page Ref: 385
   Skill: Conceptual
   Objective: 10.8

77) When her two sons fight over rights and possessions, Laura allows the boys to negotiate and work out their first ideas about justice and fairness. She then talks to them warmly and discusses moral issues with them. As a result, Laura's sons will probably
   A) have advanced moral thinking.
   B) rarely fight with each other.
   C) tend toward physical, rather than verbal, aggression in fights.
   D) experience feelings of frustration and be delayed in moral reasoning.
   Answer: A
   Page Ref: 385
   Skill: Applied
   Objective: 10.8

78) Emily is chosen as Student of the Day. Gretel is angry that she was not selected, and she calls Emily a "do-do head." This is an example of _____ aggression.
   A) hostile
   B) instrumental
   C) passive
   D) relational
   Answer: A
   Page Ref: 385
   Skill: Applied
   Objective: 10.9

79) To sit next to her mother at a restaurant, Diana pushes her little brother Mark out of the way. This is an example of _____ aggression.
   A) hostile
   B) instrumental
   C) passive
   D) relational
   Answer: B
   Page Ref: 385–386
   Skill: Applied
   Objective: 10.9

80) Rachel tells her friends, "Don't play with Jaynie. She dresses funny." This is an example of _____ aggression.
   A) hostile
   B) instrumental
   C) passive
   D) relational
   Answer: D
   Page Ref: 385–386
   Skill: Applied
   Objective: 10.9

81) Although verbal aggression is always _____, _____ aggression can be either direct or indirect.
   A) indirect; physical
   B) indirect; relational
   C) indirect; instrumental
   D) direct; relational
   Answer: D
   Page Ref: 386
   Skill: Conceptual
   Objective: 10.9

82) Which of the following is true about aggression?
   A) Proactive aggression rises over early and middle childhood and then declines steadily from adolescence to early adulthood.
   B) Although girls have a reputation for being both verbally and relationally more aggressive than boys, the sex difference is small.
   C) As soon as preschoolers are aware of gender stereotypes, physical aggression drops off more sharply for boys than for girls.
   D) Parents respond far more negatively to physical fighting in boys than they do in girls.
   Answer: B
   Page Ref: 386
   Skill: Conceptual
   Objective: 10.9

83) Which of the following statements is supported by research on aggression?
   A) Girls display overall rates of aggression that are much higher than boys.
   B) Highly aggressive children tend to be neglected by peers.
   C) Children who are high in proactive aggression often see hostile intent where it does not exist.
   D) Boys are more likely than girls to be targets of harsh, inconsistent discipline.
   Answer: D
   Page Ref: 387
   Skill: Conceptual
   Objective: 10.9

84) In the United States, _____ percent of television programs between 6 a.m. and 11 p.m. contain violent scenes.
   A) 7
   B) 17
   C) 37
   D) 57
   Answer: D
   Page Ref: 387
   Skill: Factual
   Objective: 10.9

85) Research shows that the most violent television programs are
    A) reality programs.
    B) adult medical dramas.
    C) children's cartoons.
    D) adult legal dramas.
Answer: C
Page Ref: 388
Skill: Factual
Objective: 10.9

86) Which of the following is supported by research on television violence?
    A) Children's programming is below average in violent content.
    B) Watching violence on TV does not increase the likelihood of aggressive behavior.
    C) Older children are more likely than preschoolers and young school-age children to imitate TV violence.
    D) Time spent watching TV in childhood and adolescence predicts aggressive behavior in adulthood.
Answer: D
Page Ref: 388
Skill: Conceptual
Objective: 10.9

87) Research on television violence indicates that violent TV
    A) strengthens hostility in highly aggressive children.
    B) does not spark hostile thoughts and behavior in nonaggressive children.
    C) does not cause difficulties in parent and peer relations.
    D) makes viewers less willing to tolerate violence in others.
Answer: A
Page Ref: 388
Skill: Conceptual
Objective: 10.9

88) Five-year-old Delaney watches a lot of violent television programming and also spends hours playing violent video games. Delaney probably
    A) underestimates the violence and danger in society.
    B) overestimates the violence and danger in society.
    C) is less willing to tolerate violence in others.
    D) has few hostile thoughts and behaviors.
Answer: B
Page Ref: 388
Skill: Applied
Objective: 10.9

89) The V-chip (or violence chip)
    A) violates the First Amendment right to free speech.
    B) remains optional for new television sets.
    C) is mandated in Canada.
    D) serves to make offensive television programs less appealing to children.
Answer: C
Page Ref: 388
Skill: Factual
Objective: 10.9

90) Surveys of U.S. parents indicate that _____ percent of preschoolers experience no limits on TV or computer use at home.
   A) 2 to 5
   B) 5 to 10
   C) 10 to 15
   D) 20 to 30
Answer: D
Page Ref: 389
Skill: Factual
Objective: 10.9

91) Training in _____ is an effective treatment for aggressive children.
   A) associative play
   B) social problem solving
   C) instrumental aggression
   D) inductive discipline
Answer: B
Page Ref: 389
Skill: Factual
Objective: 10.9

92) In Denyse's preschool classroom, girls spent more time in the housekeeping, art, and reading corners, while boys gathered more often in the areas devoted to blocks, woodworking, and active play. This conformity to these cultural stereotypes is known as gender
   A) typing.
   B) identity.
   C) segregation.
   D) schema.
Answer: A
Page Ref: 390
Skill: Applied
Objective: 10.10

93) Most preschoolers believe that
   A) women can be police officers.
   B) men do not wear nail polish.
   C) women can play roughly.
   D) men can take care of babies.
Answer: B
Page Ref: 391
Skill: Applied
Objective: 10.10

94) Research on biological influences on gender typing reveals that
   A) sex differences in play and personality traits only appear in Western cultures.
   B) aggression preference for same-sex playmates is widespread among mammalian species.
   C) preschool girls prefer to play in larger-group play with other girls, while boys prefer to play in pairs.
   D) prenatally administered androgens decrease active play.
Answer: B
Page Ref: 391
Skill: Conceptual
Objective: 10.10

95) The case of David Reimer, the boy who was raised as a girl after a circumcision accident, demonstrates
   A) the impact of genetic sex and prenatal hormones on a person's sense of self as male or female.
   B) that gender stereotyping can have devastating effects on self-esteem.
   C) the stronger role of the environment over heredity in determining one's gender identity.
   D) that gender reassignment surgery changes a person's sexual identity.
   Answer: A
   Page Ref: 392 Box: B&E: David: A Boy Who Was Reared as a Girl
   Skill: Conceptual
   Objective: 10.10

96) Research on gender typing reveals that
   A) beginning at birth, parents have different expectation of sons than of daughters.
   B) parents tend to describe achievement and warmth as important for sons and competition and closely supervised activities as important for daughters.
   C) parents actively reinforce closeness and independence in boys and dependency in girls.
   D) fathers are more insistent that girls rather than boys conform to gender roles.
   Answer: A
   Page Ref: 393
   Skill: Conceptual
   Objective: 10.10

97) Research on gender typing demonstrates that teachers
   A) tend to negotiate with boys who misbehave, coming up with a joint plan to improve behavior.
   B) use more disapproval and controlling discipline with girls than with boys.
   C) give girls more encouragement than boys to participate in adult-structured activities.
   D) seem to expect girls to misbehave more often than boys.
   Answer: C
   Page Ref: 394
   Skill: Conceptual
   Objective: 10.10

98) Preschoolers' same-sex peer groups
   A) increase children's tolerance for gender-inappropriate activities.
   B) serve to reduce the gender stereotypes coming from parents.
   C) make the peer context an especially potent source of gender-role learning.
   D) increase children's opportunities for cross-gender play.
   Answer: C
   Page Ref: 394
   Skill: Conceptual
   Objective: 10.10

99) Which of the following is true about gender-role learning in gender-segregated peer groups?
   A) Boys are especially intolerant of cross-gender play in other boys.
   B) Preschoolers are rarely criticized for engaging in cross-gender activities.
   C) Preschoolers play in mixed-gender groups more than they play in same-sex groups.
   D) To get their way, girls often rely on commands, threats, and physical force.
   Answer: A
   Page Ref: 394
   Skill: Conceptual
   Objective: 10.10

100) Five-year-old Susannah makes the following observations: "Boys cannot read as well as girls," "Girls are faster than boys," and "Girls are smarter than boys." Susannah is demonstrating
A) gender typing.
B) in-group favoritism.
C) gender identity.
D) androgyny.
Answer: B
Page Ref: 394
Skill: Applied
Objective: 10.10

101) Eight-year-old Ayanna is asked to rate herself on personality traits. Ayanna rates herself as ambitious, competitive, cheerful, and soft-spoken. Ayanna has a(n) _____ gender identity.
A) traditionally feminine
B) traditionally masculine
C) androgynous
D) stereotypical
Answer: C
Page Ref: 395
Skill: Applied
Objective: 10.11

102) Androgynous children and adults
A) are less adaptable than those with traditional gender identities.
B) score low on both masculine and feminine personality characteristics.
C) are less able to show feminine sensitivity than masculine individuals.
D) have higher self-esteem than feminine individuals.
Answer: D
Page Ref: 395
Skill: conceptual
Objective: 10.11

103) Five-year-old Sean realizes that his brother Shane remains a boy even when he dresses up like a girl as a joke. This demonstrates that Sean has acquired gender
A) constancy.
B) identity.
C) preference.
D) orientation.
Answer: A
Page Ref: 395
Skill: Applied
Objective: 10.11

104) If Opal is a gender-schematic child, she
A) seldom views the world in gender-linked terms.
B) applies a gender-salience filter to her experiences.
C) will play with gender-inappropriate toys.
D) will play with a toy she likes, whether or not girls typically play with it.
Answer: B
Page Ref: 396
Skill: Applied
Objective: 10.11

105) A child who believes that all firefighters are boys
    A) is a gender-aschematic child.
    B) has not yet attained gender constancy.
    C) has an incomplete gender identity.
    D) has well-formed gender schemas.
Answer: D
Page Ref: 396
Skill: Applied
Objective: 10.11

106) When Francine sees a dump truck in the sandbox, she wonders, "Do I like this toy?" She then decides to play with the truck. Francine
    A) is a gender-schematic child.
    B) is using her gender-salience filter.
    C) is a gender-aschematic child.
    D) has well-developed gender schemas.
Answer: C
Page Ref: 396
Skill: Applied
Objective: 10.11

107) When Roger sees a baby doll on the floor, he asks himself, "Do boys play with dolls?" He then decides not to play with the doll. Roger
    A) is a gender-schematic child.
    B) does not yet have well-developed gender schemas.
    C) is a gender-aschematic child.
    D) is not using his gender-salience filter.
Answer: A
Page Ref: 396
Skill: Applied
Objective: 10.11

108) Which of the following demonstrates how children's gender schemas are likely to affect memory?
    A) When shown a picture of a female wearing a dress, children may later remember her as a male.
    B) When shown a picture of a male firefighter, children may later remember him as a female.
    C) When shown a picture of a female cooking, children may later remember her as a male.
    D) When shown a picture of a male nurse, children may later remember him as a doctor.
Answer: D
Page Ref: 396–397
Skill: Conceptual
Objective: 10.11

109) By middle childhood, children who hold flexible beliefs about what boys and girls can do are
    A) more likely to engage in antisocial behavior.
    B) less likely to pursue nontraditional interests and activities.
    C) are more likely to notice instances of gender discrimination.
    D) less likely to live in nontraditional homes.
Answer: C
Page Ref: 398
Skill: Conceptual
Objective: 10.11

110) The most successful approach to child rearing is a(n) _____ style.
   A) permissive
   B) authoritarian
   C) uninvolved
   D) authoritative
   Answer: D
   Page Ref: 398
   Skill: Factual
   Objective: 10.12

111) Kevin's parents make few or no demands. They permit Kevin to make many decisions before he is ready. Kevin's parents have a(n) _____ style of child rearing.
   A) authoritarian
   B) permissive
   C) authoritative
   D) uninvolved
   Answer: B
   Page Ref: 399
   Skill: Applied
   Objective: 10.12

112) Angie's parents encourage her to express her thoughts, feelings, and desires. They make reasonable demands for her maturity and consistently enforce and explain them. Angie's parents have a(n) _____ style of child rearing.
   A) authoritative
   B) authoritarian
   C) permissive
   D) uninvolved
   Answer: A
   Page Ref: 399
   Skill: Applied
   Objective: 10.12

113) Rhoda's parents frequently degrade her. They rarely listen to her point of view. They use force and punishment and sometime threaten withdrawal of affection. Rhoda's parents have a(n) _____ style of child rearing.
   A) authoritarian
   B) permissive
   C) authoritative
   D) uninvolved
   Answer: A
   Page Ref: 399
   Skill: Applied
   Objective: 10.12

114) Riley's authoritarian parents interrupt him and put down his ideas. When Riley makes choices they disagree with, his parents withdraw their affection. Riley's parents are using _____ control to manipulate him.
   A) direct
   B) authoritative
   C) psychological
   D) permissive
   Answer: C
   Page Ref: 399
   Skill: Applied
   Objective: 10.12

115) Jamison is impulsive and rebellious. He is also overly demanding and dependent on adults. Jamison shows minimal persistence on tasks and is not doing well in school. Jamison's parents probably have a(n) _____ style of child rearing.
    A) authoritarian
    B) authoritative
    C) uninvolved
    D) permissive
Answer: D
Page Ref: 400
Skill: Applied
Objective: 10.12

116) Condi's parents are emotionally detached. Her father is depressed and her mother has little time or energy for Condi and her brother. They neglect their children and are indifferent to issues of autonomy. Condi's parents have a(n) _____ style of child rearing.
    A) permissive
    B) uninvolved
    C) authoritarian
    D) authoritative
Answer: B
Page Ref: 400
Skill: Applied
Objective: 10.12

117) Physical abuse accounts for _____ percent of reported cases of child maltreatment.
    A) 10
    B) 20
    C) 30
    D) 40
Answer: B
Page Ref: 402
Skill: Factual
Objective: 10.13

118) _____ commit the vast majority of child abuse incidents.
    A) Nonparental family members
    B) Child-care workers
    C) Parents
    D) Stepparents and foster parents
Answer: C
Page Ref: 402
Skill: Factual
Objective: 10.13

119) Which of the following is supported by research on child abuse?
    A) A single abusive personality type is a common thread among abusers
    B) Most parents who were abused as children become child abusers.
    C) Fathers engage in neglect more often than mothers.
    D) Maternal and paternal rates of physical abuse are fairly similar.
Answer: D
Page Ref: 402
Skill: Conceptual
Objective: 10.13

120) Research on child maltreatment shows that
    A) premature babies and children are rarely targets of abuse.
    B) abuse depends more strongly on child factors than on parents' characteristics.
    C) maltreating parents suffer from biased thinking about their child.
    D) abusive parents respond to stressful situations with low emotional arousal.
Answer: C
Page Ref: 403
Skill: Conceptual
Objective: 10.13

121) Which of the following is true about cultural values, laws and customs and their effect on child maltreatment?
    A) Canada prohibits corporal punishment in schools.
    B) No industrialized nations have yet outlawed physical punishment in the home.
    C) The U.S. Supreme Court rejects the right of school officials to use corporal punishment.
    D) Societies that view violence as an appropriate way to solve problems set the stage of child abuse.
Answer: D
Page Ref: 403
Skill: Conceptual
Objective: 10.13

122) Which of the following is true about the consequences of child maltreatment?
    A) While maltreated children show serious learning problems, they typically have few peer difficulties.
    B) Repeated abuse is associated with central nervous system damage, including abnormal EEG brain-wave activity.
    C) Maltreated children typically exhibit low anxiety and abnormally high self-esteem.
    D) Most parents who were maltreated as children grow up to be child abusers.
Answer: B
Page Ref: 404
Skill: Conceptual
Objective: 10.13

123) One strategy that has been quite effective in preventing child abuse is to
    A) teach child development in the regular high school curriculum.
    B) provide home visitation with a cognitive problem-solving component.
    C) arrest child abusers and make sure they serve long sentences.
    D) remove children from abusive home.
Answer: B
Page Ref: 404
Skill: Conceptual
Objective: 10.13

124) Which of the following is true about the judicial system and child maltreatment?
    A) Fewer cases of child maltreatment reach the courts than in decades past.
    B) Child maltreatment is a crime that is relatively easy to prove.
    C) In the United States, government intervention into family life is viewed as a last resort.
    D) Maltreated children and their parents are not usually attached to one another.
Answer: C
Page Ref: 405
Skill: Conceptual
Objective: 10.13

ESSAY

125) Define self-concept and self-esteem. How do they contribute to young children's development?

Answer: Self-concept is the set of attributes, abilities, attitudes, and values that an individual believes defines who he or she is. Preschoolers' self-concepts mainly consist of observable characteristics, such as their names, physical appearance, and possessions. They also describe themselves in terms of typical beliefs, emotions, and attitudes, such as "I'm happy when I play with my friends." Preschoolers' increasing self-awareness underlies struggles over their rights to objects as well as first efforts to cooperate in playing games, solving problems, and resolving disputes over objects.

Self-esteem includes the judgments an individual makes about his or her own worth and the feelings associated with those judgments. Although preschoolers' self-esteem is not yet well-defined, it is extremely high and leads young children to underestimate the difficulty of tasks. Their high self-esteem contributes greatly to their initiative during a period in which they must master many new skills. However, even a little adult disapproval can undermine a young child's self-esteem and enthusiasm for learning.

Page Ref: 365–367

126) Amelia, age 4, has an intense fear of the dark. Her parents question her and determine that Amelia is very afraid of monsters and ghosts. What advice can you give Amelia's parents to help her manage her fears?

Answer: Amelia's parents should reduce her exposure to frightening stories in books and on TV until she is better able to distinguish between appearance and reality. At night, they can make a thorough "search" of Amelia's room for monsters, showing her that none are there. They can leave a night-light burning, sit by Amelia's bed until she falls asleep, or tuck Amelia's favorite toy in for protection.

Page Ref: 370

127) Describe Mildred Parten's sequence of peer sociability, including follow-up research on the different types of play.

Answer: Mildred Parten concluded that social development begins with nonsocial activity—unoccupied, onlooker behavior and solitary play. Then it shifts to parallel play, a limited form of social participation in which a child plays near other children with similar materials but does not try to influence their behavior. At the highest level are two forms of true social interaction. In associative play, children engage in separate activities, but exchange toys and comment on one another's behavior. Finally, in cooperative play, a more advanced type of interaction, children orient toward a common goal, such as acting out a make-believe theme.

Longitudinal evidence indicates that these play forms emerge in the order Parten suggested but that later-appearing ones do no replace earlier ones in a developmental sequence. Rather, all types coexist during early childhood.

Page Ref: 372–373

128) Describe the developmental sequence of cognitive play categories. Provide examples of each.

Answer:
- Functional play: Simple, repetitive motor movements with or without objects, especially common during the first two years. Examples: Running around a room, rolling a car back and forth, kneading clay with no intent to make something.
- Constructive play: Creating or constructing something, especially common between 3 and 6 years. Examples: Making a house out of toy blocks, drawing a picture, putting a puzzle together.
- Make-believe play: Acting out everyday and imaginary roles, especially common between 2 and 6 years. Examples: Playing house, school, or police officer; acting out storybook or television characters.

Page Ref: 373

129) What is inductive discipline, and how does it motivate children's active commitment to moral standards?

Answer: Using induction, an adult helps make the child aware of feelings by pointing out the effects of the child's misbehavior on others, especially noting their distress and making clear that the child caused it. For example, a parent might say, "Your sister is crying because you took her book." When generally warm parents provide explanations that match the child's capacity to understand, while firmly insisting that the child listen and comply, induction is effective as early as age 2.

The success of induction may lie in its power to motivate children's active commitment to moral standards in the following ways:

- Induction gives children information about how to behave that they can use in future situations.
- By emphasizing the impact of the child's actions on others, induction encourages empathy and sympathetic concern, which motivate prosocial behavior.
- Giving children reasons for changing their behavior encourages them to adopt moral standards because those standards make sense.
- Children who consistently experience induction may form a script for the negative emotional consequences of harming others: Child causes harm, inductive message points out harm, child feels empathy for victim, child makes amends. The script deters future transgressions.

Page Ref: 379

130) Describe gender schema theory, and explain how it accounts for the persistence of gender stereotypes and gender-role preferences.

Answer: Gender schema theory is an information-processing approach to gender typing that combines social learning and cognitive development features. It explains how environmental pressures and children's cognition work together to shape gender role development. Beginning at an early age, children organize their experiences into gender schemas, or masculine and feminine categories, that they use to interpret their world. As soon as children can label their own gender, they begin to select gender schemas consistent with it, applying those categories to themselves. As a result, their self-perceptions become gender typed and serve as additional schemas that they use to process information and guide their own behavior. This leads to gender stereotypes and gender-role preferences in several ways. Children attend to and approach schema-consistent information, whereas they ignore, misinterpret, or reject schema-inconsistent information.

Page Ref: 396–397

131) Describe authoritative child rearing and explain what makes it effective.

Answer: The authoritative child-rearing style involves high acceptance and involvement, adaptive control techniques, and appropriate autonomy granting. Authoritative parents are warm, attentive, and sensitive to their child's needs. They establish an enjoyable, emotionally fulfilling parent-child relationship that draws the child into close connection. At the same time, authoritative parents exercise firm, reasonable control. Finally, authoritative parents engage in gradual, appropriate autonomy granting, allowing the child to make decisions in areas where he is ready to do so.

Authoritative parenting seems to create a positive emotional context for parental influences in the following ways:

- Warm, involved parents who are secure in the standards they hold for their children provide models of caring concern as well as confident, self-controlled behavior.
- Children are far more likely to comply with and internalize control that appears fair and reasonable, not arbitrary.
- By making demands and engaging in autonomy granting that matches children's ability to take responsibility for their own behavior, authoritative parents let children know that they are competent individuals who can do things successfully for themselves. In this way, parents foster favorable self-esteem and cognitive social maturity.
- Supportive aspects of the authoritative style, including parental acceptance, involvement, and rational control, are a powerful source of resilience, protecting children from the negative effects of family stress and poverty.

Page Ref: 398–400

CHAPTER 11
PHYSICAL DEVELOPMENT IN MIDDLE CHILDHOOD

MULTIPLE CHOICE

1) At age 6, the average North American child weighs about _____ pounds.
   A) 40
   B) 45
   C) 50
   D) 55
   Answer: B
   Page Ref: 412
   Skill: Factual
   Objective: 11.1

2) Between ages 6 and 8, girls are _____ boys.
   A) slightly shorter than
   B) taller than
   C) slightly heavier than
   D) the same height as
   Answer: A
   Page Ref: 412
   Skill: Factual
   Objective: 11.1

3) On average, the dramatic adolescent growth spurt occurs _____ earlier in girls than in boys
   A) 6 months
   B) 1 year
   C) 18 months
   D) 2 years
   Answer: D
   Page Ref: 412
   Skill: Factual
   Objective: 11.1

4) Seal is getting ready to start first grade. During the school years, his parents can expect him to add about _____ inches in height and _____ pounds in weight each year.
   A) 1 to 2; 3
   B) 2 to 3; 5
   C) 3 to 4; 10
   D) 4 to 5; 15
   Answer: B
   Page Ref: 412
   Skill: Applied
   Objective: 11.1

5) By age _____, the sexual difference in the growth trend reverses.
   A) 5
   B) 7
   C) 9
   D) 11
   Answer: C
   Page Ref: 412
   Skill: Factual
   Objective: 11.1

6) The _____ grow(s) the fastest in middle childhood.
   A) head
   B) upper body
   C) extremities
   D) lower body
   Answer: D
   Page Ref: 412
   Skill: Factual
   Objective: 11.1

7) Joey and Rachel are approaching adolescence. At this time, they are likely to grow out of their _____ more quickly than their _____.
   A) hats; shoes
   B) jeans; jackets
   C) shirts; jeans
   D) jackets; shoes
   Answer: B
   Page Ref: 412–413
   Skill: Applied
   Objective: 11.1

8) After age 8, girls begin _____ at a faster rate than boys.
   A) accumulating fat
   B) adding muscle
   C) pruning synapses
   D) upper body growth
   Answer: A
   Page Ref: 413
   Skill: Factual
   Objective: 11.1

9) Worldwide, a ___-inch gap exists between the smallest and the largest 8-year-olds.
   A) 3
   B) 5
   C) 7
   D) 9
   Answer: D
   Page Ref: 413
   Skill: Factual
   Objective: 11.1

10) In terms of growth norms, which of the following children is most likely to be the shortest?
    A) Shane from Australia
    B) Sayuri from Asia
    C) Daryl from Canada
    D) Alice from the United States
Answer: B
Page Ref: 413
Skill: Applied
Objective: 11.1

11) In terms of growth norms, which of the following children is most likely to be the tallest?
    A) Miguel from South America
    B) Rondi from the Pacific Islands
    C) Kota from Asia
    D) Rainer from Switzerland
Answer: D
Page Ref: 413
Skill: Applied
Objective: 11.1

12) Growth norms
    A) should be applied universally to assess secular trends.
    B) are particularly applicable to ethnic minorities.
    C) must be applied cautiously.
    D) consider height but not weight.
Answer: C
Page Ref: 413
Skill: Conceptual
Objective: 11.1

13) Body size
    A) is determined exclusively by heredity.
    B) sometimes reflects evolutionary adaptations to a particular climate.
    C) is primarily determined by environmental factors.
    D) tends to be larger in developing countries.
Answer: B
Page Ref: 413
Skill: Conceptual
Objective: 11.1

14) Tanji is long and lean. She is probably from a
    A) cold, Arctic area.
    B) region where disease is common.
    C) hot, tropical region.
    D) poor nation.
Answer: C
Page Ref: 413
Skill: Applied
Objective: 11.1

15) Physically small children tend to live in
    A) tropical climates.
    B) less developed regions.
    C) countries where food is plentiful.
    D) wealthy nations.
Answer: B
Page Ref: 413
Skill: Factual
Objective: 11.1

16) Which of the following changes could you anticipate for the child of Ethiopian immigrants who relocated to the United States?
    A) She will be taller and longer-legged than her agemates in Ethiopia.
    B) She will be heavier and have thicker bones than her agemates in Ethiopia.
    C) She will be taller than her parents, but will have shorter legs.
    D) She will be shorter and start menstruation later than her agemates in Ethiopia.
Answer: A
Page Ref: 413
Skill: Applied
Objective: 11.1

17) Secular trends in physical growth involve changes in body size from
    A) one region to another.
    B) evolutionary adaptation.
    C) one generation to the next.
    D) growth spurts.
Answer: C
Page Ref: 413
Skill: Conceptual
Objective: 11.1

18) Kristin and Katie are taller and heavier than their mother was at their age. This is an example of
    A) a generative effect.
    B) a growth spurt.
    C) a secular trend.
    D) evolutionary adaptation.
Answer: C
Page Ref: 413
Skill: Applied
Objective: 11.1

19) The larger size of today's children is mostly due to
    A) food additives.
    B) a faster rate of physical development.
    C) a cultural change in body image.
    D) widespread immunization.
Answer: B
Page Ref: 413
Skill: Conceptual
Objective: 11.1

20) In regions with widespread poverty, famine, and disease, a secular _____ has occurred.
    A) increase in height
    B) increase in weight
    C) increase in obesity
    D) decrease in body size
    Answer: D
    Page Ref: 413
    Skill: Conceptual
    Objective: 11.1

21) During middle childhood, the bones of the body
    A) stop growing.
    B) shorten and narrow.
    C) lengthen and broaden.
    D) are firmly attached to ligaments.
    Answer: C
    Page Ref: 414
    Skill: Factual
    Objective: 11.1

22) Emma, age 8, can turn cartwheels, do the splits, and do handsprings. This is probably due to which two factors of growth in middle childhood?
    A) ligaments not firmly attached to bones; increasing muscle strength
    B) hardening of the bones; tightening of ligaments
    C) muscles that are loosely attached to bones; undeveloped muscle tone
    D) underdeveloped hip and knee joints; muscles that do not fully develop until adolescence
    Answer: A
    Page Ref: 414
    Skill: Applied
    Objective: 11.1

23) Kyra's muscles are adapting to her enlarging skeleton. As a result, she will probably
    A) experience a brief period of enhanced physical coordination.
    B) display unusual physical dexterity of movement.
    C) notice a slight decrease in muscular strength.
    D) experience nighttime "growing pains."
    Answer: D
    Page Ref: 414
    Skill: Applied
    Objective: 11.1

24) Between the ages of 6 and 12, ___ primary teeth are lost and replaced by permanent teeth.
    A) 14
    B) 16
    C) 20
    D) 24
    Answer: C
    Page Ref: 414
    Skill: Factual
    Objective: 11.1

25) Grace, a third grader, is beginning to get many of her permanent teeth. Her mom is concerned because Grace's permanent teeth seem much too large. What can you tell Grace's mom?
   A) Grace's permanent teeth will appear shorter as they "settle" in to her jaw.
   B) As Grace loses all 24 of her primary teeth, the permanent teeth will appear smaller.
   C) As Grace's neck and torso grow, her teeth will appear smaller.
   D) Grace's jaw and chin bones will grow to accommodate the newly erupting teeth.
   Answer: D
   Page Ref: 414
   Skill: Applied
   Objective: 11.1

26) Most children need help with flossing until about _____ years of age.
   A) 6
   B) 9
   C) 12
   D) 15
   Answer: B
   Page Ref: 414
   Skill: Factual
   Objective: 11.1

27) Dental health affects a child's
   A) resistance to disease.
   B) personality.
   C) speech.
   D) IQ.
   Answer: C
   Page Ref: 414
   Skill: Factual
   Objective: 11.1

28) Wendi, a dental hygiene student, is visiting a second grade classroom to teach 26 children proper brushing techniques. Based on U.S. averages, how many students can she expect to see with some tooth decay?
   A) 4
   B) 9
   C) 13
   D) 20
   Answer: C
   Page Ref: 414
   Skill: Applied
   Objective: 11.1

29) Janice, age 7, is an eager thumb sucker. As a result, Janice is at risk for
   A) tooth decay.
   B) a malocclusion.
   C) gum disease.
   D) a tongue thrust.
   Answer: B
   Page Ref: 414
   Skill: Applied
   Objective: 11.1

30) A common way to treat a malocclusion is by
   A) requiring regular teeth cleaning.
   B) filling all cavities.
   C) putting braces on the teeth.
   D) flossing at least three times per week.
Answer: C
Page Ref: 414
Skill: Factual
Objective: 11.1

31) Which of the following is a cause of malocclusion?
   A) sleeping with a bottle at night
   B) eating too many sweets
   C) wearing braces
   D) crowding of permanent teeth
Answer: D
Page Ref: 414
Skill: Conceptual
Objective: 11.1

32) The weight of the brain increases by _____ percent during middle childhood and adolescence.
   A) 5
   B) 10
   C) 15
   D) 20
Answer: B
Page Ref: 414
Skill: Factual
Objective: 11.2

33) White matter
   A) increases steadily throughout childhood and adolescence.
   B) consists mostly of neurons and synapses.
   C) begins to decline in middle childhood.
   D) contains fewer myelinated nerve fibers than does gray matter.
Answer: A
Page Ref: 414
Skill: Conceptual
Objective: 11.2

34) Gray matter
   A) replaces white matter in middle childhood.
   B) consists largely of myelinated nerve fibers.
   C) increases steadily throughout childhood and adolescence.
   D) declines as synaptic pruning and death of surrounding neurons proceed.
Answer: D
Page Ref: 414
Skill: Conceptual
Objective: 11.2

35) Secretions of _____ are related to cognitive performance.
    A) the frontal lobes
    B) particular neurotransmitters
    C) the corpus callosum
    D) growth hormone
Answer: B
Page Ref: 414
Skill: Conceptual
Objective: 11.2

36) When neurotransmitters are not present in appropriate balances,
    A) cognitive performance increases.
    B) children may suffer serious developmental problems.
    C) social adjustment improves.
    D) the ability to withstand stress increases.
Answer: B
Page Ref: 415
Skill: Conceptual
Objective: 11.2

37) Milo's neurotransmitters are not present in appropriate balances. He has begun to experience seizures and loss of motor control. Milo may suffer from
    A) epilepsy.
    B) cerebral palsy.
    C) muscular dystrophy.
    D) autism.
Answer: A
Page Ref: 415
Skill: Applied
Objective: 11.2

38) Researchers believe that brain functioning may change in middle childhood because of
    A) the rapid brain growth during that time period.
    B) an overabundance of gray matter.
    C) the influence of hormones.
    D) the decrease in white matter in the corpus callosum.
Answer: C
Page Ref: 415
Skill: Conceptual
Objective: 11.2

39) Around age 7 or 8, an increase in _____ occurs in children of both sexes.
    A) androgens
    B) estrogens
    C) brain circuitry
    D) endocrine
Answer: A
Page Ref: 415
Skill: Factual
Objective: 11.2

40) Androgens
    A) decrease among boys at puberty.
    B) affect brain organization and behavior in many animal species.
    C) increase among girls at puberty.
    D) contribute to girls' lower activity level.
Answer: B
Page Ref: 415
Skill: Conceptual
Objective: 11.2

41) Eating an evening meal with parents leads to a diet
    A) lower in fruits.
    B) higher in soft drinks.
    C) lower in fried foods.
    D) lower in vegetables.
Answer: C
Page Ref: 416
Skill: Conceptual
Objective: 11.3

42) School-age children report which of the following after eating junk foods?
    A) They feel better.
    B) They focus better.
    C) They are happier.
    D) They feel sluggish.
Answer: D
Page Ref: 416
Skill: Conceptual
Objective: 11.3

43) Willemina's mom is concerned that she is not eating a well-balanced diet. One solution is to
    A) make sure she eats three healthy meals a day, but allow at least one junk food snack between meals.
    B) keep cheese, fruit, raw vegetables, and peanut butter readily available for snacks.
    C) make sure to have new, novel healthy food items available for snacks.
    D) allow her to make her own food choices because children naturally select balanced diets.
Answer: B
Page Ref: 416
Skill: Applied
Objective: 11.3

44) Pax suffers from malnutrition. Which of the following statements is probably correct?
    A) Pax will be nonresponsive to stressful situations.
    B) Pax will respond with greater fear to stressful situations.
    C) Pax will exhibit normal motor skills, but altered psychological functioning.
    D) Pax will display normal psychological functioning, but delayed motor functioning.
Answer: B
Page Ref: 416
Skill: Applied
Objective: 11.3

45) Studies conducted in Kenya, Egypt, and Mexico revealed that the
    A) quality of food strongly predicted favorable cognitive development in middle childhood.
    B) age at which government-sponsored food programs were available was more important than vitamin supplements.
    C) quantity of food strongly predicted favorable cognitive development in middle childhood.
    D) regularity of vitamin supplementation was more important than the quality of food.
    Answer: A
    Page Ref: 416
    Skill: Conceptual
    Objective: 11.3

46) An obese child is more than ____ percent over healthy weight, based on body mass index.
    A) 15
    B) 20
    C) 25
    D) 30
    Answer: B
    Page Ref: 416
    Skill: Factual
    Objective: 11.3

47) In developing countries, rates of obesity are
    A) increasing rapidly.
    B) stablizing.
    C) decreasing slowly.
    D) decreasing rapidly.
    Answer: A
    Page Ref: 417
    Skill: Factual
    Objective: 11.3

48) Childhood obesity in China
    A) is practically nonexistent.
    B) is especially high in rural regions.
    C) has reached 10 percent in cities.
    D) has decreased in the past 25 years.
    Answer: C
    Page Ref: 417
    Skill: Factual
    Objective: 11.3

49) Obese children
    A) are at a risk for social difficulties, but not emotional problems.
    B) are likely to have at least one obese parent.
    C) usually decide when to eat on the basis of hunger.
    D) are less likely than average-weight peers to spend many hours watching television.
    Answer: B
    Page Ref: 417
    Skill: Conceptual
    Objective: 11.3

50) Which of the following children is at risk for excessive weight gain?
    A) Lauralee, whose parents are average weight
    B) Stewart, who lives in a stressful family environment
    C) Donato, who was breastfed for two years
    D) Donna, whose parents are vegans
Answer: B
Page Ref: 418
Skill: Applied
Objective: 11.3

51) Jonathan, age 10, was born underweight because his mother smoked during pregnancy. Jonathan is at risk for
    A) obesity.
    B) anorexia.
    C) bulimia.
    D) a fast basal metabolism.
Answer: A
Page Ref: 418
Skill: Applied
Objective: 11.3

52) Jorda's parents are immigrants. As children, they suffered from long periods of food deprivation. As a result, they pressure Jorda to eat. This practice could contribute to
    A) disrupting Jorda's appetite control centers in the brain.
    B) Jorda becoming overweight.
    C) Jorda attaching great value to treats.
    D) Jorda becoming malnourished.
Answer: B
Page Ref: 418
Skill: Applied
Objective: 11.3

53) Obese children _____ than average-weight children.
    A) eat more slowly
    B) are more responsive to internal huger cues
    C) are less responsive to external stimuli associated with food
    D) chew their food less thoroughly
Answer: D
Page Ref: 418
Skill: Factual
Objective: 11.3

54) _____ is related to obesity.
    A) Breastfeeding
    B) Reduced sleep
    C) A fast metabolism
    D) Vegetarianism
Answer: B
Page Ref: 418
Skill: Factual
Objective: 11.3

55) As an overweight girl, Maggi is _____ than her average-weight peers.
    A) more likely to reach puberty late
    B) less likely to suffer from depression
    C) more likely to be socially isolated
    D) more likely to be given financial aid for college
Answer: C
Page Ref: 419
Skill: Applied
Objective: 11.3

56) _____ constitutes one-sixth of the caloric intake of the average American age 2 and older.
    A) Palm oil
    B) Saturated fat
    C) Fructose
    D) Fiber
Answer: C
Page Ref: 420 Box: SI: Health: The Obesity Epidemic: How Americans Became the Heaviest People in the World
Skill: Factual
Objective: 11.3

57) Research reveals that when presented with supersized food portions, individuals increase their food intake on average by _____ percent.
    A) 5 to 10
    B) 10 to 15
    C) 20 to 25
    D) 25 to 30
Answer: D
Page Ref: 420 Box: SI: Health: The Obesity Epidemic: How Americans Became the Heaviest People in the World
Skill: Factual
Objective: 11.3

58) Between the 1970s and the 1990s, due to increasingly busy lives and the growing assortment of high-calorie snack foods, average daily food intake rose by almost _____ calories.
    A) 100
    B) 200
    C) 300
    D) 400
Answer: B
Page Ref: 420 Box: SI: Health: The Obesity Epidemic: How Americans Became the Heaviest People in the World
Skill: Factual
Objective: 11.3

59) The most effective interventions for childhood obesity are
    A) family-based and focus on changing behaviors.
    B) crash diets.
    C) school-based programs.
    D) competitive sports.
Answer: A
Page Ref: 420
Skill: Factual
Objective: 11.3

60) Rewarding children for _____ seems to increase their sense of personal control of exercising.
    A) time spent exercising
    B) giving up inactivity
    C) eating less
    D) documenting daily physical activity
Answer: B
Page Ref: 421
Skill: Conceptual
Objective: 11.3

61) Schools can help reduce obesity by
    A) serving fewer meals.
    B) offering more sports.
    C) providing additional recess time.
    D) having adults chose meals for overweight children.
Answer: C
Page Ref: 422
Skill: Conceptual
Objective: 11.3

62) _____ is the most common vision problem in middle childhood.
    A) Presbyopia
    B) Tunnel vision
    C) Astigmatism
    D) Myopia
Answer: D
Page Ref: 422
Skill: Factual
Objective: 11.4

63) By the end of the school years, nearly _____ percent of all children have myopia.
    A) 15
    B) 25
    C) 35
    D) 45
Answer: B
Page Ref: 422
Skill: Factual
Objective: 11.4

64) School-age children with low birth weights show an especially high rate of
    A) myopia.
    B) otitis media.
    C) malnutrition.
    D) presbyopia.
Answer: A
Page Ref: 422
Skill: Conceptual
Objective: 11.4

65) Which of the following children is most likely to have myopia?
    A) Travis, who lives in a high-SES household
    B) Devin, whose parents have good eyesight
    C) Chen, who weighed 8 pounds at birth
    D) Hallie, whose lives in a low-SES household
    Answer: A
    Page Ref: 422
    Skill: Applied
    Objective: 11.4

66) Parents who tell their children not to read in dim light for fear of ruining their eyes are
    A) voicing well-founded concerns.
    B) repeating unfounded "old wives tales."
    C) unnecessarily scaring their children.
    D) actually putting the children at further risk for myopia.
    Answer: A
    Page Ref: 422
    Skill: Conceptual
    Objective: 11.4

67) Myopia is one of the few health conditions that
    A) decreases with age.
    B) can be entirely prevented through changes in behavior.
    C) increases with family income.
    D) is unique to industrialized nations.
    Answer: C
    Page Ref: 422
    Skill: Conceptual
    Objective: 11.4

68) The Eustachian tube becomes longer, narrow, and more slanted during middle childhood, resulting in
    A) more frequent bouts of otitis media.
    B) higher rates of strep throat.
    C) lower rates of sinus infections.
    D) reduced incidence of otitis media.
    Answer: D
    Page Ref: 422
    Skill: Factual
    Objective: 11.4

69) As many as _____ percent of low-SES children develop some hearing loss as a result of repeated middle ear infections.
    A) 5
    B) 10
    C) 20
    D) 30
    Answer: C
    Page Ref: 422
    Skill: Factual
    Objective: 11.4

70) _____ percent of U.S. school-age children suffer from nocturnal enuresis, which refers to _____.
   A) Twenty; nightmares
   B) Ten; bedwetting during the night
   C) Five; a brief period when breathing stops temporarily
   D) Ten; fear of the dark
Answer: B
Page Ref: 422
Skill: Factual
Objective: 11.5

71) One of the most common causes of enuresis is
   A) the use of prescription antidepressant drugs, which increase the amount of urine produced.
   B) abnormalities in the child's urinary tract or bladder.
   C) falling asleep in a room that is too warm or using too many blankets.
   D) a hormonal imbalance that permits too much urine to accumulate during the night.
Answer: D
Page Ref: 422–423
Skill: Conceptual
Objective: 11.5

72) The most effective treatment for enuresis is/are
   A) stimulants.
   B) a urine alarm.
   C) anxiety medication.
   D) punishment.
Answer: B
Page Ref: 423
Skill: Conceptual
Objective: 11.5

73) Seven-year-old Derek is having problems with bedwetting at night. Which of the following is probably true?
   A) Derek has not seen a health professional about his problem.
   B) Derek will outgrow this problem by age 8 or 9.
   C) When Derek's parents punish him for wetting, he wets less often.
   D) Derek's problem is a learned behavior, rather than a biological issue.
Answer: A
Page Ref: 423
Skill: Applied
Objective: 11.5

74) Mikkah is 8 years old and experiences nocturnal enuresis. His parents have decided against any type of treatment, feeling that he will "outgrow it." His parents should know that
   A) treatment in middle childhood has immediate positive psychological consequences.
   B) enuresis is not something that can be outgrown.
   C) doing nothing is, in fact, the most effective treatment for enuresis.
   D) without medical intervention, he runs a high risk of having this problem reoccur throughout his life.
Answer: A
Page Ref: 423
Skill: Applied
Objective: 11.5

75) Children experience a somewhat higher rate of illness during
   A) toddlerhood.
   B) the preschool years.
   C) the first two years of elementary school.
   D) the last two years before the onset of adolescence.
   Answer: C
   Page Ref: 423
   Skill: Factual
   Objective: 11.5

76) On average, illness causes children to miss about _____ days of school per year.
   A) 3
   B) 8
   C) 11
   D) 14
   Answer: C
   Page Ref: 423
   Skill: Factual
   Objective: 11.5

77) When Anne engages in intense exercise, particularly in cold weather or during allergy season, her bronchial tubes fill with mucus and contract. This causes her to cough and have serious breathing difficulties. Anne has
   A) nocturnal enuresis.
   B) asthma.
   C) emphysema.
   D) bronchitis.
   Answer: B
   Page Ref: 423
   Skill: Applied
   Objective: 11.5

78) The most frequent cause of school absence is
   A) oversleeping.
   B) asthma.
   C) the flu.
   D) the common cold.
   Answer: B
   Page Ref: 423
   Skill: Factual
   Objective: 11.5

79) _____ is related to asthma in middle childhood.
   A) Obesity
   B) Enuresis
   C) Otitis media
   D) Myopia
   Answer: A
   Page Ref: 423
   Skill: Factual
   Objective: 11.5

80) Which of the following is true about childhood injuries?
    A) Injury fatalities decrease from middle childhood into adolescence.
    B) Injury rates for girls rise considerable above those for boys.
    C) Motor vehicle accidents are the leading cause of injury fatalities in middle childhood.
    D) Sports-related injuries are the second leading cause of injury in middle childhood.
    Answer: C
    Page Ref: 424
    Skill: Conceptual
    Objective: 11.6

81) Parents
    A) often underestimate their child's safety knowledge.
    B) often underestimate their child's physical abilities.
    C) have little influence on children's safety knowledge.
    D) must be educated about children's age-related safety capabilities.
    Answer: D
    Page Ref: 424
    Skill: Conceptual
    Objective: 11.6

82) Which of the following children is the most likely to be a risk-taker?
    A) Betsy, whose parents are safety-conscious
    B) Frank, whose parents strictly supervise his activities
    C) Deanna, whose parents consistently enforce rules
    D) Donald, whose parents use punitive discipline
    Answer: D
    Page Ref: 424–425
    Skill: Applied
    Objective: 11.6

83) During the preschool and early school years, children
    A) have a good understanding of what is inside the body but do not apply this knowledge to explain causes of illness.
    B) do not have a good understanding of what is inside the body but do understand biological causes of illness.
    C) do not have much biological knowledge to bring to bear on their understanding of health and illness.
    D) have limited understanding of illness unless they have experienced a serious threat to their health.
    Answer: C
    Page Ref: 425
    Skill: Conceptual
    Objective: 11.6

84) If you asked 6-year-old Martin how to keep himself "healthy," he would probably say
    A) it has to do with how internal organs work.
    B) it is important to eat right so the body can build new muscles and bones.
    C) he does not understand the question.
    D) it is a matter of eating vegetables and wearing a jacket when the weather is cold.
    Answer: D
    Page Ref: 425
    Skill: Applied
    Objective: 11.6

85) Most efforts to impart health concepts to school-age children have
   A) little impact on behavior.
   B) a moderate impact on behavior.
   C) significant impact on behavior when combined with school curriculum.
   D) significant impact of behavior when combined with food rewards.
   Answer: A
   Page Ref: 425
   Skill: Conceptual
   Objective: 11.7

86) Which of the following is true about health education for school-age children?
   A) Health, particularly physical fitness, is usually an important goal for children.
   B) Children cannot see the connection between engaging in preventive behaviors now and experiencing later health consequences.
   C) Children learn health information best through the teaching of health-related facts.
   D) Children have a good sense of how internal organs work, but they do not yet connect specific behaviors with health.
   Answer: B
   Page Ref: 425
   Skill: Conceptual
   Objective: 11.7

87) Imparting health concepts to school-age children is difficult because they
   A) are far more concerned about schoolwork, friends, and play.
   B) have time perspectives that relate past, present, and future.
   C) are typically rebellious, and so information provided to them by an authority figure is likely to be ignored.
   D) are skeptical of the media and advertising, which are making a huge effort to promote healthy living.
   Answer: A
   Page Ref: 425
   Skill: Conceptual
   Objective: 11.7

88) At what age are children most likely to begin understanding that illness can be caused by contagion?
   A) 4 or 5
   B) 6 or 7
   C) 9 or 10
   D) 12 or 13
   Answer: C
   Page Ref: 426 Box: SI: Education: Children's Understanding of Health and Illness
   Skill: Factual
   Objective: 11.6

89) Which of the following children is the most likely to make the following statement: "You get a cold when your sinuses fill up with mucus. Colds come from viruses."
   A) Jared, a 6-year-old
   B) Gina, an 8-year-old
   C) David, a 10-year-old
   D) Olivia, a 13-year-old
   Answer: D
   Page Ref: 426 Box: SI: Education: Children's Understanding of Health and Illness
   Skill: Applied
   Objective: 11.6

90) School-age children sometimes believe that sharing a Coke causes AIDS because they
    A) lack the cognitive skills necessary for understanding biological causes of disease.
    B) think diseases are punishment for doing something bad.
    C) view illnesses in superstitious ways.
    D) generalize their knowledge of familiar diseases to unfamiliar ones.
Answer: D
Page Ref: 426 Box: SI: Education: Children's Understanding of Health and Illness
Skill: Conceptual
Objective: 11.6

91) Compared with preschoolers, school-age children are
    A) physically less pliable.
    B) physically more elastic.
    C) more agile, but less able to balance.
    D) stronger, but less agile.
Answer: B
Page Ref: 428
Skill: Factual
Objective: 11.8

92) At age 6, a ball thrown by a girl travels an average speed of _____ feet per second.
    A) 29
    B) 39
    C) 56
    D) 78
Answer: A
Page Ref: 428
Skill: Factual
Objective: 11.8

93) Which of the following is true about changes in running, jumping, and gait variations during middle childhood?
    A) Skipping ability, present in early childhood, decreases.
    B) Sideways stepping appears around age 9 and becomes more fluid with age.
    C) Running speed increases from 12 feet per second at age 6 to over 18 feet per second at age 12.
    D) The average 8-year-old cannot accurately jump and hop from square to square.
Answer: C
Page Ref: 428
Skill: Conceptual
Objective: 11.8

94) As Bree gets older, how will her batting abilities change?
    A) Her speed will increase but accuracy will stay the same.
    B) Her speed will stay the same but her accuracy will improve.
    C) Batting motions will involve her entire body.
    D) Batting motions will primarily involve her upper body.
Answer: C
Page Ref: 428
Skill: Applied
Objective: 11.8

95) Between 6 and 12 years of age, Hyrum demonstrates quicker, more accurate movements. This means that Hyrum has improved
   A) agility.
   B) flexibility.
   C) nimbleness.
   D) pliability.
   Answer: A
   Page Ref: 428
   Skill: Applied
   Objective: 11.8

96) Danica, age 9, executes difficult tumbling routines. Since she started gymnastics at age 4, Danica has become more pliable and elastic. This means that Danica has improved
   A) agility.
   B) flexibility.
   C) balance.
   D) force.
   Answer: B
   Page Ref: 428
   Skill: Applied
   Objective: 11.8

97) Luke, age 11, can throw a ball harder than he could at age 7. When he is jumping, he can propel himself further off the ground. This increasing ability is known as
   A) flexibility.
   B) agility.
   C) force.
   D) balance.
   Answer: C
   Page Ref: 428
   Skill: Applied
   Objective: 11.8

98) An 11-year-old's reaction time is _____ a 5-year-old's.
   A) twice as fast as
   B) half as fast as
   C) about equal to
   D) five times as fast as
   Answer: A
   Page Ref: 428
   Skill: Factual
   Objective: 11.8

99) Six-year-old Kirsten's parents are eager to have her play tennis. Because her gross-motor skills are not fully developed, a more appropriate sport or game would be
   A) softball.
   B) basketball.
   C) football.
   D) four-square.
   Answer: D
   Page Ref: 428
   Skill: Applied
   Objective: 11.8

100) Seven-year-old Alex is seldom successful at batting a thrown ball. Which of the following activities should Alex be encouraged to play at his age?
   A) T-ball
   B) tennis
   C) baseball
   D) football
Answer: A
Page Ref: 428
Skill: Applied
Objective: 11.8

101) At age 6, Shelby probably
   A) can print her first and last names legibly.
   B) will learn to write lowercase letters before uppercase letters.
   C) can learn to write in cursive as easily as printing.
   D) cannot yet integrate two-dimensional shapes into her drawings.
Answer: A
Page Ref: 429
Skill: Applied
Objective: 11.8

102) Legibility of writing gradually increases as children
   A) use larger, more uniform lettering.
   B) produce letters with uniform height and spacing.
   C) learn to make strokes with their entire arm.
   D) learn to accurately integrate two-dimensional shapes.
Answer: B
Page Ref: 429
Skill: Conceptual
Objective: 11.8

103) Around age _____ years, the third dimension is clearly evident in children's drawings.
   A) 3 or 4
   B) 5 or 6
   C) 7 or 8
   D) 9 or 10
Answer: D
Page Ref: 429
Skill: Factual
Objective: 11.8

104) _____ children excel at many motor tasks.
   A) Shorter
   B) Less muscular
   C) Taller
   D) Heavier
Answer: C
Page Ref: 430
Skill: Conceptual
Objective: 11.9

105) Which of the following is true about individual differences in motor skills?
   A) Parents tend to actively discourage girls from participating in athletic activities.
   B) Family income affects children's access to lessons needed to develop certain abilities.
   C) Boys are able to understand and process the rules of most athletic events more quickly than girls.
   D) Many low-SES children are less skilled in motor activities even when they are exposed to formal lessons.
   Answer: B
   Page Ref: 430
   Skill: Conceptual
   Objective: 11.9

106) Girls have an edge over boys in
   A) throwing.
   B) kicking.
   C) hopping.
   D) batting.
   Answer: C
   Page Ref: 430
   Skill: Factual
   Objective: 11.9

107) Boys have an edge over girls in
   A) handwriting.
   B) drawing.
   C) skipping.
   D) throwing.
   Answer: D
   Page Ref: 430
   Skill: Factual
   Objective: 11.9

108) Which of the following is true about the social environment and motor skills?
   A) Parents tend to hold higher expectations for boys' athletic performance than for girls.
   B) From first through twelfth grade, boys are less positive than girls about their own sports ability.
   C) Until adolescence, parents hold similar expectations for boys' and girls' athletic performance.
   D) Fewer girls today participate in team sports like soccer.
   Answer: A
   Page Ref: 430
   Skill: Conceptual
   Objective: 11.9

109) In order to increase girls' participation, self-confidence, and sense of fair treatment in athletics, the text recommends
   A) less emphasis on skill training for girls, as basic skills are already commensurate with those of boys.
   B) educating parents about the minimal differences in school-age boys' and girls' physical capacities.
   C) decreased attention to girls' athletic achievements, to avoid embarrassment or undue pressure.
   D) decreased attention to boys' athletic achievements because athletics are overemphasized in American culture.
   Answer: B
   Page Ref: 430
   Skill: Conceptual
   Objective: 11.9

110) Gains in _____ permit the transition to rule-oriented games.
   A) flexibility
   B) agility
   C) perspective taking
   D) fine-motor ability
Answer: C
Page Ref: 430
Skill: Conceptual
Objective: 11.10

111) Child-invented games usually rely on
   A) complex physical skills.
   B) a sizable element of luck.
   C) social problem-solving skills.
   D) an element of physical risk-taking.
Answer: B
Page Ref: 430
Skill: Conceptual
Objective: 11.10

112) Children will spend _____ of time working out the rules of a game as they will spend playing the game.
   A) twice the amount
   B) half the amount
   C) a quarter of the amount
   D) equal amounts
Answer: D
Page Ref: 430
Skill: Factual
Objective: 11.10

113) Compared with past generations, school-age children today spend more time
   A) gathering informally on sidewalks.
   B) in adult-organized sports.
   C) at playgrounds.
   D) in spontaneous play.
Answer: B
Page Ref: 431
Skill: Conceptual
Objective: 11.10

114) About ____ percent of U.S. boys and ____ percent of U.S. girls participate in organized sports outside of school hours at some time between ages 5 and 18.
   A) 40; 27
   B) 50; 32
   C) 60; 37
   D) 70; 47
Answer: C
Page Ref: 431
Skill: Factual
Objective: 11.10

115) Which of the following is true about joining community athletic teams?
  A) For most children, it is associated with increased competition and decreased social skills.
  B) Among shy children, sports participation seems to foster a decline in social anxiety.
  C) Among shy children, sports participation often contributes to an increase in social anxiety.
  D) Community sports usually allow children to naturally experiment with strategies and rules.

Answer: B
Page Ref: 431
Skill: Conceptual
Objective: 11.10

116) Critics argue that youth sports
  A) overemphasize cooperation.
  B) substitute children's natural experimentation for needed adult control.
  C) actually lead to a decrease in physical fitness activities in adulthood.
  D) overemphasize competition.

Answer: D
Page Ref: 431
Skill: Conceptual
Objective: 11.10

117) Who is most likely to affect children's athletic attitudes and capabilities?
  A) peers
  B) parents
  C) coaches
  D) teachers

Answer: B
Page Ref: 431
Skill: Factual
Objective: 11.10

118) Justine, whose mother is a fitness buff, joined a gymnastics club at the age of 2. Which of the following is a likely outcome for Justine?
  A) She will acquire the skills necessary for gymnastics earlier than her peers.
  B) She will soon lose interest in gymnastics.
  C) She will be more influenced by her coach than by her mother.
  D) She will be a lifelong sports enthusiast.

Answer: B
Page Ref: 431
Skill: Applied
Objective: 11.10

119) Henrich's parents value sports so highly that they punish him when he makes errors during games. Once, they insisted he keep playing after he sprained his ankle. Henrich is most likely to
  A) feel good about his participation and ability.
  B) put pressure on himself to practice until he becomes an elite athlete.
  C) suffer from emotional difficulties.
  D) continue in sports throughout high school and into college.

Answer: C
Page Ref: 431
Skill: Applied
Objective: 11.10

120) When parents and coaches emphasize _____, young athletes enjoy sports more and perceive themselves as more competent at their chosen sport.
    A) championship awards
    B) competition
    C) scores
    D) effort
Answer: D
Page Ref: 431
Skill: Conceptual
Objective: 11.10

121) Maurice and Samson occasionally wrestle, roll, hit, and run after one another, alternating roles while smiling and laughing. Maurice and Samson are engaged in _____ play.
    A) rough-and-tumble
    B) parallel
    C) nonsocial
    D) constructive
Answer: A
Page Ref: 431
Skill: Applied
Objective: 11.10

122) Which of the following statements is true about rough-and-tumble play?
    A) Girls do not engage in it.
    B) Boys' rough-and-tumble play consists of more running and chasing than girls'.
    C) It peaks in the preschool years.
    D) Researchers believe that it is quite distinct from aggressive fighting.
Answer: D
Page Ref: 431
Skill: Conceptual
Objective: 11.10

123) Rough-and-tumble play helps children form
    A) a dominance hierarchy.
    B) cliques.
    C) a stable gender identity.
    D) a stable self-concept.
Answer: A
Page Ref: 432
Skill: Conceptual
Objective: 11.10

124) Once school-age children establish a dominance hierarchy,
    A) aggression increases.
    B) rough-and-tumble play decreases.
    C) hostility is rare.
    D) cheating is common.
Answer: C
Page Ref: 432
Skill: Conceptual
Objective: 11.10

125) Dominance hierarchies
   A) are observed only in nonhuman primates.
   B) may serve to limit aggression among group members.
   C) promote within-group hostility.
   D) exist only for males.
   Answer: B
   Page Ref: 432
   Skill: Conceptual
   Objective: 11.10

126) Unlike children, teenage rough-and-tumble players
   A) establish a dominance hierarchy.
   B) rarely cheat.
   C) hurt their opponents.
   D) do not act aggressively.
   Answer: D
   Page Ref: 432
   Skill: Conceptual
   Objective: 11.10

127) Which of the following is true about physical activity in U.S. schools?
   A) About 45 percent of elementary and middle schools provide students with physical education at least three days a
      week.
   B) Only about 3 percent of high schools provide students with physical education at least three days a week.
   C) Elementary schools have increased recess time due to its contribution in all domains of development.
   D) Physical inactivity among U.S. school children is rare.
   Answer: B
   Page Ref: 432
   Skill: Conceptual
   Objective: 11.11

128) Which of the following is true about school recess?
   A) In recent years, recess time has increased.
   B) Recess periods tend to subtract from classroom learning.
   C) Distributing cognitively demanding tasks over a longer time by introducing recess breaks enhances attention.
   D) Classroom disruptive behavior increases for children who have more than 15 minutes of daily recess.
   Answer: C
   Page Ref: 433 Box: SI: Education: School Recess—A Time to Play, a Time to Learn
   Skill: Conceptual
   Objective: 11.11

129) School recess
   A) is one of the few remaining contexts devoted to child-organized games.
   B) inhibits classroom learning.
   C) has no effect on classroom learning.
   D) boosts classroom learning, but only when provided as an incentive to get students to work harder.
   Answer: A
   Page Ref: 433 Box: SI: Education: School Recess—A Time to Play, a Time to Learn
   Skill: Conceptual
   Objective: 11.11

130) Mr. Carter's physical education class should emphasize
    A) competitive sports.
    B) individual exercise.
    C) team success.
    D) athletic ability.
    Answer: B
    Page Ref: 434
    Skill: Applied
    Objective: 11.11

ESSAY

131) Describe the secular trends in physical growth over the past 150 years, including factors that may be responsible for changing trends.
    Answer: Over the past 150 years, secular trends in physical growth—changes in body size from one generation to the next—have occurred in industrialized nations. Children are taller and heavier than their parents and grandparents were as children. These trends have been found in Australia, Canada, Japan, New Zealand, the United States, and nearly all European countries. The secular gain appears early in life, increases over childhood and early adolescence, then declines as mature body size is reached. This pattern suggests that the larger size of today's children is mostly due to a faster rate of physical development.

    Improved health and nutrition are largely responsible for these growth gains. Secular trends are smaller for low-income children, who have poorer diets and are more likely to suffer from growth-stunting illnesses. And in regions with widespread poverty, famine, and disease, either no secular change or a secular decrease in body size has occurred. In most industrialized nations, the secular gain in height has slowed in recent decades. Weight gain, however, is continuing.
    Page Ref: 413

132) What is malocclusion and what causes it?
    Answer: Malocclusion, a condition in which the upper and lower teeth do not meet properly, occurs in one-third of school-age children. In about 14 percent of cases, serious difficulties in biting and chewing result. Malocclusion can be caused by thumb and finger sucking after permanent teeth erupt. Children who were eager thumb suckers during infancy and early childhood may require gentle but persistent encouragement to give up the habit by school entry. Another cause of malocclusion is crowding of permanent teeth. In some children, this problem clears up as the jaw grows. Others need braces, a common sight by the end of elementary school.
    Page Ref: 414

133) List and describe common factors associated with childhood obesity.
    Answer:
    - Heredity: Obese children are likely to have at least one obese parent, and concordance for obesity is greater in identical than in fraternal twins.
    - Socioeconomic status: Obesity is more common in low-SES families.
    - Early growth pattern: Infants who gain weight rapidly are at greater risk for obesity, probably because their parents promote unhealthy eating habits.
    - Family eating habits: When parents purchase high-calorie fast foods, treats, and junk food; use them as rewards; anxiously overfeed; or control their children's intake, their children are more likely to be obese.
    - Responsiveness to food cues: Obese children often decide when to eat on the basis of external cues, such as taste, smell, sight, time of day, and food-related words, rather than hunger.
    - Physical activity: Obese children are less physically active than their normal-weight peers.
    - Television viewing: Children who spend many hours watching television are more likely to become obese.
    - Early malnutrition: Early, severe malnutrition that results in growth stunting increases the risk of later obesity.
    Page Ref: 417–419

134) List some interventions for chronically ill children that foster positive family relationships, help parents and children cope with the disease, and improve adjustment.

Answer:

- Health education, in which parents and children learn about the illness and get training in how to manage it
- Home visits by health professionals, who offer counseling and social support to enhance parents' and children's strategies for handling the stress of chronic illness
- Schools that accommodate children's special health and education needs
- Disease-specific summer camps, which teach children self-help skills and give parents time off from the demands of caring for an ill youngster
- Parent and peer support groups

Page Ref: 423–424

135) List and describe advances in four basic gross-motor capacities during middle childhood.

Answer:

- *Flexibility.* Compared with preschoolers, school-age children are physically more pliable and elastic, a difference that is evident as they swing bats, kick balls, jump over hurdles, and execute tumbling routines.
- *Balance.* Improved balance supports many athletic skills, including running, hopping, skipping, throwing, kicking, and the rapid changes of direction required in many team sports.
- *Agility.* Quicker and more accurate movements are evident in the fancy footwork of dance and cheerleading and in the forward, backward, and sideways motions used to dodge opponents in tag and soccer.
- *Force.* Older children can throw and kick a ball harder and propel themselves farther off the ground when running and jumping than they could at earlier ages.

Page Ref: 428

136) School children around the world engage in an enormous variety of informally organized games. How do these activities contribute to social and emotional development?

Answer: The physical activities of school-age children reflect an important advance in quality of play: Games with rules become common. Throughout the world, children engage in a wide variety of informally organized games, including variants on popular sports such as soccer, baseball, and basketball. In addition to the best-known childhood games, such as tag, jacks, and hopscotch, children have also invented hundreds of other games, including red rover, statues, leapfrog, kick the can, and prisoner's base.

Gains in perspective taking—in particular, the ability to understand the roles of several players in a game—permit this transition to rule-oriented games. These play experiences, in turn, contribute greatly to emotional and social development. Child-invented games usually rely on simple physical skills and a sizable element of luck. As a result, they rarely become contests of individual ability. Instead, they permit children to try out different styles of cooperating, competing, winning, and losing with little personal risk. Also, in their efforts to organize a game, children discover why rules are necessary and which ones work well. In fact, they often spend as much time working out the details of how a game should proceed as they do playing the game. These experiences help children form more mature concepts of fairness and justice.

Page Ref: 430

CHAPTER 12
COGNITIVE DEVELOPMENT IN MIDDLE CHILDHOOD

MULTIPLE CHOICE

1) Piaget's concrete operational stage extends through the ages of
   A) 1 to 3.
   B) 4 to 6.
   C) 7 to 11.
   D) 12 to 15.
   Answer: C
   Page Ref: 438
   Skill: Factual
   Objective: 12.1

2) In Piaget's concrete operational stage,
   A) thought is more logical, flexible, and organized than it was during early childhood.
   B) the focus is on coordination of sensation and action through reflexive behaviors.
   C) the child learns to use and to represent objects by images, words, and drawings.
   D) individuals move beyond concrete experiences and begin to think abstractly.
   Answer: A
   Page Ref: 438
   Skill: Conceptual
   Objective: 12.1

3) Eight-year-old Daniel focuses on several aspects of a problem and relates them, rather than centering on just one. Daniel is capable of
   A) decentration.
   B) conservation.
   C) reversibility.
   D) seriation.
   Answer: A
   Page Ref: 438
   Skill: Applied
   Objective: 12.1

4) Nine-year-old Ryan thinks through a series of steps, and then mentally changes direction, returning to the starting point. Ryan is capable of
   A) conservation.
   B) reversibility.
   C) decentration.
   D) seriation.
   Answer: B
   Page Ref: 438
   Skill: Applied
   Objective: 12.1

5) _____ is part of every logical operation.
   A) Seriation
   B) Decentration
   C) Conservation
   D) Reversibility
   Answer: D
   Page Ref: 438
   Skill: Conceptual
   Objective: 12.1

6) At age 10, Paige spent hours sorting and resorting her collection of bracelets, grouping them first by color, then by size, and finally by shape. Paige has become aware of
   A) transitive inference.
   B) conservation.
   C) classification hierarchies.
   D) decentration.
   Answer: C
   Page Ref: 438
   Skill: Applied
   Objective: 12.1

7) Heather is lining up crayons in order from shortest to longest. This skill is known as
   A) continuum of acquisition.
   B) centration.
   C) conservation of length.
   D) seriation.
   Answer: D
   Page Ref: 438
   Skill: Applied
   Objective: 12.1

8) Jessica, a concrete operational child, can seriate mentally. This means that Jessica is capable of
   A) transitive inference.
   B) decentration.
   C) class inclusion.
   D) conservation.
   Answer: A
   Page Ref: 438
   Skill: Applied
   Objective: 12.1

9) Mrs. Hartley asked her second graders to draw a map of the school using their memory. The students' cognitive maps will probably
   A) have an accurate arrangement.
   B) include landmarks.
   C) incorporate map symbols and a key.
   D) depict an organized route of travel.
   Answer: B
   Page Ref: 438
   Skill: Applied
   Objective: 12.1

10) Around age 8 to 10, children's cognitive maps
    A) show scale.
    B) include map symbols.
    C) show landmarks along an organized route of travel.
    D) are accurately arranged and labeled.
Answer: C
Page Ref: 439
Skill: Conceptual
Objective: 12.1

11) Dewey has no trouble when asked to place stickers on a map to indicate the location of colored flags within a large-scale outdoor environment. Dewey is probably
    A) 5.
    B) 7.
    C) 9.
    D) 12.
Answer: D
Page Ref: 439
Skill: Applied
Objective: 12.1

12) When Kelli, a researcher, asks school-age children in a small city in India to draw maps of their neighborhood, Kelli will probably see maps that depict
    A) main streets.
    B) key directions.
    C) people and vehicles.
    D) formal, extended space.
Answer: C
Page Ref: 439
Skill: Applied
Objective: 12.1

13) A child in the concrete operational stage will have the most trouble with which of the following?
    A) abstract ideas
    B) concrete information
    C) information she can perceive directly
    D) dual representation
Answer: A
Page Ref: 440
Skill: Conceptual
Objective: 12.1

14) Brandon solves the hypothetical problem: "Marie is taller than Gina, and Gina is taller than Anna. Who is the tallest?" Brandon is probably _____ years old.
    A) 5
    B) 7
    C) 9
    D) 11
Answer: D
Page Ref: 440
Skill: Applied
Objective: 12.1

15) Eleven-year-old Nathan first grasped conservation of number, followed by length, liquid, mass, and then weight. This limitation of concrete operational thinking is known as
   A) transitive inference.
   B) continuum of acquisition.
   C) adaptability.
   D) conservation of thought.
   Answer: B
   Page Ref: 440
   Skill: Applied
   Objective: 12.1

16) Cross-cultural research suggests that
   A) compared to non-Western societies, comprehension of conservation in Western societies is greatly delayed.
   B) among the Hausa of Nigeria, the most basic conservation tasks, such as number and length, are understood as early as age 4.
   C) taking part in everyday activities helps children master conservation and other Piagetian problems.
   D) Hausa and American children attain conservation at about the same age.
   Answer: C
   Page Ref: 440
   Skill: Conceptual
   Objective: 12.2

17) The experience of going to school seems to
   A) delay mastery of conservation.
   B) promote mastery of Piagetian tasks.
   C) delay mastery of transitive inference.
   D) speed up the continuum of acquisition.
   Answer: B
   Page Ref: 440
   Skill: Factual
   Objective: 12.2

18) When children of the same age are tested, the greatest impact on transitive inference skills comes from
   A) schooling.
   B) age.
   C) gender.
   D) ethnicity.
   Answer: A
   Page Ref: 440
   Skill: Factual
   Objective: 12.2

19) On the basis of cross-cultural research, some investigators have concluded that the forms of logic required by Piagetian tasks
   A) emerge earlier in collectivist than individualist cultures.
   B) emerge spontaneously in children from diverse cultures.
   C) are heavily influenced by heredity.
   D) are heavily influenced by training, context, and cultural conditions.
   Answer: D
   Page Ref: 440–441
   Skill: Conceptual
   Objective: 12.2

20) Some Neo-Piagetian theorists like Robbie Case argue that the development of operational thinking can best be understood in terms of
   A) a sudden shift to a new developmental stage.
   B) a gradual mastery of logical concepts as children age.
   C) gains in information-processing speed.
   D) children's interaction with adults and more skilled social models.
   Answer: C
   Page Ref: 441
   Skill: Conceptual
   Objective: 12.2

21) Accordingly to Case, once the schemes of a Piagetian stage are sufficiently automatic and integrated into an improved representation, children acquire _____ that permit them to think more efficiently in a wide range of situations.
   A) abstract ideas
   B) primary systems
   C) discontinuous structures
   D) central conceptual structures
   Answer: D
   Page Ref: 441
   Skill: Conceptual
   Objective: 12.2

22) Daniella listens to and tells stories but rarely draws pictures. Daniella displays _____ advanced central conceptual structures in _____.
   A) less; storytelling
   B) no; storytelling
   C) more; storytelling
   D) more; drawing
   Answer: C
   Page Ref: 441
   Skill: Applied
   Objective: 12.2

23) Camilla, age 5, often uses an empirical approach instead of a logical approach to solve problems. After failing at a class-inclusion task at school, her teacher provided a logical explanation for solving the problem correctly. Based on recent studies, Camilla's future performance on this task should
   A) improve rapidly.
   B) be similar to that of an 8-year-old child.
   C) decrease slightly.
   D) remain the same.
   Answer: A
   Page Ref: 441–442
   Skill: Applied
   Objective: 12.2

24) Which of the following statements best characterizes Piaget's view of cognitive development in middle childhood?
   A) continuous improvement in logical skills
   B) discontinuous restructuring of children's thinking
   C) biological prewiring of processes
   D) random change in cognitive processes
   Answer: B
   Page Ref: 442
   Skill: Conceptual
   Objective: 12.2

25) Time needed to process information on a wide variety of cognitive tasks _____ between ages 6 and 12.
   A) increases slightly
   B) declines slightly
   C) declines rapidly
   D) increases rapidly
   Answer: C
   Page Ref: 442
   Skill: Factual
   Objective: 12.3

26) Digit span, which assesses the basic capacity of working memory, increases from about ____ digits at age 7 to _____ digits at age 12.
   A) 4; 5
   B) 5; 7
   C) 6; 8
   D) 7; 12
   Answer: B
   Page Ref: 442–443
   Skill: Factual
   Objective: 12.3

27) As the prefrontal cortex develops in middle childhood, children make gains in
   A) information-processing speed.
   B) information-processing capacity.
   C) inhibition.
   D) rehearsing.
   Answer: C
   Page Ref: 443
   Skill: Factual
   Objective: 12.3

28) Ten-year-old Annabelle has improved her ability to control internal and external distracting stimuli. Annabelle has made gains in
   A) mindfulness.
   B) inhibition.
   C) prohibitive concentration.
   D) process regulation.
   Answer: B
   Page Ref: 443
   Skill: Applied
   Objective: 12.3

29) During middle childhood, attention becomes
   A) less controlled.
   B) more rigid.
   C) less planful.
   D) more selective.
   Answer: D
   Page Ref: 443
   Skill: Factual
   Objective: 12.4

30) Ten-year-old Gemma is presented with a stream of numbers on a computer screen. She is asked to press a button whenever the two-digit sequence of a "5" followed by a "7" appears. Gemma's _____ attention is being tested.
    A) adaptive
    B) selective
    C) planful
    D) productive
Answer: B
Page Ref: 443
Skill: Applied
Objective: 12.4

31) Four-year-old Rolf rarely engages in attentional strategies. This is an example of a _____ deficiency.
    A) production
    B) control
    C) utilization
    D) rehearsal
Answer: A
Page Ref: 443
Skill: Applied
Objective: 12.4

32) Six-year-old Bella sometimes produces strategies, but not consistently. Bella has a(n) _____ deficiency.
    A) production
    B) control
    C) utilization
    D) organization
Answer: B
Page Ref: 443
Skill: Applied
Objective: 12.4

33) Seven-year-old Roshonda executes attentional strategies consistently, but her task performance does not improve. Roshonda is exhibiting a _____ deficiency.
    A) schematic
    B) control
    C) production
    D) utilization
Answer: D
Page Ref: 443
Skill: Applied
Objective: 12.4

34) Mrs. Rosinski gives each of her children, ages 5, 8, and 12 a shopping list of 10 items. What result can she expect to see?
    A) All of the children will immediately start to retrieve items.
    B) Her 12-year-old will probably scan the store before getting items.
    C) Her 5-year-old will probably make a plan before searching the store for items.
    D) All of the children will probably make a plan and scan the store before getting items.
Answer: B
Page Ref: 444
Skill: Applied
Objective: 12.4

35) Guy, age 10, is impulsive. During school, he drops his pencil, rearranges the papers inside his desk, and yells at people across the room. Guy is also physically awkward and fails to follow the rules when he plays games. He suffers from both academic and social problems. Guy most likely has
   A) a production deficiency.
   B) an anxiety disorder.
   C) autism.
   D) attention-deficit hyperactivity disorder (ADHD).
   Answer: D
   Page Ref: 444 Box: B&E: Children with Attention-Deficit Hyperactivity Disorder
   Skill: Applied
   Objective: 12.4

36) Which of the following is true about ADHD?
   A) Boys are diagnosed about four times as often as girls.
   B) Girls are diagnosed about twice as often as boys.
   C) ADHD affects about 15 percent of U.S. school children.
   D) All children with ADHD are hyperactive.
   Answer: A
   Page Ref: 444 Box: B&E: Children with Attention-Deficit Hyperactivity Disorder
   Skill: Conceptual
   Objective: 12.4

37) Children with ADHD
   A) tend to score higher than other children on intelligence tests.
   B) are often asymptomatic before age 7.
   C) find it hard to ignore irrelevant stimuli.
   D) have no difficulty with planning or reasoning.
   Answer: C
   Page Ref: MSP 444 Box: B&E: Children with Attention-Deficit Hyperactivity Disorder
   Skill: Conceptual
   Objective: 12.4

38) Which of the following is true about the origins of ADHD?
   A) ADHD runs in families and is highly heritable.
   B) Fraternal twins share ADHD more often than identical twins.
   C) The brains of children with ADHD grow more quickly than the brains of unaffected agemates.
   D) The brains of children with ADHD are about 3 percent larger in volume than the brains of unaffected agemates.
   Answer: A
   Page Ref: 444 Box: B&E: Children with Attention-Deficit Hyperactivity Disorder
   Skill: Conceptual
   Objective: 12.4

39) Which of the following is true about the relationship between environment factors and ADHD?
   A) Because ADHD runs in families, environmental factors have no impact on the disorder.
   B) Prenatal teratogens can combine with certain genotypes to greatly increase the risk for ADHD.
   C) A stressful home life usually causes ADHD.
   D) There is no correlation between stress factors in the home and ADHD.
   Answer: B
   Page Ref: 444 Box: B&E: Children with Attention-Deficit Hyperactivity Disorder
   Skill: Conceptual
   Objective: 12.4

40) The most common treatment for ADHD is
    A) prescription stimulant medication.
    B) family intervention.
    C) operant conditioning.
    D) therapy.
Answer: A
Page Ref: 445 Box: B&E: Children with Attention-Deficit Hyperactivity Disorder
Skill: Factual
Objective: 12.4

41) In Hong Kong,
    A) doctors are hesitant to label a child with ADHD.
    B) children are diagnosed with ADHD at less than half the rate in the United States.
    C) children are diagnosed with ADHD at more than twice the rate in the United States.
    D) girls are more likely than boys to be diagnosed with ADHD.
Answer: C
Page Ref: 445 Box: B&E: Children with Attention-Deficit Hyperactivity Disorder
Skill: Factual
Objective: 12.4

42) When her 10-year-old son comes home from school, Mrs. Calder sits down with him and organizes his homework. She makes a list for him of what to tackle first and what to put off until later. She does not ask her son to help with this task. Mrs. Calder
    A) is helping her son develop planning strategies.
    B) is helping her son with his utilization deficiency.
    C) might be robbing her son of opportunities to plan.
    D) might be creating an effective strategy use for her son.
Answer: C
Page Ref: 445
Skill: Applied
Objective: 12.4

43) When studying for her spelling test, Matilda repeats the proper spelling to herself multiple times. What memory strategy is she using?
    A) organization
    B) rehearsal
    C) elaboration
    D) chunking
Answer: B
Page Ref: 446
Skill: Applied
Objective: 12.4

44) When studying for his geography test, Brett groups states together by region. What memory strategy is he using?
    A) organization
    B) elaboration
    C) listing
    D) rehearsal
Answer: A
Page Ref: 446
Skill: Applied
Objective: 12.4

45) Five-year-old Charlotte is asked to memorize a list of words. Charlotte will probably
   A) organize well, with strong memory benefits.
   B) organize inconsistently, but still receive moderate memory benefits.
   C) switch from organization to elaboration strategies with successful memory benefits.
   D) organize inconsistently, with little or no memory benefits.
Answer: D
Page Ref: 446
Skill: Applied
Objective: 12.4

46) When studying for a test, Peter remembers the unrelated words *cellular* and *canine* by generating the following mental image, "The canine is talking on a cellular phone." Which memory strategy is Peter using?
   A) rehearsal
   B) organization
   C) elaboration
   D) chunking
Answer: C
Page Ref: 446
Skill: Applied
Objective: 12.4

47) Elaboration is a later-emerging memory strategy because it requires
   A) a great deal of mental effort and working-memory capacity.
   B) concrete pieces of information.
   C) combining rehearsal and organization.
   D) a greater digit span.
Answer: A
Page Ref: 446
Skill: Conceptual
Objective: 12.4

48) Elaboration is most likely to be used by
   A) preschoolers.
   B) children in early elementary school.
   C) adolescents and young adults.
   D) children with ADHD.
Answer: C
Page Ref: 446
Skill: Factual
Objective: 12.4

49) Children who are expert in an area
   A) are highly motivated.
   B) acquire knowledge slowly, but accurately.
   C) have difficulty making sense of information that is outside their area of expertise.
   D) have difficulty organizing information.
Answer: A
Page Ref: 447
Skill: Conceptual
Objective: 12.4

50) _____ is a person's set of beliefs about mental activities.
  A) Rote memorization
  B) Conceptual organization
  C) Elaboration
  D) Theory of mind
Answer: D
Page Ref: 447
Skill: Factual
Objective: 12.5

51) Appreciation of _____ greatly assists children in understanding others' perspectives.
  A) theory of mind
  B) second-order false belief
  C) elaboration
  D) cognitive self-regulation
Answer: B
Page Ref: 448
Skill: Conceptual
Objective: 12.5

52) Because school-age children have difficulty putting what they know about thinking into action, they are not yet good at
  A) cognitive self-regulation.
  B) metacognition.
  C) problem solving.
  D) conservation.
Answer: A
Page Ref: 449
Skill: Factual
Objective: 12.5

53) Aili is aware that she should attend closely to her teacher's directions, group items when memorizing, and reread a complicated paragraph to make sure she understands it, but she does not always engage in these activities. Aili is not yet good at
  A) sustained attention.
  B) applying memory strategies.
  C) cognitive self-regulation.
  D) metacognition.
Answer: D
Page Ref: 449
Skill: Applied
Objective: 12.5

54) Throughout elementary and secondary school,
  A) most children fail to apply memory strategies.
  B) self-regulation predicts academic success.
  C) most children show a utilization deficiency.
  D) most children show a control deficiency.
Answer: B
Page Ref: 449
Skill: Factual
Objective: 12.5

55) Children who acquire effective self-regulatory skills develop a sense of
   A) metacognition.
   B) academic integrity.
   C) academic self-efficacy.
   D) false belief.
   Answer: C
   Page Ref: 449
   Skill: Factual
   Objective: 12.5

56) As children make the transition from emergent literacy to conventional reading, _____ continues to facilitate the process.
   A) whole-language instruction
   B) private speech
   C) phonological awareness
   D) reciprocal teaching
   Answer: C
   Page Ref: 450
   Skill: Conceptual
   Objective: 12.6

57) Mrs. Markie, a first-grade teacher, believes that, from the beginning, children should be exposed to text in its complete form so that they can appreciate the communicative function of written language. Mrs. Markie takes a _____ approach to teaching reading.
   A) whole-language
   B) phonics
   C) reciprocal
   D) hierarchical
   Answer: A
   Page Ref: 450
   Skill: Applied
   Objective: 12.6

58) The phonics approach to reading
   A) claims that as long as reading is kept meaningful, children will be motivated to discover the specific skills they need.
   B) stresses the relationship between letters and sounds, thus enabling children to decode words.
   C) stresses an appreciation for word concepts in a story context.
   D) allows children to decipher meanings of words by reading the words around them.
   Answer: B
   Page Ref: 450
   Skill: Conceptual
   Objective: 12.6

59) When teachers _____, first graders show greater literacy progress.
   A) rely exclusively on the whole language approach
   B) rely exclusively on the phonics approach
   C) combine real reading and writing with teaching of phonics
   D) focus on reading aloud without stopping to concentrate on comprehension
   Answer: C
   Page Ref: 450
   Skill: Conceptual
   Objective: 12.6

60) Yolanda entered school low in phonological awareness. Without _____, Yolanda will probably be behind her agemates in text comprehension skills.
    A) early phonics training
    B) reading across the curriculum
    C) metacognitive training
    D) special education services
    Answer: A
    Page Ref: 451
    Skill: Applied
    Objective: 12.6

61) Rodney's first-grade teacher exclusively uses a phonics approach to teaching reading. She emphasizes decoding new words and learning the relationship between letters and sounds. With so much emphasis on basic skills, Rodney could
    A) become deficient in understanding the overall meaning of a passage.
    B) shift from learning to read to reading to learn.
    C) fail to master letter-sound correspondences.
    D) decrease his fluency in decoding words.
    Answer: A
    Page Ref: 451
    Skill: Applied
    Objective: 12.6

62) In teaching mathematics, teachers should focus on
    A) computation drills alone.
    B) number sense alone.
    C) a blend of the drill in computing and number sense methods.
    D) rote memorization of math facts and rules.
    Answer: C
    Page Ref: 451
    Skill: Conceptual
    Objective: 12.6

63) Encouraging students to _____ and making sure they _____ are essential for solid mastery of basic math skills.
    A) memorize math facts; remember them
    B) apply strategies; know why certain strategies work
    C) memorize math rules; have a calculator
    D) have calculators; know how to use them
    Answer: B
    Page Ref: 452
    Skill: Factual
    Objective: 12.6

64) Around age ____, IQ becomes more stable than it was at earlier ages, and it correlates well with academic achievement.
    A) 3
    B) 4
    C) 6
    D) 8
    Answer: C
    Page Ref: 453
    Skill: Factual
    Objective: 12.7

65) Test designers use _____ to identify the various abilities that intelligence tests measure.
   A) normative data
   B) observational studies
   C) confidence intervals
   D) factor analysis
Answer: D
Page Ref: 453
Skill: Factual
Objective: 12.7

66) Factor analysis identifies
   A) normative ages for correct responses to items on an IQ test.
   B) which items on an IQ test are reliable.
   C) whether an IQ test actually measures intelligence.
   D) which items on an IQ test are strongly correlated with each other.
Answer: D
Page Ref: 453
Skill: Conceptual
Objective: 12.7

67) Unlike group tests, individually administered intelligence tests
   A) permit large numbers of students to be tested at once.
   B) are useful in instructional planning.
   C) must be given by trained individuals.
   D) identify children who require more extensive group evaluation.
Answer: C
Page Ref: 453
Skill: Factual
Objective: 12.7

68) The _____ items on an intelligence test are assumed to assess more biologically based skills.
   A) verbal
   B) spatial reasoning
   C) fact-oriented
   D) culturally based
Answer: B
Page Ref: 454
Skill: Conceptual
Objective: 12.7

69) The Stanford-Binet Intelligence Scales
   A) include only a verbal mode in its 10 subtests.
   B) assess general intelligence and five intellectual factors.
   C) are only used to test children ages 6 to 16.
   D) are the most culture-free measure of intelligence available.
Answer: B
Page Ref: 454
Skill: Factual
Objective: 12.7

70) _____ was designed to downplay culture-dependent information, which is emphasized on only one factor (verbal reasoning).
    A) The Stanford-Binet Intelligence Scales, Fifth Edition,
    B) The Wechsler Intelligence Scale for Children-IV
    C) Sternberg's triarchic theory
    D) Gardner's theory of multiple intelligences
Answer: B
Page Ref: 454
Skill: Factual
Objective: 12.7

71) Many psychologists and educators came to prefer the Wechsler intelligence tests because they offered _____ long before the Stanford-Binet.
    A) both a measure of general intelligence and a variety of factor scores
    B) a measure of general intelligence
    C) fact-oriented information
    D) componential analysis
Answer: A
Page Ref: 454
Skill: Factual
Objective: 12.7

72) Professor Diaz is conducting a study to determine whether a child's information-processing speed is related to her IQ. He is conducting a
    A) functional assessment.
    B) factor analysis.
    C) componential analysis.
    D) dynamic assessment.
Answer: C
Page Ref: 454
Skill: Applied
Objective: 12.8

73) _____ is/are a good predictor of IQ.
    A) Well-developed gross-motor skills
    B) Inhibition skill
    C) Slow, steady nervous system function
    D) REM brain-wave patterns during sleep
Answer: B
Page Ref: 455
Skill: Factual
Objective: 12.8

74) A major shortcoming of the componential approach is that it
    A) focuses too much on cultural-bias in intelligence testing.
    B) regards intelligence as entirely due to causes within the child.
    C) has not generated enough research.
    D) does not try to uncover the underlying basis of IQ.
Answer: B
Page Ref: 455
Skill: Conceptual
Objective: 12.8

75) Sternberg's triarchic theory of successful intelligence is comprised of which of the following broad interacting intelligences?
   A) experiential, interpersonal, and academic
   B) fluid, crystallized, and social
   C) contextual, verbal, and spatial
   D) analytical, creative, and practical
Answer: D
Page Ref: 455
Skill: Conceptual
Objective: 12.8

76) Nianzu quickly applies learning and memory strategies to new situations and engages in self-regulation and metacognitive monitoring of her own learning. According to Sternberg, Nianzu excels in _____ intelligence.
   A) analytical
   B) creative
   C) practical
   D) experiential
Answer: A
Page Ref: 455
Skill: Applied
Objective: 12.8

77) Andrei skillfully adapts his thinking to fit with both his desires and the demands of his everyday world. When he cannot adapt to a new situation, Andrei tries to shape it to meet his needs. According to Sternberg, Andrei excels in _____ intelligence.
   A) analytical
   B) creative
   C) practical
   D) experiential
Answer: C
Page Ref: 455
Skill: Applied
Objective: 12.8

78) Noah thinks more skillfully than others when faced with novelty. Given a new task, Noah applies his information-processing skills in exceptionally effective ways, rapidly making these skills automatic so that working memory is freed for more complex aspects of the situation. According to Sternberg's theory, Noah's strengths lie in _____ intelligence.
   A) analytical
   B) creative
   C) practical
   D) experiential
Answer: B
Page Ref: 455
Skill: Applied
Objective: 12.8

79) _____ intelligence reminds us that intelligent behavior is never culture-free.
   A) Analytical
   B) Creative
   C) Practical
   D) Experiential
Answer: C
Page Ref: 456
Skill: Conceptual
Objective: 12.8

80) Which of the following parents is most likely to mention cognitive traits when asked for their idea of an intelligent first grader?
   A) Boupha, a Cambodian immigrant to the United States
   B) Lupe, a Mexican-American
   C) Chi, a Vietnamese immigrant to the United States
   D) Cindy, a Caucasian-American
Answer: D
Page Ref: 456
Skill: Applied
Objective: 12.8

81) Howard Gardner proposes at least _____ independent intelligences.
   A) two
   B) four
   C) six
   D) eight
Answer: D
Page Ref: 456
Skill: Factual
Objective: 12.8

82) Nyse has the ability to discriminate complex inner feelings and to use them to guide her own behavior. According to Gardner, Nyse has a strong _____ intelligence.
   A) intrapersonal
   B) interpersonal
   C) naturalist
   D) bodily-kinesthetic
Answer: A
Page Ref: 456
Skill: Applied
Objective: 12.8

83) Rosanna scores highly in Gardner's spatial intelligence. Based on these test results, which of the following occupations might Rosanna be best suited for?
   A) writer
   B) engineer
   C) sculptor
   D) biologist
Answer: C
Page Ref: 456
Skill: Applied
Objective: 12.8

84) Thad is sensitive to the sounds, rhythms, and meaning of words. According to Gardner's theory of multiple intelligences, Thad should consider which of the following careers?
   A) therapist
   B) navigator
   C) composer
   D) journalist
Answer: D
Page Ref: 456
Skill: Applied
Objective: 12.8

85) Kyle recognizes and classifies all varieties of animals and plants. According to Gardner, Kyle excels in _____ intelligence.
   A) spatial
   B) naturalist
   C) linguistic
   D) logico-mathematical
   Answer: B
   Page Ref: 456
   Skill: Applied
   Objective: 12.8

86) Gardner's _____ and _____ intelligences include a set of capacities for dealing with people and understanding oneself that has become known as emotional intelligence.
   A) linguistic; musical
   B) spatial; bodily-kinesthetic
   C) interpersonal; intrapersonal
   D) interpersonal; social
   Answer: C
   Page Ref: 456
   Skill: Conceptual
   Objective: 12.8

87) In school-age children, adolescents, and adults, _____ intelligence is positively associated with self-esteem, leadership skills, and life satisfaction, and negatively related to depression and aggressive behavior.
   A) spatial
   B) emotional
   C) analytical
   D) bodily-kinesthetic
   Answer: B
   Page Ref: 457 Box: SI: Education: Emotional Intelligence
   Skill: Conceptual
   Objective: 12.8

88) Mr. Klakkit provides his fourth-graders with lessons that emphasize respect and caring for others and resistance to unfavorable peer pressure. Mr. Klakkit is trying to improve his students' _____ intelligence.
   A) spatial
   B) intrapersonal
   C) emotional
   D) linguistic
   Answer: C
   Page Ref: 457 Box: SI: Education: Emotional Intelligence
   Skill: Applied
   Objective: 12.8

89) Which of the following is true about the IQ scores of American children?
   A) American white children score, on average, four to eight IQ points below American black children.
   B) Although the difference in IQ scores has been shrinking over the past several decades, a substantial gap remains.
   C) Over the past several decades, the difference in IQ scores between American white children and American black children has grown.
   D) American black children fall midway between white and Hispanic children in average IQ score.
   Answer: B
   Page Ref: 458
   Skill: Conceptual
   Objective: 12.9

90) The IQ gap between middle-SES and low-SES American children is about _____ points.
   A) 3
   B) 6
   C) 9
   D) 12
Answer: C
Page Ref: 458
Skill: Factual
Objective: 12.9

91) Arthur Jensen's "How Much Can We Boost IQ and Scholastic Achievement?" claims that _____ is largely responsible for individual, ethnic, and SES variations in intelligence.
   A) heredity
   B) educational opportunity
   C) child rearing
   D) culture
Answer: A
Page Ref: 458
Skill: Factual
Objective: 12.9

92) The most powerful evidence on the role of heredity in IQ involves
   A) adoption studies.
   B) DNA testing.
   C) twin comparisons.
   D) nontwin comparisons.
Answer: C
Page Ref: 458
Skill: Conceptual
Objective: 12.9

93) Adoption studies consistently reveal that
   A) about three-quarters of the differences in IQ among children can be traced to their genetic makeup.
   B) when young children are adopted into stimulating homes, their IQs rise substantially.
   C) adopted children from low-IQ biological mothers score below average on IQ tests during the school years.
   D) adopted children score, on average, 15 to 20 points lower in IQ than their nonadopted agemates.
Answer: B
Page Ref: 458
Skill: Conceptual
Objective: 12.9

94) Research on African-American children adopted into middle-SES white homes during the first year of life shows that
   A) these children score similarly in IQ to children who remain in low-SES homes.
   B) poverty depresses the intelligence of ethnic minority children.
   C) genetic factors have a powerful impact on African-American children's IQs.
   D) environmental factors have little impact on African-American children's IQs.
Answer: B
Page Ref: 459
Skill: Conceptual
Objective: 12.9

95) African-American parents' communication style with their children emphasizes _____ over _____.
    A) facts; emotional and social concerns
    B) quick-witted jokes; serious conversation
    C) emotional and social concerns; facts about the world
    D) facts; problem solving
Answer: C
Page Ref: 459
Skill: Factual
Objective: 12.10

96) Javier's father works together with him in a coordinated, fluid way. Each focuses on the same aspect of a problem. Javier's father prefers a(n) _____ style of communication.
    A) collaborative
    B) hierarchical
    C) abstract
    D) authoritarian
Answer: A
Page Ref: 460
Skill: Applied
Objective: 12.10

97) Mrs. Noneman directs her children to each carry out an aspect of a task. Each child is expected to work independently. Mrs. Noneman prefers a(n) _____ style of communication.
    A) collaborative
    B) hierarchical
    C) abstract
    D) authoritarian
Answer: B
Page Ref: 460
Skill: Applied
Objective: 12.10

98) Children's exposure to _____ has a profound impact on IQ test performance.
    A) a collaborative communication style
    B) high-stakes testing
    C) classroom learning
    D) digital media
Answer: C
Page Ref: 460
Skill: Factual
Objective: 12.10

99) Hershel, an African American, has heard that his test administrator believes negative stereotypes about African-American learners. He becomes anxious and distracted, which results in a lower test score. Hershel's fear is an example of
    A) stereotype threat.
    B) disengagement.
    C) dynamic assessment.
    D) test bias.
Answer: A
Page Ref: 460
Skill: Applied
Objective: 12.10

100) Over middle childhood, Reyandre, an African American, became increasingly conscious of ethnic stereotypes. By early adolescence, she stopped caring about her grades and said that school was not important to her. Reyandre's attitude is an example of
   A) stereotype threat.
   B) disengagement.
   C) dynamic assessment.
   D) an educational bias.
Answer: B
Page Ref: 461
Skill: Applied
Objective: 12.10

101) When assessing students, Mrs. Carter introduces purposeful teaching into the testing situation to find out what the child can attain with social support. Mrs. Carter is using
   A) dynamic assessment.
   B) disengagement.
   C) static assessment.
   D) stereotype assessment.
Answer: A
Page Ref: 461
Skill: Applied
Objective: 12.10

102) Dynamic assessment is consistent with _____ theory.
   A) Piaget's
   B) Vygotsky's
   C) Freud's
   D) Jensen's
Answer: B
Page Ref: 461
Skill: Factual
Objective: 12.10

103) Dynamic assessment
   A) emphasizes previously acquired knowledge.
   B) requires little knowledge of cultural values.
   C) helps identify forms of instruction best suited to the child.
   D) is quick and easy to administer.
Answer: C
Page Ref: 461
Skill: Conceptual
Objective: 12.10

104) In middle childhood, children's attitude toward language undergoes a fundamental shift as they develop
   A) metalinguistic awareness.
   B) linguistic reasoning.
   C) a theory of language.
   D) systemic linguistics.
Answer: A
Page Ref: 462
Skill: Factual
Objective: 12.11

105) On average, children in middle childhood learn about _____ new words each day.
  A) 5
  B) 10
  C) 15
  D) 20
  Answer: D
  Page Ref: 462
  Skill: Factual
  Objective: 12.11

106) When asked to define "bicycle," Emi said, "It's got wheels, a chain, and handlebars." Emi is probably
  A) a preschooler.
  B) a first grader.
  C) a sixth grader.
  D) deficient in metalinguistic awareness.
  Answer: B
  Page Ref: 463
  Skill: Applied
  Objective: 12.11

107) Which of the following classes would probably most appreciate the humor of riddles and puns?
  A) a preschool class
  B) a kindergarten class
  C) a third grade class
  D) a high school class
  Answer: C
  Page Ref: 463
  Skill: Conceptual
  Objective: 12.11

108) During the school years, English-speaking children
  A) use only the active voice.
  B) extend the passive voice to inanimate subjects.
  C) cannot understand infinitive phrases.
  D) cannot master complex grammatical constructions.
  Answer: B
  Page Ref: 463
  Skill: Conceptual
  Objective: 12.11

109) Mrs. Hopfensperger provides her second-graders with opportunities to communicate in many situations. Her students show gains in the communicative side of language. Mrs. Hopfensperger emphasizes
  A) pragmatics.
  B) semantics.
  C) grammar.
  D) syntax.
  Answer: A
  Page Ref: 463
  Skill: Applied
  Objective: 12.11

110) African-American children's narratives are usually _____ than those of Caucasian-American children.
   A) shorter and simpler
   B) about the same length as
   C) less complex
   D) longer and more complex

Answer: D
Page Ref: 464
Skill: Factual
Objective: 12.11

111) Eight-year-old Goran immigrates to the United States with his family. About how long will it take Croatian-speaking Goran to attain speaking and writing skills in English on a par with his English-speaking agemates?
   A) 1 to 2 years
   B) 3 to 5 years
   C) 5 to 7 years
   D) until he is an adult

Answer: C
Page Ref: 465
Skill: Applied
Objective: 12.12

112) Miguel is bilingual. He sometimes speaks sentences in English that contain one or more Spanish words without violating the grammar of either language. Miguel engages in
   A) topic-focused style.
   B) classic form.
   C) topic-associating style.
   D) code switching.

Answer: D
Page Ref: 465
Skill: Applied
Objective: 12.12

113) Children who become fluent in two languages
   A) develop denser white matter in areas of the right hemisphere.
   B) gradually lose their first language.
   C) outperform others on tests of cognitive flexibility.
   D) often experience difficulties in reading achievement.

Answer: C
Page Ref: 465
Skill: Conceptual
Objective: 12.12

114) Elena moved to the United States from Guatemala when she was 6 years old. Research shows that if her school curriculum integrates both Spanish and English, she will
   A) be semilingual.
   B) gradually lose her Spanish.
   C) fall behind in reading skills.
   D) acquire English more easily.

Answer: D
Page Ref: 465
Skill: Applied
Objective: 12.12

115) Hilda is moving into a new neighborhood before her son starts kindergarten. When she visits schools, Hilda should look for a class with approximately how many students to give her son the best opportunity for success?
   A) 13 to 17
   B) 18 to 21
   C) 22 to 25
   D) 26 or more
Answer: A
Page Ref: 466
Skill: Applied
Objective: 12.13

116) In a study of the impact of class size on elementary school children, placing teacher's aides in regular-size classes
   A) raised math scores.
   B) raised reading scores.
   C) had no impact.
   D) predicted higher graduation rates.
Answer: C
Page Ref: 466
Skill: Factual
Objective: 12.13

117) Mrs. Finkbiner's classroom includes richly equipped learning centers, small groups and individuals solving self-chosen problems, and a teacher who guides and supports in response to children's needs. Mrs. Finkbiner has a(n) _____ educational philosophy.
   A) constructivist
   B) traditional
   C) authoritative
   D) collectivist
Answer: A
Page Ref: 467
Skill: Applied
Objective: 12.13

118) Mr. Selkie's classroom includes students whose desks face the front of the classroom, arranged in rows. The students are relatively passive—listening to Mr. Selkie, who is the sole authority for knowledge, rules, and decision making. Mr. Selkie does most of the talking, though students are expected to respond when called on. Mr. Selkie has a(n) _____ educational philosophy.
   A) constructivist
   B) traditional
   C) authoritative
   D) collectivist
Answer: B
Page Ref: 467
Skill: Applied
Objective: 12.13

119) The _____ classroom has become increasingly pronounced as a result of the U.S. No Child Left Behind Act.
   A) collectivist
   B) authoritative
   C) traditional
   D) constructivist
Answer: C
Page Ref: 468
Skill: Factual
Objective: 12.13

120) Holly's birthday is two days before the cutoff date for kindergarten enrollment. Her parents are considering delaying her school entry by one year. They should know that research reveals that
   A) there are long-term academic benefits from delaying school entry.
   B) school readiness cannot be cultivated through classroom experiences.
   C) there are long-term social benefits from delaying school entry.
   D) younger first graders outperform same-age children a year behind them.
Answer: D
Page Ref: 468
Skill: Applied
Objective: 12.13

121) In Ms. Adkins classroom, children participate in a wide range of challenging activities with teachers and peers, with whom they jointly construct understandings. As children appropriate the knowledge and strategies generated through working together, they become competent, contributing members of their classroom. Ms. Adkins has a _____ classroom.
   A) social-constructivist
   B) traditional
   C) constructivist
   D) Piagetian-based
Answer: A
Page Ref: 468
Skill: Applied
Objective: 12.13

122) Mr. Ryan and two to four of his pupils form a cooperative learning group and take turns leading dialogues on the content of a text passage. Mr. Ryan is using
   A) an open classroom.
   B) culturally responsive instruction.
   C) reciprocal teaching.
   D) peer tutoring.
Answer: C
Page Ref: 468
Skill: Applied
Objective: 12.13

123) Reciprocal teaching focuses on which four cognitive strategies?
   A) discussion, practice, segment, and reading
   B) elaboration, rehearsal, chunking, and repetition
   C) challenging, digesting, comparing, and evaluating
   D) questioning, summarizing, clarifying, and predicting
Answer: D
Page Ref: 469
Skill: Factual
Objective: 12.13

124) Elementary and middle school students exposed to reciprocal teaching show
   A) gains in reading comprehension.
   B) gains in decoding skills.
   C) losses in reading comprehension.
   D) losses in metalinguistical skills.
Answer: A
Page Ref: 469
Skill: Factual
Objective: 12.13

125) Mrs. Nixon guides the overall process of learning in her classroom, but no other distinction is made between adult and child contributors: All participate in joint endeavors and have the authority to define and resolve problems. Mrs. Nixon is using a _____ approach to instruction.
   A) traditional
   B) communities of learners
   C) constructivist
   D) reciprocal teaching
   Answer: B
   Page Ref: 469
   Skill: Applied
   Objective: 12.13

126) Many U.S. teachers emphasize
   A) the application of abstract concepts to real-life situations.
   B) rote memorization and repetitive drills.
   C) higher-level thinking.
   D) analysis and synthesis of new information.
   Answer: B
   Page Ref: 469
   Skill: Factual
   Objective: 12.13

127) Which of the following is true about teacher–student relationships?
   A) Well-behaved, high-achieving students typically get less support from teachers because they are not as needy as other students.
   B) Overall, low-SES students have more sensitive and supportive relationships with teachers.
   C) Caring teacher–student relationships have an especially strong impact on the achievement of children at risk for learning disabilities.
   D) Teachers tend to interact in the same way with all children, regardless of student behavior or achievement.
   Answer: C
   Page Ref: 470
   Skill: Conceptual
   Objective: 12.13

128) Nora's teacher thinks she has a behavior problem. As a result, Nora starts to believe that she is a troublemaker and begins to act out in the classroom. This is an example of a(n)
   A) educational self-fulfilling prophecy.
   B) stereotype threat.
   C) collaborative identification.
   D) educational bias.
   Answer: A
   Page Ref: 470
   Skill: Applied
   Objective: 12.13

129) Which type of child–teacher relationship is most likely to lead to a negative self-fulfilling prophecy?
   A) a quiet, withdrawn student with a teacher in an open classroom
   B) a low-achieving student with a teacher who publicly compares children
   C) a high-achieving student with a teacher in a traditional classroom
   D) a low-achieving student with a teacher in an open classroom
   Answer: B
   Page Ref: 470
   Skill: Conceptual
   Objective: 12.13

130) Which of the following statements about multigrade classrooms is true?
   A) Self-esteem and attitudes toward school are usually more positive.
   B) There are no differences in academic performance between same-age and multigrade classrooms.
   C) Multigrade groupings seem to increase student competition.
   D) Pupils get more drill on basic facts and skills, a slower learning pace, and less time on academic work.

Answer: A
Page Ref: 470
Skill: Conceptual
Objective: 12.13

131) Which of the following is true about integration in American schools?
   A) School integration has increased since the 1980s.
   B) When minority students attend ethnically mixed schools, they usually do so with white students.
   C) Hispanic children are less segregated than African-American children.
   D) The racial divide in American education is gradually lessening.

Answer: C
Page Ref: 471 Box: SI: Education: Magnet Schools: Equal Access to High-Quality Education
Skill: Conceptual
Objective: 12.13

132) Which of the following is true about magnet schools?
   A) The less-segregated education provided in a magnet school enhances minority student achievement.
   B) Magnet schools are usually located in high-SES areas and bus in those from low-income, minority areas.
   C) Magnet schools are voluntarily segregated.
   D) Magnet schools typically serve a homogeneous student population.

Answer: A
Page Ref: 471 Box: SI: Education: Magnet Schools: Equal Access to High-Quality Education
Skill: Conceptual
Objective: 12.13

133) Computer programming projects in the classroom promote
   A) problem solving and metacognition.
   B) use of memory strategies.
   C) stronger math and engineering skills.
   D) reduced aggression and bullying.

Answer: A
Page Ref: 472
Skill: Factual
Objective: 12.14

134) Which of the following is true about computers and academic learning?
   A) Most U.S. low-SES families with school-age children and adolescents do not have computers or Internet access.
   B) Using the computer for word processing enables children to write freely, experimenting with letters and words without having to struggle with handwriting.
   C) Computer-written word processing products tend to be shorter and of lesser quality than handwritten products.
   D) The more low-SES middle-school students used home computers to access the Internet for personal information gathering, the lower their reading achievement.

Answer: B
Page Ref: 472
Skill: Conceptual
Objective: 12.14

135) Which of the following statements is true about the digital divide?
   A) Girls more often connect on the Internet to create Web pages, while boys emphasize instant messaging.
   B) Low-SES children who have computer and Internet access devote more time to Internet use than their higher-SES counterparts.
   C) Boys are more likely than girls to engage in writing computer programs and to rate their computer skills as "excellent."
   D) Schools can ensure that girls and low-SES students have many opportunities to benefit from computers merely by equipping classrooms with more technology.

Answer: C
Page Ref: 472
Skill: Conceptual
Objective: 12.14

136) In Mrs. Hayes's fourth grade classroom, students with learning difficulties work alongside typical students for part or all of the school day. Mrs. Hayes's classroom is
   A) ability grouped.
   B) inclusive.
   C) a resource room.
   D) constructivist.

Answer: B
Page Ref: 473
Skill: Applied
Objective: 12.15

137) Five to 10 percent of school-age children have
   A) mild mental retardation.
   B) IQs above 130.
   C) learning disabilities.
   D) autism.

Answer: C
Page Ref: 473
Skill: Factual
Objective: 12.15

138) Jaylynn has an above-average IQ, but low reading achievement scores. Jaylynn has
   A) a learning disability.
   B) mild mental retardation.
   C) an emotional disability.
   D) a behavioral disability.

Answer: A
Page Ref: 473
Skill: Applied
Objective: 12.15

139) Adam has an IQ of 68. He spends his full school day in a classroom with typical learners. Adam is experiencing
   A) a resource classroom.
   B) partial inclusion.
   C) an integrated classroom.
   D) full inclusion.

Answer: D
Page Ref: 473
Skill: Applied
Objective: 12.15

140) Which of the following is true about inclusion?
    A) All students benefit academically from inclusion, but not all benefit socially.
    B) All students benefit socially from inclusion, but not all benefit academically.
    C) Achievement gains depend on the severity of the disability and the support services available.
    D) Students with mental retardation can interact adeptly in conversations and games with their classmates and, therefore, are rarely rejected socially.
Answer: C
Page Ref: 473
Skill: Conceptual
Objective: 12.15

141) Children with special needs go to Mrs. Holman for specialized instruction for part of the day, and remain with their regular teacher for the remainder of the day. Mrs. Holman teaches in a(n)
    A) fully inclusive classroom.
    B) resource room.
    C) partially inclusive classroom.
    D) accommodation room.
Answer: B
Page Ref: 473
Skill: Applied
Objective: 12.15

142) Jeri's IQ was assessed, and she has been labeled "gifted." In other words, her IQ is over
    A) 100.
    B) 110.
    C) 120.
    D) 130.
Answer: D
Page Ref: 474
Skill: Applied
Objective: 12.16

143) If a child is creative, he or she is able to
    A) reproduce others' work with little effort.
    B) come up with original, appropriate work.
    C) think convergently.
    D) achieve outstanding scores in a specific field.
Answer: B
Page Ref: 474
Skill: Factual
Objective: 12.16

144) _____ is emphasized on intelligence tests.
    A) Divergent thinking
    B) Creativity
    C) Convergent thinking
    D) Metacognition
Answer: C
Page Ref: 474
Skill: Factual
Objective: 12.16

145) At a parent–teacher conference, Mr. Hopewell informed Juan's parents that he had been tested and was found to be a highly creative child. The test probably focused on
   A) convergent thinking.
   B) divergent thinking.
   C) fluid intelligence.
   D) spontaneous generation.
Answer: B
Page Ref: 474
Skill: Applied
Objective: 12.16

146) Marisol was selected for her school's gifted program because she had outstanding performance in mathematics. Marisol scored 119 on the IQ test. At Marisol's school, the definition of giftedness has been extended to include
   A) talent.
   B) creativity.
   C) high IQ.
   D) strong divergent thinking skills.
Answer: A
Page Ref: 474–475
Skill: Applied
Objective: 12.16

147) Carter is highly talented in art and music. His parents are likely to
   A) be warm, sensitive, and reasonably demanding.
   B) be highly intelligent.
   C) arrange for rigorous, demanding teachers when he is young.
   D) have strict rules and high expectations.
Answer: A
Page Ref: 475
Skill: Applied
Objective: 12.16

148) Gifted children
   A) have more friends than their peers.
   B) often have low self-esteem.
   C) rarely hide their abilities.
   D) usually become highly creative adults.
Answer: B
Page Ref: 475
Skill: Conceptual
Objective: 12.16

149) Gifted children fare well
   A) when they enter highly selective high schools.
   B) in programs that emphasize problem solving, critical thinking, and creativity.
   C) in programs that keep them with their agemates, but not in programs that advance them to higher grades.
   D) in programs that advance them to higher grades, but not in programs that pull them out of their regular classrooms for special instruction.
Answer: B
Page Ref: 475
Skill: Conceptual
Objective: 12.16

150) Gardner's theory has sparked the development of programs to provide enrichment to all students. Which of the following is true regarding these programs?
    A) Each student is encouraged to focus on only one specific area of interest or one particular talent.
    B) They are not useful in identifying minority children who are underrepresented in school programs for the gifted.
    C) Research has demonstrated the overwhelming effectiveness of such programs in nurturing children's talents.
    D) They highlight the strengths of students who were previously considered ordinary or even at-risk.
Answer: D
Page Ref: 475
Skill: Conceptual
Objective: 12.16

151) In international studies of reading, mathematics, and science achievement, students in the United States typically perform
    A) better than students in Korea and Japan.
    B) better than students in Canada and the Netherlands.
    C) above the international average in reading and math.
    D) at or below the international average.
Answer: D
Page Ref: 476
Skill: Factual
Objective: 12.17

152) According to international comparisons, instruction in the United States is _____ than in other industrialized countries.
    A) more challenging
    B) less focused on absorbing facts
    C) less focused on high-level reasoning
    D) more focused on critical thinking
Answer: C
Page Ref: 476
Skill: Factual
Objective: 12.17

153) Which of the following factors is a reason for the superior academic performance of Finnish as compared to American children?
    A) In Finland, all students receive the same nationally mandated, high-quality instruction.
    B) Finnish parents regard native ability as the key to academic success.
    C) Finland has a national testing system used to ability-group students.
    D) Finnish teachers are not required to participate in continuing education and, therefore, have more time to focus on the children.
Answer: A
Page Ref: 477
Skill: Conceptual
Objective: 12.17

ESSAY

154) Describe the deficiencies children must overcome to acquire selective, adaptable attentional strategies.

Answer:
- *Production deficiency.* Preschoolers rarely engage in attentional strategies. In other words, they fail to produce strategies when they could be helpful.
- *Control deficiency.* Young elementary school children sometimes produce strategies, but not consistently. They fail to control, or execute, strategies effectively.
- *Utilization deficiency.* Slightly later, children execute strategies consistently, but their performance either does not improve or improves less than that of older children.
- *Effective strategy use.* By the mid-elementary school years, children use strategies consistently, and performance improves.

These phases also characterize children's use of memory strategies. Applying a new strategy requires so much effort and attention that little remains to perform other parts of the task well. Another reason a new strategy may not lead to performance gains is that younger children are not good at monitoring their task performance. Because they fail to keep track of how well a strategy is working, they do not apply it consistently or refine it in other ways.

Page Ref: 443

155) Define cognitive self-regulation. Why does it develop gradually? How can parents help foster it?

Answer: School-age children often have difficulty putting what they know about thinking into action. They are not yet good at cognitive self-regulation, the process of continuously monitoring progress toward a goal, checking outcomes, and redirecting unsuccessful efforts. It develops gradually because monitoring learning outcomes is cognitively demanding, requiring constant evaluation of effort and progress. Parents and teachers can foster self-regulation by patiently pointing out important features of tasks and suggesting strategies. Explaining the effectiveness of strategies is particularly helpful because it provides a rationale for future action.

Page Ref: 449

156) Describe Robert Sternberg's triarchic theory of intelligence.

Answer: Sternberg's theory regards intelligence as a product of both inner and outer forces. His triarchic theory is made up of three interacting intelligences: (1) *analytical intelligence*, or information-processing skills; (2) *creative intelligence*, the capacity to solve novel problems; and (3) *practical intelligence*, application of intellectual skills in everyday situations. Intelligent behavior involves balancing all three intelligences to achieve success in life, according to one's personal goals and the requirements of one's cultural community.
- *Analytical intelligence* consists of the information-processing components that underlie all intelligent acts: applying strategies, acquiring task-relevant and metacognitive knowledge, and engaging in self-regulation.
- *Creative intelligence.* In any context, success depends not only on processing familiar information but also on generating useful solutions to new problems. People who are creative think more skillfully than others when faced with novelty. Given a new task, they apply their information-processing skills in exceptionally effective ways, rapidly making these skills automatic so that working memory is freed for more complex aspects of the situation. Consequently, they quickly move to high-level performance.
- *Practical intelligence.* Finally, intelligence is a practical, goal-oriented activity aimed at adapting to, shaping, or selecting environments. Intelligent people skillfully adapt their thinking to fit with both their desires and the demands of their everyday worlds. When they cannot adapt to a situation, they try to shape, or change, it to meet their needs. If they cannot shape it, they select new contexts that better match their skills, values, or goals. Practical intelligence reminds us that intelligent behavior is never culture-free.

Page Ref: 455–456

157) Define emotional intelligence. How is it assessed? How can teachers promote it?

Answer: Emotional intelligence refers to a set of emotional abilities that enable individuals to process and adapt to emotional information. To measure it, researchers have devised items tapping emotional skills that enable people to manage their own emotions and interact competently with others. Only a few assessments of emotional intelligence are available for children. These require careful training of teachers in observing and recording children's emotional skills during everyday activities, gathering information from parents, and taking ethnic backgrounds into account. As more and better measures are devised, they may help identify children with weak emotional and social competencies who would profit from intervention. Emotional intelligence is modestly related to IQ. And in school-age children, adolescents, and adults, it is positively associated with self-esteem, empathy, prosocial behavior, cooperation, leadership skills, and life satisfaction and negatively related to drug and alcohol use, dependency, depression, and aggressive behavior. In adulthood, emotional intelligence predicts many aspects of workplace success, including managerial effectiveness, productive co-worker relationships, and job performance.

Teachers can promote emotional intelligence by using active learning techniques that provide skill practice both in and out of the classroom. Lessons that teach emotional understanding, respect and caring for others, strategies for regulating emotion, and resistance to unfavorable peer pressure are helpful.

Page Ref: 457

158) Ms. Aragon and her young son recently moved to the United States from Mexico. She is considering whether to enroll him in a bilingual education program or immerse him in an English-only school. How would you advise her?

Answer: There are several advantages to bilingual education. Providing instruction in the native tongue lets minority children know that their heritage is respected. In addition, it prevents inadequate proficiency in both languages. When minority children gradually lose the first language as a result of being taught the second, they end up limited in both languages for a time, which can lead to serious academic difficulties. This circumstance is believed to contribute to the high rates of school failure and dropout among low-SES Hispanic youngsters. In classrooms where both languages are integrated into the curriculum, minority children are more involved in learning. They participate more actively in class discussions and acquire the second language more easily. In contrast, when teachers speak only a language children can barely understand, minority children display frustration, boredom, withdrawal, and academic failure. For U.S. non-English-speaking minority children, whose native languages are not valued by the larger society, a strategy that promotes children's native-language and literacy skills while they learn English is the best approach.

Page Ref: 465–466

159) Explain the educational benefits of a small class size in early elementary school.

Answer: In a large field experiment of more than 6,000 Tennessee kindergarteners, students were randomly assigned to "small" (13 to 17 students), "regular" (22 to 25 students) with only a teacher, and regular with a teacher plus a full-time teacher's aide. These arrangements continued into third grade. Small-class students—especially ethnic minority children—scored higher in reading and math achievement each year. Placing teacher's aides in regular-size classes had no impact. Rather, experiencing small classes from kindergarten through third grade predicted substantially higher achievement from fourth through ninth grades, after children had returned to regular-size classes. It also predicted greater likelihood of graduating from high school, particularly for low-income students.

Smaller class sizes are beneficial because with fewer children, teachers spend less time disciplining and more time teaching and giving individual attention. Also, children who learn in smaller groups show better concentration, higher-quality class participation, and more favorable attitudes toward school.

Page Ref: 466–467

160) How are gifted, creative, and talented students identified? What are some characteristics they share?
Answer:

- Gifted children display exceptional intellectual strengths. The standard definition of giftedness based on intelligence test performance is having an IQ over 130. High-IQ children have keen memories and an exceptional capacity to solve challenging academic problems. Yet recognition that intelligence tests do not sample the entire range of human mental skills, as noted earlier in this chapter, has led to an expanded conception of giftedness.
- Creative children have the ability to produce work that is original yet appropriate—something that others have not thought of that is useful in some way. A child with high potential for creativity can be designated as gifted. Tests of creative capacity tap divergent thinking—the generation of multiple and unusual possibilities when faced with a task or problem.
- Talented children have outstanding performance in a specific field, such as creative writing, mathematics, science, music, visual arts, athletics, and leadership. Highly talented children are biologically prepared to master their domain of interest, and they display a passion for doing so.

Many gifted, creative, and talented children and adolescents are socially isolated, partly because their highly driven, nonconforming, and independent styles leave them out of step with peers and partly because they enjoy solitude, which is necessary to develop their talents. Still, they desire gratifying peer relationships, and some—more often girls than boys—try to become better-liked by hiding their abilities. Compared with their ordinary agemates, gifted youths, especially girls, report more emotional and social difficulties, including low self-esteem and depression.

Page Ref: 474–476

CHAPTER 13
EMOTIONAL AND SOCIAL DEVELOPMENT
IN MIDDLE CHILDHOOD

MULTIPLE CHOICE

1) According to Erikson, the psychological conflict of middle childhood is
   A) autonomy versus shame and doubt.
   B) initiative versus guilt.
   C) industry versus inferiority.
   D) identity versus role confusion.
   Answer: C
   Page Ref: 482
   Skill: Factual
   Objective: 13.1

2) The psychological conflict of middle childhood is resolved positively when
   A) children learn to have basic confidence in the future.
   B) experiences lead children to develop a sense of competence at useful skills and tasks.
   C) experiences lead children to develop a mature identity.
   D) children learn to think in terms of conflict-free ideals, rather than conflict-laden reality.
   Answer: B
   Page Ref: 482
   Skill: Conceptual
   Objective: 13.1

3) The Ngoni of Malawi believe that when children _____, they are mature enough for intensive skill training.
   A) shed their first teeth
   B) reach puberty
   C) finish school
   D) reach the age of 10
   Answer: A
   Page Ref: 482
   Skill: Factual
   Objective: 13.1

4) Six-year-old Hector is about to start formal schooling. Hector's family life has not prepared him for school life. According to Erikson, Hector is in danger of developing a sense of
   A) shame.
   B) isolation.
   C) mistrust.
   D) inadequacy.
   Answer: D
   Page Ref: 482
   Skill: Applied
   Objective: 13.1

5) Which of the following children is the most likely to have a sense of industry?
   A) Rona, who has an overly high self-concept
   B) Jackson, who gets along with older children, but does not cooperate with agemates
   C) Boulous, who has a positive but realistic self-concept
   D) Shanna, who has little confidence in her abilities
   Answer: C
   Page Ref: 482
   Skill: Applied
   Objective: 13.1

6) When describing themselves, older school-age children are _____ likely than younger children to _____.
   A) less; include both positive and negative personality traits
   B) more; describe themselves in extreme ways
   C) less; describe themselves in comparison to peers
   D) far less; describe themselves in all-or-nothing ways
   Answer: D
   Page Ref: 483
   Skill: Conceptual
   Objective: 13.2

7) Which of the following statements accurately reflects the change in self-description that typically occurs between ages 8 and 11?
   A) Children tend to describe themselves by focusing on specific behaviors.
   B) Children will describe positive, but not negative, personality traits.
   C) Children organize their observations of behaviors and internal states into general descriptions.
   D) Children are likely to describe themselves in unrealistically extreme ways.
   Answer: C
   Page Ref: 483
   Skill: Conceptual
   Objective: 13.2

8) Jenna observes that she is better at acting than her peers but not so good at basketball. Jenna is engaging in
   A) social comparisons.
   B) perspective taking.
   C) attribution retraining.
   D) emotional self-efficacy.
   Answer: A
   Page Ref: 483
   Skill: Applied
   Objective: 13.2

9) Which of the following children is most likely to compare herself to just one other person and use that information as a basis for self-evaluation?
   A) Jessica, age 5
   B) Estelle, age 7
   C) Mariah, age 9
   D) Shelly, age 11
   Answer: A
   Page Ref: 483
   Skill: Applied
   Objective: 13.2

10) According to George Herbert Mead, _____ skills are crucial for developing a self-concept based on personality traits.
    A) social comparison
    B) emotional self-regulation
    C) perspective-taking
    D) classification
Answer: C
Page Ref: 483
Skill: Conceptual
Objective: 13.2

11) According to George Herbert Mead, as children become better at reading and internalizing others' messages, they form a(n) _____ self.
    A) real
    B) ideal
    C) inferior
    D) hierarchical
Answer: B
Page Ref: 483
Skill: Conceptual
Objective: 13.2

12) Which of the following people is Juanita, a middle-school student, most likely to look to for feedback about herself?
    A) Aunt Eva, who Juanita sees a few times a month
    B) Mr. Reckle, Juanita's science teacher
    C) Kaitlynn, Juanita's best friend
    D) Carlos, Juanita's 8-year-old brother
Answer: C
Page Ref: 483
Skill: Applied
Objective: 13.2

13) School-age children with a history of _____ have more complex, favorable, and coherent self-concepts.
    A) elaborative parent–child conversations about past experiences
    B) authoritarian parent–child interactions
    C) permissive parent–child interactions
    D) routine parent–child conversations about current events
Answer: A
Page Ref: 483
Skill: Conceptual
Objective: 13.2

14) Which child is likely to develop a self-concept based upon independence and self-assertion?
    A) Charin, from China
    B) Iniki, from Japan
    C) Pedro, from Puerto Rico
    D) Michael, from the United States
Answer: D
Page Ref: 483
Skill: Applied
Objective: 13.2

15) As children enter school and receive more feedback about how well they perform compared with their peers, self-esteem usually
   A) adjusts to an extremely high level.
   B) stays the same as it was during the preschool years.
   C) adjusts to a more realistic level.
   D) adjusts to an extremely low level.
Answer: C
Page Ref: 484
Skill: Conceptual
Objective: 13.2

16) During childhood and adolescence, _____ correlates more strongly with overall self-worth than does any other self-esteem factor.
   A) academic achievement
   B) physical appearance
   C) social competence
   D) athletic ability
Answer: B
Page Ref: 484
Skill: Factual
Objective: 13.2

17) Marcus, a self-confident preschooler, is about to enter elementary school. Based on research, Marcus's parents can expect his self-esteem to _____ over the next few years.
   A) decline
   B) increase
   C) remain at the same level
   D) fluctuate drastically
Answer: A
Page Ref: 485
Skill: Applied
Objective: 13.2

18) For most children, self-esteem rises from _____ on.
   A) preschool
   B) second grade
   C) fourth grade
   D) sixth grade
Answer: C
Page Ref: 485
Skill: Factual
Objective: 13.2

19) From middle childhood on, individual differences in self-esteem become
   A) less well-defined.
   B) increasingly stable.
   C) more flexible.
   D) less important.
Answer: B
Page Ref: 485
Skill: Conceptual
Objective: 13.2

20) Carrie, age 8, has high social self-esteem. Of the following statements, which most likely applies to Carrie?
A) She is perceived to be a bit snobbish by her classmates.
B) She outperforms the majority of her classmates in schoolwork.
C) She tends to be well-liked by her classmates.
D) She often gets other classmates into trouble.
Answer: C
Page Ref: 485
Skill: Applied
Objective: 13.2

21) Thad, age 8, has a profile of low self-esteem in all areas. Of the following statements, which most likely applies to Thad?
A) He tends to be well-liked by his classmates.
B) He suffers from anxiety or depression.
C) He relies less on social comparisons to promote his self-esteem.
D) He is a conscientious worker in his school subjects.
Answer: B
Page Ref: 485
Skill: Applied
Objective: 13.2

22) Compared with U.S. children, Asian children
A) score lower in self-esteem.
B) have lower academic achievement.
C) rely more on social comparisons to promote their self-esteem.
D) are reserved in their praise of others.
Answer: A
Page Ref: 485
Skill: Factual
Objective: 13.2

23) Steven and Stephanie have equal skill levels in math, science, and language arts. Which of the following is probably true?
A) Stephanie has higher math self-esteem.
B) Steven has higher language-arts self-esteem.
C) They have equal academic self-esteem.
D) Steven has higher math and science self-esteem.
Answer: D
Page Ref: 485
Skill: Applied
Objective: 13.2

24) Which of the following statements is true about gender differences in self-esteem?
A) Only a slight difference exists between boys and girls in overall self-esteem.
B) Boys' overall sense of self-worth is much higher than girls'.
C) Girls' overall sense of self-worth is much higher than boys'.
D) By the end of middle childhood, girls are more confident than boys about their physical appearance.
Answer: A
Page Ref: 485
Skill: Conceptual
Objective: 13.2

25) Which statement about self-esteem is true?
    A) American cultural values have deemphasized a focus on self-esteem.
    B) Compared with their Caucasian agemates, African-American children tend to have slightly higher self-esteem.
    C) Compared with U.S. children, Asian children tend to have slightly higher self-esteem.
    D) Gender-stereotyped beliefs have little, in any, effect on self-esteem.
    Answer: B
    Page Ref: 486
    Skill: Conceptual
    Objective: 13.2

26) Children whose parents use a(n) _____ child-rearing style feel especially good about themselves.
    A) authoritarian
    B) permissive
    C) authoritative
    D) uninvolved
    Answer: C
    Page Ref: 486
    Skill: Factual
    Objective: 13.2

27) _____ parenting is correlated with unrealistically high self-esteem, which undermines development.
    A) Indulgent
    B) Authoritarian
    C) Authoritative
    D) Uninvolved
    Answer: A
    Page Ref: 486
    Skill: Factual
    Objective: 13.2

28) Margaret is high in academic self-esteem and motivation. She probably credits her successes to
    A) luck.
    B) favoritism.
    C) a fixed ability.
    D) ability and effort.
    Answer: D
    Page Ref: 486
    Skill: Applied
    Objective: 13.2

29) Mastery-oriented children focus on _____ goals, while learned-helpless children focus on _____ goals.
    A) fixed; incremental
    B) incremental; learning
    C) learning; performance
    D) performance; fixed
    Answer: C
    Page Ref: 487
    Skill: Factual
    Objective: 13.2

30) Learned-helpless children
    A) are more persistent than other children.
    B) are more likely to see the connection between effort and success.
    C) attribute their failures to bad luck.
    D) hold a fixed view of ability.
Answer: D
Page Ref: 487
Skill: Conceptual
Objective: 13.2

31) When Amanda succeeds, her mother says, "You're so smart!" This type of trait statement might lead Amanda to
    A) exert more effort when faced with a challenge.
    B) question her competence in the face of a setback.
    C) focus on learning rather than performance.
    D) pay little attention to her academic achievements.
Answer: B
Page Ref: 487
Skill: Applied
Objective: 13.2

32) Teachers who emphasize learning over getting good grades tend to have
    A) average to below-average achieving students.
    B) more learned-helpless students.
    C) mastery-oriented students.
    D) students who have low motivation and achievement.
Answer: C
Page Ref: 487
Skill: Conceptual
Objective: 13.2

33) Girls more often than boys
    A) attribute poor performance to lack of ability.
    B) view failures as stemming from external factors.
    C) attribute setbacks to insufficient effort.
    D) tend to receive mastery-oriented support from teachers.
Answer: A
Page Ref: 487
Skill: Factual
Objective: 13.2

34) Asian parents and teachers are more likely than their American counterparts to
    A) hold a fixed view of ability.
    B) attend more to success than to failure.
    C) ignore a child's inadequate performance.
    D) hold an incremental view of ability.
Answer: D
Page Ref: 488
Skill: Factual
Objective: 13.2

35) Braison is receiving an intervention that encourages him to believe that he can overcome failure by exerting more effort. Braison is receiving
   A) learned success.
   B) attribution retraining.
   C) mastery orientation.
   D) academic mediation.
   Answer: B
   Page Ref: 488
   Skill: Applied
   Objective: 13.2

36) Mrs. Cybrig would like to help her low-effort daughter gain a sense of academic competence. Which of the following would you recommend to her?
   A) Select tasks that challenge, but do not overwhelm her daughter.
   B) Attribute her daughter's successes to intelligence rather than effort.
   C) Compare her daughter to her higher-achieving son by using prizes for good grades.
   D) Select tasks that her daughter can easily do, so she can have success.
   Answer: A
   Page Ref: 488
   Skill: Applied
   Objective: 13.2

37) In which of the following scenarios is Henry, age 9, the most likely to experience guilt?
   A) He accidentally knocks his friend over while running on the playground.
   B) He breaks his mother's favorite glass while trying to help her clean the dishes.
   C) He forgets to clean up his toys before leaving for school.
   D) He peeks at the answers of his classmate during a spelling quiz.
   Answer: D
   Page Ref: 489
   Skill: Applied
   Objective: 13.3

38) When 8-year-old Marcie accidentally spills orange juice and has a stain on her t-shirt for the rest of the day, she is likely to feel
   A) sad.
   B) angry.
   C) guilty.
   D) ashamed.
   Answer: D
   Page Ref: 489
   Skill: Applied
   Objective: 13.3

39) _____ prompts children to make amends.
   A) Pride
   B) Guilt
   C) Shame
   D) Anger
   Answer: B
   Page Ref: 490
   Skill: Factual
   Objective: 13.3

40) Profound feelings of shame
    A) motivate children to take on further challenges.
    B) prompt children to exert greater effort.
    C) compel children to strive for self-improvement.
    D) can trigger withdrawal and depression.
    Answer: D
    Page Ref: 490
    Skill: Factual
    Objective: 13.3

41) Between ages 6 and 12, children
    A) become more aware of circumstances likely to spark mixed emotions.
    B) are likely to explain emotion by referring to external events.
    C) only experience guilt over transgressions if an adult is present.
    D) report feeling guilt for any mishap, whether intentional or not.
    Answer: A
    Page Ref: 490
    Skill: Conceptual
    Objective: 13.3

42) Nine-year-old Simpson is emotionally understanding and empathetic. He probably
    A) also has favorable social relationships and prosocial behavior.
    B) is picked on by other children because he is "too sensitive."
    C) retreats from social situations for fear of being overwhelmed by the emotions of others.
    D) cannot yet engage in perspective taking.
    Answer: A
    Page Ref: 490
    Skill: Applied
    Objective: 13.3

43) Ten-year-old Stanley knows that his friend MaryAnn is angry because he played with Chester at recess. The next day, Stanley invites MaryAnn to play with Chester and him. Stanley is using
    A) emotion-centered coping.
    B) problem-centered coping.
    C) learned helplessness.
    D) emotional self-efficacy.
    Answer: B
    Page Ref: 490
    Skill: Applied
    Objective: 13.3

44) Kelsi's best friend tells her she does not want to be her friend anymore because she likes Jessica better. Although Kelsi is sad, she tells herself that she has many other friends to play with and she spends the evening listening to her favorite songs. Kelsi is using
    A) problem-centered coping.
    B) emotion-centered coping.
    C) learned helplessness.
    D) mastery-oriented attribution.
    Answer: B
    Page Ref: 490
    Skill: Applied
    Objective: 13.3

45) Eleven-year-old Elin is in line at the drinking fountain. When a boy pushes her from behind, Elin is most likely to respond
    A) by crying.
    B) using verbal strategies.
    C) using physical aggression.
    D) by sulking.
Answer: B
Page Ref: 491
Skill: Applied
Objective: 13.3

46) Ten-year-old Justine has a feeling of being in control of her emotional experience. Justine has acquired
    A) problem-centered coping.
    B) emotion-centered coping.
    C) emotional self-efficacy.
    D) self-conscious emotions.
Answer: C
Page Ref: 491
Skill: Applied
Objective: 13.3

47) Emotional self-efficacy
    A) enables a child to resist an impulse to engage in socially inappropriate behavior.
    B) fosters a pessimistic outlook.
    C) prevents a child from understanding and responding sympathetically to the feelings of others.
    D) fosters a favorable self-image.
Answer: D
Page Ref: 491
Skill: Conceptual
Objective: 13.3

48) In response to a story about unjust parental punishment, which of the following children is most likely to say that he or she would feel OK, rather than angry?
    A) Dalaja, a Hindu girl
    B) Joslyn, an American girl
    C) Ashoka, a Buddhist boy
    D) Samuel, an American boy
Answer: C
Page Ref: 491
Skill: Applied
Objective: 13.3

49) A'isha has the capacity to imagine what other people may be thinking and feeling. A'isha has developed
    A) social referencing.
    B) self-conceptualization.
    C) perspective taking.
    D) emotional self-efficacy.
Answer: C
Page Ref: 491
Skill: Applied
Objective: 13.4

50) Grayson understands that third-party perspective taking can be influenced by societal values. Grayson is at the stage of _____ perspective taking.
   A) undifferentiated
   B) social-informational
   C) self-reflective
   D) societal
   Answer: D
   Page Ref: 492
   Skill: Applied
   Objective: 13.4

51) Helena understands that different perspectives may result because people have access to different information. Helena is at the stage of _____ perspective taking.
   A) undifferentiated
   B) social-informational
   C) self-reflective
   D) third-party
   Answer: B
   Page Ref: 492
   Skill: Applied
   Objective: 13.4

52) Axel can "step into his brother's shoes" and view his own thoughts, feelings, and behavior from his brother's point of view. Axel is at the stage of _____ perspective taking.
   A) undifferentiated
   B) social-informational
   C) self-reflective
   D) third-party
   Answer: C
   Page Ref: 492
   Skill: Applied
   Objective: 13.4

53) Eight-year-old Rachael, a Canadian child, is likely to
   A) say that telling the truth is always good.
   B) say that telling a lie is always bad.
   C) favor lying to support the group at the expense of the individual.
   D) favor lying to support the individual at the expense of the group.
   Answer: D
   Page Ref: 493
   Skill: Applied
   Objective: 13.5

54) In one study, 8- to 10-year-olds judged the moral implications of flag burning. Which of the following was a judgment the children made?
   A) They stated that private flag burning is worse than public flag burning.
   B) They stated that burning a flag to start a cooking fire was worse than burning it accidentally.
   C) They agreed that it was never acceptable to burn a flag, even in a country that treated its citizens unfairly.
   D) They stated that burning a flag accidentally was worse than burning it to express disapproval of a country.
   Answer: B
   Page Ref: 493
   Skill: Conceptual
   Objective: 13.5

55) In middle childhood, children realize that people's _____ and _____ affect the moral implications of violating a social convention.
   A) intentions; the context of their actions
   B) age; intelligence
   C) gender; the context of their actions
   D) religion; nationality
Answer: A
Page Ref: 493
Skill: Conceptual
Objective: 13.5

56) In middle childhood, children realize that people whose _____ differs may not be equally responsible for moral transgressions.
   A) gender
   B) ethnicity
   C) knowledge
   D) nationality
Answer: C
Page Ref: 493
Skill: Conceptual
Objective: 13.5

57) As early as age 6, children
   A) recognize the importance of individual rights for maintaining a fair society.
   B) view freedom of speech and religion as individual rights.
   C) place limits on individual choice.
   D) express very few prejudices.
Answer: B
Page Ref: 493
Skill: Conceptual
Objective: 13.5

58) _____ declines in middle childhood.
   A) Moral understanding
   B) Social-conventional understanding
   C) Prejudice
   D) Children's understanding of God
Answer: C
Page Ref: 494
Skill: Factual
Objective: 13.5

59) Children everywhere seem to realize that _____ must prevail when _____ is/are at stake.
   A) higher principles; personal rights
   B) deference to authority; personal welfare
   C) respect for adults; personal matters
   D) rules; collective rights
Answer: A
Page Ref: 494
Skill: Conceptual
Objective: 13.5

60) The likelihood that a child will negatively evaluate an adult's order to commit an immoral act
    A) is much greater for a child from a collectivist, rather than an individualist, society.
    B) depends primarily on the child's gender, with boys being more likely than girls to respond negatively.
    C) is directly related to the child's socioeconomic status.
    D) is unrelated to the child's cultural background.
Answer: D
Page Ref: 494
Skill: Factual
Objective: 13.5

61) Which of the following is true about inequality?
    A) Unless their parents are racist, children rarely demonstrate negative racial attitudes.
    B) White children's parents' and friends' racial attitudes typically resemble their own.
    C) By the early school years, children associate power and privilege with white people.
    D) Most children's attitudes about group status come exclusively from explicit messages from adults.
Answer: C
Page Ref: 494
Skill: Conceptual
Objective: 13.5

62) Previous research about children's understanding of God led to a uniform conclusion that children
    A) had an abstract, mystical view of God.
    B) assigned anthropomorphic characteristics to God.
    C) saw God as omniscient and omnipotent.
    D) were not limited to parental images of God.
Answer: B
Page Ref: 495 Box: CI: Children's Understanding of God
Skill: Factual
Objective: 13.5

63) The most striking feature of children's concepts of God is
    A) how different their thinking is from that of adults.
    B) their mix of tangible and intangible features.
    C) that their representations of God are restricted to a "big person" image.
    D) that their thinking is not strongly influenced by religious education.
Answer: B
Page Ref: 495 Box: CI: Children's Understanding of God
Skill: Factual
Objective: 13.5

64) Which of the following is true about in-group and out-group racial biases?
    A) By age 5 to 7, minority children generally evaluate their own racial group favorably.
    B) After age 7 or 8, majority, but not minority, children express in-group favoritism.
    C) By age 5 to 7, white children generally evaluate other racial groups less favorably.
    D) White children's prejudice against out-group members usually strengthens after age 7 or 8.
Answer: C
Page Ref: 496
Skill: Conceptual
Objective: 13.5

65) Children _____ are _____ likely to hold racial and ethnic prejudices.
   A) who believe that personality traits are changeable; more
   B) with average to low-self esteem; more
   C) who say their own ethnicity makes them feel especially good; less
   D) with very high self-esteem; more
   Answer: D
   Page Ref: 496
   Skill: Factual
   Objective: 13.5

66) Which of the following is true about reducing prejudices?
   A) Long-term contact and collaboration in neighborhoods, schools, and communities may be the best way to reduce prejudices.
   B) Children assigned to cooperative learning groups with peers of diverse backgrounds have fewer prejudices even with regard to out-group members who are not part of the learning teams.
   C) Classrooms that expose children to broad ethnic diversity often cause children to form negative biases about out-group members.
   D) The more children believe that personalities are fixed, the more they report liking and perceiving themselves as similar to members of disadvantaged groups.
   Answer: A
   Page Ref: 497
   Skill: Conceptual
   Objective: 13.5

67) By the end of middle childhood, children form _____ on the basis of proximity, gender, ethnicity, and popularity.
   A) social clubs
   B) social networks
   C) peer groups
   D) dominance hierarchies
   Answer: C
   Page Ref: 498
   Skill: Factual
   Objective: 13.6

68) When peer groups are tracked
   A) for three to six weeks, substantial membership changes occur.
   B) from year to year, membership changes very little even though classrooms are reshuffled.
   C) from year to year, about 30 to 40 percent of groups consist mostly of the same children.
   D) for three to six weeks, membership changes very little.
   Answer: D
   Page Ref: 498
   Skill: Factual
   Objective: 13.6

69) Which of the following statements about peer groups is true?
   A) They rebuff members who deviate from their codes of dress and behavior.
   B) Religion is a primary factor in the formation of peer groups.
   C) Peer groups are diverse in terms of ethnic and gender composition.
   D) They are usually non-exclusive.
   Answer: A
   Page Ref: 498
   Skill: Conceptual
   Objective: 13.6

70) Within peer groups, children
    A) learn to embrace their individuality and uniqueness.
    B) acquire many social skills.
    C) are unlikely to endorse excluding a member.
    D) do not experience relational aggression.
Answer: B
Page Ref: 498
Skill: Conceptual
Objective: 13.6

71) Adult involvement in formal groups, such as 4-H and scouting,
    A) prevents children from realizing the gains in social maturity associated with peer groups.
    B) prevents children from realizing the gains in moral maturity associated with peer groups.
    C) holds in check the negative behaviors associated with informal peer groups.
    D) stifles children's desire for formal or informal peer group belonging.
Answer: C
Page Ref: 499
Skill: Conceptual
Objective: 13.6

72) During middle childhood, _____ is the defining feature of friendship.
    A) trust
    B) selectivity
    C) power
    D) conflict
Answer: A
Page Ref: 499
Skill: Factual
Objective: 13.6

73) Which of the following is most likely true about 8-year-old Aja?
    A) She has a lot of friends of varying ages.
    B) She has a few good friends, who do not resemble her in personality.
    C) She has only a handful of good friends, who, like Aja, are popular and do well in school.
    D) She has a lot of friends of diverse ethnic and SES groups.
Answer: C
Page Ref: 499
Skill: Applied
Objective: 13.6

74) Delia and Tanner are both aggressive girls. Which of the following is probably true about their friendship?
    A) It is low in exchange of private feelings.
    B) It is full of relational hostility.
    C) It involves frequent physical attacks.
    D) It is unlikely to include jealousy or betrayal.
Answer: B
Page Ref: 499
Skill: Applied
Objective: 13.6

75) Holden, a prosocial child, is friends with Jack, an aggressive child. Which of the following is most likely to be true?
   A) They will remain friends through adulthood.
   B) They will have a high exchange of private feelings.
   C) Each boy will be able to rely on support from the other.
   D) Their friendship will be riddled with hostile interaction.
   Answer: D
   Page Ref: 499
   Skill: Applied
   Objective: 13.6

76) Self-reports that measure social prominence assess
   A) peer acceptance.
   B) peer culture.
   C) gender typing.
   D) friendships.
   Answer: A
   Page Ref: 500
   Skill: Factual
   Objective: 13.7

77) Children's peer acceptance self-reports reveal that controversial children receive
   A) a high number of positive and negative votes.
   B) a high number of negative votes.
   C) few positive or negative votes.
   D) no extreme scores.
   Answer: A
   Page Ref: 500
   Skill: Factual
   Objective: 13.7

78) Children's peer acceptance self-reports reveal that neglected children receive
   A) a high number of positive and negative votes.
   B) a high number of negative votes.
   C) mostly positive votes, with a few negative votes.
   D) few positive or negative votes.
   Answer: D
   Page Ref: 500
   Skill: Factual
   Objective: 13.7

79) Charles received few positive and many negative votes on peer acceptance self-reports from the children in his class. How would Charles be classified?
   A) popular
   B) rejected
   C) controversial
   D) neglected
   Answer: B
   Page Ref: 500
   Skill: Applied
   Objective: 13.7

80) Charlene received many positive and no negative votes on peer acceptance self-reports from the children in her class. How would Charlene be classified?
   A) popular
   B) rejected
   C) controversial
   D) neglected
Answer: A
Page Ref: 500
Skill: Applied
Objective: 13.7

81) Jade did not receive any extreme scores on peer acceptance self-reports from the children in her class, but was not neglected either. How would Jade be classified?
   A) popular
   B) average
   C) rejected
   D) controversial
Answer: B
Page Ref: 500
Skill: Applied
Objective: 13.7

82) Which of the following children is most at risk for delinquency in adolescence and criminality in adulthood?
   A) David, an average child
   B) Marie, a rejected child
   C) Leo, a controversial child
   D) Lisa, a popular child
Answer: B
Page Ref: 500
Skill: Applied
Objective: 13.7

83) School-age children with peer-relationship problems are more likely to
   A) have experienced permissive discipline.
   B) come from middle-SES families.
   C) have weak emotional self-regulation skills.
   D) have experienced authoritative discipline.
Answer: C
Page Ref: 500
Skill: Conceptual
Objective: 13.7

84) Yvonne is well-liked by her peers. She gets good grades, solves social problems constructively, and communicates in friendly and cooperative ways. Yvonne is a popular-_____ child.
   A) prosocial
   B) antisocial
   C) aggressive
   D) neglected
Answer: A
Page Ref: 500–501
Skill: Applied
Objective: 13.7

85) Despite his aggressiveness, Tyler is admired by his peers for his sophisticated but devious social skills. Tyler is a
_____ child.
   A) rejected-withdrawn
   B) rejected-aggressive
   C) popular-antisocial
   D) popular-prosocial
Answer: C
Page Ref: 501
Skill: Applied
Objective: 13.7

86) Kristen exhibits hyperactive, inattentive, and impulsive behavior. She is deficient in perspective taking, and shows high
rates of physical and relational conflict. Kristen is a _____ child.
   A) rejected-withdrawn
   B) rejected-aggressive
   C) popular-prosocial
   D) popular-antisocial
Answer: B
Page Ref: 501
Skill: Applied
Objective: 13.7

87) Rejected-withdrawn children are
   A) impulsive and hyperactive.
   B) likely to blame others for their social difficulties.
   C) socially awkward and passive.
   D) good students who have problems with adult authority.
Answer: C
Page Ref: 501
Skill: Factual
Objective: 13.7

88) Sophia displays a blend of positive and negative social behaviors. She is disruptive, but also engages in prosocial acts.
Sophia is a _____ child.
   A) popular-antisocial
   B) rejected-aggressive
   C) neglected
   D) controversial
Answer: D
Page Ref: 501
Skill: Applied
Objective: 13.7

89) Neglected children
   A) report feeling especially lonely compared to others.
   B) are usually well-adjusted.
   C) are less socially skilled than their average peers.
   D) attempt to engage in high rates of interaction.
Answer: B
Page Ref: 501
Skill: Factual
Objective: 13.7

90) Kurt is a target of verbal abuse, physical attacks, and other forms of abuse. Kurt is
    A) a rejected-aggressive child.
    B) experiencing peer victimization.
    C) experiencing atypical bullying.
    D) a controversial-withdrawn child.
Answer: B
Page Ref: 502 Box: B&E: Bullies and Their Victims
Skill: Applied
Objective: 13.7

91) About _____ percent of children are repeatedly victimized by bullies.
    A) 3 to 7
    B) 9 to 12
    C) 15 to 30
    D) 35 to 50
Answer: C
Page Ref: 502 Box: B&E: Bullies and Their Victims
Skill: Factual
Objective: 13.7

92) Which of the following is true about bullying?
    A) Most bullies are high-status boys who are liked for their leadership or athletic abilities.
    B) Aggression and victimization are polar opposites.
    C) The best way to reduce bullying is to teach the victim to be more aggressive.
    D) Chronic victims tend to be passive when active behavior is expected.
Answer: D
Page Ref: 502 Box: B&E: Bullies and Their Victims
Skill: Conceptual
Objective: 13.7

93) Anxious, withdrawn children who _____ show fewer adjustment problems than other victimized children.
    A) have a close friend
    B) avoid interacting with others
    C) are verbally skilled
    D) can pretend as if they do not care about being teased
Answer: C
Page Ref: 502 Box: B&E: Bullies and Their Victims
Skill: Factual
Objective: 13.7

94) Many _____ children are unaware of their poor social skills and do not take responsibility for their social failures.
    A) rejected-withdrawn
    B) rejected-aggressive
    C) popular-antisocial
    D) popular-prosocial
Answer: B
Page Ref: 503
Skill: Conceptual
Objective: 13.7

95) Andy has developed a learned-helpless approach to peer acceptance—concluding, after repeated rebuffs, that he will never been liked. Andy is a _____child.
   A) rejected-withdrawn
   B) rejected-aggressive
   C) neglected
   D) controversial
Answer: A
Page Ref: 503
Skill: Applied
Objective: 13.7

96) Interventions with rejected children aim to help them attribute their peer difficulties to _____ causes.
   A) external, unchangeable
   B) external, changeable
   C) internal, changeable
   D) internal, unchangeable
Answer: C
Page Ref: 503
Skill: Factual
Objective: 13.7

97) During the school years, children's gender-stereotyped beliefs
   A) increase in obvious areas of activities and occupations.
   B) increase in less obvious areas of personality traits and achievement.
   C) decrease in both obvious and less obvious areas.
   D) decrease in less obvious areas of achievement and personality traits.
Answer: B
Page Ref: 503
Skill: Factual
Objective: 13.8

98) Parents
   A) more often praise girls for knowledge and boys for obedience.
   B) behave in more mastery-oriented ways with daughters than with sons.
   C) less often encourage girls to make their own decisions.
   D) set higher standards for girls than for boys when helping a child with a task.
Answer: C
Page Ref: 503
Skill: Conceptual
Objective: 13.8

99) Which of the following personality traits is a child most likely to describe as feminine?
   A) dependent
   B) rational
   C) dominant
   D) aggressive
Answer: A
Page Ref: 503
Skill: Applied
Objective: 13.8

100) Which of the following subjects are children most likely to regard as more for girls?
    A) mathematics
    B) physical education
    C) language arts
    D) mechanics
Answer: C
Page Ref: 503
Skill: Applied
Objective: 13.8

101) From third to sixth grade,
    A) boys' identification with their "feminine" personality traits increases.
    B) girls' identification with their "feminine" personality traits increases.
    C) girls' identification with their "masculine" personality traits declines.
    D) boys' identification with their "masculine" personality traits increases.
Answer: D
Page Ref: 505
Skill: Factual
Objective: 13.8

102) Jacob and Sarah are asked to rate the status of traditionally masculine and traditionally feminine occupations. Which of the following is most likely to be true?
    A) Both Jacob and Sarah will rate traditionally masculine occupations as having a higher status than traditionally feminine occupations.
    B) Jacob will rate traditionally masculine occupations as having a higher status than traditionally feminine occupations, and Sarah will do the opposite.
    C) Both Jacob and Sarah will rate traditionally feminine occupations as having a higher status than traditionally masculine occupations.
    D) Jacob will rate traditionally feminine occupations as having a higher status than traditionally masculine occupations, and Sarah will do the opposite.
Answer: A
Page Ref: 505
Skill: Applied
Objective: 13.8

103) Dr. Schulz is conducting a study of the degree to which children feel comfortable with their gender assignment. Dr. Schulz is examining gender
    A) typicality.
    B) contentedness.
    C) roles.
    D) stereotypes.
Answer: B
Page Ref: 505
Skill: Conceptual
Objective: 13.8

104) Which of the following statements is true about families in industrialized nations today?
    A) There are fewer never-married parents.
    B) There are more births per family unit.
    C) Families have become more diverse.
    D) Fewer mothers are entering the labor force.
Answer: C
Page Ref: 506
Skill: Conceptual
Objective: 13.9

105) In middle childhood,
    A) the amount of time children spend with parents increases dramatically.
    B) child rearing becomes easier for parents who established an authoritative style during the early years.
    C) the issues parents must deal are similar to the issues they dealt with during the preschool years.
    D) effective parents retain adult control, while ineffective parents shift control from adult to child.
Answer: B
Page Ref: 507
Skill: Conceptual
Objective: 13.9

106) Jalesa's parents exercise general oversight of her activities, while letting Jalesa take charge of moment-by-moment decision making. Jalesa and her parents are engaging in
    A) supervisory parenting.
    B) authoritarian parenting.
    C) mediation.
    D) coregulation.
Answer: D
Page Ref: 507
Skill: Applied
Objective: 13.9

107) Which of the following is true about the parent–child relationship in middle childhood?
    A) Both parents tend to devote more time to children of their own sex.
    B) Mothers tend to focus on achievement-related pursuits and chores.
    C) Fathers tend to focus on ensuring that children meet responsibilities for homework.
    D) When both parents are present, mothers engage in more caregiving than fathers.
Answer: A
Page Ref: 507
Skill: Conceptual
Objective: 13.9

108) Which of the following statements is true about sibling rivalry?
    A) It tends to decrease in middle childhood.
    B) Parental comparisons are more frequent for same-sex siblings.
    C) Same-sex siblings tend to quarrel less than other-sex siblings.
    D) Children react especially intensely when mothers prefer one child.
Answer: B
Page Ref: 507
Skill: Conceptual
Objective: 13.10

109) Differential treatment of siblings increases when
    A) siblings strive to be different from one another.
    B) parents spend more time with children.
    C) parents are dealing with financial or emotional stress.
    D) there are fewer children in the family.
Answer: C
Page Ref: 507
Skill: Factual
Objective: 13.10

110) Brothers Alan and James are very different in personality and temperament. What should their parents do to help facilitate their sibling relationship?
   A) They should maintain a "hands-off" approach and allow the boys to work independently on the relationship.
   B) They should use mediation techniques to increase the boys' awareness of each other's perspectives and reduce animosity.
   C) They should give Alan, the older brother, authority over James, the younger brother, especially in joint decision making.
   D) They should insist that the brothers rely on each other for companionship by limiting their outside friendships.
Answer: B
Page Ref: 508
Skill: Applied
Objective: 13.10

111) Which of the following is true about only children in the United States?
   A) They are spoiled and advantaged compared to children with siblings.
   B) They are lower in self-esteem compared to children with siblings.
   C) They do not differ from children with siblings in self-rated personality traits.
   D) They are better accepted in peer groups than are children from multichild families.
Answer: C
Page Ref: 508
Skill: Conceptual
Objective: 13.10

112) Only children _____ than children with siblings.
   A) do poorer in school
   B) are somewhat closer to their parents
   C) have lower achievement motivation
   D) have fewer close, high-quality friends
Answer: B
Page Ref: 508
Skill: Factual
Objective: 13.10

113) Bao, an only child, lives in China. Which of the following is probably true?
   A) Bao's development is not as favorable as only children in the United States.
   B) Bao tends to feel emotionally insecure.
   C) Bao differs from agemates with siblings in social skills.
   D) Bao does not differ from agemates with siblings in peer acceptance.
Answer: D
Page Ref: 508
Skill: Applied
Objective: 13.10

114) The most common way gay men and lesbians become parents is through
   A) previous heterosexual marriages.
   B) surrogacy.
   C) reproductive technologies.
   D) adoption.
Answer: A
Page Ref: 508
Skill: Factual
Objective: 13.11

115) Gay and lesbian adoption is illegal in
   A) the United Kingdom and Canada.
   B) Mexico and Argentina.
   C) some U.S. states.
   D) Spain and Belgium.
Answer: C
Page Ref: 508
Skill: Factual
Objective: 13.11

116) Lilly's parents are gay. Research shows that she is likely to
   A) be confused about her gender identity.
   B) suffer from poor mental health.
   C) have inadequate peer relations.
   D) be as well-adjusted as other children.
Answer: D
Page Ref: 509
Skill: Applied
Objective: 13.11

117) Children of gay and lesbian parents can be distinguished from other children by
   A) the amount of teasing they endure.
   B) issues related to living in a nonsupportive society.
   C) their higher-than-average rates of homosexuality.
   D) their gender role preferences and their gender contentedness.
Answer: B
Page Ref: 509
Skill: Factual
Objective: 13.11

118) About ___ percent of U.S. children live with a single parent who has never married and does not have a partner.
   A) 5
   B) 10
   C) 15
   D) 20
Answer: B
Page Ref: 509
Skill: Factual
Objective: 13.12

119) African-American young women
   A) make up the largest group of never-married parents.
   B) postpone childbirth more than women in other U.S. ethnic groups.
   C) postpone marriage less than women in other U.S. ethnic groups.
   D) are less likely than Caucasian young women to raise a child in a single-parent household.
Answer: A
Page Ref: 509
Skill: Factual
Objective: 13.12

120) The rate of divorce in the United States is
    A) the lowest in the world.
    B) the same as most Western nations.
    C) the highest in the world.
    D) increasing at a steady pace.
Answer: C
Page Ref: 510
Skill: Factual
Objective: 13.13

121) Seven-month-old Tristan's parents are divorcing. If Tristan is like the average child of divorce, which of the following is likely to happen?
    A) Tristan will spend about a third of his childhood in a single-parent family.
    B) Neither of Tristan's parents will remarry.
    C) Tristan will reside with his father.
    D) Tristan will spend about two-thirds of his childhood in a single-parent family.
Answer: A
Page Ref: 510
Skill: Applied
Objective: 13.13

122) Approximately _____ of divorced parents remarry; and approximately _____ percent of those second marriages end in a divorce.
    A) one-third; 45
    B) one-half; 50
    C) one-half; 75
    D) two-thirds; 50
Answer: D
Page Ref: 510
Skill: Factual
Objective: 13.13

123) Samantha has recently divorced. She and her 2-year-old are likely to experience which of the following in the initial period after the divorce?
    A) remaining in the family home
    B) an increase in income due to child support payments
    C) a sharp drop in income
    D) a stronger relationship
Answer: C
Page Ref: 511
Skill: Applied
Objective: 13.13

124) Trent's parents are divorced and he resides with his mother. Trent's father sees him only occasionally. His father's parenting style is likely to be
    A) uninvolved, but loving.
    B) harsh, but consistent.
    C) authoritative and warm.
    D) permissive and indulgent.
Answer: D
Page Ref: 511
Skill: Applied
Objective: 13.13

125) Which child is the most likely to blame himself for his parents' divorce?
    A) Dewayne, age 4
    B) Emmit, age 9
    C) Gregory, age 12
    D) Killian, age 15
Answer: A
Page Ref: 511
Skill: Applied
Objective: 13.13

126) Which of the following children has the highest risk for poor academic achievement and emotional adjustment?
    A) Zane, a boy who lives with his divorced mother
    B) Logan, a boy who lives with his divorced father
    C) Madisyn, a girl who lives with her divorced mother
    D) Kennedy, a girl who lives with her divorced father
Answer: A
Page Ref: 511–512
Skill: Applied
Objective: 13.13

127) Most children show improved adjustment to their parents' divorce after
    A) 6 months.
    B) 1 year.
    C) 18 months.
    D) 2 years.
Answer: D
Page Ref: 512
Skill: Factual
Objective: 13.13

128) The overriding factor in positive adjustment after divorce is
    A) the gender of the child.
    B) effective parenting.
    C) the custody and residential arrangements.
    D) the temperament of the child.
Answer: B
Page Ref: 512
Skill: Factual
Objective: 13.13

129) Outcomes for sons are better when the
    A) mother is the sole custodian.
    B) parents equally split parenting time.
    C) father has no visitation.
    D) father is the custodial parent.
Answer: D
Page Ref: 512
Skill: Factual
Objective: 13.13

130) Cheryl and Saul are getting a divorce. They are meeting together with a trained professional in order to reduce family conflict, including legal battles over property division and child custody. Cheryl and Saul are participating in
  A) marriage counseling.
  B) joint custody.
  C) divorce mediation.
  D) family arbitration.
Answer: C
Page Ref: 513
Skill: Applied
Objective: 13.13

131) Nikki and Alex are divorcing. The court grants both of them an equal say in important decisions about their children's upbringing. This arrangement is known as
  A) coparenting.
  B) shared custody.
  C) custodial mediation.
  D) joint custody.
Answer: D
Page Ref: 513
Skill: Applied
Objective: 13.13

132) Which child is the most likely to be well-adjusted after a divorce?
  A) Corez, whose parents have joint custody
  B) Sequoia, who lives in a sole maternal-custody home
  C) Amanda, who lives in a sole paternal-custody home
  D) Gillian, who lives with her grandmother and neither parent
Answer: A
Page Ref: 513
Skill: Applied
Objective: 13.13

133) Which of the following parents is the most likely to pay regular child support?
  A) Betty, a noncustodial mother who sees her son only occasionally
  B) Barney, a noncustodial father who has supervised visitation with his son
  C) Fred, a noncustodial father who sees his daughter often
  D) Wilma, a noncustodial mother who has no visitation rights
Answer: C
Page Ref: 513
Skill: Applied
Objective: 13.13

134) Seven-year-old Matthew and 14-year-old Molly have been living with their mother since their parents' divorce two years ago. If their mother remarries, you would expect
  A) Matthew to show more adjustment problems than Molly.
  B) Molly to show more adjustment problems than Matthew.
  C) neither child to show many adjustment problems.
  D) both children to have a very difficult adjustment.
Answer: B
Page Ref: 514
Skill: Applied
Objective: 13.13

135) Stepfathers
A) who marry rather than cohabit are usually more involved in parenting.
B) generally disrupt the close ties many boys have with their mothers.
C) are usually welcomed by girls, regardless of the girl's age.
D) tend to be more welcomed by older school children than by younger ones.
Answer: A
Page Ref: 514
Skill: Factual
Objective: 13.13

136) Which of the following is true about father–stepmother families?
A) Boys, especially, have a hard time getting along with their stepmothers.
B) The longer children live in father–stepmother households, the more negative the interaction with them becomes.
C) When fathers have custody, children typically react negatively to remarriage.
D) Remarriage of noncustodial fathers usually leads to increased contact with their biological children.
Answer: C
Page Ref: 515
Skill: Conceptual
Objective: 13.13

137) In the United States today, about _____ of mothers with school-age children are employed.
A) one-third
B) one-half
C) two-thirds
D) three-quarters
Answer: D
Page Ref: 515
Skill: Factual
Objective: 13.14

138) Regardless of SES, daughters of employed mothers
A) are more achievement- and career-oriented.
B) show lower self-esteem.
C) perceive women's roles as involving less satisfaction.
D) devote fewer hours to doing homework under parental guidance.
Answer: A
Page Ref: 515
Skill: Factual
Objective: 13.14

139) When working mothers enjoy their jobs and remain committed to parenting, children show
A) lower self-esteem.
B) less positive family and peer relations.
C) less gender-stereotyped beliefs.
D) poorer academic achievement.
Answer: C
Page Ref: 515–516
Skill: Factual
Objective: 13.14

140) The Fishers are a dual-earner family. The Fisher children probably _____ than their friends in single-earner households.
   A) participate in fewer household chores
   B) have more rigid gender-role attitudes
   C) have more behavioral and academic problems
   D) devote more daily hours to doing homework under parental guidance
Answer: D
Page Ref: 516
Skill: Applied
Objective: 13.14

141) Samantha is a stay-at-home mother who is considering going back to work. She is concerned about the impact on her children's adjustment. To provide her children with the greatest benefits, Samantha could
   A) work part-time with a flexible work schedule.
   B) select a job that she does not really enjoy so that she will not be tempted to get caught up in her work.
   C) remain a stay-at-home mom until her kids leave home.
   D) select a full-time job that will quickly get her acclimated to being away from her family.
Answer: A
Page Ref: 516
Skill: Applied
Objective: 13.14

142) Alicia, a fourth-grader, regularly looks after herself for two to three hours after she gets home from school and before her mother gets home from work. Alicia is a
   A) home-based child.
   B) neglected child.
   C) self-care child.
   D) afternoon orphan.
Answer: C
Page Ref: 516
Skill: Applied
Objective: 13.14

143) Which of the following 11-year-old children is the most likely to have adjustment difficulties when left alone at home?
   A) Genevieve, who has a history of authoritative parenting
   B) Trenton, who is left to his own devices for five hours a day
   C) Teresa, who is monitored by parental telephone calls
   D) Alexia, who has regular after-school chores
Answer: B
Page Ref: 516
Skill: Applied
Objective: 13.14

144) In middle childhood, children's anxieties are directed toward the realities of the wider world, such as a fear of
   A) the dark.
   B) supernatural beings.
   C) thunder and lightning.
   D) war and disaster.
Answer: D
Page Ref: 517
Skill: Factual
Objective: 13.15

145) Yolanda has developed an intense, unmanageable fear of the dark. Yolanda has a(n)
    A) anxiety disorder.
    B) social disorder.
    C) phobia.
    D) typical childhood fear.
Answer: C
Page Ref: 517
Skill: Applied
Objective: 13.15

146) Jane feels severe apprehension about attending school. She often gets dizzy or nauseous and complains of stomachaches. Jane is likely to have
    A) a school bully.
    B) overindulgent parents.
    C) a permissive teacher.
    D) harsh living conditions.
Answer: A
Page Ref: 517
Skill: Applied
Objective: 13.15

147) Hymie has developed a school phobia. Hymie's parents should
    A) tell him to be braver and send him to school anyway.
    B) insist that he return to school after providing training in how to cope.
    C) arrange a shortened school day for him.
    D) give him tangible rewards for each day he attends school without complaining.
Answer: B
Page Ref: 518
Skill: Applied
Objective: 13.15

148) Children who live in the midst of constant danger, chaos, and deprivation,
    A) tend to cope better with phobias.
    B) have fewer anxieties than children with inhibited temperaments.
    C) are at risk for long-term emotional distress and behavior problems.
    D) have some short-term, but few long-term, emotional problems.
Answer: C
Page Ref: 518
Skill: Factual
Objective: 13.15

149) When war and social crises are temporary, most children
    A) cannot be comforted.
    B) do not show long-term emotional difficulties.
    C) lose their sense of safety.
    D) build a pessimistic view of the future.
Answer: B
Page Ref: 518 Box: CI: The Impact of Ethnic and Political Violence on Children
Skill: Factual
Objective: 13.15

150) The best protection against lasting problems for children of war is
   A) parental affection and reassurance.
   B) religious involvement.
   C) training in offensive and defensive maneuvers.
   D) participating in recreational programs.
Answer: A
Page Ref: 518 Box: CI: The Impact of Ethnic and Political Violence on Children
Skill: Factual
Objective: 13.15

151) Which child of war, who is separated from her parents, is likely to experience the most emotional stress?
   A) Gasira, who lives with her grandparents
   B) Sentwali, who lives in a shelter
   C) Amira, who lives with a neighboring family
   D) Farrah, who lives with her older sister
Answer: B
Page Ref: 518 Box: CI: The Impact of Ethnic and Political Violence on Children
Skill: Applied
Objective: 13.15

152) Which of the following is true about child sexual abuse?
   A) Children with disabilities are abused less than their typically developing peers.
   B) Sexual abuse is committed against children of both sexes, but more often against girls.
   C) Most cases begin in middle childhood and are not reported until adulthood.
   D) Typically, the abuser is a nonrelative whom the child does not know very well.
Answer: B
Page Ref: 519
Skill: Conceptual
Objective: 13.16

153) A child sexual abuser is most likely to be
   A) the victim's mother or stepmother.
   B) a stranger or someone the victim does not know very well.
   C) male, and either a parent or someone the parent knows well.
   D) someone the victim does not trust.
Answer: C
Page Ref: 519
Skill: Factual
Objective: 13.16

154) Which of the following is true about child sexual abusers?
   A) Most offenders live in middle- to high-income households and are strangers to the child.
   B) Most offenders prefer a victim who is physically strong and has an assertive personality.
   C) Most offenders do not suffer from any psychological disorders.
   D) Many offenders deny their own responsibility, blaming the abuse on the willing participation of a seductive youngster.
Answer: D
Page Ref: 519
Skill: Conceptual
Objective: 13.16

155) Children who _____ are especially vulnerable to child sexual abuse.
    A) live in economically advantaged homes
    B) live in homes with a constantly changing cast of characters
    C) are physically strong and emotionally stable
    D) are socially popular and have no disabilities
Answer: B
Page Ref: 519
Skill: Conceptual
Objective: 13.16

156) Younger children who are sexually abused frequently react
    A) with generalized fearfulness.
    B) by running away.
    C) by attempting suicide.
    D) with substance abuse.
Answer: A
Page Ref: 519
Skill: Factual
Objective: 13.16

157) Ellie was sexually abused as a child. This increases her chances of _____ in adulthood.
    A) engaging in authoritative parenting
    B) engaging in coercive parenting
    C) choosing a nonabusive partner
    D) avoiding sexual activity
Answer: B
Page Ref: 520
Skill: Applied
Objective: 13.16

158) The best way to reduce the suffering of victims of child sexual abuse is
    A) by prosecuting the offender.
    B) by short-term therapy for the victim.
    C) to prevent sexual abuse from continuing.
    D) by teaching them to recognize inappropriate sexual advances.
Answer: C
Page Ref: 520
Skill: Factual
Objective: 13.16

159) Research indicates that _____ relationship exists between stressful life experiences and psychological disturbance in childhood.
    A) a very strong
    B) only a modest
    C) a very weak
    D) no
Answer: B
Page Ref: 520
Skill: Factual
Objective: 13.17

160) Marni, an easy-going third-grader with favorable self-esteem, has faced school difficulties, family transitions, and early maltreatment. Yet, Marni is well-adjusted. Marni is
   A) a stress-resilient child.
   B) probably living with an adoptive family.
   C) at great risk for psychological problems in adulthood.
   D) unlikely to have any warm, supportive adults in her life.
Answer: A
Page Ref: 520
Skill: Applied
Objective: 13.17

161) Until recently, children were not assumed fully competent to testify in court cases involving child abuse until age
   A) 3.
   B) 5.
   C) 7.
   D) 10.
Answer: D
Page Ref: 521 Box: SI: Children's Eyewitness Testimony
Skill: Factual
Objective: 13.16

162) Compared with preschoolers, school-age children who give eyewitness testimony are
   A) better at inferring other's motives and intentions.
   B) less resistant to misleading questions.
   C) less likely to give detailed narrative accounts.
   D) less able to recall events accurately.
Answer: A
Page Ref: 521 Box: SI: Children's Eyewitness Testimony
Skill: Factual
Objective: 13.16

163) To maximize the accuracy of children's testimony,
   A) children should be interviewed repeatedly and carefully coached.
   B) interviewers should use a confrontational style of questioning.
   C) very young children should be questioned using anatomically correct dolls.
   D) children should be prepared ahead of time, so they know what to expect.
Answer: D
Page Ref: 521 Box: SI: Children's Eyewitness Testimony
Skill: Conceptual
Objective: 13.16

164) Children in second through sixth grades who participated in the *Resolving Conflict Creatively Program*
   A) showed increased relational aggression.
   B) showed gains in prosocial behavior, but losses in academic achievement.
   C) less often behaved aggressively and engaged in more prosocial behavior.
   D) did not benefit from a second year of the intervention.
Answer: C
Page Ref: 523
Skill: Factual
Objective: 13.17

ESSAY

165) How does children's self-esteem change from early to middle childhood?

   Answer: Most preschoolers have extremely high self-esteem. But as children enter school and receive much more feedback about how well they perform compared with their peers, self-esteem differentiates and also adjusts to a more realistic level. By age 6 to 7, children in diverse Western cultures have formed at least four broad self-evaluations: academic competence, social competence, physical/athletic competence, and physical appearance. Within these are more refined categories that become increasingly distinct with age. Self-esteem takes on a hierarchical structure. Children attach greater importance to certain self-evaluations than to others, giving them more weight in the total picture. Self-esteem declines during the first few years of elementary school as children's performances are increasingly judged in relation to those of others, and as they become cognitively capable of social comparison. To protect their self-worth, children eventually balance social comparisons with personal achievement goals. Perhaps for this reason, the drop in self-esteem in the early school years usually is not harmful. Then, from fourth grade on, self-esteem rises for the majority of young people, who feel especially good about their peer relationships and athletic capabilities

Page Ref: 484–485

166) What are some ways that schools can prevent learned helplessness and foster a mastery-oriented approach to learning?

   Answer:
   - *Provision of tasks*: Select tasks that are meaningful, responsive to a diversity of student interests, and appropriately matched to current competence so that the child is challenged but not overwhelmed.
   - *Parent and teacher encouragement*: Communicate warmth, confidence in the child's abilities, the value of achievement, and the importance of effort in success. Model high effort in overcoming failure. Teachers should communicate often with parents, suggesting ways to foster children's effort and progress. Parents should be encouraged to monitor schoolwork; provide scaffolded assistance that promotes knowledge of effective strategies and self-regulation.
   - *Performance evaluations*: Make evaluations private; avoid publicizing success or failure through wall posters, stars, privileges to "smart" children, and prizes for "best" performance. Emphasize individual progress and self-improvement.
   - *School environment*: Offer small classes, which permit teachers to provide individualized support for mastery. Provide for cooperative learning and peer tutoring, in which children assist one another; avoid ability grouping, which makes evaluations of children's progress public. Accommodate individual and cultural differences in styles of learning. Create an atmosphere that sends a clear message that all pupils can learn.

Page Ref: 489

167) Describe personal and situational factors that affect the extent to which children hold racial and ethnic biases.

   Answer:
   - *A fixed view of personality traits*. Children who believe that people's personality traits are fixed rather than changeable often judge others as either "good" or "bad." Ignoring motives and circumstances, they readily form prejudices on the basis of limited information. For example, they might infer that a new child at school who tells a lie to get other kids to like her is simply a bad person.
   - *Overly high self-esteem*. Children and adults with very high self-esteem are more likely to hold racial and ethnic prejudices. These individuals seem to belittle disadvantaged individuals or groups to justify their own extremely favorable self-evaluation. Children who say their own ethnicity makes them feel especially "good"—and thus perhaps socially superior—are more likely to display in-group favoritism and out-group prejudice.
   - *A social world in which people are sorted into groups*. The more adults highlight group distinctions for children and the less interracial contact children experience, the more likely white children are to display prejudice.

Page Ref: 494–497

168) Describe the features of friendship in middle childhood.

Answer: During the school years, friendship becomes more complex and psychologically based. Friendship is no longer just a matter of engaging in the same activities. Instead, it is a mutually agreed-on relationship in which children like each other's personal qualities and respond to one another's needs and desires. Once a friendship forms, trust becomes its defining feature. School-age children state that a good friendship is based on acts of kindness that signify each person can be counted on to support the other. Consequently, violations of trust, breaking promises, and gossiping behind the other's back are serious breaches of friendship.

School-age friendships are more selective. Whereas preschoolers say they have lots of friends, by age 8 or 9, children name only a handful of good friends. Girls, especially, are exclusive in their friendships because they demand greater closeness than boys. Children tend to select friends like themselves in age, sex, race, ethnicity, and SES. Friends also resemble one another in personality, peer popularity, prosocial behavior, and academic achievement.

High-quality friendships remain stable over middle childhood, with most lasting over a school year, and some for several years. Friendships of relationally aggressive girls are high in exchange of private feelings but full of jealousy, conflict, and betrayal. Among boys, talk between aggressive friends contains frequent coercive statements and attacks.

Page Ref: 499–500

169) Describe the characteristics of, and explain the difference between, popular-prosocial and popular-antisocial children.

Answer: Popular children are those who are well-liked or admired by their peers. The majority of popular-prosocial children combine academic and social competence. They perform well in school, communicate with peers in friendly and cooperative ways, and solve social problems constructively. But other popular children are admired for their socially adept yet belligerent behavior. This smaller subtype, popular-antisocial children, includes "tough" boys—athletically skilled but poor students who cause trouble and defy adult authority—and relationally aggressive boys and girls who enhance their own status by ignoring, excluding, and spreading rumors about other children. Despite their aggressiveness, peers view these youths as "cool," perhaps because of their athletic ability and sophisticated but devious social skills. Although peer admiration gives these children some protection against lasting adjustment difficulties, their antisocial acts require intervention. With age, peers like these high-status, aggressive youths less and less, a trend that is stronger for relationally aggressive girls. The more socially prominent and controlling these girls become, the more they engage in relational aggression. Eventually peers condemn their nasty tactics and reject them.

Page Ref: 500–501

170) Discuss sibling rivalry, and explain how parents contribute to it.

Answer: Sibling rivalry tends to increase in middle childhood. As children participate in a wider range of activities, parents often compare siblings' traits and accomplishments. The child who gets less parental affection, more disapproval, or fewer material resources is likely to be resentful and show poorer adjustment over time. For same-sex siblings who are close in age, parental comparisons are more frequent, resulting in more quarreling and antagonism and in poorer adjustment. This effect is particularly strong when parents are under stress as a result of financial worries, marital conflict, single parenthood, or child negativity. Parents whose energies are drained become less careful about being fair. Perhaps because fathers, overall, spend less time with children than mothers, children react especially intensely when fathers prefer one child. Parents can limit these effects by making an effort not to compare children, but some feedback about their competencies is inevitable.

Providing parents with training in mediation—how to get siblings to lay down ground rules, clarify their points of disagreement and common ground, and discuss possible solutions—increases siblings' awareness of each other's perspectives and reduces animosity.

Page Ref: 507–508

171) Discuss blended families and describe some support options available to them.

Answer: When divorced parents remarry, cohabit, or share a sexual relationship and a residence with a partner outside of marriage, the parent, stepparent, and children form a new family structure called a blended, or reconstituted, family. For some children, this expanded family network is positive, bringing greater adult attention. But overall, children in blended families have more adjustment problems—including internalizing and externalizing symptoms and poor school performance—than children in stable, first-marriage families. Switching to stepparents' new rules and expectations can be stressful, and children often regard steprelatives as intruders. How well they adapt is, again, related to the quality of family functioning. This depends on which parent forms a new relationship, the child's age and sex, and the complexity of blended-family relationships. Girls of all ages, older school-age children, and adolescents seem to have the most adjustment difficulties.

Parenting education and couples counseling can help parents and children adapt to the complexities of blended families. Effective approaches encourage stepparents to move into their new roles gradually by first building a warm relationship with the child. Only when a warm bond has formed between stepparents and stepchildren is more active parenting possible. Counselors can offer couples guidance in coparenting to limit loyalty conflicts and provide consistency in child rearing. This allows children to benefit from the increased diversity that stepparent relationships bring to their lives.

Page Ref: 513–515

172) Describe some of the consequences of child sexual abuse from early childhood to adulthood.

Answer: The adjustment problems of sexually abused children are often severe. Depression, low self-esteem, mistrust of adults, anger, and hostility can persist for years after the abusive episodes. Younger children react with sleep difficulties, loss of appetite, and generalized fearfulness. Reactions of adolescents include severe depression, suicidal impulses, substance abuse, early sexual activity with more partners, running away, and delinquency. At all ages, persistent abuse accompanied by force, violence, and a close relationship to the perpetrator (incest) has a more severe impact. And repeated sexual abuse, like physical abuse is associated with central nervous system damage.

Sexually abused children frequently display sexual knowledge and behavior beyond their years. In adolescence, abused young people often become promiscuous, and as adults, they show increased arrest rates for sex crimes and prostitution. Women who were sexually abused are likely to choose partners who abuse both them and their children. As mothers, they often engage in irresponsible and coercive parenting, including child abuse and neglect. In these ways, the harmful impact of sexual abuse is transmitted to the next generation.

Page Ref: 519–520

CHAPTER 14
PHYSICAL DEVELOPMENT IN ADOLESCENCE

MULTIPLE CHOICE

1) Franca, age 11, recently started contradicting and disagreeing with her parents. She is self-conscious and often goes to her room and closes the door. Franca is a head taller and several pounds heavier than most girls in her sixth-grade class. Franca has probably
   A) developed an eating disorder.
   B) entered adolescence.
   C) reached full maturation.
   D) developed a social phobia.
   Answer: B
   Page Ref: 530
   Skill: Applied
   Objective: 14.1

2) The beginning of adolescence is marked by
   A) reaching full adult height.
   B) assumption of adult roles.
   C) the onset of puberty.
   D) secretion of the growth hormone.
   Answer: C
   Page Ref: 530
   Skill: Factual
   Objective: 14.1

3) Jean-Jacques Rousseau believed that
   A) the biological upheaval of puberty triggers heightened emotionality, conflict, and defiance of adults.
   B) the social environment has a greater impact on adolescent behavior than the biological events associated with puberty.
   C) adolescence resembles the period in which humans evolved from savages into civilized beings.
   D) during adolescence, instinctual drives shift to the genital region of the body, resulting in conflict and volatile, unpredictable behavior.
   Answer: A
   Page Ref: 530
   Skill: Conceptual
   Objective: 14.1

4) _____ viewed the teenage years as a biologically based, universal "developmental disturbance."
   A) Jean-Jacques Rousseau
   B) Margaret Mead
   C) G. Stanley Hall
   D) Anna Freud
   Answer: D
   Page Ref: 530
   Skill: Factual
   Objective: 14.1

5) G. Stanley Hall described adolescence as
    A) the period of calm after the storm of childhood.
    B) the stage in which sexual impulses reawaken and trigger volatile behavior.
    C) a cascade of instinctual passions.
    D) a period of harmony and predictability of behaviors.
Answer: C
Page Ref: 530
Skill: Conceptual
Objective: 14.1

6) _____ viewed adolescence as a period so turbulent that it resembled the era in which humans evolved from savages into civilized beings.
    A) G. Stanley Hall
    B) Sigmund Freud
    C) Jean-Jacques Rousseau
    D) Anna Freud
Answer: A
Page Ref: 530
Skill: Factual
Objective: 14.1

7) In Freud's genital stage,
    A) social forces determine the young person's reaction to puberty.
    B) sexual impulses reawaken, triggering psychological conflict and volatile behavior.
    C) sexual impulses remain dormant for a short period of time.
    D) the major conflict is called Oedipal conflict.
Answer: B
Page Ref: 530
Skill: Conceptual
Objective: 14.1

8) Contemporary research suggests that the storm-and-stress notion of adolescence is
    A) the most accurate perspective.
    B) greatly understated.
    C) slightly accurate because most teens experience emotional turbulence.
    D) greatly exaggerated.
Answer: D
Page Ref: 530
Skill: Conceptual
Objective: 14.1

9) The overall rate of psychological disturbance _____ from childhood to adolescence, when it is about _____ percent.
    A) rises slightly; 15
    B) rises sharply; 35
    C) stays about the same; 10
    D) decreases slightly; 5
Answer: A
Page Ref: 530
Skill: Factual
Objective: 14.1

10) _____ was the first researcher to point out the wide variability in adolescent adjustment.
   A) Sigmund Freud
   B) Margaret Mead
   C) G. Stanley Hall
   D) Anna Freud
Answer: B
Page Ref: 530
Skill: Factual
Objective: 14.1

11) Margaret Mead showed that
   A) to understand adolescent development, researchers must pay greater attention to social and cultural influences.
   B) Samoan adolescents had a similar adolescent experience as young people in Western societies.
   C) the period of adolescence is greatly extended in non-Western societies.
   D) not all cultures have an intervening phase between childhood and adulthood.
Answer: A
Page Ref: 530
Skill: Conceptual
Objective: 14.1

12) Which of the following statements about adolescence is true?
   A) The length of adolescence does varies little from culture to culture.
   B) In modern industrialized societies, the adolescent transition to adulthood is relatively short.
   C) The biological changes of adolescence are universal, found in all primates and all cultures.
   D) Many cultures do not have an intervening phase between childhood and the full assumption of adult roles.
Answer: C
Page Ref: 531
Skill: Conceptual
Objective: 14.1

13) _____ vary/varies substantially among cultures.
   A) Feelings of uncertainty and self-doubt
   B) The length of adolescence
   C) The biological changes of adolescence
   D) The social expectations that accompany adolescence
Answer: B
Page Ref: 531
Skill: Conceptual
Objective: 14.1

14) Shannon is in early adolescence. Shannon is between the ages of
   A) 10 and 12.
   B) 11 and14.
   C) 14 and 16.
   D) 16 and 18.
Answer: B
Page Ref: 531
Skill: Applied
Objective: 14.1

15) Kai has achieved his full adult appearance and anticipates assumption of adult roles. Kai is in which phase of adolescence?
    A) early adolescence
    B) middle adolescence
    C) late adolescence
    D) emerging adulthood
Answer: C
Page Ref: 531
Skill: Applied
Objective: 14.1

16) Fourteen-year-old Per has been experiencing pubertal changes, which are now nearly complete. Per is in which phase of adolescence?
    A) early adolescence
    B) middle adolescence
    C) late adolescence
    D) emerging adulthood
Answer: B
Page Ref: 531
Skill: Applied
Objective: 14.1

17) Which of the following individuals would you expect to spend the greatest amount of time in adolescence?
    A) Aapep, who lives in a tribal society
    B) Chimalma, who lives in a village society
    C) Desta, who lives in a nonindustrialized country
    D) Brayden, who lives in an industrialized country
Answer: D
Page Ref: 531
Skill: Applied
Objective: 14.1

18) On the average, girls reach puberty _____ boys.
    A) slightly earlier than
    B) two years earlier than
    C) at the same time as
    D) slightly later than
Answer: B
Page Ref: 531
Skill: Factual
Objective: 14.2

19) The hormonal changes that underlie puberty occur gradually and are under way by age
    A) 6 or 7.
    B) 8 or 9.
    C) 10 or 11.
    D) 12 or 13.
Answer: B
Page Ref: 531
Skill: Factual
Objective: 14.2

20) Secretions of _____ and _____ increase during puberty, leading to tremendous gains in body size and to attainment of skeletal maturity.
   A) melatonin; GH
   B) epinephrine; adrenal androgens
   C) GH; thyroxine
   D) insulin; gastrin
   Answer: C
   Page Ref: 531
   Skill: Factual
   Objective: 14.2

21) Sexual maturation is controlled by
   A) androgens and estrogens.
   B) estrogens and insulin.
   C) adrenal androgens and melatonin.
   D) testosterone and cortisol.
   Answer: A
   Page Ref: 531
   Skill: Factual
   Objective: 14.2

22) The boy's testes release large quantities of _____, which leads to muscle growth, body and facial hair, and other male sex characteristics.
   A) adrenal androgens
   B) estrogens
   C) the androgen testosterone
   D) cortisol and thyroxine
   Answer: C
   Page Ref: 531
   Skill: Factual
   Objective: 14.2

23) Which of the following is true about sex hormones?
   A) Boys have only male hormones called androgens.
   B) Girls have only female hormones called estrogens.
   C) Neither androgens nor estrogens are present in the average boy.
   D) Both androgens and estrogens are present in different amounts in boys and girls.
   Answer: D
   Page Ref: 531
   Skill: Conceptual
   Objective: 14.2

24) _____ influence girls' height spurt and stimulate growth of underarm and pubic hair.
   A) Adrenal androgens
   B) Estrogens
   C) Testosterones
   D) A combination of GH and estrogen
   Answer: A
   Page Ref: 532
   Skill: Factual
   Objective: 14.2

25) The first outward sign of puberty is
   A) menarche.
   B) spermarche.
   C) the growth spurt.
   D) the cephalocaudal trend.
   Answer: C
   Page Ref: 532
   Skill: Factual
   Objective: 14.2

26) On average, the growth spurt of puberty is underway for girls shortly after age ___ and for boys around age ____.
   A) 8½; 10
   B) 9; 11½
   C) 10; 12½
   D) 10½; 13
   Answer: C
   Page Ref: 532
   Skill: Factual
   Objective: 14.2

27) Altogether, adolescents add _____ inches in height and _____ pounds in weight.
   A) 6 to 7; 25 to 35
   B) 8 to 9; 35 to 50
   C) 10 to 11; 50 to 75
   D) 12 to 14; 60 to 80
   Answer: C
   Page Ref: 533
   Skill: Factual
   Objective: 14.2

28) Fifteen-year-old Jesse is growing at his peak. He will probably add more than ___ inches and ____ pounds this year.
   A) 2; 16
   B) 4; 26
   C) 6; 10
   D) 8; 20
   Answer: B
   Page Ref: 533
   Skill: Applied
   Objective: 14.2

29) During puberty,
   A) the hands, legs, and feet accelerate first.
   B) growth follows the cephalocaudal trend.
   C) the torso accelerates first.
   D) children grow from the head first, then the torso.
   Answer: A
   Page Ref: 533
   Skill: Factual
   Objective: 14.2

30) Which of the following is true about body proportions during puberty?
   A) Boys' hips broaden relative to the waist.
   B) Girls' shoulders broaden relative to the hips.
   C) Girls' hips broaden relative to the shoulders.
   D) Girls' legs become longer in relation to the rest of the body.
   Answer: C
   Page Ref: 533
   Skill: Conceptual
   Objective: 14.2

31) Which of the following statements is true about muscle–fat makeup in adolescence?
   A) Although both sexes gain in muscle, the increase is 150 percent greater in boys.
   B) Arm and leg fat decreases in adolescent girls.
   C) Altogether, girls gain far more muscle strength than boys.
   D) Around age 8, boys start to add more fat than girls on their arms, legs, and trunk.
   Answer: A
   Page Ref: 533
   Skill: Conceptual
   Objective: 14.2

32) Twins, Jake and Molly, age 15, are both athletic. Which of the following is probably true?
   A) Jake's gains in gross-motor performance are slow and gradual.
   B) Molly is experiencing a dramatic spurt in strength, speed, and endurance.
   C) By mid-adolescence, Jake will run faster and throw farther than Molly.
   D) By late-adolescence, Molly will jump farther than Jake.
   Answer: C
   Page Ref: 534
   Skill: Applied
   Objective: 14.2

33) Gregor, a high-school senior, has begun taking creatine to enhance his performance on the basketball court. Which of the following side effects are possible?
   A) diabetes
   B) brain seizures
   C) damage to the reproductive organs
   D) a loss in muscle power
   Answer: B
   Page Ref: 534
   Skill: Applied
   Objective: 14.2

34) Which of the following did researchers find about rates of physical activity from ages 9 to 15?
   A) Fewer than one-third of sampled youths met the U.S. government recommendation of at least 60 minutes of moderate to strenuous physical activity per day.
   B) From ages 9 to 15, physical activity increased by about 40 minutes per day for sampled youths.
   C) In U.S. high schools, about 75 percent of girls and 80 percent of boys are enrolled in physical education courses.
   D) Only one-half of all U.S. high school students participate in a daily physical education class.
   Answer: A
   Page Ref: 534
   Skill: Conceptual
   Objective: 14.2

35) Which of the following athletes is especially likely to continue her activity into adulthood?
    A) Ellen, a softball player
    B) Gerda, a volleyball player
    C) Justine, a basketball player
    D) Alena, a cross-country runner
Answer: D
Page Ref: 535
Skill: Applied
Objective: 14.2

36) Which of the following is an example of a secondary sexual characteristic?
    A) changes in the uterus
    B) changes in the scrotum
    C) breast development
    D) changes in the testes
Answer: C
Page Ref: 535
Skill: Conceptual
Objective: 14.2

37) Primary sexual characteristics
    A) are visible on the outside of the body.
    B) involve the reproductive organs directly.
    C) are unrelated to sexual functioning.
    D) do not develop in a standard sequence.
Answer: B
Page Ref: 535
Skill: Factual
Objective: 14.2

38) Female puberty usually begins with
    A) menarche.
    B) the budding of the breasts.
    C) significant weight gain.
    D) the appearance of pubic hair.
Answer: B
Page Ref: 536
Skill: Factual
Objective: 14.2

39) The average age of menarche in North America is
    A) 11.
    B) 12½.
    C) 13.
    D) 14.
Answer: B
Page Ref: 536
Skill: Factual
Objective: 14.2

40) Menarche takes place
    A) after the peak of the height spurt.
    B) approximately one year before the height spurt.
    C) before pubic hair appears.
    D) after breast growth is completed.
Answer: A
Page Ref: 536
Skill: Factual
Objective: 14.2

41) The first sign of puberty in boys is
    A) the appearance of pubic hair.
    B) the height spurt.
    C) the enlargement of the testes.
    D) deepening of the voice.
Answer: C
Page Ref: 536
Skill: Factual
Objective: 14.2

42) Spermarche occurs
    A) before the height spurt begins.
    B) after the peak strength spurt.
    C) between ages 10 and 11.
    D) before facial hair begins to grow.
Answer: D
Page Ref: 536
Skill: Factual
Objective: 14.2

43) In boys, the voice change
    A) begins after facial and body hair emerge.
    B) occurs before enlargement of the penis and testes.
    C) takes place at the beginning of the growth spurt.
    D) often is not complete until puberty is over.
Answer: D
Page Ref: 536
Skill: Factual
Objective: 14.2

44) The first ejaculation occurs around age
    A) 12.
    B) 13½.
    C) 14.
    D) 15½.
Answer: B
Page Ref: 536
Skill: Factual
Objective: 14.2

45) Julianna is obese. She is likely to experience puberty
    A) earlier than other girls.
    B) at the same time as other girls.
    C) slightly later than other girls.
    D) much later than other girls.
    Answer: A
    Page Ref: 536
    Skill: Applied
    Objective: 14.3

46) Gemma eats very little. She is likely to experience puberty
    A) much earlier than other girls.
    B) slightly earlier than other girls.
    C) around the same time as the average girl.
    D) later than other girls.
    Answer: D
    Page Ref: 536
    Skill: Applied
    Objective: 14.3

47) Which of the following is true about body fat and puberty?
    A) Breast and pubic hair growth occur later for heavier girls.
    B) Few studies report a link between body fat and puberty in boys.
    C) Few studies report a link between body fat and puberty in girls.
    D) Obese girls tend to experience later puberty.
    Answer: B
    Page Ref: 536
    Skill: Applied
    Objective: 14.3

48) Which girl is likely to reach menarche first?
    A) A'akia, who lives in a poverty-stricken village in Ethiopia
    B) Anya, who comes from a low-income family in Sweden
    C) Alexis, who is a middle-income Caucasian American
    D) Angelique, who is a middle-income African American
    Answer: D
    Page Ref: 536–537
    Skill: Applied
    Objective: 14.3

49) Tamineh has a history of family conflict and has experienced harsh parenting. Tamineh will probably reach puberty
    A) earlier than other girls.
    B) at the same time as the average girl.
    C) slightly later than other girls.
    D) much later than other girls.
    Answer: A
    Page Ref: 537
    Skill: Applied
    Objective: 14.3

50) When children's safety and security are at risk, it is adaptive for them to
    A) reproduce early.
    B) reproduce later.
    C) fail to reproduce.
    D) fail to reach menarche or spermarche.
Answer: A
Page Ref: 537
Skill: Conceptual
Objective: 14.3

51) _____ increase(s) during middle childhood and adolescence.
    A) Gray matter
    B) Sleep time
    C) White matter
    D) Neurons in the prefrontal cortex
Answer: C
Page Ref: 537
Skill: Factual
Objective: 14.4

52) Which of the following is true about brain development in adolescence?
    A) Adolescents tend to recruit the prefrontal cortex's network of connections with other brain areas more effectively than adults do.
    B) Adolescents tend to perform better than adults on tasks requiring inhibition and future orientation.
    C) In humans and other mammals, neurons become less responsive to excitatory neurotransmitters during puberty.
    D) Adolescents react more strongly to stressful events than adults do and experience pleasurable stimuli more intensely.
Answer: D
Page Ref: 538
Skill: Conceptual
Objective: 14.4

53) Enhanced _____ sensitivity helps explain why young adolescents are so self-conscious and sensitive to others' opinions.
    A) gray matter
    B) oxytocin
    C) insulin
    D) estrogen
Answer: B
Page Ref: 538
Skill: Factual
Objective: 14.4

54) The combination of a sleep "phase delay" and evening activities, phones, and computers has resulted in
    A) today's teenagers getting much less sleep than those of previous generations.
    B) teenagers who are better able to cope with sleep loss than previous generations.
    C) teenagers who are less likely to rely on sleep rebound on weekends.
    D) teenagers who get a better night's rest than those in previous generations.
Answer: A
Page Ref: 539
Skill: Conceptual
Objective: 14.4

55) Sleep rebound on weekends
    A) helps teenagers perform better in school during the weekdays.
    B) is vitally important to teenage sleep patterns.
    C) can lead to difficulty falling asleep on subsequent evenings.
    D) decreases the sleep phase delay.
    Answer: C
    Page Ref: 539
    Skill: Conceptual
    Objective: 14.4

56) Girls typically react to menarche with
    A) surprise.
    B) joy.
    C) fear.
    D) depression.
    Answer: A
    Page Ref: 539
    Skill: Factual
    Objective: 14.5

57) Grace's grandma recalls menarche as a traumatic experience. She would like things to be different for Grace. What advice can you give her?
    A) She should let Grace be surprised by menarche and then answer any questions she has about puberty.
    B) She should explain to Grace that menarche is an unpleasant but necessary experience.
    C) She should prepare Grace in advance and treat it as an important milestone.
    D) She should provide Grace with biological information but deliver the information as clinically as possible.
    Answer: C
    Page Ref: 540
    Skill: Applied
    Objective: 14.5

58) Boys typically respond to spermarche with
    A) fear.
    B) mixed feelings.
    C) depression.
    D) joy.
    Answer: B
    Page Ref: 540
    Skill: Factual
    Objective: 14.5

59) Boys _____ about ejaculation before spermarche.
    A) usually know
    B) usually talk with their peers
    C) usually find out from their fathers
    D) rarely know
    Answer: A
    Page Ref: 540
    Skill: Factual
    Objective: 14.5

60) Trevor just experienced spermarche. Which of the following is likely to be true?
    A) Trevor did not know about ejaculation ahead of time.
    B) Trevor obtained information about ejaculation from reading material or websites.
    C) Trevor's first ejaculation was later than he expected.
    D) Trevor will eventually tell a friend that he experienced spermarche.
    Answer: B
    Page Ref: 540
    Skill: Applied
    Objective: 14.5

61) Haeata lives in a tribal society and just experienced menarche. Which of the following is probably true?
    A) Haeata will feel ashamed and will not tell anyone about the onset of puberty.
    B) Haeata will still be regarded as a child by her parents and family.
    C) The tribe will celebrate the onset of puberty with an initiation ceremony.
    D) The tribe will acknowledge the onset of puberty, but it will not mark a change in Haeata's social status.
    Answer: C
    Page Ref: 540
    Skill: Applied
    Objective: 14.5

62) Western adolescents
    A) celebrate the onset of puberty with a ritualized announcement.
    B) are granted partial adult status at many different ages.
    C) are formally initiated into adulthood through ceremonies like the quinceanera.
    D) usually have an earlier transition to adulthood than those in tribal or village societies.
    Answer: B
    Page Ref: 540
    Skill: Factual
    Objective: 14.5

63) Higher pubertal hormone levels are _____ moodiness.
    A) strongly linked to greater
    B) strongly linked to lesser
    C) modestly linked to greater
    D) the primary cause of
    Answer: C
    Page Ref: 540
    Skill: Factual
    Objective: 14.5

64) Which of the following statements is true about adolescent mood variation?
    A) High points tend to occur around noon each day.
    B) Low points tend to occur during times spent with friends.
    C) High points tend to occur during self-chosen leisure activities.
    D) Low points tend to occur on Friday nights.
    Answer: C
    Page Ref: 541
    Skill: Conceptual
    Objective: 14.5

65) In a study comparing mood swings, those between the ages of _____ most often shifted from cheerful to sad and back again.
    A) 9 and 11
    B) 12 and 16
    C) 17 and 19
    D) 20 and 25
Answer: B
Page Ref: 541
Skill: Factual
Objective: 14.5

66) Which of the following is true about the parent–child relationship in adolescence?
    A) Contrary to popular media portrayals, there is a decline in the intensity of parent–child conflict.
    B) Psychological distancing, common in village and tribal societies, is less common in Western cultures.
    C) The larger the gap between parents' and adolescents' views of teenagers' readiness for new responsibilities, the more they quarrel.
    D) Parent–son conflict tends to be more intense than conflict with daughters.
Answer: C
Page Ref: 541
Skill: Conceptual
Objective: 14.5

67) The majority of parent–adolescent disagreements focus on
    A) everyday matters such as driving and curfews.
    B) the adolescent's future plans.
    C) philosophical and religious issues.
    D) school achievement.
Answer: A
Page Ref: 541
Skill: Factual
Objective: 14.5

68) _____ is a modern substitute for the physical departure of the adolescent from the home.
    A) An initiation ceremony
    B) A rite of passage
    C) Psychological distancing
    D) A cultural script
Answer: C
Page Ref: 541
Skill: Factual
Objective: 14.5

69) Ethan is an early-maturing boy. He is probably perceived by both adults and peers as
    A) unpopular.
    B) self-confident.
    C) withdrawn.
    D) prone to depression.
Answer: B
Page Ref: 542
Skill: Applied
Objective: 14.6

70) Carter is a late-maturing adolescent boy. He is likely to report more _____ than his on-time counterparts.
    A) psychological stress
    B) sexual activity
    C) aggression
    D) anxiety
Answer: D
Page Ref: 542
Skill: Applied
Objective: 14.6

71) Chinara is an early-maturing girl. She is most likely to be perceived as _____ by her peers.
    A) popular
    B) withdrawn
    C) independent
    D) relaxed
Answer: B
Page Ref: 542
Skill: Applied
Objective: 14.6

72) Maggi is a later-maturing girl. She is most likely to be regarded as
    A) a leader at school.
    B) unpopular.
    C) lacking in self-confidence.
    D) withdrawn.
Answer: A
Page Ref: 542
Skill: Applied
Objective: 14.6

73) _____ -maturing Caucasian girls tend to report a _____ positive body image than other girls.
    A) Early; more
    B) Late; less
    C) Early; less
    D) On-time; less
Answer: C
Page Ref: 542
Skill: Factual
Objective: 14.6

74) Adolescents feel _____ comfortable with peers who _____.
    A) more; mature sooner than they do
    B) most; match their own level of biological maturity
    C) more; mature later than they do
    D) least; match their own level of biological maturity
Answer: B
Page Ref: 543
Skill: Factual
Objective: 14.6

75) _____ maturers in _____-income neighborhoods are especially vulnerable to establishing ties with deviant peers.
   A) Late; high
   B) Late; low
   C) Early; middle
   D) Early; low
Answer: D
Page Ref: 543
Skill: Factual
Objective: 14.6

76) Research shows that _____ tend to have lasting adjustment problems in later life.
   A) early-maturing boys
   B) late-maturing boys
   C) late-maturing girls
   D) early-maturing girls
Answer: D
Page Ref: 543
Skill: Factual
Objective: 14.7

77) Of all age groups, adolescents are most likely to
   A) be obese.
   B) skip breakfast.
   C) make healthy food choices.
   D) need less protein.
Answer: B
Page Ref: 544
Skill: Factual
Objective: 14.7

78) The most common nutritional problem of adolescence is _____ deficiency.
   A) riboflavin
   B) magnesium
   C) iron
   D) calcium
Answer: C
Page Ref: 544
Skill: Factual
Objective: 14.7

79) Janelle, a teenager, is chronically tired, but she appears to be growing normally. She should have a medical checkup because she might be suffering from
   A) anemia.
   B) obesity.
   C) diabetes.
   D) anorexia nervosa.
Answer: A
Page Ref: 544
Skill: Applied
Objective: 14.7

80) Mr. and Mrs. Falk want to improve their teenagers' diets. One simple and proven way they can do this is to
    A) forbid them from eating fast foods.
    B) give them limited spending money.
    C) find a way to eat together as a family most nights of the week.
    D) remove all sweets from the home.
Answer: C
Page Ref: 545
Skill: Applied
Objective: 14.7

81) Vegetarian adolescents
    A) are far less likely than their nonvegetarian counterparts to have healthy eating habits.
    B) may have diets that are deficient in certain nutrients.
    C) are prone to fad dieting, which can lead to later weight gain.
    D) usually consume too few calories and nutrients.
Answer: B
Page Ref: 545
Skill: Conceptual
Objective: 14.7

82) Which girl is the most at risk for an eating problem?
    A) Angela, who reached puberty late
    B) Bea, who grew up in a home with no weight concerns
    C) Caity, who reached puberty early
    D) Desiree, whose friends are overweight
Answer: C
Page Ref: 545
Skill: Applied
Objective: 14.8

83) _____ is the strongest predictor of the onset of an eating disorder in adolescence.
    A) Severe dieting
    B) Obsessive behavior
    C) Erratic behavior
    D) Parental discord
Answer: A
Page Ref: 545
Skill: Factual
Objective: 14.8

84) Renae has a compulsive fear of getting fat. As a result, she is starving herself. Renae has
    A) bulimia nervosa.
    B) typical adolescent insecurities.
    C) a 10 percent chance of a full recovery.
    D) anorexia nervosa.
Answer: D
Page Ref: 545
Skill: Applied
Objective: 14.8

85) Boys account for _____ percent of anorexia cases.
   A) 5 to 10
   B) 10 to 15
   C) 15 to 20
   D) 20 to 25
   Answer: B
   Page Ref: 545
   Skill: Factual
   Objective: 14.8

86) Which of the following girls is the least likely to develop anorexia nervosa?
   A) Aaliyah, a Caucasian American
   B) Brenda, an Asian American
   C) Cheyanne, an African American
   D) Deliah, a Hispanic American
   Answer: C
   Page Ref: 545
   Skill: Applied
   Objective: 14.8

87) Girls who develop anorexia nervosa typically have
   A) at least one overweight parent.
   B) a long history of yo-yo dieting.
   C) poor academic performance at school.
   D) unrealistically high standards for their own performance.
   Answer: D
   Page Ref: 546
   Skill: Conceptual
   Objective: 14.8

88) Fathers of daughters with anorexia nervosa tend to be
   A) overprotective and controlling.
   B) sensitive to adolescent autonomy.
   C) punitive or indulgent.
   D) emotionally distant.
   Answer: D
   Page Ref: 546
   Skill: Conceptual
   Objective: 14.8

89) The most successful treatment for anorexia nervosa is
   A) family therapy and medication.
   B) behavior modification.
   C) in-patient hospitalization.
   D) outpatient education.
   Answer: A
   Page Ref: 546
   Skill: Factual
   Objective: 14.8

90) Connie's teenage daughter follows a strict diet during the day, exercises strenuously, binge eats in the evening, and often takes laxatives. Connie should be concerned that her daughter has
   A) anorexia nervosa.
   B) obsessive compulsive disorder.
   C) bulimia nervosa.
   D) a severe hormone imbalance.
   Answer: C
   Page Ref: 546
   Skill: Applied
   Objective: 14.8

91) Compared to anorexics, adolescents with bulimia nervosa
   A) do not have a pathological fear of getting fat.
   B) feel guilty or depressed about their eating habits.
   C) experience their parents as emotionally available and involved.
   D) do not want help for their problem.
   Answer: B
   Page Ref: 546
   Skill: Conceptual
   Objective: 14.8

92) Most girls with bulimia nervosa
   A) are underweight.
   B) were later maturers.
   C) are impulsive.
   D) are perfectionists.
   Answer: C
   Page Ref: 546
   Skill: Conceptual
   Objective: 14.8

93) _____ is/are the leading killer of U.S. teenagers.
   A) Firearms
   B) Automobile accidents
   C) Suicide
   D) Sports-related injuries
   Answer: B
   Page Ref: 547
   Skill: Factual
   Objective: 14.9

94) Which of the following is true about automobile accidents and adolescent drivers?
   A) Graduated licensing laws reduce adolescent traffic fatalities by 6 to 11 percent.
   B) Parent–child communication has no preventive effect on automobile accidents.
   C) Contrary to media portrayals, alcohol use is not a leading cause of teen auto accidents.
   D) Automobile accident account for about 25 percent of teen deaths in the United States.
   Answer: A
   Page Ref: 547
   Skill: Conceptual
   Objective: 14.9

95) Which of the following is true about firearms and adolescent injury?
   A) Firearms are the leading cause of adolescent fatalities in the United States.
   B) Violence-related behaviors among high school students have increased in the past decade.
   C) Rates of gun violence are highest in poverty-stricken inner-city neighborhoods.
   D) Metal detectors in schools have had little impact on preventing youth violence.
Answer: C
Page Ref: 547
Skill: Factual
Objective: 14.9

96) Which of the following is true about sports-related injuries in adolescence?
   A) More than one-half of high school students are involved in sports injuries that require medical attention.
   B) Coaches sometimes make unreasonable demands of players that can lead to injury.
   C) Many coaches match competitors on the basis of pubertal maturity rather than age and weight.
   D) The safest athletic activities during the pubertal growth period are team sports.
Answer: B
Page Ref: 547
Skill: Conceptual
Objective: 14.9

97) The production of _____ in young people of both sexes leads to an increase in sex drive.
   A) estrogens
   B) adrenaline
   C) androgens
   D) oxytocin
Answer: C
Page Ref: 548
Skill: Factual
Objective: 14.10

98) Which of the following adolescents is the most likely to have parents with a permissive attitude about sex?
   A) Iryana, an Iranian
   B) Kirsten, a Canadian
   C) Madison, an American
   D) Fau, a Papua New Guinean
Answer: D
Page Ref: 548
Skill: Applied
Objective: 14.10

99) Sexual attitudes in the U.S. are
   A) extremely liberal.
   B) fairly open.
   C) relatively restricted.
   D) highly restricted.
Answer: C
Page Ref: 548
Skill: Factual
Objective: 14.10

100) The majority of U.S. teens learn about sex from their
   A) friends or the media.
   B) mothers.
   C) fathers.
   D) teachers.
   Answer: A
   Page Ref: 548
   Skill: Factual
   Objective: 14.10

101) Which of the following is true about sex education and the media?
   A) Most prime-time TV shows today depict sexual partners who act responsibly.
   B) In several studies, teenagers' media exposure to sexual content positively predicted current sexual activity.
   C) The Internet offers young people a safe, anonymous place to learn about sex.
   D) Youths who feel depressed, are bullied by peers, or are involved in delinquent activities have fewer encounters with Internet pornography.
   Answer: B
   Page Ref: 548
   Skill: Conceptual
   Objective: 14.10

102) Which of the following is true about adolescent sexual attitudes and behavior?
   A) Rates of extramarital sex among U.S. young people are on the rise.
   B) Overall, teenage sexual activity rates are lower in the United States than in other Western countries.
   C) U.S. youths become sexually active later than their Canadian and European counterparts.
   D) Most teenagers have had only one or two sexual partners by the end of high school.
   Answer: D
   Page Ref: 549
   Skill: Conceptual
   Objective: 14.10

103) Which of the following teens is more likely to have early sex or frequent teenage sexual activity?
   A) Uli, who feels a strong sense of personal control over life events
   B) Howie, whose family is actively involved in their church
   C) Darwin, who was a late maturer
   D) Ryan, whose parents do not monitor his activities
   Answer: D
   Page Ref: 549
   Skill: Applied
   Objective: 14.10

104) Early sexual activity is more common among young people from _____ homes.
   A) high-income
   B) economically disadvantaged
   C) middle-income
   D) two-parent
   Answer: B
   Page Ref: 549
   Skill: Factual
   Objective: 14.10

105) Brad's parents provide him with information on sex and contraception, and convey their values. As a result, Brad is likely to
   A) take sexual risks.
   B) engage in sex at a young age.
   C) adopt his parents' sexual values.
   D) fail to take his parents seriously.
   Answer: C
   Page Ref: 550 Box: SI: Education: Parents and Teenagers (Don't) Talk About Sex
   Skill: Applied
   Objective: 14.10

106) When Monica's parents sit down to talk with her about sex, she laughs and tells them that they are too late. She assures them that she already knows everything she needs to know. Chances are high that
   A) Monica is right, and they do not need to have "the talk."
   B) Monica will abstain from sex until she reaches adulthood.
   C) Monica will adopt her parents' sexual values.
   D) Monica's actual knowledge is far less than her perceived knowledge.
   Answer: D
   Page Ref: 550 Box: SI: Education: Parents and Teenagers (Don't) Talk About Sex
   Skill: Applied
   Objective: 14.10

107) Mr. Linden wants to discuss sex with his teenage daughter. Which of the following would you recommend to him?
   A) a parent-dominated explanation about the facts of life
   B) a give-and-take conversation between parent and child
   C) a child-led question/answer session
   D) a conversation in which the parent provides judgmental comments about the child's questions
   Answer: B
   Page Ref: 551 Box: SI: Education: Parents and Teenagers (Don't) Talk About Sex
   Skill: Applied
   Objective: 14.10

108) Teenagers who talk openly with their parents about sex and contraception
   A) are just as likely as other teens to fail to use contraception.
   B) report having more unprotected sex than teens who do not discuss sex.
   C) have higher pregnancy rates than other teens.
   D) are more likely than other teens to use birth control if they have intercourse.
   Answer: D
   Page Ref: 552
   Skill: Factual
   Objective: 14.10

109) Approximately ____ percent of 15- to 44-year-olds identify as lesbian, gay, or bisexual.
   A) 2
   B) 4
   C) 6
   D) 10
   Answer: B
   Page Ref: 552
   Skill: Factual
   Objective: 14.11

110) Studies involving genetic influences in homosexuality indicate that
    A) homosexuality is more common on the paternal side of families.
    B) fraternal twins are more likely to share a homosexual orientation than identical twins.
    C) adoptive relatives are as likely to share a homosexual orientation as biological relatives.
    D) homosexual brothers often have an identical segment of DNA on the X chromosome.
Answer: D
Page Ref: 552
Skill: Factual
Objective: 14.11

111) Jose is a homosexual man. Which of the following is most likely to be true?
    A) He has a higher-than-average number of older brothers.
    B) He has a higher-than-average number of younger sisters.
    C) He is an only child.
    D) He is a first-born child.
Answer: A
Page Ref: 552
Skill: Applied
Objective: 14.11

112) Which of the following accurately characterizes the three-phase sequence that many gay and lesbian adolescents and adults move through in coming out to themselves and others?
    A) feeling different, confusion, self-acceptance
    B) confusion, feeling accepted, announcement
    C) feeling different, self-acceptance, integration
    D) feeling rejected, confusion, self-acceptance
Answer: A
Page Ref: 553 Box: B&E: Gay, Lesbian, and Bisexual Youths: Coming Out to Oneself and Others
Skill: Conceptual
Objective: 14.11

113) Ned is a gay man. He recalls feeling different from other children when he was young. If Ned is typical, when did this first sense of his biologically determined sexual orientation appear?
    A) between ages 2 and 4
    B) between ages 6 and 12
    C) between ages 10 and 13
    D) after age 14
Answer: B
Page Ref: 553 Box: B&E: Gay, Lesbian, and Bisexual Youths: Coming Out to Oneself and Others
Skill: Applied
Objective: 14.11

114) Suzanne responded to her daughter's coming out positively. She is understanding and accepting of the teenager's same-sex romantic relationship. However, Suzanne is concerned about her daughter's self-acceptance. Suzanne should know that
    A) coming out to family impedes a young person's view of homosexuality as a valid and fulfilling identity.
    B) contact with other gays and lesbians can interfere with a young person's self-acceptance.
    C) coming out to friends often brings a backlash that impedes many aspects of adolescent development.
    D) the strongest predictor of favorable adjustment for gay and lesbian youths is parental understanding.
Answer: D
Page Ref: 553 Box: B&E: Gay, Lesbian, and Bisexual Youths: Coming Out to Oneself and Others
Skill: Applied
Objective: 14.11

115) Fifteen-year-old Anna is attracted to her best friend, Eva, and her boyfriend, Emory. Which of the following is the most likely to be true?
    A) Anna is gender-deviant in dress.
    B) Eva and Emory are gender-deviant in behavior.
    C) Anna identifies as heterosexual.
    D) Anna's bisexuality is a transient state: she will eventually identify as either straight or lesbian.
Answer: C
Page Ref: 553
Skill: Applied
Objective: 14.11

116) Out of all age groups, adolescents have the highest rate of
    A) criminal behavior.
    B) sexually transmitted diseases.
    C) asthma and severe seasonal allergies.
    D) sexual experimentation.
Answer: B
Page Ref: 554
Skill: Factual
Objective: 14.12

117) Which of the following STDs usually disappears on its own?
    A) chlamydia
    B) gonorrhea
    C) cytomegalovirus
    D) syphilis
Answer: C
Page Ref: 554
Skill: Factual
Objective: 14.12

118) Teenagers at the greatest risk for STDs are
    A) poverty-stricken teenagers who feel a sense of hopelessness.
    B) high-income teenagers whose parents are permissive.
    C) middle-income teenagers whose parents have high expectations.
    D) impossible to identify; all teenagers are equally at risk for STDs.
Answer: A
Page Ref: 555
Skill: Factual
Objective: 14.12

119) Which of the following is true about HIV and AIDS?
    A) In the United States, less than 5 percent of those infected with HIV are teens.
    B) It is twice as easy for a female to infect a male with HIV, as for a male to infect a female.
    C) The risk for heterosexual spread of AIDS is higher for those teens with more than one partner in the previous 18 months.
    D) In the United States, females account for about 15 percent of new cases of HIV among adolescents and young adults.
Answer: C
Page Ref: 555
Skill: Conceptual
Objective: 14.12

120) As a result of school courses and media campaigns,
    A) about 90 percent of high school students are aware of basic facts about AIDS, but are poorly informed about other STDs.
    B) about 90 percent of middle and high school students are aware of basic facts about most STDs.
    C) most sexually active high school students report using STD protection during oral sex.
    D) few high school students report engaging in oral sex with multiple partners, and most who do are well-informed about STDs.
Answer: A
Page Ref: 555
Skill: Conceptual
Objective: 14.12

121) Among U.S. teenage girls, an estimated _____ percent of those who had sexual intercourse became pregnant in the most recently reported year.
    A) 10
    B) 20
    C) 30
    D) 40
Answer: B
Page Ref: 556
Skill: Factual
Objective: 14.13

122) The U.S. adolescent pregnancy rate is _____ than that of other industrialized nations.
    A) much lower
    B) slightly lower
    C) slightly higher
    D) much higher
Answer: D
Page Ref: 556
Skill: Factual
Objective: 14.13

123) One factor that heightens the incidence of adolescent pregnancy is
    A) exposure to sex education in middle and high school.
    B) easy availability of low-cost contraceptive services.
    C) a history of family poverty, which encourages risk-taking behavior.
    D) early puberty for boys and late puberty for girls.
Answer: C
Page Ref: 556
Skill: Factual
Objective: 14.13

124) The number of American teenage births is lower than it was 50 years ago because
    A) one-third of adolescent pregnancies end in abortion.
    B) of more effective sex education programs in public schools.
    C) convenient contraceptive services are more readily available.
    D) more girls give up their infants for adoption.
Answer: A
Page Ref: 556
Skill: Factual
Objective: 14.13

125) Today, the majority of pregnant adolescents
    A) marry and keep their babies.
    B) abort their pregnancies.
    C) put their babies up for adoption.
    D) stay unmarried and keep their babies.
Answer: D
Page Ref: 556
Skill: Factual
Objective: 14.13

126) Which of the following teens is most likely to have an adolescent pregnancy?
    A) Wynn, a middle-income African American
    B) Kim, a high-income Asian American
    C) Selena, a low-income Hispanic American
    D) Bella, a middle-income Caucasian American
Answer: C
Page Ref: 556
Skill: Applied
Objective: 14.13

127) Teenage motherhood _____ the likelihood of _____.
    A) reduces; marriage
    B) increases; earning a high school diploma
    C) reduces; divorce
    D) increases; future contraceptive use
Answer: A
Page Ref: 556
Skill: Factual
Objective: 14.13

128) Compared with adult mothers, adolescent mothers
    A) deliver healthier babies.
    B) know less about child development.
    C) have low expectations for their infants.
    D) less often engage in child abuse.
Answer: B
Page Ref: 557
Skill: Conceptual
Objective: 14.13

129) In the United States, the most controversial aspect of adolescent pregnancy prevention efforts is
    A) the promotion of abstinence.
    B) requiring sex education courses in school.
    C) teaching social skills for handling sexual situations.
    D) increasing the availability of contraceptives.
Answer: D
Page Ref: 557
Skill: Conceptual
Objective: 14.13

130) Which of the following statements regarding the intergenerational continuity of adolescent pregnancy and parenthood is true?
    A) Becoming a second-generation teenage parent is inevitable for individuals born to an adolescent mother.
    B) Intergenerational continuity in adolescent daughters is far greater when teenage mothers marry.
    C) Marriage may limit the negative impact of teenage childbearing on development by reducing family stress.
    D) Adolescent parenthood does not increase the chances of teenage childbearing the next generation.
Answer: C
Page Ref: 558: Box: SI: Health: Like Parent, Like Child: Intergenerational Continuity in Adolescent Parenthood
Skill: Conceptual
Objective: 14.13

131) Which of the following adolescent mothers in the most likely to break the intergenerational cycle of adolescent parenthood?
    A) Prudence, who marries her daughter's father
    B) Heidi, who obtains a low HOME score
    C) Natalia, who does not earn her high school diploma
    D) Emma, who moves to low-income housing and remains unmarried
Answer: A
Page Ref: 558 Box: SI: Health: Like Parent, Like Child: Intergenerational Continuity in Adolescent Parenthood
Skill: Conceptual
Objective: 14.13

132) Radio and TV campaigns promoting contraceptive use—used widely in Africa, Europe, India, and South America—are associated with a(n)
    A) reduction in early sexual activity.
    B) increase in teenage sexual activity.
    C) decrease in teenagers' use of birth control.
    D) increase in teenage abortion rates.
Answer: A
Page Ref: 558–559
Skill: Factual
Objective: 14.13

133) _____ is linked to delayed initiation of sexual activity and to reduced teenage pregnancy.
    A) Abstinence-based sex education
    B) Even limited sex education
    C) Early pubertal development
    D) School involvement
Answer: D
Page Ref: 559
Skill: Factual
Objective: 14.13

134) Older adolescent mothers display more effective parenting when they
    A) live with one or both of their own parents until the child is school-age.
    B) avoid child-care assistance from the baby's father in order to establish their independence.
    C) cut off ties with their friends and relatives during the early childhood years.
    D) establish their own residence with the help of relatives.
Answer: D
Page Ref: 559
Skill: Conceptual
Objective: 14.13

135) By the time a child of adolescent parents start school,
    A) fewer than one-fourth have regular contact with their fathers.
    B) nearly half visit with their fathers regularly.
    C) less than two-thirds receive financial assistance from their fathers.
    D) most have established lasting ties to their fathers.
Answer: A
Page Ref: 559
Skill: Factual
Objective: 14.13

136) Teenage alcohol and drug use rates in the United States have _____ since the mid-1990s.
    A) risen sharply
    B) slowly increased
    C) slowly decreased
    D) substantially declined
Answer: D
Page Ref: 560
Skill: Factual
Objective: 14.14

137) By tenth grade, 38 percent of teenagers in the United States have experimented with at least one illegal drug, usually
    A) painkillers.
    B) cocaine.
    C) marijuana.
    D) alcohol.
Answer: C
Page Ref: 560
Skill: Factual
Objective: 14.14

138) The majority of teenagers who dabble in alcohol, tobacco, and marijuana
    A) will become addicted to at least one substance.
    B) are not headed for a life of decadence and addiction.
    C) are either psychologically unhealthy or socially awkward.
    D) are self-medicating from the stress of high school.
Answer: B
Page Ref: 560
Skill: Factual
Objective: 14.14

139) Brad is a teen who has experimented minimally with alcohol. Brad is likely to
    A) be a healthy, curious young person.
    B) become an addict in adulthood.
    C) be less sociable than his peers who do not experiment.
    D) choose not to drink alcohol in college.
Answer: A
Page Ref: 560
Skill: Applied
Objective: 14.14

140) _____ is one of the deadliest substance abuse issues.
   A) Alcohol use
   B) Marijuana smoking
   C) Caffeine use
   D) Cigarette smoking
Answer: D
Page Ref: 561
Skill: Factual
Objective: 14.14

141) Which of the following teens with family difficulties has an especially high risk of substance abuse?
   A) Jake, whose mother is unemployed
   B) Ken, whose peers use and provide drugs
   C) Walt, whose sister used drugs but is now in recovery
   D) Paul, who has a below-average school performance
Answer: B
Page Ref: 561
Skill: Applied
Objective: 14.14

142) Mr. Wellington wants to reduce drug experimentation among the teens in his community program. He should
   A) teach parents that teens need freedom from activity monitoring.
   B) teach students skills for resisting peer pressure.
   C) deemphasize parent education.
   D) acknowledge the social acceptability of drug use.
Answer: B
Page Ref: 561
Skill: Applied
Objective: 14.14

143) Which of the following is true about adolescent drug abuse treatment?
   A) Individual, rather than family, therapy is the best treatment.
   B) Even comprehensive programs have alarmingly high relapse rates.
   C) Support-group session interventions often increase drug taking in the short term.
   D) Comprehensive programs that focus on individual and family therapy have modest to low relapse rates.
Answer: B
Page Ref: 561
Skill: Conceptual
Objective: 14.14

ESSAY

144) Explain why adolescence is extended in industrialized nations, including the three phases of adolescence.
   Answer: In industrialized nations, successful participation in economic life requires many years of education. Most tribal and village societies have only a brief intervening phase between childhood and full assumption of adult roles. In industrialized nations, young people face extra years of dependence on parents and postponement of sexual gratification while they prepare for a productive work life. As a result, adolescence is greatly extended, and researchers commonly divide it into three phases:
   1. Early adolescence, from 11 or 12 to 14 years of age, a period of rapid pubertal change
   2. Middle adolescence, from 14 to 16 years, when pubertal changes are nearly complete
   3. Late adolescence, from 16 to 18 years, when the young person achieves his or her full adult appearance and faces a more complete assumption of adult roles

Page Ref: 531

145) Describe the secular trend in pubertal timing in industrialized nations.

Answer: Children in industrialized nations grow faster and larger than in past generations. Similarly, age of menarche declined steadily—by about 3 to 4 months per decade—from 1900 to 1970, a period in which nutrition, health care, sanitation, and control of infectious disease improved greatly. Boys, too, have reached puberty earlier in recent decades. This secular trend in pubertal timing lends added support to the role of physical well-being in adolescent growth.

While the secular gain in height has slowed and the trend toward earlier menarche has stopped or undergone a slight reversal in most industrialized nations, in the United States and a few European countries, soaring rates of overweight and obesity are responsible for a modest, continuing trend toward earlier menarche. A worrisome consequence is that girls who reach sexual maturity at age 10 or 11 will feel pressure to act much older than they are. Early-maturing girls are at risk for unfavorable peer involvements, including sexual activity.

Page Ref: 537

146) Describe the long-term consequences of pubertal timing, especially for early-maturing girls. What are some possible reasons for the difficulties early-maturing girls face?

Answer: Follow-up studies reveal that early-maturing girls, especially, are prone to lasting difficulties. In one study, depression subsided by age 13 in early-maturing boys but tended to persist in early-maturing girls. In another study, which followed young people from ages 14 to 24, early-maturing boys again showed good adjustment. But early-maturing girls reported poorer-quality relationships with family and friends, smaller social networks, and lower life satisfaction into early adulthood than did their on-time counterparts. Similarly, in a Swedish investigation, achievement and substance-use difficulties of early-maturing girls lingered, in the form of greater alcohol abuse and lower educational attainment than their agemates.

Childhood family conflict and harsh parenting are linked to earlier pubertal timing, more so for girls than for boys. Perhaps many early-maturing girls enter adolescence with emotional and social difficulties. As the stresses of puberty interfere with school performance and lead to unfavorable peer pressures, poor adjustment extends and deepens. Clearly, interventions that target at-risk early-maturing adolescents are needed. These include educating parents and teachers and providing adolescents with counseling and social supports so they will be better prepared to handle the emotional and social challenges of this transition.

Page Ref: 542–543

147) What are some characteristics of sexually active adolescents? Which children are more likely than others to engage in early and frequent teenage sexual activity?

Answer: Early and frequent teenage sexual activity is linked to personal, family, peer, and educational characteristics. These include childhood impulsivity, weak sense of personal control over life events, early pubertal timing, parental divorce, single-parent and stepfamily homes, large family size, little or no religious involvement, weak parental monitoring, disrupted parent–child communication, sexually active friends and older siblings, poor school performance, lower educational aspirations, and tendency to engage in norm-violating acts, including alcohol and drug use and delinquency. Because many of these factors are associated with growing up in a low-income family, it is not surprising that early sexual activity is more common among young people from economically disadvantaged homes. Living in a neighborhood high in physical deterioration, crime, and violence also increases the likelihood that teenagers will be sexually active. In such neighborhoods, social ties are weak, adults exert little oversight and control over adolescents' activities, and negative peer influences are widespread. Early and prolonged father absence also predicts higher rates of intercourse and pregnancy among adolescent girls, after many family background and personal characteristics are controlled.

Page Ref: 549–552

148) Discuss the role of heredity and prenatal biological influences in the development of sexual orientation. How might heredity lead to homosexuality?

Answer: Heredity makes an important contribution to sexual orientation. Although definitive conclusions await further research, the evidence to date suggests that genetic and prenatal biological influences are largely responsible for homosexuality. Identical twins of both sexes are much more likely than fraternal twins to share a homosexual orientation; the same is true for biological as opposed to adoptive relatives. Male homosexuality tends to be more common on the maternal than the paternal side of families, suggesting that it might be X-linked. One gene-mapping study found that among 40 pairs of homosexual brothers, 33 (82 percent) had an identical segment of DNA on the X chromosome. One or several genes in that region might predispose males to become homosexual.

According to some researchers, certain genes affect the level or impact of prenatal sex hormones, which modify brain structures in ways that induce homosexual feelings and behavior. Consistent with early, hormonal influences, childhood gender nonconformity—boys' preference for quiet, "feminine" play and girls' preference for active, "masculine" pursuits—is strongly linked to homosexuality.

Girls exposed prenatally to abnormal levels of androgens or estrogens—either because of a genetic defect or drugs given to the mother to prevent miscarriage—are more likely to become homosexual or bisexual. Furthermore, homosexual men tend to have a later birth order and a higher-than-average number of older brothers. One proposal is that mothers with several male children sometimes produce antibodies to androgens, which reduce the prenatal impact of male sex hormones on the brains of later-born boys.

Page Ref: 552–554

149) Describe an effective sex education program. What key elements should be included?

Answer: Sex education must provide factual information, but also help teenagers build a bridge between what they know and what they do. Too often, sex education courses are given late (after sexual activity has begun), last only a few sessions, and are limited to a catalogue of facts about anatomy and reproduction. Sex education that goes beyond this minimum does not encourage early sex, as some opponents claim. It does improve awareness of sexual facts—knowledge that is necessary for responsible behavior. Knowledge, however, is not enough. Effective sex education programs combine several key elements:

- They teach techniques for handling sexual situations—including refusal skills for avoiding risky sexual behaviors and communication skills for improving contraceptive use—through role-playing and other activities in which young people practice those behaviors.
- They deliver clear, accurate messages that are appropriate in view of participating adolescents' culture and sexual experiences.
- They last long enough to have an impact.
- They provide specific information about contraceptives and ready access to them.

Many studies show that sex education that includes these components can delay the initiation of sexual activity, increase contraceptive use, change attitudes (for example, strengthen future orientation), and reduce pregnancy rates.

Page Ref: 557–559

150) Principal Jaster wants to reduce drug experimentation among his high school students. Describe the components of an effective drug prevention program.

Answer: School and community programs that reduce drug experimentation typically combine several features:

- They promote effective parenting, including monitoring of teenagers' activities.
- They teach skills for resisting peer pressure.
- They reduce the social acceptability of drug taking by emphasizing health and safety risks.

But some drug taking seems inevitable, so interventions that prevent teenagers from harming themselves and others when they do experiment are essential. Many communities offer weekend on-call transportation services that any young person can contact for a safe ride home, with no questions asked. Providing appealing substitute activities, such as drug-free dances and sports activities, is also helpful.

Page Ref: 561–562

CHAPTER 15
COGNITIVE DEVELOPMENT IN ADOLESCENCE

MULTIPLE CHOICE

1) Veronique can think abstractly about things she cannot perceive concretely. She is in Piaget's _____ stage.
   A) concrete operational
   B) formal operational
   C) emerging adulthood
   D) hypothetical reasoning
   Answer: B
   Page Ref: 566
   Skill: Applied
   Objective: 15.1

2) A person in Piaget's formal operational stage
   A) can come up with general logical rules through internal reflection.
   B) is able to use inductive reasoning for the first time.
   C) can only "operate on reality."
   D) has just learned that hypotheses must be confirmed by appropriate evidence.
   Answer: A
   Page Ref: 556
   Skill: Conceptual
   Objective: 15.1

3) In biology class, Zia had to determine which of two fertilizers was best for growing African violets. She tested not just for type of fertilizer but also for its concentration and frequency of use. Zia used
   A) hypothetico-deductive reasoning.
   B) propositional thought.
   C) hierarchical classification.
   D) transitive inference.
   Answer: A
   Page Ref: 556
   Skill: Applied
   Objective: 15.1

4) Lourdes is capable of hypothetico-deductive reasoning. When faced with a problem, which of the following will she do first?
   A) Develop a general theory of all possible variables that might affect the outcome.
   B) Deduce specific hypotheses about what might happen in a situation.
   C) Test her hypotheses in an orderly fashion to see which ones work in the real world.
   D) Examine the most obvious predictions about a situation.
   Answer: A
   Page Ref: 556
   Skill: Applied
   Objective: 15.1

5) In trying to solve the pendulum problem, formal operational adolescents usually
   A) fail to notice variables not suggested by the concrete materials of the task.
   B) think of many possible hypotheses.
   C) have difficulty separating out the effects of variables.
   D) are totally stumped; the problem is not solved until adulthood.
   Answer: B
   Page Ref: 566
   Skill: Conceptual
   Objective: 15.1

6) In watching a concrete operational child and a formal operational adolescent solve the pendulum problem, what difference would be evident?
   A) The concrete operational child will be completely unable to solve the problem.
   B) The formal operational adolescent will solve the problem intuitively, without experimentation.
   C) The formal operational adolescent will systematically test alternative hypotheses.
   D) None; both will use similar strategies.
   Answer: C
   Page Ref: 557
   Skill: Conceptual
   Objective: 15.1

7) Marcus is able to evaluate the logic of verbal statements without making reference to real-world circumstances. Marcus is engaging in
   A) hypothetico-deductive reasoning.
   B) propositional thought.
   C) concrete operational thought.
   D) cognitive intuition.
   Answer: B
   Page Ref: 567
   Skill: Applied
   Objective: 15.1

8) Bryan hears the following statement: "Either the train is moving or it is not moving." If Bryan is in the formal operational stage, he will say that
   A) he needs to see the train to determine whether the statement is true or false.
   B) the statement is true.
   C) the statement is false.
   D) the statement is both true and false at the same time.
   Answer: B
   Page Ref: 567
   Skill: Applied
   Objective: 15.1

9) An experimenter hides a poker chip in her hand and asks children to indicate whether the following statement is true, false, or uncertain: "Either the chip in my hand is green or it is not green." A concrete operational child will say the statement is _____. A formal operational adolescent will say the statement is _____.
   A) uncertain; true
   B) true; uncertain
   C) uncertain; false
   D) true; false
   Answer: A
   Page Ref: 567
   Skill: Applied
   Objective: 15.1

10) For adolescents, propositional thought
    A) limits their reasoning to the here and now.
    B) prevents them from solving the red-and-green poker chip problem.
    C) provides them with access to new realms of knowledge, such as higher math.
    D) enables them to get along better with their peers.
Answer: C
Page Ref: 567
Skill: Conceptual
Objective: 15.1

11) Six-year-old children can understand that hypotheses must be confirmed by the appropriate evidence, and they can sort out evidence concerning _____ variable(s).
    A) only one
    B) one or two
    C) three
    D) four or more
Answer: B
Page Ref: 567
Skill: Conceptual
Objective: 15.2

12) The teacher says, "If mice are bigger than cats, and cats are bigger than elephants, then mice are bigger than elephants." This statement is likely to be judged
    A) false by 11-year-old Craig.
    B) false by 13-year-old Michael.
    C) true by 9-year-old Rana.
    D) true by 12-year-old Paige.
Answer: D
Page Ref: 568
Skill: Applied
Objective: 15.2

13) School-age children have difficulty drawing accurate conclusions from propositional statements because they
    A) find it more difficult to inhibit activation of well-learned knowledge.
    B) adhere rigidly to the logical necessity of the statement.
    C) are unable to think logically about any problem.
    D) cannot yet understand the concept of a hypothesis.
Answer: A
Page Ref: 568
Skill: Conceptual
Objective: 15.2

14) The _____ of propositional reasoning can be explained as the understanding that the accuracy of conclusions drawn from premises rests on the rules of logic, not on real-world confirmation.
    A) major premise
    B) logical necessity
    C) secondary premise
    D) metacognitive understanding
Answer: B
Page Ref: 568
Skill: Factual
Objective: 15.2

15) Twelve-year-old Alicia hears the following: "A spoon is something that can be used to stir. Suppose something is not a spoon. Can it be used to stir?" Alicia will
   A) say that she needs to see the object in question.
   B) be able to reason correctly after hearing the statement.
   C) say "no."
   D) say "only if it is a fork."
   Answer: B
   Page Ref: 568
   Skill: Applied
   Objective: 15.2

16) Many college students and adults are not fully formal operational because
   A) they lack extensive experience on the specific tasks that are being assessed.
   B) they are not motivated to solve formal operational tasks.
   C) only the very brightest people become fully formal operational.
   D) they are more interested in socializing than in thinking.
   Answer: A
   Page Ref: 568
   Skill: Conceptual
   Objective: 15.2

17) Taking college courses
   A) has no measurable impact on formal operational reasoning.
   B) leads to improvements in formal operational reasoning on all kinds of tasks.
   C) improves formal operational reasoning on tasks related to course content.
   D) improves propositional thought but not hypothetico-deductive reasoning.
   Answer: C
   Page Ref: 568
   Skill: Conceptual
   Objective: 15.2

18) An English student who excels at analyzing the themes of a play
   A) will also excel at analyzing political events.
   B) can apply her formal operational abilities to mathematics problems.
   C) may not be especially good at formal operational tasks in another subject area.
   D) simultaneously develops formal operations that can be applied to academic tasks, but not real-world problems.
   Answer: C
   Page Ref: 568
   Skill: Applied
   Objective: 15.2

19) One reason that adolescents and adults do not always engage in formal operational thinking is that they
   A) lack educational experiences that foster abstract reasoning.
   B) may be capable of it, but fall back on less demanding intuitive judgments.
   C) lack the motivation for higher-level thinking and problem solving.
   D) prefer to make trial-and-error judgments.
   Answer: B
   Page Ref: 569
   Skill: Factual
   Objective: 15.2

20) Research into the development of formal operational tasks among peasants in tribal and village societies found that
   A) formal operational thought occurs more often in women than men.
   B) they often reason at a much higher level than young people in industrialized nations.
   C) people can be capable of formal operational thought even if they rarely display it in everyday life.
   D) they are incapable of mastering formal operational tasks.
   Answer: C
   Page Ref: 569
   Skill: Factual
   Objective: 15.2

21) Piaget acknowledged that
   A) formal operational thinking is culturally transmitted from parents or more expert peers to children.
   B) achievement of the formal operational stage probably occurs as a result of new information-processing abilities.
   C) very few adults are capable of formal operational thinking.
   D) people in some societies may not demonstrate formal operations as a result of lack of experience with hypothetical problems.
   Answer: D
   Page Ref: 569
   Skill: Conceptual
   Objective: 15.2

22) Researchers regard _____ as central to the development of abstract thought.
   A) processing capacity
   B) application of memory strategies
   C) metacognition
   D) attentional self-regulation
   Answer: C
   Page Ref: 569
   Skill: Conceptual
   Objective: 15.3

23) The heart of scientific reasoning is
   A) coordinating theories with evidence.
   B) designing experiments.
   C) developing hypotheses.
   D) conducting statistical analyses of data.
   Answer: A
   Page Ref: 570
   Skill: Factual
   Objective: 15.3

24) According to Kuhn, young children faced with the sports ball problem
   A) are skilled at coordinating theory with evidence but fail to apply strategies consistently.
   B) use logical rules to examine the relationship between multiple variables.
   C) often reason much like adolescents and young adults.
   D) often ignore conflicting evidence or distort it in ways consistent with their own theories.
   Answer: D
   Page Ref: 570
   Skill: Conceptual
   Objective: 15.3

25) A high-school science teacher, Mr. Reidy, wants to increase his students' skills at coordinating theory with evidence. He wonders if he should provide them with traditional scientific tasks, or allow them to engage in informal reasoning. What should you tell him?
   A) Scientific reasoning is influenced by years of schooling that can involve either of the two methods.
   B) Neither of the methods has been proven effective for increasing scientific reasoning.
   C) Traditional scientific tasks are the only problems that improve scientific reasoning.
   D) Informal reasoning tasks are the only problems that improve scientific reasoning.
   Answer: A
   Page Ref: 570
   Skill: Applied
   Objective: 15.4

26) Charquinta is trying to solve a scientific problem and applies logic more effectively to the theory that she doubts than to the theory that she favors. Charquinta
   A) is lacking in scientific reasoning skills.
   B) has acquired scientific reasoning skills.
   C) has developed the metacognitive capacity to evaluate her own objectivity.
   D) has developed a flexible, open-minded approach to cognitive problem-solving.
   Answer: A
   Page Ref: 570
   Skill: Applied
   Objective: 15.4

27) Cristina feels that she is a fairly objective person, but she also knows there are times when her opinions are completely biased and fail to take into account factual evidence. In all likelihood, Cristina
   A) has difficulty solving abstract problems.
   B) tends to be more fair-minded rather than self-serving.
   C) is generally disliked by her peers for being selfish.
   D) is still a concrete thinker.
   Answer: B
   Page Ref: 570
   Skill: Applied
   Objective: 15.4

28) Research indicates that when solving novel problems (for example, causal-experimental) in various task domains, adolescents
   A) master component skills in no particular order.
   B) fail to formulate and test the appropriate hypotheses.
   C) construct a general model that can be applied to many instances of a given type of problem.
   D) formulate appropriate hypotheses but have difficulty applying effective strategies.
   Answer: C
   Page Ref: 570
   Skill: Conceptual
   Objective: 15.4

29) Information-processing findings confirm that scientific reasoning
   A) results from abrupt, stagewise change.
   B) develops gradually.
   C) is fully developed by age 12.
   D) is more advanced in boys than girls.
   Answer: B
   Page Ref: 571
   Skill: Conceptual
   Objective: 15.4

30) Since Sheila has become a teenager, she tends to be idealistic, more critical of her parents, and generally indecisive. Which of the following statements regarding Sheila is true?
   A) She is showing signs of a possible learning disability.
   B) She is displaying characteristics of adolescence that will probably benefit her in the long run.
   C) She probably has severe psychological problems and bends easily to peer pressure.
   D) She probably has a history of attachment insecurity with one or both parents.
   Answer: B
   Page Ref: 571
   Skill: Applied
   Objective: 15.5

31) Why should parents refrain from finding fault with their teenagers in public?
   A) Teens already tend to believe that they are the focus of everyone else's attention and concern, so critical remarks in public can be mortifying.
   B) Parents tend to judge teen behavior incorrectly, so they run a higher risk of being critical without a legitimate reason.
   C) The best way to ride out the storminess of adolescence is to appease teens as much as possible; being critical will only create more problems.
   D) Recent research has found that adolescents who suffer such public criticism engage in higher levels of delinquency than their peers.
   Answer: A
   Page Ref: 572
   Skill: Conceptual
   Objective: 15.5

32) Mr. Conwell's son is expressing an exaggerated sense of personal uniqueness. What would be the best way for Mr. Conwell to handle this situation?
   A) acknowledge his son's unique qualities, but also look for moments to point out that he, too, felt similarly as a teenager
   B) be sensitive but firm in telling his son that he is not really unique at all; that human beings are all much more similar than different
   C) cater to his son's sense of self until about the age of 18 when his son should be ready to hear a more balanced perspective
   D) completely ignore his son's sense of self; most adolescents resolve these issues on their own
   Answer: A
   Page Ref: 572
   Skill: Applied
   Objective: 15.5

33) _____ lead(s) adolescents to think more about themselves.
   A) Overly permissive child rearing and a lack of structure
   B) The ability to reflect on their thoughts, combined with physical and psychological changes,
   C) Individualistic values and a disregard for others' feelings
   D) Selfishness and poor problem-solving skills
   Answer: B
   Page Ref: 572
   Skill: Factual
   Objective: 15.5

34) According to Piaget, the new form of egocentrism that appears at adolescence involves an inability to distinguish
   A) the self from the surrounding world.
   B) another person's view of an object from one's own view.
   C) subjective and objective aspects of experience.
   D) perspectives of self and others.
   Answer: D
   Page Ref: 572
   Skill: Factual
   Objective: 15.5

35) Young teenagers are convinced that they are the object of everyone else's attention and concern. This feature of adolescent thought is called
   A) propositional reasoning.
   B) the imaginary audience.
   C) the personal fable.
   D) rule assessment.
   Answer: B
   Page Ref: 572
   Skill: Factual
   Objective: 15.5

36) Gina has a bruise on her leg. She turned down an invitation to a swim party, explaining, "I can't possibly wear a swim suit with this ugly bruise. Everyone will notice how ugly I look!" Gina's response reveals that her thinking is characterized by
   A) paranoia.
   B) argumentativeness.
   C) the imaginary audience.
   D) the personal fable.
   Answer: C
   Page Ref: 572
   Skill: Applied
   Objective: 15.5

37) _____ helps explain the long hours adolescents spend inspecting every detail of their appearance and why they are so sensitive to public criticism.
   A) Egocentrism
   B) Concrete thinking
   C) The imaginary audience
   D) Metacognition
   Answer: C
   Page ref: 572
   Skill: Conceptual
   Objective: 15.5

38) While out shopping, Mrs. Salveson becomes upset with her teenage daughter's sarcastic responses to her questions. Understanding the concept of the imaginary audience, how would you advise Mrs. Salveson to react to her daughter's behavior?
   A) Address the problem immediately when it happens to avoid the likelihood of it recurring.
   B) Wait until she can speak to her daughter alone, and address the problem then.
   C) Ignore the behavior and hope that it will disappear as she matures.
   D) Have another respected adult, like a teacher or counselor, deal with the behavior.
   Answer: B
   Page Ref: 572
   Skill: Applied
   Objective: 15.5

39) As teenagers become sure that others are observing and thinking about them, they start to feel special and unique. This feature of adolescent thought is called
    A) propositional reasoning.
    B) the imaginary audience.
    C) the personal fable.
    D) rule assessment.
Answer: C
Page Ref: 572
Skill: Factual
Objective: 15.5

40) After getting rejected for a date, Kelsey's father attempts to comfort him. Kelsey responds, "Leave me alone, Dad! You'll never understand what I'm going through!" This common adolescent distortion is known as
    A) logical necessity.
    B) hypothetico-deductive reasoning.
    C) the imaginary audience.
    D) the personal fable.
Answer: D
Page Ref: 572
Skill: Applied
Objective: 15.5

41) The personal fable contributes to
    A) risk taking.
    B) disengagement from others.
    C) poor schoolwork.
    D) peer conformity.
Answer: A
Page Ref: 573
Skill: Conceptual
Objective: 15.5

42) The personal fable may help young people cope with the challenges of adolescence by
    A) discouraging reckless behavior.
    B) decreasing the importance of the imaginary audience.
    C) focusing attention on the opinions of others.
    D) enabling them to view themselves as influential and capable.
Answer: D
Page Ref: 573
Skill: Applied
Objective: 15.5

43) When dealing with the personal fable, adolescents are concerned about the opinions of others because
    A) others' evaluations have real consequences in terms of self-esteem, peer acceptance, and social support.
    B) such opinions help them transition smoothly from adolescence to adulthood.
    C) they lack the ability to think independently and are unable to develop opinions of their own.
    D) they do not trust their own opinions or judgments.
Answer: A
Page Ref: 573
Skill: Factual
Objective: 15.5

44) Young people with _____ and _____ scores tend to take more sexual risks, more often use drugs, and commit more delinquent acts than their agemates.
   A) low personal-fable; high sensation-seeking
   B) high personal fable; high sensation-seeking
   C) high self-esteem; low sensation-seeking
   D) low self-esteem; high idealism
Answer: B
Page Ref: 573
Skill: Conceptual
Objective: 15.5

45) Adolescent idealism often leads young people to become
   A) more cooperative at home.
   B) more critical of parents and siblings.
   C) better students at school.
   D) more realistic in their evaluations of others.
Answer: B
Page Ref: 573
Skill: Conceptual
Objective: 15.5

46) Elizabeth has developed an idea of what the "perfect family" should look and act like and constantly criticizes her siblings and parents when they do not measure up. Elizabeth's parents should
   A) ignore her comments and hope she outgrows this behavior as she matures.
   B) use authoritarian child-rearing techniques and punish her after every critical remark.
   C) develop a hierarchy of negative consequences that should be implemented immediately after each critical remark.
   D) respond patiently to her remarks, but point out the positive features of each family member to help her see that all people are blends of virtues and imperfections.
Answer: D
Page Ref: 573
Skill: Applied
Objective: 15.5

47) Teenagers struggle to make plans and decisions because they
   A) think more rationally than adults.
   B) are better at making abstract judgments than real-world decisions.
   C) have not yet mastered abstract thought.
   D) have difficulty inhibiting emotions and impulses.
Answer: D
Page Ref: 573
Skill: Factual
Objective: 15.5

48) When making decisions, adolescents are likely to emphasize _____ over _____
   A) short-term goals; long-term goals.
   B) logic; irrationality.
   C) metaevaluation.
   D) source monitoring.
Answer: A
Page Ref: 574
Skill: Factual
Objective: 15.5

49) Adolescents' planning and decision making are
    A) easy for tasks of daily life, but are undeveloped for schoolwork.
    B) much improved for schoolwork, but are still difficult in daily life.
    C) very effective in both schoolwork and daily life.
    D) poorly developed in both schoolwork and daily life.
Answer: B
Page Ref: 574
Skill: Factual
Objective: 15.5

50) When making decisions, adolescents often depend on
    A) logical and rational thinking.
    B) cognitive self-regulation.
    C) intuitive judgments.
    D) evaluations from strangers.
Answer: C
Page Ref: 574
Skill: Conceptual
Objective: 15.5

51) Sixteen-year-old Solomon seems unable to make any decisions, from what outfit to wear to which classes he wants to take next year. His mother should
    A) just make the decisions for him until he snaps out of this phase.
    B) model good decision-making skills, but refrain from making decisions for him.
    C) know that this phase will eventually pass, and that she should just wait patiently until it does.
    D) provide him with more opportunities to make decisions.
Answer: B
Page Ref: 574
Skill: Applied
Objective: 15.5

52) Who is most likely to be referred for remedial reading instruction?
    A) Rachel, who is 6 years old
    B) Betsy, who is 8 years old
    C) Eric, who is 10 years old
    D) Allison, who is 12 years old
Answer: C
Page Ref: 575
Skill: Applied
Objective: 15.6

53) Which of the following is consistent with current research on gender differences in intellectual performance?
    A) In early childhood, boys are slightly ahead in verbal ability.
    B) By early childhood, girls do better at abstract mathematical problem solving.
    C) By adolescence, girls are far ahead in verbal ability.
    D) Girls score higher on tests of verbal ability throughout the school years.
Answer: D
Page Ref: 575
Skill: Factual
Objective: 15.6

54) Females may show an advantage in verbal skills because
   A) the left hemisphere of the cerebral cortex develops earlier in girls than in boys.
   B) they rely on sensory brain regions to process spoken and written words.
   C) they tend to work harder in school than boys.
   D) they are more likely to attend college than boys.
Answer: A
Page Ref: 575
Skill: Factual
Objective: 15.6

55) When do boys start to outperform girls in mathematics?
   A) from preschool age
   B) by the age of 7 or 8
   C) by early adolescence
   D) by late adolescence
Answer: C
Page Ref: 576
Skill: Factual
Objective: 15.6

56) Boys' superiority over girls in mathematics
   A) is steadily increasing in industrialized nations.
   B) has remained steady over the last 30 years.
   C) has greatly diminished.
   D) is actually a myth.
Answer: C
Page Ref: 576
Skill: Factual
Objective: 15.6

57) Sex differences on _____ tasks are weak or nonexistent.
   A) spatial visualization
   B) mental rotation
   C) spatial perception
   D) visual orientation
Answer: A
Page Ref: 576 Box: B&E: Sex Differences in Spatial Abilities
Skill: Factual
Objective: 15.6

58) Some researchers hypothesize that prenatal exposure to _____ enhances right hemispheric functioning, giving males an advantage in spatial abilities.
   A) estrogens
   B) endorphins
   C) androgens
   D) adrenaline
Answer: C
Page Ref: 576 Box: B&E: Sex Differences in Spatial Abilities
Skill: Conceptual
Objective: 15.6

59) Research indicates that boys and girls who regularly engage in activities like _____ do better on spatial tasks.
   A) playing board games
   B) diving
   C) riding a bicycle
   D) building models
Answer: D
Page Ref: 577 Box: B&E: Sex Differences in Spatial Abilities
Skill: Factual
Objective: 15.6

60) Fabian and his sister Felicity regularly play computer games that require rapid mental rotation of visual images. You would expect
   A) both children to show decreased spatial abilities in school.
   B) both children to show enhanced scores on spatial tasks.
   C) Felicity to show enhanced spatial scores, and Fabian's scores to be unaffected.
   D) Fabian to show enhanced spatial scores, and Felicity's scores to be unaffected.
Answer: B
Page Ref: 577 Box: B&E: Sex Differences in Spatial Abilities
Skill: Applied
Objective: 15.6

61) In elementary school,
   A) girls more often blame math errors on lack of ability than boys.
   B) both boys and girls view math as a "female domain."
   C) girls believe they do not have to work as hard as boys in math.
   D) boys regard math as less useful for their future lives than girls.
Answer: A
Page Ref: 577
Skill: Conceptual
Objective: 15.6

62) With regard to computer use, Angelique is more likely to _____, while Brendan is more likely to _____.
   A) write computer programs; use e-mail
   B) use instant messaging; use graphics software
   C) analyze data; gather information for homework assignments
   D) use e-mail; use instant messaging
Answer: B
Page Ref: 577–578
Skill: Applied
Objective: 15.6

63) Which of the following is a critical factor in eliminating gender differences in math and science?
   A) finding a way to reduce genetic differences between the genders
   B) creating all-girl science classes so that they will not be compared to boys
   C) decreasing the amount of emphasis for boys to excel at math and science
   D) promoting girls' interest and confidence in math and science
Answer: D
Page Ref: 578
Skill: Conceptual
Objective: 15.6

64) One way to enhance girls' math skills is to
   A) focus more on their verbal processing skills.
   B) focus less on spatial skills and more on computational skills.
   C) teach them how to apply effective spatial strategies.
   D) wait until secondary school, when higher order skills are being utilized, to intervene.
   Answer: C
   Page Ref: 578
   Skill: Factual
   Objective: 15.6

65) Gains in language development during adolescence are largely due to
   A) biological maturation.
   B) reading adult literary works.
   C) improved capacity for reflective thought and abstraction.
   D) adult instruction.
   Answer: C
   Page Ref: 578
   Skill: Conceptual
   Objective: 15.7

66) During adolescence, vocabulary growth involves the addition of many
   A) abstract words.
   B) compound words.
   C) action words.
   D) modifiers.
   Answer: A
   Page Ref: 578
   Skill: Factual
   Objective: 15.7

67) Compared to school-age children, adolescents are better at
   A) defining concrete words.
   B) understanding figurative language.
   C) turn taking in conversations.
   D) applying the basic rules of grammar.
   Answer: B
   Page Ref: 579
   Skill: Conceptual
   Objective: 15.7

68) Research shows that in adolescence, the ability to understand proverbs is positively related to
   A) peer acceptance.
   B) spatial skills.
   C) reading proficiency.
   D) interest in political issues.
   Answer: C
   Page Ref: 579
   Skill: Conceptual
   Objective: 15.7

69) Sixteen-year-old Alyssa speaks differently to her boss at work, her parents at home, and her friends at school. Alyssa demonstrates an improved mastery of
    A) vocabulary.
    B) grammar.
    C) pragmatics.
    D) pronunciation.
Answer: C
Page Ref: 579
Skill: Applied
Objective: 15.7

70) Teenage slang is an example of adolescents'
    A) mastery of language style.
    B) poor use of grammar.
    C) egocentrism.
    D) capacity for second-language learning.
Answer: A
Page Ref: 579
Skill: Conceptual
Objective: 15.7

71) Compared to their elementary school teachers, students say junior high teachers
    A) care less about them.
    B) are more friendly.
    C) care more about them.
    D) grade more fairly.
Answer: A
Page Ref: 580
Skill: Conceptual
Objective: 15.8

72) Research on school transitions shows that _____ declines for both genders after each school change.
    A) self-esteem
    B) grade-point average
    C) loneliness
    D) dating
Answer: B
Page Ref: 580
Skill: Factual
Objective: 15.8

73) Joshua recently switched from elementary school to middle school. He feels less academically competent and his liking for school has declined. Which of the following best explains the cause of his feelings?
    A) He comes from a high-SES background.
    B) The class sizes are bigger, and the school work is more challenging.
    C) Middle school teachers tend to be less caring and supportive than elementary school teachers.
    D) Boys, more so than girls, tend to struggle with school transitions.
Answer: B
Page Ref: 580
Skill: Conceptual
Objective: 15.8

74) In general, research shows that the earlier the school transition, the
    A) more powerful its impact, especially for boys.
    B) more powerful its impact, especially for girls.
    C) less its impact, especially for boys.
    D) less its impact, especially for girls.
Answer: B
Page Ref: 580
Skill: Factual
Objective: 15.8

75) Which of the following adolescents are at greatest risk for academic and emotional difficulties after a school transition? Those who
    A) move from a large elementary school to a small junior high school.
    B) were good students in elementary school.
    C) attend a single-sex school.
    D) have to cope with added life strains, such as family disruption or poverty.
Answer: D
Page Ref: 581
Skill: Conceptual
Objective: 15.8

76) Students who had academic difficulties in addition to mental health problems during junior high _____ after the transition to high school.
    A) showed grade improvements
    B) showed increased out-of-school problem behaviors
    C) experienced an increase in self-esteem
    D) had fewer mental health problems
Answer: B
Page Ref: 581
Skill: Factual
Objective: 15.8

77) School transitions typically lead to environmental changes that fit poorly with adolescents' developmental needs, including
    A) disruption of close relationships with teachers at a time when adolescents need adult support.
    B) an emphasis on sophisticated academic collaboration during a period of heightened self-focusing.
    C) increased expectation for independent decision making.
    D) lowered academic demands as students are sorted into academic and nonacademic tracks.
Answer: A
Page Ref: 581
Skill: Conceptual
Objective: 15.8

78) Teenagers who perceive their school learning environments to be _____ have more successful school transitions.
    A) more rigid and strict than their middle school environments
    B) competitive
    C) easy and unstructured
    D) sensitive and flexible
Answer: D
Page Ref: 581
Skill: Conceptual
Objective: 15.8

79) An effective way to ease the strain of school transition in adolescence is to
   A) assign students to classes with several familiar peers or a constant group of new peers.
   B) make sure that academic expectations in junior high are tougher than in elementary school.
   C) reduce students' need to conform by encouraging anonymity.
   D) reduce the number of extracurricular activities available in high school.
   Answer: A
   Page Ref: 581–582
   Skill: Conceptual
   Objective: 15.8

80) Crystal, age 16, is allowed to work at her part-time job for no more than 15 hours a week, and she tends to make decisions jointly with her parents. Which of the following statements about Crystal is most likely to be true?
   A) Crystal will likely grow up to have a poor work ethic as an adult.
   B) Crystal will likely grow up to be a permissive parent.
   C) Crystal is likely to do very well in her academic work.
   D) Crystal is likely to lack motivation in doing her school work.
   Answer: C
   Page Ref: 582
   Skill: Applied
   Objective: 15.9

81) Which of the following child-rearing styles is associated with superior school performance in adolescence?
   A) authoritarian
   B) authoritative
   C) permissive
   D) inconsistent
   Answer: B
   Page Ref: 582
   Skill: Conceptual
   Objective: 15.9

82) Authoritative child rearing is related to _____ for _____.
   A) higher grades; both boys and girls, regardless of SES
   B) higher grades; both boys and girls but only in middle-and upper-SES groups
   C) lower grades; girls in lower-SES groups
   D) lower grades; boys in lower-SES groups
   Answer: A
   Page Ref: 582
   Skill: Conceptual
   Objective: 15.9

83) _____ child rearing predicts the poorest school performance in adolescence.
   A) Authoritarian
   B) Authoritative
   C) Permissive
   D) Uninvolved
   Answer: D
   Page Ref: 582
   Skill: Conceptual
   Objective: 15.9

84) Adolescents whose parents engage in _____ show especially positive outcomes.
   A) joint decision making
   B) authoritarian parenting
   C) uninvolved parenting
   D) mastery-oriented behavior
   Answer: A
   Page Ref: 582
   Skill: Conceptual
   Objective: 15.9

85) Mr. and Mrs. Fischman keep tabs on their teenager's school progress and communicate with her teachers frequently. However, as their daughter moves into high school, they wonder whether they should decrease their level of involvement. What should you tell them?
   A) They should continue to stay involved; these efforts are just as important during high school as they were earlier.
   B) They should decrease their level of school involvement, so as not to embarrass their daughter.
   C) Parents' school involvement has no correlation to grade-point average or other indicators of school success.
   D) Children pay no attention to their parents' level of school involvement, so they should do whatever feels best to them.
   Answer: A
   Page Ref: 582–583
   Skill: Applied
   Objective: 15.9

86) Parent involvement in eighth grade predicted tenth-grade GPA for
   A) white students only.
   B) white and black students only.
   C) Asian and Native-American students only.
   D) white, black, Asian, and Native-American students.
   Answer: D
   Page Ref: 583
   Skill: Conceptual
   Objective: 15.9

87) Which of the following explains the level of school involvement for many low-income parents?
   A) They tend to be unconcerned with academic matters.
   B) They face daily stresses that reduce the energy they have for school involvement.
   C) They purposely avoid school involvement so as not to increase the strain on their relationships with their teenagers.
   D) They already have strained relationships with school personnel and try to avoid further conflict.
   Answer: B
   Page Ref: 583
   Skill: Factual
   Objective: 15.9

88) One way to increase parent involvement in school during adolescence is
   A) by requiring a certain number of volunteer hours from the parent in exchange for their teenager's enrollment.
   B) to hold the parents responsible for their teenager's actions.
   C) to remove parents' burden of involvement in school planning and government.
   D) by fostering personal relationships between parents and teachers.
   Answer: D
   Page Ref: 583
   Skill: Conceptual
   Objective: 15.9

89) Adolescents whose parents value achievement
   A) most often rebel and choose friends who are low-achievers.
   B) choose friends who are popular because of sports or musical abilities.
   C) choose friends who share that value.
   D) tend to be rejected by their peers.
Answer: C
Page Ref: 583
Skill: Conceptual
Objective: 15.9

90) Which child is likely to show an especially large drop in school enjoyment after a school transition?
   A) Joshua, whose friends dislike school
   B) Jasmine, whose friends are all high-achieving students
   C) Jared, whose friends like school
   D) Julie, whose friends call each other to check answers to homework problems
Answer: A
Page Ref: 583
Skill: Applied
Objective: 15.9

91) Adolescents most commonly "media multitask" by
   A) surfing the Internet while in class.
   B) listening to music while doing homework or talking with friends.
   C) watching TV while eating dinner with their families.
   D) using cell phones while watching TV.
Answer: B
Page Ref: 585 Box: SI: Media Multitasking Disrupts Attention and Learning
Skill: Factual
Objective: 15.9

92) Research has shown that media multitasking
   A) fragments the attention span.
   B) helps train adolescents' brains to attend to more than one task at the same time.
   C) has little effect on teenagers' ability to focus.
   D) helps improve use of explicit memory.
Answer: A
Page Ref: 585 Box: SI: Media Multitasking Disrupts Attention and Learning
Skill: Factual
Objective: 15.9

93) Frequent media multitaskers may find it difficult to
   A) utilize implicit memory.
   B) focus on more than one task at a time.
   C) ignore irrelevant stimuli in the environment.
   D) shift attention from one task to another.
Answer: C
Page Ref: 585 Box: SI: Media Multitasking Disrupts Attention and Learning
Skill: Factual
Objective: 15.9

94) A recent study showed that seventh-grade students who moved into eighth-grade classes that emphasized competition and public comparison of students
   A) performed better academically than peers in classrooms that emphasized cooperation and mutual respect.
   B) showed increased perseverance and improved study habits.
   C) showed declines in motivation and self-regulation.
   D) showed better attendance than peers in classrooms that emphasized cooperation and shared classroom control.
   Answer: C
   Page Ref: 584
   Skill: Factual
   Objective: 15.9

95) A factor that promotes school attendance and achievement is
   A) teachers who expect students to perform well and encourage high-level thinking.
   B) the use of high-level textbooks.
   C) classrooms that require few assignments.
   D) placing students in ability-grouped classes.
   Answer: A
   Page Ref: 584
   Skill: Factual
   Objective: 15.9

96) Johann, a low-achieving student, is placed in a mixed-ability group. Research shows that Johann will
   A) be intimidated by the higher achievers.
   B) benefit socially and intellectually from the mixed grouping.
   C) stifle the achievement of the higher achievers.
   D) feel that he is superior to the higher achievers.
   Answer: B
   Page Ref: 585
   Skill: Applied
   Objective: 15.9

97) The No Child Left Behind Act requires that
   A) every child will have access to high-quality education and extracurricular activities, regardless of race, class, or sex.
   B) by the year 2011, every child will need to attend at least two years of college.
   C) every country in the world will provide an education for all children regardless of sex.
   D) each state must evaluate every public school's performance through annual achievement testing and publicize the results.
   Answer: D
   Page Ref: 586 Box: SI: Education: High-Stakes Testing
   Skill: Factual
   Objective: 15.9

98) Alan's elementary school has been labeled a "failing" school according to No Child Left Behind standards. Alan's parents will probably
   A) have the option of transferring him to a higher-performing school.
   B) be asked to provide additional tutoring for Alan, at their own expense.
   C) hear that his school has received additional federal funding to improve student achievement.
   D) learn that his teachers have received financial bonuses.
   Answer: A
   Page Ref: 586 Box: SI: Education: High-Stakes Testing
   Skill: Applied
   Objective: 15.9

99) Accumulating evidence on high-stakes testing indicates that it
    A) often undermines the quality of education.
    B) provides motivation for upgrading teaching and learning.
    C) encourages teachers to focus on more in-depth, critical thinking tasks in their lessons.
    D) accurately indicates the academic abilities of students.
Answer: A
Page Ref: 586 Box: SI: Education: High-Stakes Testing
Skill: Factual
Objective: 15.9

100) The reliance on test scores for making decisions about students
    A) sharply reduces the high school dropout rate, particularly among ethnic minorities.
    B) amplifies achievement gaps between racial and gender groups.
    C) is more accurate than taking teacher-assigned grades into account.
    D) coincides with the emphasis on teaching for deeper understanding in high-achieving nations like Japan.
Answer: B
Page Ref: 586 Box: SI: Education: High-Stakes Testing
Skill: Factual
Objective: 15.9

101) High-stakes testing prompts teachers to spend more class time
    A) on research projects.
    B) administering rote exercises that resemble test items.
    C) explaining the importance of doing well on tests.
    D) developing students' writing skills.
Answer: B
Page Ref: 586 Box: SI: Education: High-Stakes Testing
Skill: Conceptual
Objective: 15.9

102) In high school, _____ students are assigned in large numbers to noncollege tracks.
    A) female
    B) male
    C) middle-SES
    D) low-SES minority
Answer: D
Page Ref: 587
Skill: Factual
Objective: 15.9

103) Quinn is a capable student who is placed in a low academic track. Research indicates that Quinn will probably
    A) show large performance gains because the subject matter is better geared toward his level.
    B) get better quality instruction than his peers in high-ability classrooms.
    C) "sink" to the performance level of his trackmates.
    D) maintain his friendships with peers from high- and mixed-ability groups.
Answer: C
Page Ref: 587
Skill: Applied
Objective: 15.9

104) Students who are not assigned to a college preparatory track or who do poorly in high school can still get a college education in
   A) China.
   B) Japan.
   C) Western Europe.
   D) the United States.
Answer: D
Page Ref: 587
Skill: Factual
Objective: 15.9

105) The American high school dropout rate is highest for _____ teenagers.
   A) female
   B) rural
   C) African-American
   D) low-SES, ethnic minority
Answer: D
Page Ref: 587
Skill: Factual
Objective: 15.10

106) While many high school dropouts show a persistent pattern of disruptive behavior and poor academic achievement, a large number
   A) drop out for the lure of high-paying jobs in technical fields.
   B) quietly disengage from school after experiencing academic failure.
   C) drop out in order to earn money to support unemployed parents.
   D) are pushed out by teachers who fear repercussions from the No Child Left Behind Act.
Answer: B
Page Ref: 588
Skill: Factual
Objective: 15.10

107) Typically, parents of students who drop out of school
   A) encourage achievement but just are not successful.
   B) completed high school themselves.
   C) show little involvement in their child's education.
   D) have serious emotional problems.
Answer: C
Page Ref: 588
Skill: Conceptual
Objective: 15.10

108) Recent reports indicate that over _____percent of students in some inner-city high schools do not graduate.
   A) 30
   B) 40
   C) 50
   D) 60
Answer: C
Page Ref: 588
Skill: Factual
Objective: 15.10

109) Compared to students in an academic program, students in general education and vocational tracks are _____ likely to drop out.
    A) no more
    B) three times as
    C) six times as
    D) ten times as
Answer: B
Page Ref: 588
Skill: Factual
Objective: 15.10

110) Many students at risk for dropping out benefit from
    A) remedial instruction in small classes.
    B) greater emotional distance from teachers.
    C) less focus on vocations and more emphasis on basic academics.
    D) larger classes where they feel less "on the spot."
Answer: A
Page Ref: 589
Skill: Conceptual
Objective: 15.10

111) Involvement in extracurricular activities
    A) interferes with academic performance.
    B) increases the dropout rate.
    C) is promoted by small school size.
    D) results in negative peer pressure.
Answer: C
Page Ref: 589
Skill: Factual
Objective: 15.10

112) The percentage of North American adolescents completing high school has risen to just over ____ percent.
    A) 39
    B) 54
    C) 90
    D) 98
Answer: C
Page Ref: 590
Skill: Factual
Objective: 15.10

113) The percentage of American high school graduates who earn college degrees is nearly ____ percent.
    A) 30
    B) 40
    C) 50
    D) 60
Answer: B
Page Ref: 590
Skill: Factual
Objective: 15.10

114) Lindsey is in the fantasy period of vocational development. She is probably _____ years old.
   A) 10
   B) 13
   C) 16
   D) 19
   Answer: A
   Page Ref: 590
   Skill: Applied
   Objective: 15.11

115) Leilani thinks that she wants to be an actress or a ballerina when she grows up. Her brother Reilly wants to be a football player or a motorcycle racer. Leilani and Reilly are currently in the _____ period of vocational development.
   A) fantasy
   B) tentative
   C) realistic
   D) decisive
   Answer: A
   Page Ref: 590
   Skill: Applied
   Objective: 15.11

116) Libby is good at playing the flute and likes the pleasure music gives to others. As a result, she thinks she might want to be a musician. She is likely in the _____ phase of vocational development.
   A) capability
   B) tentative
   C) realistic
   D) fantasy
   Answer: B
   Page Ref: 590
   Skill: Applied
   Objective: 15.11

117) Which period of vocational development characterizes early and middle adolescence?
   A) fantasy
   B) tentative
   C) realistic
   D) exploratory
   Answer: B
   Page Ref: 590
   Skill: Factual
   Objective: 15.11

118) The correct order of the phases of vocational development is:
   A) fantasy period, tentative period, realistic period.
   B) tentative period, realistic period, fantasy period.
   C) fantasy period, realistic period, tentative period.
   D) realistic period, fantasy period, tentative period.
   Answer: A
   Page Ref: 590–591
   Skill: Conceptual
   Objective: 15.11

119) Adolescents begin to narrow their options in the _____ period of vocational development.
   A) fantasy
   B) tentative
   C) realistic
   D) appraisal
   Answer: C
   Page Ref: 591
   Skill: Conceptual
   Objective: 15.11

120) During the _____ phase of the _____ period of vocational development, an individual typically gathers more information about a set of possibilities that blends with his or her personal characteristics.
   A) exploration; fantasy
   B) exploration; tentative
   C) crystallization; realistic
   D) exploration; realistic
   Answer: D
   Page Ref: 591
   Skill: Factual
   Objective: 15.11

121) Lyndall is a sophomore in college and has decided that he wants to be an engineer. He plans to take introductory courses in both electrical and mechanical engineering to help him decide. Lyndall is in the _____ phase of the _____ period of vocational development.
   A) exploration; fantasy
   B) crystallization; tentative
   C) crystallization; realistic
   D) exploration; realistic
   Answer: C
   Page Ref: 591
   Skill: Applied
   Objective: 15.11

122) Based upon the fact that people are attracted to occupations that complement their personalities, John Holland identified _____ that affect vocational choice.
   A) 6 interest areas
   B) 6 personality types
   C) 10 vocational areas
   D) 8 personality subgroups
   Answer: B
   Page Ref: 591
   Skill: Factual
   Objective: 15.11

123) Nissa wants to be a physicist or an engineer. According to Holland, she is a(n) _____ person.
   A) realistic
   B) conventional
   C) investigative
   D) enterprising
   Answer: C
   Page Ref: 591
   Skill: Applied
   Objective: 15.11

124) The social person is likely to select which of the following occupations?
    A) anthropologist
    B) counselor
    C) plumber
    D) musician
Answer: B
Page Ref: 591
Skill: Conceptual
Objective: 15.11

125) Kyle enjoys construction and carpentry. Which of the following personality types best describes him?
    A) conventional
    B) enterprising
    C) investigative
    D) realistic
Answer: D
Page Ref: 591
Skill: Applied
Objective: 15.11

126) The artistic person is likely to select which of the following occupations?
    A) engineer
    B) teacher
    C) surveyor
    D) writer
Answer: D
Page Ref: 591
Skill: Conceptual
Objective: 15.11

127) Meredith likes well-structured tasks, values material possessions, and is concerned about her social status. Meredith demonstrates personality traits associated with a(n) _____ person.
    A) enterprising
    B) realistic
    C) conventional
    D) antisocial
Answer: C
Page Ref: 591
Skill: Applied
Objective: 15.11

128) Cynthia is adventurous and exciting. Because of her strong leadership skills and persuasive personality, people are drawn to her. Cynthia displays personality characteristics of a(n) _____ person.
    A) enterprising
    B) investigative
    C) social
    D) conventional
Answer: A
Page Ref: 591
Skill: Applied
Objective: 15.11

129) Ty's dad is a doctor and his mom is an engineer. To which of the following occupations is Ty most likely to aspire?
    A) construction worker
    B) lawyer
    C) painter
    D) flight attendant
Answer: B
Page Ref: 591
Skill: Applied
Objective: 15.11

130) Which of the following is a behavior displayed by lower-SES parents that influences career choices of their children?
    A) engaging in a wide range of strategies to promote a child's progress
    B) gathering information on colleges and areas of study
    C) emphasizing conformity and obedience
    D) identifying knowledgeable professionals who can help children make vocational decisions
Answer: C
Page Ref: 592
Skill: Conceptual
Objective: 15.11

131) Which of the following statements is true?
    A) Adolescents' career choices are largely a matter of chance.
    B) Teachers play a powerful role in adolescents' career decisions.
    C) Family background has little to do with vocational choice.
    D) Peers have a major impact on vocational choice.
Answer: B
Page Ref: 592
Skill: Conceptual
Objective: 15.11

132) Nicole is in high school. Which of the following people is especially likely to help her foster high career aspirations?
    A) her high school principal
    B) her friends
    C) people at her after-school job
    D) her high school teachers
Answer: D
Page Ref: 592
Skill: Applied
Objective: 15.11

133) Women's progress entering and excelling at male-dominated professions has been
    A) slow.
    B) moderate.
    C) rapid.
    D) nonexistent.
Answer: A
Page Ref: 592
Skill: Factual
Objective: 15.11

134) The gender gap in career attainment is partially accounted for by
   A) the fact that boys' grades are higher than girls' grades.
   B) boys' superior efforts.
   C) innate ability.
   D) girls' underestimation of their own achievement.
Answer: D
Page Ref: 593
Skill: Conceptual
Objective: 15.11

135) Based on the 2010 U.S. Census Bureau's statistics on women in various professions, which of the following professions do women dominate most?
   A) teacher
   B) lawyer
   C) business executive
   D) doctor
Answer: A
Page Ref: 593
Skill: Applied
Objective: 15.11

136) Janetta and four friends chose a vocational track in high school, similar to those chosen by their parents. None of these students was interested in going to college. They will
   A) probably end up working in technical or medical fields.
   B) have more work opportunities available to them than their parents did.
   C) have fewer work opportunities than their parents did several decades ago.
   D) probably receive a lot of vocational counseling and job placement services as they transition from school to work.
Answer: C
Page Ref: 593
Skill: Applied
Objective: 15.12

137) Which of the following statements about teenage employment is true?
   A) Most teenagers work to receive vocational training or to prepare for the transition to college.
   B) Most teenagers plan to continue in the same vocational area as their afterschool job once they graduate.
   C) The more teenagers work, the poorer their school attendance and the less likely they are to participate in extracurricular activities.
   D) Middle- and high-income young people make up the majority of the teenage workforce.
Answer: C
Page Ref: 594
Skill: Factual
Objective: 15.12

138) American high school students who work many hours a week and hold a heavy commitment to their job
   A) usually have stimulating, well-paid jobs.
   B) do better in school than their unemployed counterparts.
   C) tend to be depressed and disliked by peers.
   D) earn lower grades and report more drug and alcohol use.
Answer: D
Page Ref: 594
Skill: Factual
Objective: 15.12

139) High school work-study programs are related to
   A) positive school and work attitudes.
   B) good teacher and peer relations.
   C) poor achievement.
   D) high dropout rates among low-income youths.
   Answer: A
   Page Ref: 594
   Skill: Conceptual
   Objective: 15.12

140) High-quality vocational preparation programs in high schools
   A) have resulted in improved academic achievement and reduced delinquency.
   B) are widespread in both the United States and Canada.
   C) are typically available in North American schools, but only for industrial occupations and manual trades.
   D) have shown no influence on attitudes or vocational outcomes for high school students.
   Answer: A
   Page Ref: 594
   Skill: Factual
   Objective: 15.12

141) Which of the following statements about Germany's work-study apprenticeship system is true?
   A) Government regulations require that businesses carry the entire costs of the program.
   B) Businesses provide financial support because they know that the program guarantees a competent, dedicated work force.
   C) The German government provides the full funding for the program, because it guarantees a competent, dedicated work force.
   D) The program is funded entirely through philanthropic donations.
   Answer: B
   Page Ref: 594
   Skill: Factual
   Objective: 15.12

142) One challenge that Germany's apprenticeship program still faces is
   A) preventing low-SES youths from being concentrated in the lowest-skilled apprenticeship placements.
   B) lack of participation due to minimal public awareness about the program.
   C) enrollment numbers that are too high to ensure quality apprenticeships for each student.
   D) low enrollments due to increased interest in college preparatory programs.
   Answer: A
   Page Ref: 594
   Skill: Factual
   Objective: 15.12

ESSAY

143) Twelve-year-old Tamika is a formal operational thinker. What are the major characteristics of her thought processes?

Answer: At the formal operational stage, Tamika reasons much like a scientist searching for solutions in the laboratory. She no longer requires concrete things and events as objects of thought. Instead, she can come up with new, more general logical rules through internal reflection. Tamika is capable of hypothetico-deductive reasoning, which means that when faced with a problem, she starts with a general theory of all possible factors that might affect the outcome—even those not immediately suggested by concrete features of the situation—and deduces from it specific hypotheses about what might happen. Then, she tests these hypotheses in an orderly fashion to see which ones work in the real world. Tamika also demonstrates propositional thought by evaluating the logic of propositions (verbal statements) without referring to real-world circumstances. Language is more important to Tamika now, as abstract thought requires language-based systems of representation that do not stand for real things, such as those that exist in higher mathematics. Tamika can reason verbally about abstract concepts, such as morality and justice.

Page Ref: 566–567

144) Compared to school-age children, adolescents show improved ability to think scientifically. What factors contribute to this improvement?

Answer: Adolescents benefit from exposure to increasingly complex problems and instruction that highlights critical features of tasks and effective strategies. Consequently, scientific reasoning is strongly influenced by years of schooling, whether individuals grapple with traditional scientific tasks (like Piaget's pendulum problem) or engage in informal reasoning—for example, justify a theory about what causes children to fail in school.

Many investigators believe that sophisticated metacognitive understanding is at the heart of advanced cognitive development. When children receive continuous opportunities to pit theory against evidence, eventually they reflect on their current strategies, revise them, and become aware of the nature of logic. Then, they apply their abstract appreciation of logical necessity to a wide variety of situations. Although much better at scientific reasoning than children, adolescents and adults continue to show a self-serving bias in their thinking. They apply logic more effectively to ideas they doubt than to ones they favor. Reasoning scientifically, however, requires the metacognitive capacity to evaluate one's objectivity—a disposition to be fair-minded rather than self-serving. Information-processing research reveals that scientific reasoning does not result from an abrupt, stagewise change, as Piaget believed. Instead, it develops gradually out of many specific experiences that require children and adolescents to match theory against evidence and reflect on their thinking.

Page Ref: 570–571

145) Tija has noticed that her adolescent daughter is very self-conscious. Explain why this is so, and be sure to use the terms *imaginary audience* and *personal fable* in your explanation.

Answer: Adolescents' ability to reflect on their own thoughts, combined with the physical and psychological changes they are undergoing, means that they start to think more about themselves. Piaget's followers suggest that as a result, two distorted images of the relation between self and other appear. The first is called the *imaginary audience.* Young teenagers regard themselves as always on stage. They are convinced that they are the focus of everyone else's attention and concern. As a result, they become extremely self-conscious (as Tija observed with her daughter), often going to great lengths to avoid embarrassment. To teenagers, who believe that everyone is monitoring their performance, a critical remark from a parent or teacher can be mortifying. Another cognitive distortion is the *personal fable.* Because teenagers are so sure that others are observing and thinking about them, they develop an inflated opinion of their own importance. They start to feel that they are special and unique. Many view themselves as reaching great heights of glory as well as sinking to unusual depths of despair-experiences that others could not possibly understand.

Page Ref: 572–573

146) Explain why teenagers have difficulty with decision making.

Answer: Being "first-timers," teenagers do not have enough knowledge to consider the pros and cons of many experiences and to predict how they might react to them. At the same time, they encounter many more complex situations involving competing goals—for example, how to maintain standing in the peer group while avoiding getting drunk at a party. Teenagers often feel overwhelmed by their expanding range of options—abundant school courses, extracurricular activities, social events, and material goods to choose from. They also depend on intuitive judgments and value short-term rather than long-term goals. As a result, their efforts to choose frequently break down, and they resort to habit, act on impulse, or postpone decision making.

Page Ref: 573–574

147) Do sex differences in mental abilities exist during childhood and adolescence? Explain.

Answer: Boys and girls do not differ in general intelligence. They do, however, vary in specific mental abilities. Girls are ahead in early language development. Throughout the school years, they attain higher scores in reading and writing, and account for a lower percentage of children referred for remedial reading instruction. Girls continue to score slightly higher on tests of verbal ability in adolescence. Girls show a biological advantage in earlier development of the left hemisphere of the cerebral cortex, where language is localized. Girls also receive more verbal stimulation from mothers in the preschool years, and view reading as a "feminine" subject.

Sex differences in mathematical ability are apparent by first grade, with boys outperforming girls. Girls more often depend on concrete manipulatives to solve basic math problems, whereas boys more often mentally represent numbers and rapidly retrieve answers from memory. Boys continue to do better in math in secondary school, especially on tests of abstract reasoning, primarily complex word problems and geometry. The difference is evident in many countries, and it extends to science achievement, where boys' advantage increases as problems become more difficult. Although it is diminishing, the gender gap is largest among the academically talented.

Page Ref: 575–578

148) Ashley has just graduated from sixth grade; in the fall, she will be starting junior high school. Based on what you have learned about the impact of school transitions, what can you predict about Ashley's adjustment at her new school? Suggest ways to minimize the stress of these changes.

Answer: School transitions can create adjustment problems. Ashley's course grades will probably drop, partly because of the tighter academic standards, but also because the junior high is likely to offer less personal attention, more whole-class instruction, and fewer opportunities to participate in classroom decision making. Ashley will probably rate her learning experiences in junior high less favorably than she did her elementary school experiences and believe that her teachers care less about her, are less friendly, grade less fairly, and stress competition more and mastery and improvement less. Consequently, Ashley may feel less academically competent and her motivation may drop. Her participation in extracurricular activities may also decline. If Ashley also has to cope with added transitions, such as family disruption, parental unemployment, or a shift in residence, or if she is a poor achiever or poverty-stricken, she is at even greater risk for academic and emotional difficulties.

Enhanced support from parents, teachers, and peers eases the strain of school transition. Parental involvement, monitoring, and gradual autonomy granting are associated with better adjustment after entering junior high. Homerooms can be provided where teachers offer academic and personal counseling and work closely with parents to promote favorable school adjustment. Ashley or her parents can also check with the school administration to see if students can be assigned to classes with several familiar peers or a constant group of new peers—arrangements that promote emotional security and social support. Finally, the school can work to foster students' growing capacity for autonomy and responsibility by making sure to avoid handing down rules that students see as unfair and punitive.

Page Ref: 580–582

149) Doug has decided to find a job and not to attend college. What problem is Doug likely to face? Suggest ways to minimize or alleviate these problems.

Answer: Doug may have difficulty finding work in anything other than the job he held during high school. In contrast to college students, Doug has few resources for vocational counseling and job placement. If he does find work, it will probably be a low-paid, unskilled job. American employers prefer to hire young adults, regarding the recent high school graduate as poorly prepared for a demanding, skilled occupation.

When work experiences are specially designed to meet educational and vocational goals, outcomes are different. Participation in work-study programs is related to positive school and work attitudes and improved academic achievement among low-SES teenagers. High-quality vocational preparation for adolescents who do not go to college is scarce in the United States. Unlike some European nations, the United States and Canada have no widespread training systems to prepare youths for skilled business and industrial occupations and manual trades. The success of the German system suggests that a national apprenticeship program would improve the transition from high school to work for North American young people. Currently, small-scale school-to-work projects are underway in an effort to solve these problems.

Page Ref: 593–594

150) Describe the German apprenticeship system. What are the challenges to implementing a similar system in the United States?

Answer: In Germany, adolescents who do not go to a college-preparatory high school have access to one of the most successful work-study apprenticeship systems in the world for entering business and industry. Two-thirds of adolescents participate in the apprenticeship system, making it the most common form of secondary education. After completing full-time schooling at age 15 or 16, adolescents spend the remaining 2 years of compulsory education in the *Berufsschule*, which offers part-time vocational courses that they combine with an apprenticeship, which is jointly planned by educators and employers. Students train in work settings for more than 400 blue- and white-collar occupations. Apprentices who complete training and pass a qualifying examination are certified as skilled workers and earn union-set wages for that occupation. Implementing an American apprenticeship system poses major challenges. Perhaps the greatest is overcoming the reluctance of employers to assume part of the responsibility for vocational training, ensuring cooperation between schools and businesses, and preventing low-income youths from being concentrated in the lowest skilled apprenticeship placements—an obstacle that Germany itself has not yet fully overcome.

Page Ref: 594

CHAPTER 16
EMOTIONAL AND SOCIAL DEVELOPMENT
IN ADOLESCENCE

MULTIPLE CHOICE

1) Jos, age 16, thinks, "What am I really like? Who will I become?" These remarks
   A) are signs of identity development.
   B) indicate that Jos lacks self-confidence.
   C) reveal that Jos has a serious adjustment problem.
   D) indicate that Jos is ready for Erikson's intimacy stage.
   Answer: A
   Page Ref: 599
   Skill: Applied
   Objective: 16.1

2) Erikson's theory recognizes _____ as the major personality achievement of adolescence.
   A) autonomy
   B) identity
   C) guilt
   D) diffusion
   Answer: B
   Page Ref: 600
   Skill: Conceptual
   Objective: 16.1

3) Defining who you are, what you value, and the directions you choose to pursue in life is part of
   A) constructing an identity.
   B) moral development.
   C) gender intensification.
   D) commitment.
   Answer: A
   Page Ref: 600
   Skill: Conceptual
   Objective: 16.1

4) Identity can be described as an explicit theory of oneself as a(n)
   A) complex unit with varying personalities and desires.
   B) rational agent who acts on the basis of reason and takes responsibility for those actions.
   C) interpersonal being whose decisions are made within a wider social context.
   D) entity who must explain its randomly occurring behavior.
   Answer: B
   Page Ref: 600
   Skill: Factual
   Objective: 16.1

5) According to Erikson, resolution of the adolescent psychological conflict requires
    A) successful outcomes at earlier stages.
    B) an above-average IQ.
    C) a variety of sexual partners.
    D) permissive parenting.
Answer: A
Page Ref: 600
Skill: Conceptual
Objective: 16.1

6) According to Erikson, the psychological conflict of adolescence is identity versus
    A) autonomy.
    B) role confusion.
    C) exploration.
    D) commitment.
Answer: B
Page Ref: 600
Skill: Conceptual
Objective: 16.1

7) Kelly has reached adolescence and experiences difficulty having faith in ideals, such as truth, freedom, and honesty. According to Erikson, Kelly
    A) has a weak sense of trust.
    B) has poor initiative.
    C) lacks a sense of industry.
    D) recently overcome an identity crisis.
Answer: A
Page Ref: 600
Skill: Applied
Objective: 16.1

8) According to Erikson, a temporary period of confusion and distress as adolescents experiment with alternatives before settling on a set of values is known as
    A) diffusion.
    B) a critical period.
    C) identity formation.
    D) an identity crisis.
Answer: D
Page Ref: 600
Skill: Conceptual
Objective: 16.1

9) Current theorists believe that the typical adolescent's approach to forming a mature identity starts with _____ and is then followed by _____.
    A) industry; autonomy
    B) trust; initiative
    C) exploration; commitment
    D) confusion; calm
Answer: C
Page Ref: 600
Skill: Conceptual
Objective: 16.1

10) Erin has no real interests or hobbies, and she cannot stay committed to an activity, a part-time job, or her school work. Some of her peers have called her "shallow," and her aunt complains that she is "directionless." Erikson would say that Erin
    A) is currently in the commitment phase of identity development.
    B) is experiencing role confusion.
    C) has successfully resolved the intimacy stage of identity development.
    D) is having trouble with her sense of industry.
Answer: B
Page Ref: 600
Skill: Applied
Objective: 16.1

11) According to Erikson, an identity crisis involves
    A) questioning the values of one's society and culture.
    B) experimenting with alternatives before deciding on values and goals.
    C) rejecting previous identities in favor of a new vision of the self.
    D) limiting one's choices and desires.
Answer: B
Page Ref: 600
Skill: Conceptual
Objective: 16.1

12) Lauren first described herself as "attractive." A moment later she said she was "sort of plain." These contradictory assertions suggest Lauren is about _____ years of age.
    A) 10
    B) 13
    C) 16
    D) 18
Answer: B
Page Ref: 601
Skill: Applied
Objective: 16.2

13) Compared to school-age children, adolescents place more emphasis on _____ in their self-descriptions.
    A) physical appearance
    B) favorite activities
    C) social virtues
    D) school performance
Answer: C
Page Ref: 601
Skill: Conceptual
Objective: 16.2

14) _____ is/are a key theme in older adolescents' self-concepts.
    A) Being smart
    B) Wearing the right clothes
    C) Personal possessions
    D) Personal and moral standards
Answer: D
Page Ref: 601
Skill: Conceptual
Objective: 16.2

15) During the adolescent years, self-esteem generally
    A) rises.
    B) declines.
    C) fluctuates a great deal.
    D) remains stable.
    Answer: A
    Page Ref: 601
    Skill: Factual
    Objective: 16.2

16) As Milee transitions from childhood to adolescence, she will likely add several new dimensions of self-evaluations—
    A) athletic skill, academic competence, and moral understanding.
    B) identity, autonomy, and initiative.
    C) close friendship, romantic appeal, and job competence.
    D) popularity, future aspirations, and spirituality.
    Answer: C
    Page Ref: 602
    Skill: Applied
    Objective: 16.2

17) A study of self-esteem in 13 industrialized countries showed that the majority of teenagers had
    A) low self-esteem.
    B) a negative attitude toward school and work.
    C) a pessimistic outlook on life.
    D) confidence in their ability to cope with life's problems.
    Answer: D
    Page Ref: 602
    Skill: Factual
    Objective: 16.2

18) Fifteen-year-old Tyson feels poorly about his academic abilities and family relationships. Tyson is
    A) probably an early maturer.
    B) at risk for adjustment difficulties.
    C) probably experimenting with different identities.
    D) a typical teenager.
    Answer: B
    Page Ref: 602
    Skill: Applied
    Objective: 16.2

19) Which of the following teenagers will probably experience weekly self-esteem shifts?
    A) Sally, who is overly dependent on peer social approval
    B) Donald, who is somewhat dependent on peer social approval
    C) Anne, who does not depend on peer social approval at all
    D) Lisa, who actively despises peer approval
    Answer: A
    Page Ref: 602
    Skill: Applied
    Objective: 16.2

20) Lou's parents give him feedback that is primarily negative or inconsistent. The chances are high that Lou
   A) will become increasingly resilient with age.
   B) will rely more on adults than peers to affirm his self-esteem.
   C) has a relatively stable, if negative, self-worth.
   D) is in need of constant reassurance.
Answer: D
Page Ref: 603
Skill: Applied
Objective: 16.2

21) Which of the following statements is true?
   A) Caucasian-American adolescents have higher self-esteem than African-American adolescents.
   B) Warm, extended families and a strong sense of ethnic pride lead to more positive self-esteem for African-American adolescents than for Caucasian-American adolescents.
   C) Caucasian-American girls are more satisfied with their peer relationships than African-American girls.
   D) There are no significant SES or ethnic differences in adolescent self-esteem.
Answer: B
Page Ref: 603
Skill: Conceptual
Objective: 16.2

22) Hillary, an African-American adolescent, would have higher self-esteem
   A) if she was the only African-American girl in an otherwise all-white school.
   B) in a school with just a few other African-American students.
   C) in a school with many other African-American students.
   D) if she was home schooled by a female relative.
Answer: C
Page Ref: 603
Skill: Applied
Objective: 16.2

23) Tony has thought long and hard about music as a career. When asked if he would change his mind if something better came along, he replied, "I doubt it." Which identity status characterizes Tony?
   A) identity achievement
   B) moratorium
   C) identity foreclosure
   D) identity diffusion
Answer: A
Page Ref: 603
Skill: Applied
Objective: 16.3

24) Suzanne questions her parents' religious beliefs and has begun to visit other churches to find out about alternatives. What identity status characterizes Suzanne?
   A) identity achievement
   B) identity moratorium
   C) identity foreclosure
   D) identity diffusion
Answer: B
Page Ref: 603
Skill: Applied
Objective: 16.3

25) Katy accepts her family's political and religious beliefs without question. Which identity status characterizes Katy?
   A) identity achievement
   B) moratorium
   C) identity foreclosure
   D) identity diffusion
   Answer: C
   Page Ref: 603
   Skill: Applied
   Objective: 16.3

26) Heather is a foreclosed teenager. Which of the following statements is Heather likely to make?
   A) "I don't care about finding a so-called value system. What does it matter anyway?"
   B) "I believe what my parents have taught me and have no reason to doubt that they are right."
   C) "I've explored many options and have settled on the value system that makes the most sense to me."
   D) "I'm still exploring my options for the future."
   Answer: B
   Page Ref: 603
   Skill: Applied
   Objective: 16.3

27) When asked about his career plans, Rodney responds, "Haven't thought about it. Doesn't make too much difference to me what I do." What identity status characterizes Rodney?
   A) identity achievement
   B) moratorium
   C) identity foreclosure
   D) identity diffusion
   Answer: D
   Page Ref: 603
   Skill: Applied
   Objective: 16.3

28) A diffused adolescent would most likely say that she
   A) shares the political perspective of her parents because "it works for them."
   B) is currently considering several different political perspectives.
   C) does not really care about politics and is not interested in exploring alternative viewpoints.
   D) has considered various viewpoints and has decided to commit to a particular political party.
   Answer: C
   Page Ref: 603
   Skill: Applied
   Objective: 16.3

29) Which of the following is true?
   A) Once adolescents enter an identity status, they tend to remain in that status until early adulthood.
   B) Most adolescents start out as foreclosed or diffused, but by late adolescence they move toward moratorium and identity achievement.
   C) Most adolescents start out in moratorium, but by late adolescence they move toward foreclosure and diffusion.
   D) Most adolescents start out in foreclosure, but by late adolescence they move toward diffusion and identity achievement.
   Answer: B
   Page Ref: 604
   Skill: Conceptual
   Objective: 16.3

30) After high school, Tom entered college while his brother Jay went to work. Which of the following is true?
   A) Jay will probably settle on a self-definition before Tom.
   B) Jay is unlikely to reach identity achievement.
   C) Tom is at greater risk for identity diffusion than Jay.
   D) Tom and Jay are unlikely to differ in their paths to identity.
Answer: A
Page Ref: 604
Skill: Applied
Objective: 16.3

31) Recent research on gender differences in identity development reveals that girls
   A) focus on intimacy development before they become concerned with establishing an identity.
   B) show less sophisticated reasoning about identity issues related to intimacy than do boys.
   C) are fairly similar to boys in that they typically make progress on identity concerns before experiencing genuine intimacy in relationships.
   D) are more identity diffused than boys and, therefore, experience intimacy in relationships before boys.
Answer: C
Page Ref: 604
Skill: Conceptual
Objective: 16.3

32) _____ is seen as a psychologically healthy route to a mature identity.
   A) Diffusion
   B) Foreclosure
   C) Moratorium
   D) Conventionalism
Answer: C
Page Ref: 604
Skill: Conceptual
Objective: 16.3

33) Compared to the other identity statuses, young people who are identity achieved or actively exploring
   A) have lower self-esteem.
   B) report a larger discrepancy between their ideal selves and their real selves.
   C) are more self-conscious and self-focused.
   D) are more advanced in moral reasoning.
Answer: D
Page Ref: 604
Skill: Factual
Objective: 16.3

34) Which identity status is associated with a dogmatic, inflexible cognitive style?
   A) diffusion
   B) foreclosure
   C) achievement
   D) moratorium
Answer: B
Page Ref: 604
Skill: Conceptual
Objective: 16.3

35) Which of the following teenagers is at highest risk for peer pressure and drug abuse?
   A) Hayden, who has adopted his parents' values without question
   B) Danica, who entrusts her fate to luck but has a sense of hopelessness about the future
   C) Deon, who is actively exploring various belief systems but has not yet settled on one that "fits"
   D) Makenna, who has committed to a particular religious faith after considering several alternatives
   Answer: B
   Page Ref: 605
   Skill: Applied
   Objective: 16.3

36) What can happen to identity formation when either an individual or a context changes?
   A) There is a possibility for identity reformulation.
   B) Identity formation is interrupted.
   C) Identity formation is damaged.
   D) Individual and contextual changes have no impact on identity formation.
   Answer: A
   Page Ref: 605
   Skill: Conceptual
   Objective: 16.3

37) Adolescents who assume that absolute truth is always attainable tend to be
   A) foreclosed.
   B) identity diffused.
   C) in a state of moratorium.
   D) identity achieved.
   Answer: A
   Page Ref: 605
   Skill: Conceptual
   Objective: 16.3

38) Tate's father wants to support his identity development. He should
   A) limit Tate's participation in extracurricular activities so he has more time to spend at home.
   B) discourage Tate from talking to others about identity concerns, as this will be confusing in his own identity search.
   C) encourage him to avoid vocational training programs during adolescence because this makes teens feel "locked in" to a certain career choice.
   D) collaborate with Tate when solving problems and allow Tate to voice his own opinions.
   Answer: D
   Page Ref: 605
   Skill: Applied
   Objective: 16.3

39) The lowest levels of warm, open communication at home are reported by adolescents who are
   A) foreclosed.
   B) identity diffused.
   C) in a state of moratorium.
   D) identity achieved.
   Answer: B
   Page Ref: 605
   Skill: Factual
   Objective: 16.3

40) Hannah has warm, trusting peer ties. Recent research suggests that Hannah will also be
    A) more involved in exploring relationship issues.
    B) less involved in career exploration.
    C) higher in identity diffusion.
    D) foreclosed.
Answer: A
Page Ref: 605
Skill: Applied
Objective: 16.3

41) Which of the following statements regarding schools and identity development is true?
    A) Over the past 20 years, schools have had an increasingly negative impact on identity development.
    B) Schools foster identity development by promoting high-level thinking.
    C) Schools often interfere with identity development by emphasizing competition over learning.
    D) In school settings, boys tend to receive more encouragement than girls to develop a secure identity.
Answer: B
Page Ref: 605
Skill: Conceptual
Objective: 16.3

42) Maria feels a strong sense of ethnic-group membership and has attitudes and feelings associated with that membership. Maria is displaying
    A) a bicultural identity.
    B) an ethnic identity.
    C) identity foreclosure.
    D) identity confusion.
Answer: B
Page Ref: 607 Box: CI: Identity Development Among Ethnic Minority Adolescents
Skill: Applied
Objective: 16.3

43) For teenagers who are members of minority groups, a sense of ethnic-group membership
    A) is central to the quest for identity.
    B) often leads to distancing from the majority culture.
    C) is less important than a secure identity.
    D) can interfere with identity development.
Answer: A
Page Ref: 607 Box: CI: Identity Development Among Ethnic Minority Adolescents
Skill: Conceptual
Objective: 16.3

44) Adolescents who immigrate with their family to the United States from a collectivist culture demonstrate _____ the longer their family has been in the United States.
    A) increased rejection of mainstream U.S. values
    B) increased commitment to fulfilling family obligations and learning about their collectivist culture
    C) decreased ability to fit in with mainstream U.S. culture
    D) decreased commitment to obeying their parents and fulfilling family obligations
Answer: D
Page Ref: 607 Box: CI: Identity Development Among Ethnic Minority Adolescents
Skill: Factual
Objective: 16.3

45) Psychological distress resulting from conflict between the minority and host culture is called
   A) cognitive dissonance.
   B) a culture war.
   C) acculturative stress.
   D) xenophobia.
Answer: C
Page Ref: 607 Box: CI: Identity Development Among Ethnic Minority Adolescents
Skill: Factual
Objective: 16.3

46) Noelle is an African-American teenager who has explored and adopted the values from her own culture, as well as from the dominant Caucasian-American culture. Noelle has formed a _____ identity.
   A) weak
   B) diffused
   C) foreclosed
   D) bicultural
Answer: D
Page Ref: 607 Box: CI: Identity Development Among Ethnic Minority Adolescents
Skill: Applied
Objective: 16.3

47) The Heinz dilemma is a(n)
   A) classic example of an adolescent in moratorium, deliberating between two career choices.
   B) narrative used to assess adolescents' understanding of social conventions.
   C) example of an everyday moral conflict that young people encounter.
   D) story that presents a genuine conflict between two moral values.
Answer: D
Page Ref: 608
Skill: Factual
Objective: 16.4

48) According to Kohlberg, which is the most important factor in determining the maturity of responses to moral dilemmas?
   A) the reasoning behind the answer
   B) whether the child considers anyone else's perspective
   C) how the child uses emotion in determining the answer
   D) whether the child answers like other children his age
Answer: A
Page Ref: 608
Skill: Conceptual
Objective: 16.4

49) Kohlberg's moral stages correspond to
   A) Selman's perspective-taking stages.
   B) Erikson's psychosocial theory.
   C) Freud's psychosexual stages.
   D) Vygotsky's sociocultural theory.
Answer: A
Page Ref: 609
Skill: Conceptual
Objective: 16.4

50) Kohlberg and Piaget both believed that moral understanding
   A) continues to evolve over the course of the lifespan.
   B) could be reached by adhering closely to parental and cultural directives.
   C) was gained by actively grappling with moral issues and perspective taking.
   D) could lead to close-mindedness and intolerance if it was not grounded in a religious faith.
Answer: C
Page Ref: 609
Skill: Conceptual
Objective: 16.4

51) At which of Kohlberg's levels is morality externally controlled?
   A) preconventional
   B) conventional
   C) postconventional
   D) autonomous
Answer: A
Page Ref: 609
Skill: Factual
Objective: 16.4

52) At which of Kohlberg's stages would a child reason, "You do this for me, and I'll do this for you"? The _____ orientation.
   A) punishment and obedience
   B) instrumental purpose
   C) good boy-good girl
   D) social-order-maintaining
Answer: B
Page Ref: 609
Skill: Applied
Objective: 16.4

53) In response to the Heinz dilemma, Jolee explains, "If Heinz cares at all about what his family thinks of him, he won't let his wife die. He'd be a disgrace to his family's name." Jolee is in which of Kohlberg's stages?
   A) punishment and obedience orientation
   B) instrumental purpose orientation
   C) "good boy-good girl" orientation
   D) social-order-maintaining orientation
Answer: C
Page Ref: 610
Skill: Applied
Objective: 16.4

54) In response to the Heinz dilemma, Oliver explains, "Heinz shouldn't steal the drug because it's his duty as a citizen to obey the law. If everyone started breaking the law, there'd be no civilization!" Oliver is in which of Kohlberg's stages?
   A) punishment and obedience orientation
   B) instrumental purpose orientation
   C) "good boy-good girl" orientation
   D) social-order-maintaining orientation
Answer: D
Page Ref: 610
Skill: Applied
Objective: 16.4

55) In response to the Heinz dilemma, Mara explains, "Heinz ought to steal the drug. Obeying the law in this case goes against the reason for which the law was originally created. The law should be reinterpreted to take account of Heinz's right to save his wife's life." Mara is in which of Kohlberg's stages?
   A) instrumental purpose orientation
   B) social-order-maintaining orientation
   C) social contract orientation
   D) universal ethical principle orientation
   Answer: C
   Page Ref: 610
   Skill: Applied
   Objective: 16.4

56) In response to the Heinz dilemma, Seth explains, "If Heinz doesn't do everything he can to save his wife's life, he's valuing something more than the value of life. People have a mutual duty to save one another from dying." Seth is in which of Kohlberg's stages?
   A) instrumental purpose orientation
   B) social-order-maintaining orientation
   C) social contract orientation
   D) universal ethical principle orientation
   Answer: D
   Page Ref: 610–611
   Skill: Applied
   Objective: 16.4

57) Research on Kohlberg's stage sequence
   A) supports the order of the stages.
   B) indicates that movement through the stages is quite rapid.
   C) confirms the existence of Stage 6.
   D) shows that postconventional morality is common in adulthood.
   Answer: A
   Page Ref: 611
   Skill: Factual
   Objective: 16.4

58) Research on Kohlberg's stage sequence indicates that by early adulthood, Stage _____ is the typical response; few people move beyond it.
   A) 2
   B) 3
   C) 4
   D) 5
   Answer: C
   Page Ref: 611
   Skill: Factual
   Objective: 16.4

59) Which of the following statements is true?
   A) Responses to moral dilemmas tend to generalize to everyday moral conflicts.
   B) Adolescents rarely report feeling confused or tempted over real-life dilemmas.
   C) Situational factors seem to play a very small part in people's responses to moral dilemmas.
   D) Real-life problems seem to elicit reasoning below a person's actual capacity.
   Answer: D
   Page Ref: 611
   Skill: Conceptual
   Objective: 16.4

60) Research on Kohlberg's theory indicates that
   A) most young people reach Stage 6 by the end of high school.
   B) few people move beyond Stage 4.
   C) males are more advanced in moral reasoning than females.
   D) real-life moral reasoning is based on social conformity.
   Answer: B
   Page Ref: 611
   Skill: Conceptual
   Objective: 16.4

61) Like Piaget's cognitive stages, Kohlberg's moral stages
   A) are loosely organized and overlapping.
   B) facilitate concrete reasoning.
   C) are hypothetical.
   D) are universal.
   Answer: A
   Page Ref: 611
   Skill: Conceptual
   Objective: 16.4

62) According to Gilligan, feminine morality is based on
   A) rights and justice.
   B) an ethic of care.
   C) irrational reasoning.
   D) the same principles as male morality.
   Answer: B
   Page Ref: 612
   Skill: Conceptual
   Objective: 16.5

63) According to Gilligan, a concern for others is
   A) a different, but no less valid, basis of morality.
   B) a less valid basis for morality than justice.
   C) highly valued in Kohlberg's theory.
   D) limited in young women.
   Answer: A
   Page Ref: 612
   Skill: Conceptual
   Objective: 16.5

64) Most recent studies _____ Gilligan's claim that Kohlberg's approach underestimates the moral maturity of females.
   A) support
   B) do not support
   C) are inconclusive about
   D) have failed to test
   Answer: B
   Page Ref: 612
   Skill: Factual
   Objective: 16.5

65) Research shows that on both hypothetical and real-life moral dilemmas,
    A) themes of justice occur more often than caring.
    B) males reason at a much lower level than females.
    C) females actually emphasize themes of justice over caring.
    D) themes of justice and caring appear in the responses of both males and females.
Answer: D
Page Ref: 612
Skill: Factual
Objective: 16.5

66) Research shows that although the morality of males and females taps the orientations of both justice and care, females do tend to stress
    A) empathic perspective taking.
    B) justice.
    C) justice and care equally.
    D) rights.
Answer: A
Page Ref: 612
Skill: Factual
Objective: 16.5

67) It is likely that Norwegian males and females score similarly on complex reasoning about care issues because
    A) civic engagement is required for graduation in all Norwegian high schools.
    B) Norwegian culture induces boys and men to think deeply about interpersonal obligations.
    C) Norwegian females are less concerned with the ethic of care than females from other cultures.
    D) most public schools incorporate a moral curriculum beginning in the elementary years.
Answer: B
Page Ref: 612
Skill: Factual
Objective: 16.5

68) As they work to reconcile personal rights and community obligations, adolescents increasingly consider the overlap between
    A) preconventional morality and racial prejudice.
    B) moral education and role confusion.
    C) identity development and matters of personal choice.
    D) moral imperatives and social conventions.
Answer: D
Page Ref: 613
Skill: Factual
Objective: 16.6

69) Which adolescent is likely to experience greater gains in moral reasoning?
    A) Bradley, who is very competitive
    B) Brenda, who is open-minded
    C) Brady, who is confident
    D) Butler, who is introverted
Answer: B
Page Ref: 613
Skill: Applied
Objective: 16.6

70) A powerful predictor of moral reasoning is
    A) personality type.
    B) religious affiliation.
    C) years of schooling completed.
    D) independence from parents.
Answer: C
Page Ref: 614
Skill: Factual
Objective: 16.6

71) Which of the following is true about the impact of peer interaction on moral reasoning?
    A) Due to high rates of peer pressure, peer interaction in adolescence often interferes with advanced moral reasoning.
    B) The more time young people spend with peers, the less mature their moral reasoning.
    C) Interaction among peers who confront and engage each other about moral issues leads to gains in moral reasoning.
    D) Throughout adolescence, peers are more influential in moral decision making than parents.
Answer: C
Page Ref: 614
Skill: Conceptual
Objective: 16.6

72) Reasoning at Kohlberg's Stage 4 and above depends on
    A) understanding the role of larger social structures in resolving moral conflict.
    B) understanding the content of hypothetical moral dilemmas.
    C) the age and gender of the respondent.
    D) the ability to deal with day-to-day conflict, particularly with parents.
Answer: A
Page Ref: 614
Skill: Conceptual
Objective: 16.6

73) In which of the following cultural environments is moral development especially advanced?
    A) United States cities
    B) tribal and village cultures
    C) Israeli cities
    D) Israeli kibbutzim
Answer: D
Page Ref: 614
Skill: Factual
Objective: 16.6

74) In a study conducted in India, the most morally mature individuals
    A) were those who had access to a moral curriculum in high school.
    B) reached Stage 5 or 6 during the transition to high school. .
    C) were females who grew up in large extended-family households. .
    D) explained that a moral solution should not be the burden of a single individual.
Answer: D
Page Ref: 615
Skill: Factual
Objective: 16.6

75) Collectivist cultures place moral responsibility on the entire society. This raises a question about whether Kohlberg's highest stages
    A) represent a culturally specific rather than universal way of thinking.
    B) represent hypothetical constructs or real-life dilemmas.
    C) are limited to non-Western societies.
    D) can be attained by young people in industrialized nations.
Answer: A
Page Ref: 615
Skill: Factual
Objective: 16.6

76) As a teenager, John shows higher-stage thinking on Kohlberg's dilemmas. Compared with his peers, John is likely to
    A) state that people should help others, but is unlikely to do so in real life.
    B) help others and defend victims of injustice.
    C) cheat in school just as much as other teens.
    D) emphasize an ethic of care.
Answer: B
Page Ref: 615
Skill: Applied
Objective: 16.6

77) In which country do the greatest percentage of the population report being religious?
    A) Italy
    B) Great Britain
    C) Germany
    D) the United States
Answer: D
Page Ref: 615, 617
Skill: Factual
Objective: 16.6

78) Teenagers with a sense of civic responsibility are most likely to identify _____ as a cause for homelessness.
    A) low intelligence
    B) lack of job skills
    C) unfair government practices
    D) personal problems
Answer: C
Page Ref: 616 Box: SI: Education: Development of Civic Responsibility
Skill: Conceptual
Objective: 16.6

79) Schools that have _____ promote a sense of civic responsibility.
    A) a democratic climate
    B) a diverse range of mentors
    C) vocational courses
    D) a range of extracurricular opportunities
Answer: A
Page Ref: 616 Box: SI: Education: Development of Civic Responsibility
Skill: Factual
Objective: 16.6

80) Miguel spent a year volunteering in a homeless shelter. At the end of the year, Miguel is likely to
   A) attribute homelessness to personal or individual factors.
   B) become overwhelmed by social injustices.
   C) become desensitized to social injustices.
   D) redefine his own identity to include a responsibility to combat the misfortunes of others.
   Answer: D
   Page Ref: 616 Box: SI: Education: Development of Civic Responsibility
   Skill: Applied
   Objective: 16.6

81) Which of the following statements about formal religious involvement during adolescence is true?
   A) Formal religious involvement declines during adolescence.
   B) Formal religious involvement increases during adolescence.
   C) Nearly 70 percent of U.S. adolescents attend church on a weekly basis.
   D) Many young people change religious denominations during high school or college.
   Answer: A
   Page Ref: 617
   Skill: Conceptual
   Objective: 16.6

82) The development of a personally meaningful, religious identity
   A) is usually resolved by the late teens or early twenties.
   B) is not resolved until middle adulthood or later.
   C) usually begins during early childhood and is complete by adolescence.
   D) coincides with increased participation in religious activities during adolescence.
   Answer: A
   Page Ref: 617
   Skill: Factual
   Objective: 16.6

83) Opponents of Kohlberg's theory argue in favor of a
   A) more flexable framework for moral development.
   B) new emphasis on social order and ideal reciprocity.
   C) pragmatic approach to morality.
   D) instrumental stage of civic responsibility.
   Answer: C
   Page Ref: 617
   Skill: Factual
   Objective: 16.7

84) Gender intensification refers to
   A) a cognitive distortion.
   B) gender-role flexibility.
   C) increased gender stereotyping of attitudes and behavior.
   D) reduced gender-role bias by parents and teachers.
   Answer: C
   Page Ref: 618
   Skill: Factual
   Objective: 16.8

85) How does gender stereotyping change during adolescence for girls?
   A) Gender intensification decreases among girls.
   B) Gender intensification is stronger for girls.
   C) Girls feel more free to experiment with "other-gender" activities.
   D) Gender stereotyping inteferes with girls' involvement in mixed-sex cliques.
   Answer: B
   Page Ref: 618
   Skill: Factual
   Objective: 16.8

86) Which of the following tends to be associated with better-than-average psychological health in adolescence, especially for girls?
   A) gender intensification
   B) a feminine gender-role identity
   C) an androgynous gender-role identity
   D) gender-typed pressures from others
   Answer: C
   Page Ref: 619
   Skill: Factual
   Objective: 16.8

87) As Juanita tries to develop a separate sense of self, she tries to rely less on her parents and more on herself. Juanita is striving for
   A) moral self-relevance.
   B) an ideal self.
   C) a secure identity.
   D) autonomy.
   Answer: D
   Page Ref: 619
   Skill: Applied
   Objective: 16.9

88) During adolescence, teenagers deidealize their parents. This contributes to
   A) warmer sibling ties.
   B) a rise in parent-child conflict.
   C) a shift from authoritative to authoritarian child rearing.
   D) a decline in academic achievement.
   Answer: B
   Page Ref: 619
   Skill: Factual
   Objective: 16.9

89) The _____ child-rearing style is most effective in supporting cognitive and social development in adolescence.
   A) authoritarian
   B) permissive
   C) authoritative
   D) controlling
   Answer: C
   Page Ref: 620
   Skill: Conceptual
   Objective: 16.9

90) Parent-child relations can be better understood if we keep in mind that
    A) both parents and teenagers are undergoing a major life transition.
    B) parents are undergoing a major life transition, but teenagers are not.
    C) teenagers are undergoing a major life transition, but parents are not.
    D) teenagers are often moody and irrational.
Answer: A
Page Ref: 620
Skill: Conceptual
Objective: 16.9

91) Compared to non-immigrant parents, immigrant parents
    A) usually grant their adolescents more freedom.
    B) engage in harsher, more coercive parenting.
    C) react more strongly to adolescent disagreements.
    D) actively discourage other-sex friendships.
Answer: C
Page Ref: 621
Skill: Factual
Objective: 16.9

92) The Marinuzzis are a well-functioning family who are experiencing mild conflicts with their teenage son. They should know that these conflicts
    A) will facilitate identity and autonomy by helping their son learn to express and tolerate disagreement.
    B) will continue to escalate throughout the high school years and then will gradually decrease.
    C) are common among young people who are abusing alcohol or drugs.
    D) are unusual for most adolescents and may indicate that their son is depressed.
Answer: A
Page Ref: 621
Skill: Applied
Objective: 16.9

93) Throughout adolescence, what is the single most consistent predictor of a teenager's mental health?
    A) academic achievement
    B) peer group affiliation
    C) SES
    D) parent-child relationship
Answer: D
Page Ref: 621
Skill: Conceptual
Objective: 16.9

94) Mr. and Mrs. Green are financially secure and have careers that do not introduce a lot of stress into their lives. When dealing with their teenage son, the Greens will probably
    A) engage in permissive child rearing.
    B) provide him with too little autonomy.
    C) provide him with too much autonomy.
    D) find it easier to grant him the appropriate amount of autonomy.
Answer: D
Page Ref: 621
Skill: Applied
Objective: 16.9

95) Compared to childhood, adolescent sibling relationships
    A) become more intense.
    B) become less intense.
    C) are characterized by greater competition.
    D) become hostile and quarrelsome.
    Answer: B
    Page Ref: 622
    Skill: Factual
    Objective: 16.9

96) Teenagers in the United States spend more time together outside the classroom than teenagers in Europe or East Asia. The difference is probably due to
    A) lower rates of maternal employment in the United States.
    B) less demanding academic standards in the United States.
    C) fewer public gathering places for adolescents in the United States.
    D) greater flexibility in school hours in Europe and East Asia.
    Answer: B
    Page Ref: 622
    Skill: Conceptual
    Objective: 16.10

97) When asked about the meaning of friendship, teenagers stress which of the following characteristics?
    A) attractiveness, compatibility, and loyalty
    B) common interests and trust
    C) attractiveness, similarity, and common interests
    D) intimacy, mutual understanding, and loyalty
    Answer: D
    Page Ref: 622–623
    Skill: Factual
    Objective: 16.10

98) Compared to childhood friends, adolescent friends
    A) know each other better as personalities.
    B) compete more and cooperate less.
    C) do not have to work as hard to preserve the relationship.
    D) are less sensitive to one another's needs and desires.
    Answer: A
    Page Ref: 623
    Skill: Conceptual
    Objective: 16.10

99) Research shows that compared to girls, boys
    A) tend to corumniate among their friends.
    B) focus on competition and conflict when talking with friends.
    C) form friendships that are more intimate.
    D) have fewer friends.
    Answer: B
    Page Ref: 624
    Skill: Factual
    Objective: 16.10

100) Which of the characteristics of close friendships can trigger anxiety and depression?
   A) loyalty
   B) trustworthiness
   C) corumination
   D) faithfulness
   Answer: C
   Page Ref: 624
   Skill: Factual
   Objective: 16.10

101) Of the following, who is MOST likely to have other-sex friends?
   A) Cassidy, an average student who is not well-known
   B) Marie, who reached puberty earlier than her classmates
   C) Chase, who frequently plays sports with his many male friends
   D) Gwenneth, who is neither popular nor unpopular
   Answer: B
   Page Ref: 624
   Skill: Applied
   Objective: 16.10

102) Self-disclosure to friends is greater than self-disclosure to romantic partners
   A) until fifth grade.
   B) until late adolescence.
   C) until the college years.
   D) from childhood onward.
   Answer: C
   Page Ref: 624
   Skill: Factual
   Objective: 16.10

103) Among boys who lack same-sex friends, friendships with girls are associated with
   A) increased aggression and antisocial behavior.
   B) a higher risk of being bullied by peers.
   C) increased feelings of competence.
   D) greater motivation in school.
   Answer: C
   Page Ref: 624
   Skill: Conceptual
   Objective: 16.10

104) Why is building Internet relationships so appealing to young people?
   A) It allows them to anonymously engage in antisocial behavior without fear of getting caught.
   B) As teens strive for autonomy and identity, the Internet opens up vast alternatives beyond their immediate community.
   C) Because teens tend to be more secretive, the Internet allows them a space to maintain their private lives apart from their parents and friends.
   D) The Internet is an emotionally safer place to develop relationships, particularly romantic relationships, than school.
   Answer: B
   Page Ref: 625
   Skill: Conceptual
   Objective: 16.10

105) Which of the following is true about adolescent friendships?
   A) They limit opportunities for self-exploration.
   B) They reduce adolescents' positive feelings about school.
   C) They lead to daily hassles in getting along with others.
   D) They are related to psychological health and competence.
   Answer: D
   Page Ref: 625
   Skill: Conceptual
   Objective: 16.10

106) Ella has five good friends with whom she spends most of her time. This group of girls, who resemble each other in family background, attitudes, and values, is called a
   A) crowd.
   B) clique.
   C) club.
   D) peer group.
   Answer: B
   Page Ref: 626
   Skill: Applied
   Objective: 16.10

107) Which of the following is true about adolescent crowds?
   A) They promote intimate interaction with the other sex.
   B) They grant adolescents an identity within the larger social structure of the school.
   C) They encourage delinquency and antisocial behavior.
   D) They have little impact, either positive or negative, on social development.
   Answer: B
   Page Ref: 626
   Skill: Conceptual
   Objective: 16.10

108) Adolescents who describe their parents as authoritative tend to be members of _____ crowds.
   A) "popular"
   B) "jock"
   C) "nerd"
   D) "druggie"
   Answer: A
   Page Ref: 626
   Skill: Factual
   Objective: 16.10

109) The positive impact of having competent and self-controlled peers is greatest for teenagers whose own parents are
   A) authoritative.
   B) authoritarian.
   C) permissive.
   D) uninvolved.
   Answer: A
   Page Ref: 627
   Skill: Conceptual
   Objective: 16.10

110) One benefit of _____ is that they provide a supportive context for boys and girls to get to know one another and offer models for how to interact with the other sex without having to be intimate.
   A) same-sex cliques
   B) mixed-sex cliques
   C) crowds
   D) groups
Answer: B
Page Ref: 627
Skill: Factual
Objective: 16.10

111) As young people progress through the adolescent years,
   A) crowd membership becomes more important.
   B) mixed-sex cliques gain importance.
   C) deviant crowds lose members.
   D) deviant crowds gain members.
Answer: C
Page Ref: 627
Skill: Factual
Objective: 16.10

112) The "crowd" offers adolescents
   A) a place for trying out roles in the absence of adult monitoring.
   B) a situation for experimenting with values.
   C) a context for acquiring new social skills.
   D) the security of a temporary identity as they separate from the family.
Answer: D
Page Ref: 627
Skill: Conceptual
Objective: 16.10

113) When asked about her reason for wanting to date, 14-year-old Kayla is most likely to say she wants to
   A) gain status with her peers.
   B) share interesting activities with someone.
   C) please her parents.
   D) find someone who would make a good permanent partner.
Answer: A
Page Ref: 627
Skill: Applied
Objective: 16.10

114) During adolescence, intimacy in dating relationships typically _____ intimacy in same-sex friendships.
   A) is advanced compared to
   B) lags behind
   C) appears at about the same time as
   D) substitutes for
Answer: B
Page Ref: 627
Skill: Factual
Objective: 16.10

115) Early and frequent dating is associated with
    A) mature behavior.
    B) high academic achievement.
    C) drug use and delinquency.
    D) intimacy.
Answer: C
Page Ref: 628
Skill: Factual
Objective: 16.10

116) Thirteen-year-old Donna, whose family life is marked by abuse, has already started dating. There is a strong potential for Donna to
    A) practice sexual abstinence.
    B) become more popular among her peers.
    C) engage in unhealthy eating behaviors.
    D) experience dating violence.
Answer: D
Page Ref: 628
Skill: Applied
Objective: 16.10

117) The short duration of high school romances is probably
    A) exaggerated; first romances are usually long-lasting.
    B) due to competition and jealousy from friends.
    C) due to difficulties caused by one partner moving away for college or work.
    D) a result of young people still forming their identities.
Answer: D
Page Ref: 628
Skill: Conceptual
Objective: 16.10

118) Which of the following is true about peer conformity?
    A) Most teenagers blindly do what their peers ask, regardless of their age or relationship with parents.
    B) Adolescents feel most pressured to conform to obvious aspects of peer culture, such as grooming and participation in social activities.
    C) Peer pressure to engage in antisocial acts is greater than peer pressure to engage in proadult behavior.
    D) Authoritarian child rearing is related to adolescents resisting peer pressure.
Answer: B
Page Ref: 628
Skill: Factual
Objective: 16.11

119) As Stan progresses through adolescence, his parents will probably find that they have the greatest influence on his
    A) educational plans.
    B) friends.
    C) grooming.
    D) dating.
Answer: A
Page Ref: 628–629
Skill: Applied
Objective: 16.11

120) Which of the following is the most common psychological problem of the teenage years?
   A) anorexia nervosa
   B) drug abuse
   C) depression
   D) social anxiety
Answer: C
Page Ref: 629
Skill: Factual
Objective: 16.12

121) Derek is chronically depressed, which means that he
   A) experiences mild to moderate feelings of depression.
   B) is gloomy and self-critical for many months and sometimes even years.
   C) bounces back after short periods of depression.
   D) is experiencing an incurable and lifelong condition.
Answer: B
Page Ref: 629
Skill: Applied
Objective: 16.12

122) In industrialized nations, depression
   A) occurs at the same rate in adolescence as it did in middle childhood.
   B) symptoms increase sharply between the ages of 12 and 16.
   C) occurs equally as often in girls as in boys.
   D) does not seem to affect identity development.
Answer: B
Page Ref: 630
Skill: Factual
Objective: 16.12

123) Which of the following statements is true?
   A) Adolescent girls experience depressive symptoms more often than adolescent boys, but this difference disappears in early adulthood.
   B) In most cultures, there are no gender differences in the frequency of depressive symptoms.
   C) Adolescent girls experience depressive symptoms more often than adolescent boys, and this difference is sustained throughout the lifespan.
   D) Adolescent boys experience depressive symptoms more often than adolescent girls, and this difference is sustained throughout the lifespan.
Answer: C
Page Ref: 630
Skill: Factual
Objective: 16.12

124) Genes can induce depression by affecting
   A) quality and quantity of sleep.
   B) the overall quantity of neurotransmitters in the brain.
   C) the development of brain regions involved in inhibiting negative emotion.
   D) the development of social skills.
Answer: C
Page Ref: 630
Skill: Conceptual
Objective: 16.12

125) Depression is more likely to occur in
    A) adolescents who experience learned helplessness.
    B) fraternal twins than in identical twins.
    C) high-SES adolescent boys.
    D) adolescents with a masculine gender identity.
Answer: A
Page Ref: 630
Skill: Factual
Objective: 16.12

126) Rates of adolescent depression are similar for males and females in
    A) developing countries.
    B) industrialized nations.
    C) adolescence, but not in adulthood.
    D) inner-cities.
Answer: A
Page Ref: 630
Skill: Factual
Objective: 16.12

127) The suicide rate
    A) is highest during the adolescent years.
    B) increases over the lifespan but jumps sharply at adolescence.
    C) remains steady over the lifespan.
    D) declines slightly in adolescence.
Answer: B
Page Ref: 631
Skill: Factual
Objective: 16.12

128) Of the following, suicide rates are highest in
    A) Canada.
    B) Japan.
    C) the United States.
    D) Finland.
Answer: D
Page Ref: 631
Skill: Factual
Objective: 16.12

129) Which of the following is true?
    A) The adolescent suicide rate is 3 to 4 times higher among boys than girls.
    B) Boys attempt suicide more often than girls.
    C) Compared to boys, girls are more likely to use suicide methods that lead to instant death.
    D) The adolescent suicide rate is about the same for boys and girls.
Answer: A
Page Ref: 631
Skill: Factual
Objective: 16.12

130) Which of the following young people is at greatest risk for suicide?
   A) Jennifer, who is Hispanic
   B) Claire, who is African American
   C) Alyssia, who is Native American
   D) Leah, who is Caucasian American
Answer: C
Page Ref: 631
Skill: Factual
Objective: 16.12

131) The largest group of teenagers who commit suicide
   A) are withdrawn.
   B) show antisocial tendencies.
   C) are highly intelligent.
   D) are girls.
Answer: B
Page Ref: 632
Skill: Factual
Objective: 16.12

132) Events like conflict with parents, the breakup of an important relationship, or the humiliation of being caught engaging in irresponsible or antisocial acts are all
   A) stressors that can foster depression, but typically do not lead to a suicide attempt.
   B) triggers that result in more delinquent acts.
   C) contributing factors to the imaginary audience and the personal fable.
   D) stressors that can trigger a suicide attempt.
Answer: D
Page Ref: 632
Skill: Factual
Objective: 16.12

133) Of the following, which factors contribute to the sharp rise in suicide from childhood to adolescence?
   A) adolescent impulsiveness and teenagers' stormy nature
   B) improved ability to plan ahead and learned helplessness
   C) increased emotional distance from parents and high SES
   D) teenagers' inability to think about the future
Answer: B
Page Ref: 632
Skill: Factual
Objective: 16.12

134) Grant's parents have noticed that he seems to be putting his affairs in order — smoothing over troubled relationships and giving away treasured possessions. This indicates that Grant may
   A) be contemplating suicide.
   B) be entering Erikson's stage of identity confusion.
   C) have reached Kohlberg's "good boy-good girl" orientation.
   D) be about to run away from home.
Answer: A
Page Ref: 633
Skill: Applied
Objective: 16.12

135) Lydia says, "I hate my life and I just want to die. Besides, everyone would be better off without me — better if I had never been born." You should
    A) try to take her mind off her problems by taking her to a movie or some other activity.
    B) agree with her initially. If she thinks you are on her side by not opposing her plan, she is more likely to be convinced by you later.
    C) make her get professional help right away. Do not try to talk with her yourself, as untrained counseling can actually increase the risk of suicide.
    D) empathize as much as you can and ask if she has a plan for killing herself. If her plan involves a method and a time, the risk of suicide is very high.
Answer: D
Page Ref: 633
Skill: Applied
Objective: 16.12

136) Which of the following statements is true?
    A) According to your text, gun control legislation would have no impact on the number of teenage suicides.
    B) Thoughts of suicide should be viewed as normal and just a passing phase.
    C) Most, if not all, successful suicides are sudden and impulsive.
    D) Teenage suicides often occur in clusters.
Answer: D
Page Ref: 633
Skill: Factual
Objective: 16.12

137) When teenagers are asked directly and confidentially, _____ admit that they are guilty of a delinquent offense.
    A) almost none
    B) about half
    C) almost all
    D) only boys
Answer: C
Page Ref: 634
Skill: Factual
Objective: 16.13

138) Delinquency usually _____ over adolescence and then _____.
    A) declines; rises
    B) rises; rises further
    C) declines; declines further
    D) rises; declines
Answer: D
Page Ref: 634
Skill: Factual
Objective: 16.13

139) For the majority of adolescents, a minor brush with the law
    A) does not lead to a life of antisocial behavior.
    B) is an early warning of more serious problems in the future.
    C) is a sign of drug abuse.
    D) is usually the result of peer pressure.
Answer: A
Page Ref: 634
Skill: Factual
Objective: 16.13

140) Low-SES ethnic minority teenagers
    A) commit the majority of major crimes in this country.
    B) have a greater propensity to engage in violence and other lawbreaking acts.
    C) are more likely to be arrested, charged, and punished for crimes than their higher-SES white and Asian counterparts.
    D) are arrested, charged, and punished less often than their higher-SES white and Asian peers.
Answer: C
Page Ref: 634
Skill: Factual
Objective: 16.13

141) Chronic delinquents typically
    A) experience peer rejection in childhood.
    B) show few academic problems in childhood.
    C) behave rebelliously despite good parental discipline.
    D) are unresponsive to pressures of the peer group.
Answer: A
Page Ref: 634
Skill: Conceptual
Objective: 16.13

142) Which of the following consistently characterizes delinquent youths?
    A) social competence
    B) permissive parenting
    C) low-warmth, high-conflict families
    D) authoritarian child rearing
Answer: C
Page Ref: 634
Skill: Conceptual
Objective: 16.13

143) Why do delinquent youths tend to stick together?
    A) to avoid social isolation and bolster their fragile self-esteem
    B) to more effectively commit crimes
    C) because larger groups tend to gain more status and respect in local communities
    D) because they have similar interests and values
Answer: A
Page Ref: 634
Skill: Conceptual
Objective: 16.12

144) The mayor of Central City wants to reduce its youth crime rate. Based on research findings, which of the following would you recommend?
    A) Start school earlier in the day and end it later in the day.
    B) Require ongoing extracurricular involvement in public high schools.
    C) Decrease the amount of homework assigned to students in an effort to bridge the adult-adolescent divide.
    D) Promote high-quality teaching in schools and create work-study vocational education programs.
Answer: D
Page Ref: 634
Skill: Applied
Objective: 16.13

145) For disruptive, peer-rejected adolescents, antisocial friends facilitate each other's violent behavior while also
    A) relieving loneliness.
    B) lifting depressive moods.
    C) enhancing popularity.
    D) fostering a more realistic self-esteem.
Answer: A
Page Ref: 634
Skill: Conceptual
Objective: 16.13

146) Rick has overly high self-esteem, despite his academic difficulties and status as a social outcast. When another student challenges his arrogant behavior, he is likely to
    A) withdraw and become depressed.
    B) lash out in anger.
    C) respond with relational aggression.
    D) reconsider his behavior and display more socially appropriate responses.
Answer: B
Page Ref: 635
Skill: Applied
Objective: 16.13

147) The best way to combat adjustment problems in adolescence is through
    A) strict parental supervision.
    B) rigorous academic requirements in high school.
    C) police curfews that keep teenagers off the streets at night.
    D) prevention, beginning early in life.
Answer: D
Page Ref: 635
Skill: Factual
Objective: 16.13

148) Treating serious offenders
    A) is best accomplished by addressing one aspect of delinquency at a time.
    B) with short-term comprehensive interventions is most effective.
    C) with work experience programs and summer camps has been shown to be ineffective.
    D) combines family and peer intervention in order to integrate youths into more positive environments.
Answer: D
Page Ref: 635
Skill: Conceptual
Objective: 16.13

149) Longitudinal research reveals that compared to conduct problems that begin in adolescence, early-onset delinquency
    A) is less likely to lead to a life-course pattern of criminality.
    B) involves less severe crimes.
    C) often emerges out of dysfunctional peer relations.
    D) is more likely to lead to a life-course pattern of criminality.
Answer: D
Page Ref: 636 Box: B&E: Two Routes to Adolescent Delinquency
Skill: Factual
Objective: 16.13

150) Children with early-onset delinquency
    A) feel closer to their families than those whose delinquent behavior begins in adolescence.
    B) have subtle deficits in cognitive functioning.
    C) show restlessness and willfulness as early as age 7.
    D) often outgrow their dysfunctional behavior by late adolescence.
Answer: B
Page Ref: 636 Box: B&E: Two Routes to Adolescent Delinquency
Skill: Factual
Objective: 16.13

151) Compared to their early-onset counterparts, adolescent-onset delinquent teenagers
    A) are more socially isolated and violent.
    B) often have moderate to severe learning difficulties.
    C) are much more likely to demonstrate continued criminal behavior into adulthood.
    D) have conduct problems that arise from the peer context of early adolescence.
Answer: D
Page Ref: 636 Box: B&E: Two Routes to Adolescent Delinquency
Skill: Factual
Objective: 16.13

152) Johnson County officials are considering four options to help late-onset adolescent delinquents. Based upon research findings, which proposal would you recommend?
    A) Proposal 1: Implement longer prison terms for repeat offenders.
    B) Proposal 2: Eliminate juvenile court and prosecute teenagers in adult court.
    C) Proposal 3: Hold parents of delinquent youths legally accountable for their children's behavior.
    D) Proposal 4: Help young people to find satisfying jobs.
Answer: D
Page Ref: 637 Box: B&E: Two Routes to Adolescent Delinquency
Skill: Applied
Objective: 16.13

153) Research shows that most teenagers
    A) engage in serious antisocial acts, although they are rarely caught or prosecuted.
    B) do not show serious depression, suicidal tendencies, or persistent antisocial behavior.
    C) experience severe bouts of depression, especially those in industrialized nations.
    D) seriously consider suicide, although few actually make an attempt.
Answer: B
Page Ref: 636
Skill: Factual
Objective: 16.14

154) Which of the following resources are shown to faciliate resilience in adolescents?
    A) working a full-time job
    B) early dating
    C) affiliation with a religious organization
    D) other-sex friendships
Answer: C
Page Ref: 637
Skill: Conceptual
Objective: 16.14

ESSAY

155) Describe the four identity statuses described by James Marcia, and cite factors that promote identity development.

Answer: Using a clinical interviewing procedure devised by James Marcia, researchers evaluate adolescents' progress in identity development on two key criteria derived from Erikson's theory: exploration and commitment. Their various combinations yield four identity statuses: 1) identity achievement, commitment to values, beliefs, and goals following a period of exploration; 2) identity moratorium, exploration without having reached commitment; 3) identity foreclosure, commitment in the absence of exploration; and 4) identity diffusion, an apathetic state characterized by lack of both exploration and commitment.

A wide variety of factors affect identity development. Personality characteristics—in particular, a flexible, open-minded approach to grappling with competing beliefs and values—are important. Also, when the family serves as a "secure base" from which teenagers can confidently move out into the wider world, identity development is enhanced. Classrooms that promote high-level thinking; extracurricular and community activities that permit teenagers to take on responsible roles; teachers and counselors who encourage low-SES and ethnic minority students to go to college; and vocational training programs that immerse adolescents in the real world of adult work foster identity development. Finally, the larger cultural context and historical time period influence the timing of exploration and commitment in specific areas, such as political beliefs, gender-role preference, and vocational choice.

Page Ref: 603–606

156) Explain why students from ethnic minority backgrounds face difficulties in developing an identity, and give suggestions on how to help minority adolescents resolve identity conflicts constructively.

Answer: As they develop cognitively and become more sensitive to feedback from the social environment, minority youths become painfully aware that they are targets of prejudice and discrimination. This discovery complicates their efforts to develop a sense of cultural belonging and a set of personally meaningful goals.

Minority youths often feel caught between the standards of the larger society and the traditions of their culture of origin. In many immigrant families from collectivist cultures, adolescents' commitment to obeying their parents and fulfilling family obligations lessens as the family spends more time in their new country. Other minority teenagers react to years of shattered self-esteem, school failure, and barriers to success in the mainstream culture by defining themselves in contrast to majority values.

Because it is painful and confusing, minority high school students often dodge the task of forming an ethnic identity. Many are diffused or foreclosed on ethnic identity issues. But when family members encourage them to deal with prejudice and discrimination proactively, by disproving stereotypes of low achievement and antisocial behavior, young people generally are highly committed to their ethnicity. In addition, adolescents whose families taught them the history, traditions, values, and language of their ethnic group and who frequently interact with same-ethnicity peers are more likely to forge a favorable ethnic identity.

Society can help minority adolescents resolve conflicts constructively by: 1) promoting effective parenting in which children and adolescents benefit from family ethnic pride yet are encouraged to explore the meaning of ethnicity in their own lives; 2) ensuring that schools respect minority youths' native languages, unique learning styles, and right to a high-quality education; and 3) fostering contact with peers of the same ethnicity along with respect between ethnic groups.

Page Ref: 607

157) What types of moral dilemmas do people face in real life, and how do they resolve them? How does this compare to their approach to hypothetical problems like Kohlberg's Heinz dilemma?

Answer: Kohlberg's theory emphasizes rationally weighing alternatives when solving hypothetical moral dilemmas. Real-life conflicts, such as whether to continue helping a friend who is taking advantage of you, often elicit moral reasoning below a person's actual capacity because they bring out practical considerations and mix cognition with intense emotion. In working through these challenges, people most often use reasoning, but they also mention other strategies, such as talking through issues with others, relying on intuition that their decision was right, and calling on religious and spiritual ideas. And they report feeling drained, confused, and torn by temptation—an emotional side of moral judgment not tapped by hypothetical situations.

Page Ref: 611, 615

158) Renee is approaching early adolescence. How will Renee's gender-typed behavior likely change as she moves through adolescence? What factors will likely contribute to these changes?

Answer: Research suggests that early adolescence is a period of gender intensification-increased gender stereotyping of attitudes and behavior. Although it occurs for both sexes, it is stronger for girls. Compared to the middle school years, girls like Renee feel less free to experiment with "other-gender" activities and behavior. Gender intensification seems to decline by middle to late adolescence. Biological, social, and cognitive factors are involved in gender intensification. Puberty magnifies sex differences in appearance, causing teenagers to spend more time thinking about themselves in gender-linked ways. Pubertal changes also prompt gender-typed pressures from others. Parents—especially those with traditional gender-role beliefs—may encourage "gender-appropriate" activities and behavior to a greater extent than they did in middle childhood. And when adolescents start to date, they often become more gender typed as a way of increasing their attractiveness to other-sex peers. Finally, cognitive changes—in particular, greater concern with what others think—make young teenagers more responsive to gender-role expectations.

Page Ref: 618–619

159) Describe adolescent dating. Why do teenagers date? What are the positive and/or negative consequences of dating in adolescence? How do circumstances differ for homosexual young people?

Answer: The beginning of dating is regulated by cultural expectations. Western societies tolerate and even encourage romantic involvements between teens, which typically begin in junior high school. Younger teens are more likely to say that they date for recreation and to achieve status with their peers, whereas older adolescents are looking for someone who offers personal compatibility, companionship, affection, and social support. Early, frequent dating does not foster social maturity. Instead, it is related to drug use, delinquency, and poor academic achievement. While early adolescent boys involved in dating gain in status among their same-sex peers, girls often experience more conflicts due to competition and jealousy from other girls. Furthermore, romantic relationships often draw adolescents away from time with friends. As long as it does not begin too soon, dating provides adolescents with lessons in cooperation, etiquette, and dealing with people in a wide range of situations. As teenagers form a close emotional tie, sensitivity, empathy, capacity for intimacy, and identity development are enhanced. First romances usually serve as practice for later, more mature bonds.

Among homosexual young people, first dating relationships are often short-lived, with little emotional commitment, but for reasons different from those of heterosexual adolescents. Homosexual youths fear peer harassment and rejection and, as a result, may retreat into heterosexual dating. Often their first contacts with other sexual-minority youths occur in support groups, where they are free to date publicly.

Page Ref: 627–628

160) You have been asked to give a talk on preventing adolescent suicide at a local high school. Using research from the text as a guide, what will you say in your lecture?

Answer: Picking up on the signals that a troubled teenager sends is a crucial first step in preventing suicide. Parents and teachers need to be familiar with warning signs. Schools can help by providing sympathetic counselors, peer support groups, and information about telephone hot lines. Once a teenager takes steps toward suicide, staying with the young person, listening, and expressing sympathy and concern until professional help can be obtained are essential. Intervention with depressed and suicidal adolescents takes many forms, from antidepressant medication to individual, family, and group therapy, and sometimes hospitalization to ensure safety and swift entry into treatment. Until the adolescent improves, parents are usually advised to remove weapons, knives, razors, scissors, and drugs from the home. On a broader scale, gun control legislation that limits adolescents' access to the most frequent and deadly suicide method would greatly reduce both the number of suicides and the high teenage homicide rate.

Page Ref: 631–633

161) Which adolescents are at greatest risk for becoming delinquent? What are some suggestions for prevention of delinquency?

Answer: Boys are much more likely than girls to commit major crimes, especially when they are targets of angry, inconsistent discipline. Although SES and ethnicity are strong predictors of arrests, they are only mildly related to teenagers' self-reports of antisocial acts. The difference is due to the tendency to arrest, charge, and punish low-SES ethnic minority youths more often than their higher-SES white and Asian counterparts. A variety of child characteristics—difficult temperament, low intelligence, poor school performance, and peer rejection—are linked to chronic delinquency. One of the most consistent findings about delinquent youths is that their family environments are low in warmth, high in conflict, and characterized by inconsistent discipline. Because marital transitions often contribute to disrupted parenting, boys experiencing parental separation and divorce are especially prone to deviant behavior.

Factors beyond the family and peer group also contribute to delinquency. Students enrolled in schools that fail to meet their developmental needs—those with large classes, poor-quality instruction, and rigid rules—show higher rates of lawbreaking, even after other influences are controlled. And in poverty-stricken neighborhoods with fragmented community ties and adult criminal subcultures, teenagers have few constructive alternatives to antisocial behavior.

Because delinquency often has roots in childhood and results from events in several contexts, prevention must start early and take place at multiple levels. Helping parents to use authoritative parenting, high-quality teaching in schools, and communities with healthy economic and social conditions would go a long way toward reducing adolescent criminality. Treating serious offenders also requires an approach that recognizes the multiple determinants of delinquency; when interventions address only one aspect, they are generally ineffective. Delinquents who engage in serious, violent crimes usually must be removed from the community and placed in a correctional facility. Regardless of where treatment takes place, approaches that work best are lengthy and intensive and use problem-focused methods that teach cognitive and social skills needed to overcome family, peer, and school difficulties. Intensive efforts to create nonaggressive environments—at the family, community, and cultural levels—are needed to support interventions for delinquent youths and to foster healthy development for all young people.

Page Ref: 633–637

CHAPTER 17
EMERGING ADULTHOOD

MULTIPLE CHOICE

1) Lincoln, an American adult, is asked: "Do you consider yourself to have reached adulthood?" He responds that he feels that he is truly an adult. Lincoln is probably _____ years old.
   A) 18 or 19
   B) 20 to 22
   C) 23 to 25
   D) 26 to 35
   Answer: D
   Page Ref: 643
   Skill: Applied
   Objective: 17.1

2) Emerging adulthood
   A) spans from ages 16 to 18 years old.
   B) is a new transitional period extending from the late teens to the mid-twenties.
   C) is evident in nonindustrialized countries.
   D) is a time of certainty and focus.
   Answer: B
   Page Ref: 644
   Skill: Factual
   Objective: 17.1

3) Which of the following is true about emerging adulthood?
   A) It is primarily found in low-SES ethnic minority groups.
   B) Emerging adults are actually adolescents who take on adult responsibilities.
   C) Most parents of emerging adults view their children as not yet fully adult.
   D) Adult milestones are highly consistent in time and order across individuals.
   Answer: C
   Page Ref: 644
   Skill: Conceptual
   Objective: 17.1

4) Extended education, delayed career entry, and postponed marriage all result in _____ for those in emerging adulthood.
   A) great residential instability
   B) an inability to commit to long-term romantic relationships
   C) long-term career stability
   D) a great sense of security
   Answer: A
   Page Ref: 645
   Skill: Factual
   Objective: 17.1

5) Nearly half of American 18- to 25-year olds
    A) earn a bachelor's degree by age 22.
    B) enter graduate school.
    C) return to their parents' home for brief periods after first leaving.
    D) view marriage and parenthood as crucial markers of adult status.
Answer: C
Page Ref: 645
Skill: Factual
Objective: 17.1

6) Which of the following young adults is the most likely to live independently?
    A) Alan, a Caucasian American
    B) Isaiah, an African American
    C) Jesus, a Hispanic American
    D) Tommy, a Native American
Answer: A
Page Ref: 645
Skill: Applied
Objective: 17.1

7) Research suggests that emerging adulthood
    A) greatly speeds up identity development.
    B) is a cultural construction.
    C) is a time of financial independence.
    D) primarily occurs in low-SES ethnic minority groups.
Answer: B
Page Ref: 645
Skill: Conceptual
Objective: 17.2

8) Which of the following young adults is more likely to experience emerging adulthood?
    A) Indira, who comes from a low-income family in India
    B) Mae Ling, who comes from a wealthy family in China
    C) Isabel, who comes from a middle-income family in Brazil
    D) Estevan, who comes from a low-income family in Mexico
Answer: B
Page Ref: 646
Skill: Applied
Objective: 17.2

9) The overwhelming majority of young people in traditional, non-Western countries
    A) experience a prolonged emerging adulthood.
    B) enter marriage late.
    C) enter lifelong work late.
    D) have no emerging adulthood.
Answer: D
Page Ref: 646
Skill: Factual
Objective: 17.2

10) Matthew comes from a low-SES American family. He dropped out of high school and, at age 19, is unemployed. Matthew will probably
    A) encounter a "floundering period."
    B) experience an extended period of emerging adulthood.
    C) experience excitement during the transition to adulthood.
    D) experience a wide array of personal expansion.
Answer: A
Page Ref: 646
Skill: Applied
Objective: 17.2

11) One criticism of the concept of emerging adulthood is
    A) emerging adulthood fails to describe the experiences of most young people in industrialized nations.
    B) research on emerging adulthood largely emphasizes its societal benefits.
    C) at no time has adulthood in complex societies been attained at a distinct moment.
    D) emerging adulthood is rapidly expanding in developing nations.
Answer: C
Page Ref: 647 Box: CI: Is Emerging Adulthood Really a Distinct Period of Development?
Skill: Conceptual
Objective: 17.2

12) Proponents of emerging adulthood as a distinct period note that
    A) it fails to describe the experiences of most of the world's youths.
    B) it applies to most young people in industrialized societies.
    C) it occurs across diverse cultures and SES groups.
    D) emerging adults are part of a general trend toward blurring of age-related expectations.
Answer: B
Page Ref: 647 Box: CI: Is Emerging Adulthood Really a Distinct Period of Development?
Skill: Conceptual
Objective: 17.2

13) Dr. Thayer's research shows that college students make impressive strides in cognition. She focuses on cognitive development beyond Piaget's formal operational stage. Dr. Thayer studies
    A) preoperational thought.
    B) postformal thought.
    C) globalization.
    D) postoperational thought.
Answer: B
Page Ref: 648
Skill: Applied
Objective: 17.3

14) Our reflections on how we arrived at facts, beliefs, and ideas are called
    A) dualistic thinking.
    B) cognitive dissonance.
    C) relativistic thinking.
    D) epistemic cognition.
Answer: D
Page Ref: 648
Skill: Factual
Objective: 17.3

15) Jermaine, a college sophomore, was asked, "If two people disagree on the interpretation of a poem, how would you decide which one is right?" He replied, "You'd have to ask the poet. It's his poem." Jermaine is displaying
    A) dualistic thinking.
    B) cognitive dissonance.
    C) relativistic thinking.
    D) epistemic cognition.
Answer: A
Page Ref: 648
Skill: Applied
Objective: 17.3

16) Maribeth views all knowledge as embedded in a framework of thought. She believes that each person, in arriving at a position, creates her own "truth." Maribeth uses
    A) dualistic thinking.
    B) cognitive dissonance.
    C) relativistic thinking.
    D) epistemic cognition.
Answer: C
Page Ref: 648
Skill: Applied
Objective: 17.3

17) Eventually, the most mature individuals progress to
    A) dualistic thinking.
    B) commitment within relativistic thinking.
    C) cognitive dissonance.
    D) intuitive rationality.
Answer: B
Page Ref: 648
Skill: Factual
Objective: 17.3

18) When college students tackle challenging, ill-structured problems, interaction among individuals who are _____ is beneficial.
    A) equal in authority but greater in knowledge
    B) roughly equal in authority and knowledge
    C) greater in authority and equal in knowledge
    D) lesser in authority and knowledge
Answer: B
Page Ref: 649
Skill: Conceptual
Objective: 17.3

19) Exposure to multiple viewpoints during emerging adulthood
    A) often confuses young people, thereby delaying commitment to life goals.
    B) encourages young people to adopt rigid values and beliefs.
    C) often causes young people to rebel against their family values for a period of time.
    D) encourages young people to look more closely at themselves, thereby developing a more complex self-concept.
Answer: D
Page Ref: 649
Skill: Conceptual
Objective: 17.3

20) Which of the following is true about identity development in emerging adulthood?
    A) Young people usually explore in depth, but not in breadth.
    B) Young people usually explore in breadth, but not in depth.
    C) Young people usually explore possibilities in breadth and then in depth.
    D) Most college students make commitments, but fail to evaluate them.
Answer: C
Page Ref: 649–650
Skill: Conceptual
Objective: 17.3

21) According to your text, advances in identity occur in which three domains?
    A) love, work, and worldview
    B) career, financial security, and love
    C) job security, financial security, and marital status
    D) religiosity, spirituality, and work
Answer: A
Page Ref: 650
Skill: Factual
Objective: 17.3

22) Which of the following is true about romantic ties in emerging adulthood?
    A) Nearly 60 percent of emerging adults have had more than two sexual partners in the past year.
    B) Until the mid-20s, few romantic relationships last longer than six months.
    C) With age, emerging adults' romantic ties last longer and involve greater trust.
    D) The majority of emerging adults have more than one sexual partner over the course of a year.
Answer: C
Page Ref: 650
Skill: Conceptual
Objective: 17.3

23) Nearly all U.S. young people are sexually active by age
    A) 18.
    B) 20.
    C) 22.
    D) 25.
Answer: D
Page Ref: 650
Skill: Factual
Objective: 17.3

24) Ray and his girlfriend, Amy, do not have similar attitudes, personalities, or political beliefs. They subscribe to the popular belief that "opposites attract." Which of the following is most likely to be true?
    A) They will be more satisfied with their relationship than with previous relationships.
    B) They are less likely to stay together than two people who are similar to each other.
    C) They are just as likely to stay together as are two similar people.
    D) They are more likely to choose marriage over cohabitation.
Answer: B
Page Ref: 651
Skill: Applied
Objective: 17.3

25) Identity achievement in the vocational realm
    A) is more challenging for women than for men.
    B) usually occurs by age 21.
    C) is easier for women in male-dominated careers.
    D) is more challenging for men than for women.
Answer: A
Page Ref: 652
Skill: Conceptual
Objective: 17.3

26) Many ethnic minority young people
    A) experience a longer period of emerging adulthood than their Caucasian agemates.
    B) arrive at emerging adulthood with experiences that compromise their academic preparedness for college.
    C) complete their college degrees by age 23 and enroll in graduate school shortly thereafter.
    D) focus on career goals over finding a long-term romantic partner.
Answer: B
Page Ref: 653
Skill: Conceptual
Objective: 17.3

27) Andrew is an emerging adult. He is likely to say that _____ is essential for him to attain adult status.
    A) getting married
    B) settling into a career
    C) finishing his education
    D) constructing a worldview
Answer: D
Page Ref: 654
Skill: Applied
Objective: 17.3

28) Which of the following is true?
    A) More U.S. young people today vote than in previous generations.
    B) More U.S. young people today engage in political party activities than in previous generations.
    C) During emerging adulthood, attendance at religious services drops to its lowest level throughout the lifespan.
    D) Emerging adults who view religion as important in their lives engage in less community service.
Answer: C
Page Ref: 655
Skill: Conceptual
Objective: 17.3

29) Rita is similar to the average emerging adult. Which of the following is probably true?
    A) She sustains regular, formal religious activities.
    B) She does not vote.
    C) She sees work as merely a way to obtain spending money.
    D) She does not believe in cohabitation.
Answer: B
Page Ref: 655
Skill: Applied
Objective: 17.3

30) Which of the following activities peaks between ages 18 and 24?
   A) drug taking
   B) religious service attendance
   C) political activism
   D) community involvement
Answer: A
Page Ref: 656
Skill: Factual
Objective: 17.4

31) Annika, an emerging adult, lives with her overprotective mother. Annika's mother calls her employer when she has to be absent from work and helps her complete her community college homework. Annika probably
   A) feels connected and secure.
   B) has high self-esteem.
   C) is poorly adjusted.
   D) is identity achieved.
Answer: C
Page Ref: 658
Skill: Applied
Objective: 17.4

32) During emerging adulthood, supportive family, school, and community environments
   A) are crucial, just as they were at earlier stages of development.
   B) are not nearly as important as they were in earlier stages of development.
   C) can sometimes interfere with mature identity development.
   D) are more important to affluent young people than their lower-SES counterparts.
Answer: A
Page Ref: 658
Skill: Conceptual
Objective: 17.4

ESSAY

33) Explain how young people find lasting intimate relationships. How does partner similarity contribute to long-term relationships?
   Answer: Young people who establish happy, lasting intimate relationships usually meet in conventional ways: Family members or friends introduce them, or they get to know each other at work, school, or social events where people similar to themselves congregate. Sustaining an intimate tie is easier when couples share interests and values and when people they know approve of the match.

   Over the past decade, the Internet has become an increasingly popular way to initiate relationships, with more than one-third of single adults going to dating websites or other online venues in search of romantic partners. Success rates, however, are much lower than with conventional strategies.

   Contrary to the popular belief that "opposites attract," couples tend to resemble each other—in attitudes, personality, intelligence, educational plans, physical attractiveness, ethnicity, and (to a lesser extent) religious and political beliefs. The more alike two people are, the more satisfied they tend to be with their relationship, and the more likely they are to stay together.
   Page Ref: 651

34) List personal attributes (cognitive, emotional, and social) and social supports that foster resilience in emerging adulthood.

Answer: *Cognitive attributes:*
- Effective planning and decision making
- Information-gathering cognitive style
- Good school performance
- Knowledge of vocational options and skills

Emotional and social attributes:
- Positive self-esteem
- Good emotional self-regulation and flexible coping strategies
- Good conflict-resolution skills
- Confidence in one's ability to reach one's goals
- Sense of personal responsibility for outcomes
- Persistence and good use of time
- Healthy identity development—movement toward exploration in depth and commitment certainty
- Strong moral character
- Sense of meaning and purpose in life, engendered by religion, spirituality, or other sources
- Desire to contribute meaningfully to one's community

Social supports:
- Positive relationships with parents, peers, teachers, and mentors
- Sense of connection to social institutions, such as school, church, workplace, and community center

Page Ref: 657